SOJOURNING SISTERS

The Lives and Letters of Jessie and Annie McQueen

SOJOURNING SISTERS

The Lives and Letters of
Jessie and Annie McQueen

JEAN BARMAN

Feb 2003

leah —
In appreciation to you —

UNIVERSITY OF TORONTO PRESS
Toronto Buffalo London

© University of Toronto Press Incorporated 2003
Toronto Buffalo London
Printed in Canada

ISBN 0-8020-3697-X (cloth)

Printed on acid-free paper

Life and Letters Series

National Library of Canada Cataloguing in Publication

Barman, Jean, 1939–
Sojourning sisters : the lives and letters of Jessie and Annie
McQueen / Jean Barman.

Includes bibliographical references and index.
ISBN 0-8020-3697-X

1. McQueen, Jessie.   2. McQueen, Annie.   3. Women – British
Columbia – Biography.   I. McQueen, Jessie.   II. McQueen, Annie.   III. Title.

FC3826.1.M33B37 2003   971.1′0082   C2002-902950-3
F1088.M23B37 2003

University of Toronto Press acknowledges the financial assistance to its
publishing program of the Canada Council for the Arts and the
Ontario Arts Council.

This book has been published with the help of a grant from the Humanities
and Social Sciences Federation of Canada, using funds provided by the
Social Sciences and Humanities Research Council of Canada.

University of Toronto Press acknowledges the financial support for its
publishing activities of the Government of Canada through the Book
Publishing Industry Development Program (BPIDP).

Contents

Maps follow page viii
Illustrations follow page 150

Acknowledgments

Many people have given assistance in telling Jessie and Annie McQueen's stories. Family letters were gathered together by their grandniece Relief Williams Mackay of Pictou County, Nova Scotia, who used them to write a family history, *Simple Annals*, and, with another family member, Margaret McCurrach of Victoria, British Columbia, deposited them in archives in the two provinces. The British Columbia Archives, Nicola Valley Archives, Rossland Archives, and Provincial Archives of Nova Scotia have each given encouragement toward publication. Access to the Nova Scotia portion of the correspondence was facilitated by the initiative taken by Alison Prentice to have it transcribed by Sandra Berry, and I am extraordinarily grateful to both of them. My understanding of McQueen family dynamics has been enormously enriched by ongoing contact with Annie McQueen's granddaughter Bridget Gordon Mackenzie of Dornoch, Sutherland, Scotland, and with the sisters' grand-nieces, Margaret McCurrach and the late Relief Mackay. Rev. Glen Macdonald of Sutherland River's Presbyterian Church generously took me, in the summer of 2001, through the church and McQueen family home. He introduced me to Marjorie Scott, Betty MacNeil, and George Mackenzie, all members of the extended McQueen family still living in Nova Scotia. Judith Priestman of the Bodleian Library at Oxford University, Cathleen Blackburn of Manches Solicitors in Oxford, and Douglas A. Anderson have facilitated my understanding of the relationship between Annie McQueen's younger son, E.V. Gordon, and J.R.R. Tolkien. Among others who have helped along the way are Edward Affleck, Bill Barlee, Anita Bonson, Randy Bouchard, George Brandak, Margaret Conrad, Ross

Douglas, Elizabeth Duckworth, Elizabeth (Phillipps) Gravelle, Frances Gundry, Chris Hanna, Lily Kuhn, Shirley Morrison, Patricia Roy, Lotus Fraser Ruckle, Bob Stewart, Bette Sulz, Lyn Tait, Edna Wallace, Bruce Watson, Derryll White, and Dana Whyte. Bridget Mackenzie, Margaret McCurrach, Roderick J. Barman, and two anonymous reviewers insightfully critiqued the manuscript. Phil Buckner commented on the Nova Scotia sections, and Jeremy Mouat on Rossland. The Social Sciences and Humanities Research Council of Canada and the Humanities and Social Sciences Federation of Canada have both given important financial support. I thank you all, and, most of all, I thank Jessie and Annie McQueen for writing in the first place.

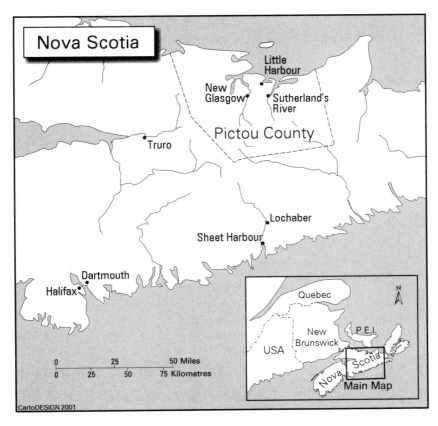

Central Nova Scotia

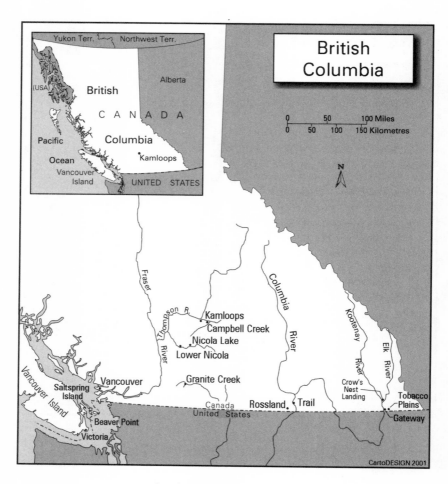

Southern British Columbia

SOJOURNING SISTERS

The Lives and Letters of Jessie and Annie McQueen

Chapter One

Sojourning Sisters

Two strong women have lived with me for a long time. They're hung around the house, woken me up in the middle of the night, become real nuisances. Tell our story, they say. Parts of it I have already put in print, but they are not satisfied.[1] Write it all down, they say, so we can be on our way. The time has come, they prod me, and so I do so here.

Each of the McQueen sisters has told me what she wants me to say. She left a trace during her lifetime. Indeed, that's how Jessie, Annie, and I became acquainted in the first place. Most women and men live and die without the trace that makes it possible to tell their stories. The McQueen sisters did not. Their correspondence survives. At the same time, how a trace is turned into a narrative gives the teller enormous power. Jessie's and Annie's lives cannot be recaptured. At best I can tell a story about their lives. It is a story based on the traces they left behind, but it is a story nonetheless.

Turning lives into stories in no way reduces our obligation to take the past seriously. In *Women on the Margins*, Natalie Zemon Davis perceptively notes about the three seventeenth-century women whose stories she recounts that 'at one time they were flesh and blood; then, what was left were memories, portraits, their writings, and their art.'[2] It is much the same with the McQueen sisters. They left traces, from which meaning must be inferred. As Kerwin Lee Klein reminds us in *Frontiers of Historical Imagination*, 'the process of reaching agreement on which narratives are plausible and which are not does not differ in kind from the process of reaching agreement on which statements of historical fact are plausible.'[3] We do our best, knowing that at some point in time we must free our subjects.

Sojourning Sisters tells a story that, for me at least, embodies tremendous human interest. The McQueen sisters arrived in British Columbia from Pictou County, Nova Scotia, during 1887–8 in the wake of the transcontinental railroad. They came to teach, considering that at the end of three years they would return home. They saw themselves as sojourners, having gone west temporarily, primarily for economic reasons. In the event, the sisters continued to make their lives between the two provinces until the second sister's death early in the Second World War.

Jessie and Annie McQueen brought with them a way of life, an outlook, that they took for granted. Their Scots Presbyterian upbringing imbued them with an everyday ethic that for the next half century they exemplified and transferred to others. Neither sister was a hero in the traditional sense of the word. They were highly unlikely to be so, in any case, given their gender. Their participation in the places around them was of a more prosaic nature: they taught school, they supported their local church, they were social beings. In these ways, Jessie and Annie McQueen participated in the transformation of British Columbia from a remote frontier of the Canadian nation, still largely the home of Aboriginal people, into a 'modern' urban entity. They were part of the people power that brought the two keystones of Canadian society – school and church – to distant parts of the province. The Nicola Valley, Kamloops, Campbell Creek, Salmon Arm, Rossland, the southeastern Kootenays, Salt Spring Island, Victoria – the sisters were there at some point in time. Jessie and Annie McQueen were not just there, they were active agents, as well as observers, in whatever setting their circumstances placed them. The actions of thousands of Jessies and Annies, much more than those of a handful of politicians or other 'heroes,' brought Canada together into the nation we know today.

It is important to emphasize that the McQueen sisters would not have seen themselves as making Canada, certainly not in the sense in which the process was understood at the time. Nation building was long equated with the power exercised by men in the public domain. Women like Jessie and Annie rarely discussed politics, and when they did, it was most often prior to an election, and then in fairly prosaic terms. Numerous scholars remind us that the achievement and sustenance of nationhood are far more complex than political acts and government decrees. 'Until well after the beginning of the twentieth century,' historian Margaret Prang explains, Canada 'was overwhelmingly a collection of rural societies in which local values and allegiances were dominant, as they had been in the decades before Confederation. In these circumstances, the political parties and the patronage system provided a minimal organizing and unifying force in a country where most of the citizens rarely felt the impact of the national government in their lives.'[4] 'Local values and allegiances' did not, of course, exist in isolation. They were shaped by 'broader currents of thought,' to pick up on Gerald Friesen's phrase from *Citizens and Nation*.[5] Jessie and Annie McQueen absorbed, and passed on, values and ideas consistent with their upbringing that were made explicit by men at the podium, in the pulpit, or writing in the press.[6]

The McQueen sisters acted within the settings deemed acceptable for women, and it was precisely by doing so that they effected change. In order to understand how a nation acquires its force, we must take both genders into account. Benedict Anderson evokes the nation as an 'imagined community' that, to possess legitimacy, must acquire a taken-for-granted quality. 'Members of even the smallest nation will never know most of their fellow-members, meet them, or even hear of them, yet in the minds of each lives the image of their communion.'[7] The means through which an imagined community emerges Eric Hobsbawm describes as 'invented traditions.' Ceremonies and public monuments, primary education, and organized sports serve to 'inculcate certain values and norms of behaviour by repetition.'[8] Other aspects of everyday life encouraging the imagined community that is the nation include common language, origins, and beliefs. Then there are the myths, images, and stories to do with, in the case of Canada, the United Empire Loyalists, Royal Canadian Mounted Police, canoes and the wilderness, the North, and so on, as detailed by Daniel Francis and Norman Knowles.[9] Friesen emphasizes the act of communication itself. People talk and write to each other. The ways in which they do so create shared understandings that feed into the nation. All of these elements operate most powerfully at the local level and encompass the lives of women as much as those of men. Whether persons are in direct contact with each other or not, they come to behave in similar fashion toward the nation.

The Canada fostered by women like the McQueen sisters was not inclusive of all its residents. Nova Scotia was a British possession at the time of their births, and the decision to enter the Canadian Confederation in 1867 did little to alter the set of attitudes associated with colonialism. Jessie and Annie came of age in a colonized and colonizing world. Colonialism was premised on fundamental divisions based in race and gender that they and their fellow Canadians mostly accepted without question. The European nations that exercised control over much of the world justified their doing so by the superiority of their ways of life.

A variety of scientific manipulations were used to organize persons hier-archically according to skin colour into what were termed races. Data ranging from the technical and economic advances flowing from coloni-zation to the different ways of life followed by darker skinned people whose territories had been occupied, reassured colonizers that persons looking like themselves were destined to rule. Gender divisions pre-dated colonization, being grounded in Christianity. Males had long legitimized what they perceived as their inherent superiority over females by the biblical narrative of Adam and Eve, in which Eve's innate weakness led to the sin of apple picking. Colonization was presented as a Christian enterprise, thereby encouraging the interpretation of bio-logical differences between men and women in such a way as to make male attributes the norm, those of females aberrations from them.

The logic of colonialism meant that only some persons were welcome in the nation. Very pale or 'white' skin pigment was essential. The reli-ance on skin colour as a visual marker to distinguish colonizers from the colonized had an unwanted complexity. Gender assumptions meant that it was almost wholly male colonizers who fanned out across the world, certainly in the first generation. These men sometimes engaged in sex-ual dalliances or longer-term unions with local women, whose darker skin tones limited the respect shown to them or to the resulting off-spring. Mixed-race persons straddled societies. In their appearance and otherwise, they were neither colonists nor the colonized, combining aspects of both in their persons. They occupied an in-between or liminal space, being in general more easily accepted in contact zones, where the boundaries between newcomers and indigenous persons were not yet fixed, than in racially homogeneous societies. Cultural theorists Robert Young, Avtar Brah, and Annie Coombes use the concept of 'hybridity' to describe such persons, the term signifying the potential for hardier vari-eties resulting from the crossing of two species, while also acknowledging the threat posed to proponents of racial purity.[10]

Gender boundaries were equally complex during Jessie and Annie's time. Although women were prohibited as a matter of course from exer-cising the franchise, they were accorded an important role in nation building and, more generally, in colonialism. Theirs was the domestic realm. In a narrow sense, domesticity was equated with the home, but the term was sometimes expanded to encompass such 'maternal' occu-pations as teaching. The practice of domesticity gave the means for women to transfer accepted patterns of behaviour from one setting to another. Race and gender worked together. Anne McClintock is among several scholars who have examined the ways in which colonial women interacted with colonized peoples so that, as she puts it, 'domestic space became racialized, colonial space became domesticated.'[11]

Some women, like the McQueen sisters, domesticated within a political entity, engaging in a kind of internal colonialism that served the cause of nation building. They went from a settled area to a contact zone or frontier, a place in space and time in which the winners and losers were not yet determined. It is on frontiers that peoples and the societies of which they are a part come together and for a time interact before again drawing apart. Alexandra Harmon uses the image of shifting lines in sand to evoke the fluidity that exists on the frontier in relations between original inhabitants and newcomers.[12] In 1901 the *Oxford English Dictionary* defined a frontier as 'that part of a country which forms the border of its settled or inhabited regions' and 'the outlying districts of civilization.'[13] The language of this definition, in particular the use of the word 'civilization,' which at the time was equated with Christianity, usefully reminds us that it is newcomers, the colonizers, who, historically, have imposed themselves on indigenous peoples, a process long eulogized as pioneering or colonization.

As sojourners intending to remain in British Columbia only over the short term, Jessie and Annie McQueen largely acted as they would have done at home. By virtue of doing so, they domesticated in two distinct but linked meanings of the word. They turned the frontier that was most of British Columbia in the direction of settlement, and they nudged the province as a whole closer toward the rest of Canada. The conversations the sisters had, the causes they supported, the friends they made, the books that they read, all served, in small but incremental fashion, to encourage British Columbians to think and act in ways familiar to the sisters. It was through such means, rather than any single political act, although the Canadian Pacific Railway was very important, that the province was domesticated into Canada. The frontier receded and British Columbia became more like Nova Scotia, and more like the imagined community that was Canada, not in a single swoop but as a matter of accretion. It is as though Prang had Jessie and Annie in mind in reflecting, 'There have been many bands of "hopeful travelers" in Canadian history, usually moving westward, but we know all too little about the consequences of the transfer of their social and cultural baggage. Thus, in a general way, the influence of the migrating Pictou county Scots on education, religion, and commerce has often been noticed but seldom studied.'[14]

Sojourning Sisters is told from Jessie and Annie McQueen's perspectives through the letters they exchanged with each other and with family members. Once they headed west, letter writing became the sole means for sustaining contact with parents, four older sisters, and a brother, each a continent away. The practice signalled far more than the pieces of paper themselves. It gave a routine to daily life. 'You see we have only two mails in a week, & I seldom mail more than two letters at a time, & some days I mail none at all.' From a particularly isolated location, Jessie lamented how 'there is so little to mark the days off from one another – not even a regular mail day ... I never knew before what good land-marks mail days make, to say nothing of the comfort of knowing when to expect & send letters.' At a trying point in her life, she described what the practice meant to her: 'As for the letters they are just like our talks, about anything & everything, & might be read by anyone for that matter.'[15]

Over five hundred letters survive to or from Jessie or Annie McQueen, together with a larger number between their parents and siblings. Spanning the years 1860–1930, the letters total 835,000 words. Many other letters have disappeared, some in the course of being passed around the family.[16] 'Mother remailed me your letter only about a week ago and I remailed to [sister] Mary same week,' Jessie was told about a letter long since gone astray. Another time Annie assured her mother that 'your letter and Jessie's, enclosing Mary B.'s, came to hand today, and glad I was to get them all.' The letters are limited by their writers and intended recipients. The sisters' father wrote infrequently, perhaps because his wife took such a strong lead but also because he was less literate. Jessie once observed how composing a letter was 'harder on the dear man than a day's work.' Correspondence with parents was more guarded than between siblings. Jessie reassured her mother about an earlier letter to one of her sisters: 'When I wrote to Liz, I didn't think of your being there, but of course you are welcome to read any of my letters. I shouldn't have written as I did, I suppose.' Another time Jessie simply acknowledged, a bit wearily, 'I know most letters are common property.'[17]

For all of their limitations, the letters tell a story. The correspondence opens up a new window onto the histories of Nova Scotia, British Columbia, and Canada. It is revealing of the practices of domesticity and colonialism, of how they were effected and then reinforced, mentored, and surveilled through the written word. The established character of letter writing in the McQueen family accustomed its members to share the details of their everyday worlds in unaffected fashion. Jessie, Annie, and their sisters echo the lives of a generation of women. The diaries and letters of the fifteen Nova Scotian women included in the innovative anthology *No Place like Home* begin rather than close off the discussion.[18] While aspects of these women's lives are similar to those of the McQueens, none of them headed west within Canada and, given the constraints of the volume, none of the narratives extends over the lifespan. With a couple of possible exceptions, none comes from a family that was quite so ordinary.[19]

Neither have published accounts of newcomer or settler women in British Columbia, particularly on the frontier, spanned everyday experience over time so honestly as do the McQueen sisters' letters.[20] Susan Allison composed her memoir of early newcomer settlement in the southern interior in old age, carefully honing its contents to obscure the hybridity all around her, including her own stepchildren and grandchildren having Aboriginal mothers.[21] The four women given voice by Kathryn Bridge similarly sculpted their accounts, writing in retrospect or at a momentous point in their lives.[22] Most newcomer women whose lives have made it into print were urban creatures, at the most visiting the frontier or living there briefly.[23] The McQueen correspondence gives an unequalled look into the everyday life of newcomer women in British Columbia from the late nineteenth century through the interwar years.

The McQueen letters also speak to the complexities, for women in particular, of family ties. Daughterhood's obligations and sisterhood's bonds marked Jessie and Annie McQueen's lives, as it did many others of their time. Judith Fingard found that, for women attending Dalhousie University in Halifax during the last two decades of the nineteenth century, 'dutiful obligation to family as adults' loomed large.[24] The McQueen sisters might cross a continent, but they did not escape the associations that the accident of birth gave. They took for granted they would remain daughters so long as their parents, and in particular their mother, lived. Marriage gave a certain release, but for single women there was no escape. Jessie and Annie accepted their obligation in different ways at different times in their lives, but it was always there, its most enduring manifestation being, of course, the letters themselves. The bonds that sisterhood gave were equally long lived. There were Jessie and Annie, and there were four more sisters back in the Maritimes, as Nova Scotia, New Brunswick, and Prince Edward Island were known collectively. All six were linked through correspondence by sisterhood's bonds.

Jessie and Annie McQueen's very ordinariness, not to mention their gender, makes it easy to discount persons like them in the shaping of

British Columbia and Canada. The proportion of the British Columbian population born in other parts of Canada has never been that large, nor have the outward manifestations of a distinctly Canadian nation been a prominent feature of provincial life. Yet, somehow, British Columbia became, and remains, part of the entity we know as Canada. The McQueen sisters were a means by which it did so and by which Canada as a nation has endured. Be it Annie who revelled in attention or the much quieter Jessie, many of the changes they wrought were almost imperceptible. Others took their acts of kindness, of gentle persuasion if you will, for granted. It was precisely because sojourners like the sisters were so unmemorable that they were such powerful agents of change.

Chapter Two

Pictou County Origins

The house still stands where Jessie was born on Christmas Eve, 1860, and her sister Annie, in the summer of 1865, to Daniel and Catherine Mc-Queen.[1] Cape Cod style with clapboard siding, many small-paned windows, and a stone chimney, its one-and-a-half stories look remarkably as they did at the sisters' births. The farmhouse sits on a rise, facing over the valley of Sutherland's River. Below the farmhouse is a bridge crossing the river to the Presbyterian church that can be glimpsed from the upper hall window. A spire has been added, but otherwise the church too is mostly unchanged. The surrounding country is now substantially wooded; during the sisters' childhoods, it would have been interspersed with fields. All their lives, they recalled the setting with tenderness. Sent a dried mayflower, Jessie exclaimed: 'It just took me back to the woods at home with a rush, & I all but *saw* the Mayflowers growing deep down in the moss under the spruce trees, out by the "back fence."' The farm came constantly to mind. 'I think I can see our garden now – that long grassy strip behind the house with the branches of the trees sweeping it.'[2]

The view from the farmhouse door does not reach quite as far as the sea, or, more precisely, the Northumberland Strait, which divides Nova Scotia from Prince Edward Island. Yet the sea, to which Sutherland's River flows, is the key to understanding the McQueen family and their world. The sea brought the first wave of immigrants to the area. In 1773 the brig *Hector* carried to this northeastern shore of the British colony of Nova Scotia 178 Scots Highlanders, most of them Gaelic-speaking. The defeat of their clan chiefs by the English in the mid-eighteenth century accelerated the decline of feudal relationships whereby the many tenant-farmed for the few. Nova Scotia gave the Highlanders the opportunity to own their own farms and also to engage in fishing and lumbering. Among their number was John Sutherland who settled at the mouth of the river that bears his name. A popular historian has described the *Hector*'s voyage as 'the beginning of the Scottish-Canadian community of the entire nation' of Canada.[3] As the forests began to be cleared, Pictou, as the district was known, attracted more and more newcomers from Scotland. They and their fellow settlers elsewhere in Nova Scotia swept aside, virtually without noticing them, the Mi'kmaq peoples who occupied the land. There were 865 Mi'kmaq recorded in the Pictou district at the time of the *Hector*'s arrival, but just a hundred by the time of Jessie's and Annie's births.[4]

Refugees and disbanded soldiers arriving after the war of the American Revolution doubled Nova Scotia's population to 40,000 by 1790. Among them was Alexander McQueen, an illiterate labourer from the island of Skye, who in 1778 at the age of thirty had enlisted as a private in the 82nd Regiment of Foot, assembled in Scotland to fight the American rebels. Landing at the capital of Halifax, the regiment spent the war in garrison duty there, apart from an expedition to Maine to construct a fort intended to interrupt shipping in and out of Boston. At peace the regiment was disbanded in Halifax. A tract of 26,000 acres (10,530 hectares) lying about 150 kilometres to the northeast in the Pictou district was set aside for them. The land was divided into lots, and the men drew for their particular piece of property. In 1783 Alexander McQueen acquired a hundred acres (40.5 hectares) at Little Harbour, about eight kilometres west along the coast from Sutherland's River. While numerous men sold out and re-enlisted at Halifax, he was among the fifty or so who persevered and raised their families in the Pictou district. His son Angus McQueen fathered a dozen children at Little Harbour, including Daniel, born in July 1818, by which time Pictou's population had reached 8,000. Over 90 per cent of them were, like the McQueens, Presbyterian by religious conviction. Many of them were from the Scottish Highlands, where evictions to make way for grazing sheep combined with overpopulation to encourage thousands to leave during the first decades of the nineteenth century.

The McQueen family was modest but respectable. Offspring were expected to better themselves through hard work and initiative. Young Daniel served a four-year apprenticeship as a joiner, a carpenter specializing in house construction. A building boom was under way thanks to an expanding population, a flourishing economy, and a road that made it possible to travel to Halifax via the market town of Truro in two days. Daniel did fairly well with what he termed 'my little business,' but, however good he was as a joiner, he showed no great skill or resilience in handling the pressures of life.[5] It was no wonder that in his late twenties he looked for a wife who possessed the qualities he lacked. His gaze lit on Catherine Olding, four years his junior.

Daniel McQueen showed a considerable degree of courage in courting Kate, as she was known as a young woman. The McQueens were without pretensions, cut from ordinary cloth, unlike the Oldings, who were among the leading Pictou families. Catherine's grandfather, Nicholas Purdue Olding, was English, not Scots. Said to be from a family 'of some rank in the County of Kent' and educated at Oxford University, he set up a legal practice in the then British colony of New York. During the American Revolution, he served as a chasseur, or light horseman, on the British side. At war's end, he resettled his family in Halifax and subsequently became the first practising lawyer in the Pictou district.[6] In 1795 he was made a captain of the Pictou militia unit, a sign of high social standing, and two years later received a land grant on Betsy Island off the mouth of Sutherland's River. Born an Anglican, he astutely joined the Presbyterian Church. Catherine's obituary would eulogize her father, 'Squire Olding,' as 'educated, refined, and possessed of means,' and the Olding family as 'superior people' possessed of 'superior articles of decoration – silver, paintings, and such like.'[7] Local historians celebrate him as 'the father of the Bar of Nova Scotia,' and as 'not only the father but the grandfather of the Bar.'[8] The squire's son John, who was Catherine's father, served as both a justice of the peace and a major in the militia.

Daniel McQueen was not viewed favourably by Kate's family. The courtship had to be carried on covertly, with Daniel, who hated writing, being forced to send supplicating and deferential letters to his beloved and to space out his visits to her home. In Daniel's favour were his comely looks and his willingness to subscribe to Kate's views. Finally, late in March 1849, they told their respective parents of their determination to marry and were wed on the last day of that month in the nearby shipbuilding and market town of New Glasgow. Daniel was thirty and Catherine twenty-six, the average ages of the day for getting married in Nova Scotia.[9]

Two and a half years later, Daniel McQueen bought a farm for £260 near the mouth of Sutherland's River. His first act was to construct a fine new house, which he probably did himself. Its respectability spoke to Catherine's aspirations for the marriage. By this time the couple had two children, Jane, born in the late winter of 1850, and Mary Belle, eighteen months later in the autumn of 1851.[10] The move to Sutherland's River may explain the break before Eliza's birth in late winter 1854. Susan Dove came along in the summer of 1856, to be followed by George in late 1858. Margaret Janet, always called Jessie, appeared on Christmas Eve, 1860. A second son, Daniel, born in the summer, died at just over a year of age. Catherine, by then aged forty-one, conceived once again, and her final child, a daughter named Annie Lowden, was born on 31 July 1865. By this time, the McQueen family had been farming for almost a quarter century at Sutherland's River.

The character of Pictou County, as it was called from 1836, was by now fixed. Stretching 80 kilometres along Nova Scotia's north coast and 30 kilometres inland, it contained 32,000 people; that is, 8 per cent of Nova Scotians lived there. In 1871 about two-thirds of family heads were, like Daniel McQueen, farmers. Another quarter were labourers, mostly mining coal, building ships, tanning leather, or manufacturing cloth. The rest were merchants, businessmen, or professionals, who, like many of the labourers, mostly lived in the two largest settlements, New Glasgow or Pictou, with populations of two to three thousand each.

Occupational stability was strengthened by common origins. Whereas the Scots were the strongest ethnic group across Nova Scotia at just over a third, in Pictou County they reigned supreme. Fully 85 per cent of Pictonians claimed Scots descent. A county atlas published in 1879 showed 94 per cent of rural property owners as having Scots surnames.[11] By this time, the Scots character of Pictou County Scots had moved beyond stereotypical attributes into a way of life. By 1871 over 85 per cent of Pictonians had been born in Nova Scotia, a proportion climbing to 90 per cent over the next decade. An American visitor shortly after the McQueens' marriage caught the essence of this shift. 'I have a reasonable amount of respect for a Highlander in full costume,' he opined, but Pictonians were 'denationalized.' He described them as 'a sorry sight' for wearing 'breaches and round hats' useful for farming, rather than being decked out, as he would have preferred, in 'plaids and ... buckles, hose and bonnets.' They were 'without bagpipes or pistols, sporrans [pouches worn in front of kilts] or philabegs [kilts]; there was not even a solitary thistle to charm the eye.'[12]

Of the attributes that held, the most noticeable was the Gaelic language, brought over from the Highlands. It remained sufficiently commonplace that the older McQueen children interspersed it in their letters home as a matter of course. 'Thereby hangs a tale which maybe I'll tell you wherry [*sic*] I see you and say *Cimeer hasn un dhu.*' Another time, a possible misspelling was followed by an apology for how 'my Gaelic limps.' There was also the matter of a Scots accent. Jessie described a newcomer she met at the age of sixteen as 'very Scotchy, says "verra" & "thocht" & all the rest.' She reflected many years later from British Columbia how she thought she 'was pretty well up in the Scottish tongue,' until two others 'get talking sometimes in Scotch so broad that it is utterly beyond my pen.'[13]

Presbyterianism went hand in hand with Scots descent. Twenty-five per cent of Nova Scotians were Presbyterian, and a comparable number Catholic, they being the two dominant faiths. In Pictou County, over 80 per cent were Presbyterian, about 9 per cent Catholic. In 1871, 39 of the county's 52 churches were Presbyterian. Pictou County was at the fore in reconciling competing factions within the denomination, each guided by well-educated clergy who assumed their right to lead social and cultural endeavours, including all levels of education. According to a local account, it was the distances involved in attending their respective churches that led parishioners settled near Sutherland's River to a more practical alternative. The church erected there in 1854 was the first in Nova Scotia to house the feuding factions in a single structure. It was built by voluntary labour, including that of Daniel McQueen, who, according to the minute book, 'furred the door and lathed the ceiling.'[14] At the church's completion in December 1858, its forty-five boxed pews were sold at auction, the most desirable being nearest the front. Daniel McQueen was one of the elders, part of the church's governing body. Perhaps it was that position, or perhaps it was Catherine's strong sense of self, that secured the family the second box back on the right-hand side, no mean feat. At first the factions held separate services whenever an itinerant minister could be had, but in 1871 two of them amalgamated in the hopes of securing a permanent minister, the third joining a decade later. When the long-sought minister arrived, it was the McQueens, just across the river, who gave him room and board.

The other fundamental attribute of Pictou County, growing out of Scots descent and Presbyterianism, was a commitment to literacy. As an early historian put it, 'they believed profoundly in the Word of God and the blessings of education.'[15] The Protestant Reformation of the sixteenth century had as its basic tenet the necessity for everyone to acknowledge, on an individual basis, that he or she was born in sin and needed God's grace to be saved. The alternative was to go, at death, to eternal hell as opposed to heaven, a fate no one wanted to chance. The means to salvation was 'the word of God' in the form of the Bible, which each person had to read and study by him- or herself. There was no possibility of an intermediary, as was the case in the previously dominant Catholic Church, where the priest alone had access to the Bible. Nor would good works do the trick. The Calvinist version of Protestantism, out of which Presbyterianism emerged, quickly took hold in Scotland. With it came a commitment to making literate all persons, male and female, rich and poor. Scotland was a leader in establishing local schools. In Pictou County, where the best-known school was Pictou Academy, founded in 1816 to educate promising young men contemplating the Presbyterian ministry, the push to make schooling generally available was widespread. A school opened at Little Harbour, home to the McQueen clan, in 1822. The earliest literacy figures are from 1871, when just 700, or 4 per cent, of Pictou County adults were unable to read. Even though writing was not essential to faith, only 10 per cent, mostly Pictou women, could not do so.

The McQueens exemplified Pictou County. They were Scots, they were Presbyterian, they were literate, and they farmed. The society in which the McQueens lived was homogeneous and self-referential. The Pictonians' distinctive qualities were visible to outsiders, as with the visitor who found them 'generally a very moral and religious people, indulging in few of the luxuries and beverages of modern society.'[16] For families like the McQueens, the qualities and values they held were not just the right ones, they were the only ones conceivable. 'Believe the Bible, believe that when God says he will direct your path if you commit your way to Him, He will really do it,' Catherine McQueen once explained to Jessie. There was no room for pluralism or diversity, for God knew best. He guided the faithful in the direction he chose for them. 'When I trusted to Providence I didn't go astray,' Catherine confided to Jessie at a trying moment. As Jessie's older sister Mary Belle put it, 'God's providence rules everywhere.'[17]

The concept of providence, used frequently in the McQueens' correspondence, was gentler than the older Calvinist concept of predestination, with its notion of an 'elect' who by their piety and right behaviour indicated that they had been chosen by God for salvation even before their birth. Both concepts had a sense of inevitability about them. Whatever happened was for the best because it was God's will. Providence also embodied an element of free will. The more persons accommodated themselves to God's will by studying the Bible and following its precepts, the more likely it was they would find providence pleasing. Catherine urged her children to have 'faith that God will guide you and, by guiding, help you to do your best and that having done your best, you may trust Him to supply all your needs.' Because death, upon which an individual went irrevocably to heaven or hell, might come to anyone at any moment, the need was, as Catherine McQueen reminded Mary Belle, when informing her of a neighbour's 'call,' to 'be ye also ready.'[18] The tenets of Presbyterianism, defined by historian Michael Gauvreau as a mixture of 'original sin, human depravity, God's absolute sovereignty, and the apparent contradictions of predestination, free will, and divine grace,' worked powerfully to enforce conformity.[19]

In the farmhouse at Sutherland's River, the guardian of the faith was Catherine McQueen, who held strong views on belief and even stronger opinions about conduct. As a great-granddaughter put it, Catherine 'had definite ideas about religion and deportment.' Like Presbyterians in general, she was cautious and conservative. She valued duty, self-denial, and thrift. 'You can work all the better, can you not, thinking of the wonderful Counsellor, then you must believe in His providence,' Catherine admonished. This ethic she was determined to inculcate into her offspring. Writing to her youngest daughter, Annie, Catherine typically observed: 'Well Annie Dear you are 16 & makes me feel old, my Baby 16 & it makes me sad too, when I think how far short I've come in doing my duty to her & training her for a higher life than this.' If Catherine came short in her self-appointed task, it was not for want of trying. Morning and evening prayers were held without fail in the McQueen household. Before the start, Catherine took care to extinguish the candle because the children were meant to have their eyes shut.[20]

Sundays were dedicated to religion. Nothing profaned the sabbath. All activity stopped, including work on the farm. Even the precious letter writing ceased on Sunday, apart from exceptional circumstances. In 1848, when Daniel was courting her, Catherine praised him with the words, 'I was happy to see by the conclusion of your letter that though your time was limited you would not encroach on the sabbath by writing even to me.'[21] Reading material was confined to the Bible and the *Witness*, a Presbyterian newspaper. No travel was possible except to the church located just over the bridge spanning Sutherland's River. The McQueen family proudly occupied their box pew, whose narrow ledge for sitting bordered all four sides except for its door.

Whatever the day of the week, entertainment in the form of dancing, card-playing, and games using dice was strongly disapproved of. One of the games that Catherine permitted, perhaps because of its educational value, was logomachy, in which cards containing separate letters were joined together to form words. Music with a religious character was encouraged. Both Jessie and Annie learned to play the meloden, a small organ. In 1879 Annie proudly announced: 'I can play "Mary and Martha," "Come unto me," and the air of "Yankee Doodle" and "Men of Harlech," I am going at "The Anthem for Dedication" and I expect I'll have it too before long.' Writing from British Columbia, Annie took pleasure in telling her mother that in the upcoming Sunday school concert 'we are to sing one of your old favourites, "I'll do my daily duty ere the sun goes down."' Reflecting on her upbringing, Annie added, 'I think of you every time the children practice it.'[22]

Presbyterianism went hand in hand with temperance, which grew in appeal during these years. The first organized temperance group in Nova Scotia, said to be the first in British North America, began in Pictou County in 1827, and by mid-century the movement, spearheaded by the Presbyterian and other Protestant churches, was widespread.[23] It was no coincidence that New Glasgow's churches were constructed on Temperance Street, or that it was so named in the first place. The most imposing of the town's Presbyterian churches was located at the very end of Temperance Street at an angle, where it still keeps watch over the town. When Daniel was courting her in 1848, Catherine gave him a lecture on the subject of temperance: 'I think you are already aware of my aversion to the use of intoxicating liquors and I think I have said in your presence that I never would unite with one who used them (or something to that effect). I must now tell you frankly, my opinion and determination are still the same.'[24] Liquor was banned from the farmhouse. Supporters of the campaign to prohibit, or at the least get tight control over, alcohol in the interests of a higher morality were convinced that God was on their side.

Temperance meetings mimicked church services with sermons, prayers, and singing. The parallels made acceptable a whole range of activities that came to be associated with temperance. One of the few opportunities that the McQueen children had for socialization with their own age group outside of the family was through lodges committed to the cause. In December 1868, Jane, George, and Dove took eight-year-old Jessie with them to a meeting of the Mayflower Juvenile Lodge. The minute book recorded – all in the name of temperance – collection of dues, a secret password, recitations, songs, speeches from special guests, and debates on such topics as whether ships or railroads were more beneficial or whether it 'is best for a man to have a clean cross wife or a good natured dirty wife.'[25]

The young McQueens' other regular activity away from the farm was the school. Until 1864 Nova Scotia families had to pay toward their children's schooling, and somehow the McQueens scraped together the money to send their five eldest children to school. Two new Public School Acts made elementary and secondary education available free of charge. Families like the McQueens responded enthusiastically. Daniel donated land at the corner of the farm for a public school at Sutherland's River and may have built it himself. Officially Nova Scotia possessed a single non-denominational system as opposed to religiously based schools under the oversight of particular denominations. In practice, as historian Robert Nicholas Bérard points out, schools were overseen, and their pupils examined by, the local Presbyterian minister, who sought to ensure that the pupils were instructed in the word of God. Appointments to teaching positions went to young men intending to enter the clergy or some other worthy occupation, and to their female counterparts awaiting the time to marry.[26] Five years after Daniel McQueen's young brother Duncan qualified as a teacher, he headed off to Boston to better himself. For the McQueen children, the values of home and school were mutually reinforcing.

Scots Presbyterianism accorded virtue not just to temperance and learning, but also to hard work. It was a good thing, too, given how much needed to be done around the McQueen household. The census of 1871 recorded the farm, which totalled 130 acres, as consisting of 70 acres that had been improved, being cleared of trees, and another 5 in pasture. There were 4 acres of dykeland hay, 1 of potatoes, ½ each of wheat and of garden and orchard. Livestock consisted of 4 milch cows, 2 horned cattle, 12 sheep, 1 pig, and 1 horse. The census failed to record the flock of hens that the family also kept. The produce on hand was noted as 80 bushels of potatoes, 65 of oats, 20 of barley, 5 of spring wheat, together with 4 tons of hay. Over the past year, the cows had yielded 240 pounds of butter and the sheep 30 pounds of wool, which were sold for needed cash. Of farm machinery, the census recorded two carts and wagons and one plough.

The farm at Sutherland's River was of average size for mid-nineteenth-century Nova Scotia.[27] The census data make clear that it was not organized for commercial production. As son George once commented, 'at most a farm in Pictou only gives a living.'[28] At its best, it provided subsistence for the family members with a sufficient surplus to acquire through sale and barter the products that could not be produced on the farm itself. Little or no margin existed as a cushion against a year of poor crops or a sudden surge in family expenditures. The McQueens' situation was in no way unusual. As scholars of Nova Scotia have described, very few families were able to subsist from farming alone. Most heads of households had other occupations for at least part of the year, and even then the combined family income might not be sufficient to cover necessary expenses.[29] Two factors combined to intensify the McQueen family's economic difficulties.

The first factor was the gender of the McQueen children. Instead of six sons and one daughter, offspring who would have provided ample labour for the effective running of the farm, there were six daughters and only one son. Catherine's sense of family pride worsened the situation. She would not permit George, the great-grandson of 'Squire Olding,' to become a mere farmhand. George was not given encouragement to work on the farm, smugly remarking, 'I am hardly built heavily enough for farm work especially as I lack early training on that score,' although he did spend what he later termed 'the old carpenter days' with his father. The McQueens had accordingly to find the wages for a labourer, who did the heavy work. From an early age, the McQueen daughters were expected to participate in the tasks of farming, so much so that the yearly round became intrinsic to their lives. In October 1888, far away from home, Jessie lamented, 'I'd a 'nuff rather go home & pick potatoes for a day or two, for you must be needing a hand about this time.'[30] The McQueen daughters learned the ethic of hard work from an early age.

The second and far more serious problem was Daniel McQueen himself. He was much loved by his children, but even they recognized his limitations. Eliza, the third daughter, once reflected how 'we were brought up on a farm where there was no farmer.' Her father simply did not possess the resolute temperament and steady application needed for farming. His carpentry jobs brought in some needed cash, but they also took him away from home, wherever jobs were to be had, for indeterminate periods of time. Sometimes he returned with payment, but other times only a promise of eventually being paid for his labour or even his materials. A letter beseeching him to 'finish the remainder of the loft' took care not to raise expectations: 'I do not know if I will be able to pay you all this fall but it will not be long if I can.'[31]

George McQueen wrote a self-analysis in 1892 which applied with equal force to Daniel: 'My life has been one of ups and downs; the ups higher and the downs lower than I in young days dreamed of or could imagine.' Both father and son were subject to mercurial swings in mood. Both committed themselves, when in their upswings, to projects that promised great fortunes but invariably ended up in disaster. Since the farm lay on a stagecoach route, Daniel's first scheme was to convert the house into an inn that would provide rest and refreshment for travellers. Since refreshment meant the consumption of hard liquor on the premises, Catherine vetoed this scheme. She did not so intervene when at the end of 1864 Daniel went into partnership to run a tannery in Sutherland's River. His partner does not seem to have paid his share of the purchase price. Within a year, the venture failed, with the partnership dissolved and Daniel responsible for its liabilities. So heavy was the burden of these debts that in 1869 Daniel even considered making a fresh start in the United States. His younger brother Duncan, living in Indiana, learned of the proposal and wrote a letter of passionate objection. 'In reference to breaking up the associations of a life-time, ... the cost should be counted, not in Dollars and cents, but in the sundering of the ties of affection and society ... Ah Dan, it is not a light matter to pull up stakes, and move out into a hollow, heartless world.'[32]

Catherine McQueen's burden – a houseful of daughters and an unreliable husband – was experienced by many other wives of these years. The basic response of such women was never to give way under the strain and never to allow their situation to destroy the fabric of family life. This response was expressed in two ways. First, the physical world over which they had authority was closely controlled. Order, cleanliness, punctuality, and frugality characterized the house, the yard, and the garden. These same qualities were expressed in the clothing and the appearance of the women and children. Available resources were stretched as far as they could go, and indeed farther. Secondly, the tasks that had to be done were turned into an elaborate routine, to be scrupulously followed. The mundane became the indispensable, almost sacrosanct. In the poet's words, 'who sweeps a room, as for thy laws, makes that and th'action fine.' Routine became a ritual that not only made 'drudgery divine' but gave those involved a sense of community and even of purpose in life.[33] Carrying out household tasks, particularly shared tasks, became a refuge and a comfort from the larger problems about which those involved could do little or nothing. The domestic realm served as a haven amidst the surrounding difficulties.

Domesticity, as these practices may be termed, was as much about goals as actualities. Domesticity emphasized appearances rather than realities. As Julie Jeffrey emphasizes in her classic study of American frontier women, and Cynthia Comacchio affirms for Canada, 'domesticity described norms, not the actual conduct.' It is precisely this that gives the concept of domesticity its force. 'Norms were important because they established the behavioral context for those who tried to reject them as much as for those who attempted to realize them. They existed as goals ... and provided a source for identity and self-esteem.' Domesticity's power lay, as literary critic Elizabeth Langland reminds us, in its markers or signs. These functioned, as an etiquette book of the time put it, as 'an effectual barrier against the innovations of the vulgar; a rubicon, [that] the uncouth in manner and low in speech can never hope to pass.' Catherine McQueen and her daughters carried with them, no matter where they went, expectations about right behaviour, and, as Jeffrey puts it, 'even if it was impossible initially to live up to domestic and cultural ideals, these ideals helped women retain their sense of self.'[34] The story is still told at Sutherland's River of Catherine reprimanding a daughter for scrubbing the floor on her hands and knees. Olding women bent their knees when washing the floor. It was beneath their dignity ever to get on hands and knees.[35] Jeffrey emphasizes frontier women's 'desire to hold on to the conventions of female culture no matter how unfavorable the circumstances seemed.'[36]

The tannery fiasco intensified traits already visible in Catherine McQueen's personality. She had always been frugal, someone who did not believe in spending money on oneself. Now she became utterly parsimonious and self-denying. Her daughter Jessie, aged six at the time of the tannery disaster, came to emulate her mother, recalling later in life how, 'from my childhood, I always liked to "save" things – the best to the last.' Catherine expected her offspring to put the family's interests first. Work took priority even over schooling. The youngest children were kept home whenever, as Annie put it in 1877 at age thirteen, 'Ma needs me.' Catherine McQueen watched every penny and tried to make as much as possible selling and trading eggs, butter, and other produce. The large size of her family meant that she could not avoid running up bills with New Glasgow merchants. Among the McQueen papers in the Provincial Archives of Nova Scotia are bills for boots, fabric, tea, and chewing tobacco. Some notes were more serious than others. 'I beg leave to inform you that your bill of taxes is still unpaid amount $4.73. As I am about coming the tax up I will be under the necessity of taken [sic] legal steps against if not settle [sic] at once.'[37] New sources of income had to be found, and it was the duty of the McQueen children to provide them. The most obvious solution was for

the eldest daughters to qualify as schoolteachers, as did many neighbouring offspring.

The Public School Acts of 1864 and 1865, which made education free
of charge, caused more children to go to school longer. The demand for
teachers soared, and it was the daughters of modest families like the
McQueens who seized the opportunity. By doing so, they both reflected
and contributed to a rise in the percentage of female teachers in Pictou
County from just over 25 per cent in 1860, the year Jessie was born, to
almost 60 per cent by the time she took charge of a classroom.[38] The law
set sixteen as the minimum age for holding a teaching post. In 1855 the
eldest McQueen daughter, Jane, reached that age. It was not, however,
possible for her to undertake this work. Family tradition states that a bad
fall she suffered in her teens arrested her emotional development, but
her problem seems to have been that she suffered in an extreme form
from the mood swings that marked both her father and brother and also
her maternal grandfather. Squire Olding, the story goes, was unable to
plead in court in case he suddenly went out of control, a circumstance
some attributed to a wound in the head. It is said to have been this circumstance that precipitated the move from Halifax to the more remote
Pictou district. Jane could write letters and her behaviour was in general
kind and considerate. She certainly did her share of the household
chores and worked in the barn. She often took care of her younger siblings. Mary Belle perceptively portrayed her as 'the dear sister who did so
much for the rest of us.'[39] However, Jane could suddenly become angry
and hostile, a condition that deteriorated into fits of physical violence as
she grew older.

The duty of increasing the McQueen family income fell on Mary
Belle, who in 1868, at the age of seventeen, secured a temporary licence
to teach and thereafter took jobs wherever they could be found, a term
at a time. In 1872 a school inspector, whose job was to monitor the province's somewhat motley teaching force, reported, 'Pupils registered 57,
present 38, average to date 36 ... There is entirely too much labor for
one teacher; there should be an assistant. The work is all carried on with
a masterly hand by Miss Mary B. McQueen, Grade B, salary $75.' This
salary was not for the month but for the school term of six months
minus a three-week break between terms. At first, Mary Belle taught at
schools within walking distance of her home, so that most of her pay
could go to meet the family's necessities and cover debts. When Mary
Belle moved a bit further away, Catherine ensured she knew she was still
being monitored. 'Mary tho absent you're not forgot there is not a day

passes over my head but I think of you and your welfare.' Having heard a dance was in the offing, Catherine pronounced: 'I hope you will take no part in such parties (even if I should never know) they will never never give real pleasure.'[40]

One salary was not enough. In May 1869, Eliza passed her teacher's examination, but her licence was endorsed in red ink: 'Mis McQ. is not authorized to take charge of a school till 16 years of age, without the Inspector's approval.' That birthday still lay some eleven months into the future, whereupon she too taught. For a time, she kept a journal, one of its first entries reading a bit ambiguously: 'Resolved to work as faithfully and diligently as possible for the good of my little charges ... Truly a teacher has much to answer for.'[41] Next, it was Dove's turn. The sums the daughters got seem to have been sufficient to set the family finances in order by the middle of the 1870s, and their absence meant that many fewer mouths to feed.

Escape from debt proved to be a dubious blessing since it allowed Daniel McQueen to embark once more on his fortune-making ventures. Coal had been mined in Pictou County since the early nineteenth century, and he decided to get in on the action. A letter sent by Jane to her sister Mary Belle early in March 1874 explained that 'Pa had [someone] digging for coal, though the precious metal is mighty frightened and keeps clear of them.' Mary Belle wrote in reply: 'Fact is you are all famous letter-writers ... I don't know about Pa, though I suspect a wealthy coal speculator has not time for such small matters.' A couple of months later, Mary Belle mused a bit wistfully in anticipation of coming home between terms: 'What is Pa doing in town? I'm afraid we're out of any improvements at home this summer and I'm very sorry, for though it is the pleasantest place in the world to me yet, it might be made more comfortable and enjoyable by a little professional work. But oh, dear, we must wait I suppose.'[42] It was likely a long wait, for from this fancy Daniel McQueen moved on to riskier ventures.

Daniel and Catherine McQueen's attitude toward their only son contributed to the family's financial straits. Late in 1875, George, then almost seventeen, enrolled at Dalhousie College in Halifax. A little over a decade old, the officially non-denominational post-secondary institution was effectively Presbyterian. As the only son in what was a sharply gendered world, it was simply assumed that the family would rally around putting him through college. He managed to win a scholarship, but the amount was not sufficient to cover his expenses. George relied on money from home, so he confided to Mary Belle: 'I'm clean out of cash, haven't even enough to pay this week's board. I wrote home last week but haven't received an answer yet. Of course if there is not money at home I don't wish them to go to any trouble or bother until some comes in, but I would like to know just how matters are.' George's older sisters assisted, as indicated by a reference in one of Eliza's letters to 'Geo's expenses – I can't bear to think of him going to a less comfortable boarding-house he musn't *lodge* whatever he does.' In March 1878, George had his photograph professionally taken, sending copies to his sisters in remuneration for their generosity. Jessie's response in her journal was to be expected. 'Ain't I hopping glad. It's a perfect beauty.'[43]

It was George's needs and other financial pressures that caused the family, which now had only Jane, Jessie, and Annie at home, to take in the new Presbyterian minister at Sutherland's River. Soon joined by his bride, he was allocated the front bedroom and front parlour, the family being relegated to the back of the house and upstairs bedrooms. Worse was to follow. Daniel McQueen, gregarious by nature and easily misled, was talked into signing a note guaranteeing the moneys owed by a friend of his, a New Glasgow businessman. The merchant's death brought the business crashing down. Daniel found himself liable for debts of about $4,000. At the start of September 1878, he was able to convince the creditors to settle at 25¢ on the dollar.[44] To find this sum, he had to mortgage the farm to the Bank of Nova Scotia. His brother Angus McQueen shortly thereafter took over the loan, and the bank released Daniel from the mortgage. However, in 1880, Angus called in his money, and the family had to scramble to find alternative means to finance the remaining debt.

Catherine McQueen's reaction to the financial crisis is revealed in a letter she wrote her daughter Eliza at a moment when Daniel, assisted by George, was in New Glasgow trying to settle the debt at a reduced rate. 'They have not returned, yet I know the Lord rules over & above all and however the matter may be settled he can & will provide, such is my trust, strong & clear & I am not so cast down or sad as you might suppose, and surely I should be thankful too, that he enables me to trust it all with him.' Always a hard, demanding person, she briefly gave way to a physical and emotional breakdown, but thereafter ruled those around her with a rod of iron, her husband included. She fretted whenever Daniel 'commenced the tobacco again.' He had to chew it in secret, going behind the barn to escape his wife's wrath. Indicative of Catherine's priorities was a letter she wrote Eliza in 1879. 'The finances at home are a little low, but the word of truth holds good. "The Lord will provide" & not one word more about not being able to help.'[45]

Catherine's assumptions about her daughters' work were, as Louise Tilly and Joan Scott have demonstrated for England and France during these years, absolutely typical. 'Not only did parents expect contributions from their daughters, but daughters expected to contribute to the family fund.'[46] The guilt that they were made to feel comes out vividly in a letter from Dove, in which she detailed down to the last cent her expenses over the past term of teaching. 'I was quite surprised to find that you thought me parsimonious as regards money matters ... I feel sorry that I could not do more if you are in need of anything cannot you get things in my name or your own with the understanding that I will pay for them in the fall ... I am as fond of the old home as any of them and I've been homesick often enough this winter.'[47] So long as daughters remained single, they belonged, and were responsible, to their parents' household.

The McQueens' only son continued to be exempted from the rule that family obligations came first. When the financial crisis of 1878 struck, George was about to start his fourth year at Dalhousie. As a friend remarked, 'if George were only through College he would be in a better position to get along, as it is he will be thrown entirely on his own resources for a sufficiency to complete his College course.' Forced to drop out, George took a teaching job, but predictably, given the occupation's gendered character, he soon decided he deserved more. Within the year, he was off to New York City for a job in publishing whose impetus lay in a Pictou County connection. While at university, George got to know Will Munro, whose father, a Pictou farmer's son, had made a fortune in New York by publishing cheap reprints of good fiction. At first, George not only worked for the Munro publishing firm, he lived with the family, moving out after a year but holding onto the job for a couple more, after which he struck out on his own. The reasons for leaving the Munros' home in Brooklyn are unclear, apart from a comment that Will, whom George still considered 'my friend and may be more than ever,' was now moving 'in a circle much too expensive for me.' Lest his mother think that he would soon settle down into conventionality, George warned her that 'it's going to be a regular stunner of a girl that will ever take the place in my affections that my family and tried and true boy friends hold.'[48]

Whereas the McQueen daughters were Catherine's milch cows, George was her pet and he knew it. To sidestep any opposition to his being in New York rather than at home in Nova Scotia, he claimed 'a kind Providence' had directed him there. 'Everything indeed has been for the best,' he assured his doting mother. From time to time, George would promise the sky, how, very soon, 'I shall be in a position to give the home crowd that help which now has to go to the daughters.' He bragged in 1881 how he was earning $1,400 a year and, as soon as he cleared his debts, there would be 'a margin for sundry little checks payable to my dear Mrs McQueen.' The debts must have been considerable, for he was soon equivocating. 'I feel disappointed to think that the girls have to teach as I expected by this time that it would have been unnecessary, but there's many a slip.' About the same time, George remonstrated Jessie, after an illness, not to hasten to accept another teaching job since 'I'll guarantee to make good all the money lost by your needed rest.' Out of work for a time, George got a new job in the spring of 1884, whereupon Catherine slipped him the money to buy an entire wardrobe commensurate with his status – 'shoes, socks, shirts, drawers, coat, pants, vest, hat, collars, necktie, everything.' His response was to complain how 'it rather hurt me to be even a temporary burden to you whom I ought to be keeping' and how 'the little girls Annie & Jessie never give me a quiet conscience.' George repeatedly employed verbal acrobatics, not just to assuage his guilt but to justify not returning home. 'As to my financial status, I know perfectly well that you don't want me to think that you are in need of money at home but I know that you are miserably short of cash for necessary comforts.' So George stayed put, despite his sisters sometimes feeling that he should 'do his duty' and return home to help on the family farm.[49]

The freedom that George took as his due fired his sisters' imaginations. His letters tantalized them with the possibilities lying beyond Pictou County and Nova Scotia. To Jessie, then in her early twenties: 'We have the great apostle of the English aesthetes here now, name Oscar Wild [sic] age between twenty five and thirty, dress fur coat or robe knee-breeches, silk stocking creed, there is beauty in everything, and his practice is to carry around lilies and sunflowers, the one the type of chaste and pure the other of gaudy leonine beauty.' George hastened to assure his younger sister that neither he nor she could possibly be tempted by such a lifestyle. 'My opinion of him and his disciples is they're fools and short lived ones at that for I've seen women in the back woods of Pictou who never heard of this latest renaisance [sic] who put into practice in the decoration of her parlor more than all the really practical the whole lot of them possesses.'[50] He might dally, but the domestic realm was, from George's perspective, his sister's lot as a duti-ful daughter of Pictou County.

Dreams of adventure surfaced among McQueen daughters at least from 1874, when Eliza, living at home and teaching, inquired of her older sister Mary Belle, working a ways away, 'Have you thought of what you are going to do next term at all? I wish we could both pull up stakes and go West and do something worth while, but it seems harder to me than ever.' Three years later, Eliza mulled the invitation of a friend who 'intends going to the States about the middle of October and would like very well to go down with me.' In 1880 Dove began to 'talk of going to Colorado.'[51] In the event, all three, on reaching the average age for marriage for women in Nova Scotia, found themselves husbands. Mary Belle and Eliza were married in 1880 at the ages of twenty-nine and twenty-six respectively, the first to businessman Freeman Wisdom, the second to medical doctor Norman Cunningham. Four years later, at the age of twenty-seven, Dove married an itinerant Baptist preacher, Edwin Crowell. Their departures – Mary Belle to Saint John, New Brunswick, Eliza to Dartmouth, which was adjacent to Halifax, and Dove to various locations across the Maritimes – put additional pressures on the two youngest McQueen sisters, still at home.

Perhaps because Jessie was a middle child, she did not develop a strong sense of self. When sickness kept her away from school for two weeks at age thirteen, she fretted to Mary Belle that her fellow 'scholars are forgetting there ever was a Jessie McQueen.' Mary Belle praised Jessie's 'quiet wholesome fun homelike ways.' Rather than preening upon acquiring a new dress, Jessie worried that she might stand out. 'I'm muchly afraid that I'll look like an exaggerated "cherry-bush" as the frills are rather full. When I put it on I'll just have to smile and smile.' For Jessie, more with any of the other sisters, family took priority. Jessie qual-ified as a teacher in October 1876 when she was, as with her older sister Eliza, not yet sixteen. It was 'the deepest, blackest thunder-cloud' of the family's debt that impelled Jessie to try for her first teaching job at age sixteen in the fall of 1877. Unsuccessful, she returned to high school and was reduced to a single black dress when one of her older sisters came to the rescue. 'I feel sorry for Jessie working so bravely at home & sent her and the rest a few things.' Even so, the young Jessie had moments of despair over what she termed 'the burden of life.' 'There are times I think when everything in the world looks blue – when one can take no pleasure in past present or future views, when everything ahead looks as though all to be done was the most dismal routine imaginable & in the end it came to nothing.'[52]

A year later, Jessie once again tried for a teaching job. School boards voted in a somewhat idiosyncratic fashion 'for a female' or male teacher. It was only in October 1878, two months after the teaching year began when only the least desirable jobs were still unfilled, that she could report, 'I've got a school at last.' The job was about as far away from home as it was possible to be. It was located at Lochaber, 'a poor section' where 'they all have work in the woods,' almost twenty kilometres inland from Sheet Harbour along Nova Scotia's south shore. From the onset, Jessie was ambivalent about the opportunity, and her fears were soon realized. 'The school is so horrid I never disliked anything so much. The children are so dirty and stupid and they all have colds and go snuffing & snorting round.' Jessie simply could not cope. At the beginning of December, she wrote in her diary: 'No school today & I'm not sorry. It's the most unsatisfactory kind of work I have ever tried.' Anything else had to be better. 'I feel as though I could do everything at home kindle fires attend the barn and all kinds of work ... I know quite well that when I do get home I'll be apt through time to get somewhat discontented with my lot but then you see I'll have this spell of misery to look back on.'[53]

Jessie's desire to return home was reinforced by her mother's state of mind in her absence. Catherine groused to Mary Belle: 'I have to be stable boy & maid of all work, so that sometimes I feel almost like giving up (don't mention this to Jessie).' Catherine's response to Jessie's plight was, perhaps inadvertently, calculated to create in her a lifelong sense of guilt for not being as true a daughter as she ought. 'My Dear little girl, my heart aches for you & if I could, I would run to you with all my heart, & cheer you up. But don't fret, we will only be too glad to have you home again, & we will be trying & considering what will be the best way, don't trouble about the money or expenses (although with us now money may be necessary) it don't weigh a strain in comparison with your happiness.' Still wearing 'the black dress that I took away in such a dilapidated state,' Jessie slunk home at Christmas and stayed there. More than ever before, she felt the family's penury. 'Oh the blues! the blues! work, they say is the great panacea & if that's so I must go into it strong to keep these vapours off my yearning "spirit" ... And all because we *have* to scratch & toil for money, money, money.'[54]

Over the next several years, Jessie taught whenever and wherever she could get a job in Pictou County.[55] She quit writing in her journal in the misery of Lochaber, but eighteen months later penned a reflective afterword. 'I've changed my mind [about teaching] since that time and think it's splendid on the whole. Of course I've got better schools though. The Sheet Harbor one was a weariness to the flesh. The Mills [likely MacPherson's Mills on Upper Sutherland's River] even was better & Fraser's Mt. [outside of New Glasgow toward Sutherland's River] is best of all. There never was a rose though without a thorn, but there are some with only a few prickles & I guess this is one of them.' About this time, her sister Eliza described, as she left Pictou County a married woman, 'dear little Jess at her school-house door – the dear lonely little figure I'll never forget it.' The imagery was apt, for each sister's marriage put a greater 'obligation on the others left behind. Jessie was left only to dream, confiding to a cousin how 'Sutherland River is destitute of young men.' The actual situation may have embodied an element of pathos, for a family story has Jessie engaged to a young man who died of fever. Three months into the 1882 school year, Jessie secured the still vacant school at Sutherland's River. The appointment triggered a letter from Eliza, six years her senior, which was revealing of teachers' circumstances. 'I think $55 [a term] is a pitiful salary for S.R. to offer a teacher – but for you is as much as you'd clear elsewhere and is so nice for the rest at home to have you.'[56]

To the extent Jessie was comforted in her lot, it was by her younger sister, Annie, known affectionately as Nan. Physically, the two were much alike, Jessie once being asked repeatedly 'if I weren't a sister of Miss [Annie] McQueen's, you look *so* much like her.' They were both tiny women, Jessie observing when walking with two female friends that 'I am a mere speck beside them, and when I get on the outside turning a corner, am sure to be left half-a-dozen steps behind.' Jessie had blue eyes, and Annie 'black eyes shining more than the traditional burnt holes.' If the sisters did not wear spectacles, they should have. Their mother wrote in the spring of 1878, after a period of illness, that 'their eyesight is weak, they cannot write, nor read large print without blundering, I thought it was caused by their reading too soon [after being ill], but I find tis a general complaint with the recovered ones.' George recalled five years later how 'Nan with her spectacles calmly surveys the world with her eyes twinkling with mischief.' Jessie's eyesight wavered, and hence such observations as 'my eyes are stronger now, for I've given them quite a rest this week.'[57]

Similar in appearance, the sisters were opposites in personality. Annie considered that she and her father 'are a good deal alike, we both take up readily with new acquaintances and surroundings.' Jessie resembled her mother, whose cautions to her children were routine. In many ways, the sisters were mirror images. Annie was exuberant, while Jessie held back. Annie met life head on, and Jessie steeled herself in order to be able to cope. Jessie once observed how 'Nan was all life & go,' whereas she was 'very quiet.' Jessie wanted nothing so much as to please. Her older sister Eliza recalled about her as a child that 'if Jessie had a peppermint lozenge she wasn't happy till she had shared it all round.' Annie was much more her own person, willing to face off even her mother from time to time. 'I can skip pretty well now, I skipped to two hundred and seven the other day, but ma will not let me skip any at all today.' Presbyterianism was massaged to serve her needs, as in cajoling her mother, while on a visit to Eliza, about how she had been lent 'a green dress' and would have to 'trust in Providence' for a replacement when she got home. If, as Eliza put it judiciously, Annie cared overly much for her own 'amusements,' she was also generous of spirit. When Jessie got so horribly lonely her first term of teaching, it was Annie at age fourteen who tried to cheer her up by offering to 'take your place; wouldn't it be jolly? I'd like it splendidly wouldn't I look dignified and order the scholars round.' In turn, Jessie mused about the 'poor little thing,' now forced to take up the burden of work at home, that 'perhaps a little won't hurt her.' Unlike Jessie, Annie exuded the confidence inherent to good teaching. From her first opportunity, while still a pupil: 'I like it splendidly.' As soon as she was old enough, Annie, like her older sisters, taught in various locations, including nearby Little Harbour.[58]

Daughterhood's obligations loomed large for the two youngest McQueens. Staying a few extra days on a visit to her married sister Eliza, Jessie at age twenty-four fretted, 'I do hope you won't think it too bad of me – the temptation was very strong ... Be sure and send me word mother dear for I begin to feel mean about it. In any case tell Ann I'll be home in time to help her with her dress.' Two days later, it was Eliza who queried whether 'Jessie *might* stay a few days longer.' Annie and Catherine were left with the chores, and Eliza reminded the pair about Jessie that 'I know that *she* would be willing to do as much for Annie under similar circumstances.' Faced with a fait accompli, the mother and sister left behind ensured that Jessie realized the full extent to which she was shirking her obligations. From Annie: 'Monday afternoon after you left, I set to work first to wash the army of dishes and ... after that, I swept out the front bedroom, hall, dining-room and kitchen, cleaned the closet ... and then went to milk feeling pretty blue ... Same repeated each time ... On Wednesday I washed a big tubful of clothes, but it rained in the afternoon, so I had to leave all the flannels and calicoes, and the second tubful of white clothes until the next day ... Today, I baked, ironed and churned, & I am pretty tired ... Now, you know that it is utterly impossible for you to make that dress in time, as you are going to stay "a few days beyond Tuesday," so if I do go [on a planned outing], which is doubtful, I will [have to] go without it.' Annie saved her best shot for the postscript: 'Suit yourself (as far as I am concerned) about what time to come back. You know the facts of the case better than I can tell you.'[59]

In November 1884, Jessie took her courage in her hands and enrolled in the Provincial Normal School at Truro.[60] In 1853 it was decided to establish rail service from Halifax to Truro, from where lines would fan out across Nova Scotia. Truro's new status as rail hub caused the teacher's training institution, legislated a year later, to be located there. An imposing new building constructed in 1878 was the centerpiece of a bustling commercial and industrial town with a population approaching 4,000, about 500 more than New Glasgow. Jessie was encouraged in her decision by the ease of rail transportation, as well as the opportunity to gain a professional qualification and so a higher salary. Rail service, completed from Halifax to Truro in 1858, reached New Glasgow in 1867, being extended to Sutherland's River in 1878. With Annie in the classroom, Jessie could afford to take a year off.

Jessie's experience at Truro reinforced the familiar. Over two terms, the school offered content courses similar to what was taught in school together with methods courses and classroom practice. By Jessie's estimate, fully half of the two hundred 'Normalites' were Presbyterian, and all but twenty-five or thirty, female. As to there being 'six or seven *ladies* to every gentleman,' Jessie professed, at least to her mother, to be 'truly thankful that it *is* so.' Although boarding away from home, Jessie continued to seek Catherine's approval. When the 'teacher's govt. money' which subsidized Jessie's attendance did not arrive in time, she felt it necessary to ask whether 'I might indulge in some Xmas cards mother.' Repeatedly, she fretted that she 'had no business to stay here, when I must be so much needed' by 'poor mother.' Jessie rationalized that 'surely sometime I'll get the worth of this winter in hard cash.'[61] The expectation of higher wages made her year away from teaching worthwhile.

At Truro, Jessie was reminded of schooling's purposes, as summed up by educational historian Janet Guildford, to 'provide moral training for the young and produce a generation of hard-working, law-abiding citizens.' Even though Jessie remained, as recalled by one of her instructors, 'a remarkably modest, unassuming young lady,' it was 'the inculcation of these social and moral values' on distinctly religious lines that gave her a greater sense of self-assurance as to teaching's obligations. At Truro there was even 'a "talk" from a lady Doctor' after 'all the "male men" were dismissed,' which included 'remarks about dress – food &c [that] coincided with our own views & practice pretty muchly so.'[62]

Jessie was not a stellar student. Writing to Annie in February 1885, she lamented, 'I despise myself that I can't do better ... Oh Nan I wish I'd been born clever – it would be so nice to feel oneself progressing.' Jessie considered that she made progress slowly. 'Did I tell you I had taught, for the second time? I didn't howl this time – till I got home I mean – but I felt that this attempt was even worse than the last. It's no good to fret though!' The next week: 'Oh do you know I'm doing *far* better this month (Feb. I mean) ... I'm improving slowly. I actually got through a recitation in Dr. Hall's today without stammering – it was only a short paragraph, but showed me that I was gaining a little confidence.' Two months later: 'I taught on Thursday (the fourth time for me) a lesson on fractions, and Mr. [John B.] Calkin [head of the normal school] said it was as good a lesson as he had heard this year – and that he was very much pleased with it ... I shook dreadfully at first, but before I was done I felt wonderfully at ease and dismissed my class in a very composed manner.' Jessie became confident enough to take pleasure that 'I got my photos – $2 a doz – tell me how you like them.' By the end of the academic year: 'Nan dear I did wish that you could come to closing ... I am to teach mind you, little did I think last summer that such a thing would ever be.' Jessie was awarded 'a Superior Diploma,' for which she was roundly congratulated by her fellow students.[63]

With no one younger to take their place to help support the family, Jessie and Annie seemed caught in a web of familial obligations. Jessie noted as she was about to return home from Truro that 'Nan & I are the only men on the farm to help father with the hay &c &c.' Jessie felt it necessary to cajole her mother 'if it would be too much for me to ask for a day of rest for myself after' completing government examinations. 'Don't think that I am altogether selfish mother dear, but you know I never was among such a lot of people before, and I have made *some* friends, and after we leave here we are scattered all over the Province & may never see one another again ... I don't ask to stay so long, (for I *do* so want to be home too, in fact, I'm quite torn in two by conflicting emotions).' Jessie was soon back at her former existence at Sutherland's River. As well as teaching, she made do for others, at times for her married sisters. Eliza had only a momentary pang of conscience that, later the same summer, 'perhaps I was selfish to give Jessie so much sewing to do.'[64]

A year later, in the fall of 1886, with Jessie in the classroom, Annie got her turn at the Truro Normal School. Now aged twenty-one, Nan was much more of a social being, reporting back to Jessie how 'Valentine's day came, and how the Vals did fly! ... I had to travel up there [to receive them at the front of the Assembly room] *four* times, the fourth time, the 2nd Class boys began to clap me, and even Mr Calkin laughed.' Annie's great strength was that she liked herself. She described how she 'skipped up gaily' to the front of the class to recite and how 'the crowd [of boys] all say that I am the favourite, the boys are awfully good to me in lots of ways, and no mashing about it.' Annie ended up overextending herself, becoming ill, and finished the year with a Pass Certificate.[65] The die seemed cast that Annie would return home and, like her older sister Jessie, soon be back in the classroom.

Even as Nan was reconciling herself to her fate, a providential letter arrived. A Presbyterian minister settled in the distant Canadian province of British Columbia wrote at the beginning of April 1887 about a teaching post that would shortly become open. The Rev. John Chisholm was a family friend from Pictou County. The teaching vacancy for which he sought Annie was not far from his parish at Kamloops, a former fur-trading post in the province's southern interior, now a divisional point on the new transcontinental rail line. His purpose was straightforward, to stack British Columbia public schools with young Presbyterian women who would inculcate in their pupils the same values he was preaching from the pulpit, much as occurred back home in Pictou County. His goal was about as close to colonization as it was possible to get within a nation. Chisholm more or less promised Annie the position if she would only apply for it. Moreover, once she got settled, she could keep an eye out for a vacancy for Jessie, who could then follow her west.[66] The recent completion of the Canadian Pacific Railway meant that the trip itself was a matter of days instead of weeks or months. Suddenly a new and different future opened up, not just for Annie but also for her shyer older sister Jessie.

Chapter Three

Nova Scotia to British Columbia

When Annie McQueen and then, nine months later, her sister Jessie boarded the train for British Columbia, they embarked on a trip taking just eight days. It was, however, much longer in the making. The decision as to whether they would be allowed to go was not taken easily and consumed a considerable period of time. The circumstances that finally permitted them to leave were far older than they were. The trip from Nova Scotia to British Columbia was no small undertaking.

The idea of sojourning, of going elsewhere to work for a time, as Annie was now invited to do, had become widely accepted in Nova Scotia and across the Maritime provinces. Many families found themselves unable to survive on the resources available close to home. Even though the McQueens grew much of their own food and some cash flowed in from the sale of eggs and butter, Daniel's building jobs, and daughters' wages, finances were always tight for the growing family. The impetus behind their son George's heading to New York City, and their daughters' dreaming of faraway places, lay in larger shifts taking place in Nova Scotia.

Daniel and Catherine McQueen's childhoods were spent, at least in retrospect, during a period of prosperity for Nova Scotia. Fishing, lumbering, wooden shipbuilding, coal mining, and trade complemented a principal reliance on agriculture. Halifax, whose origins harked back to the mid-eighteenth century, built on its strategic coastal location to become Nova Scotia's political, economic, and cultural centre. The city's sense of permanence was encouraged by amenities as diverse as stoves, handlooms, and bookstores. The founding of colleges and associations helped to develop a sense of identity distinctive from the United States to the south.

By the 1840s, the British colony of Nova Scotia ceased to be a frontier attracting newcomers with the promise of cheap land. Thereafter growth came primarily through natural increase, which consolidated a commitment to place. It was not just Pictou County that was acquiring a sense of permanence. By 1871 fully 90 per cent of Nova Scotia's population of 387,800, climbing to 440,000 over the decade, was born in the province. Over three-quarters were British in origin, and another 20 per cent, northern European. Almost all Nova Scotians lived next door to someone as comfortably pale skinned as they themselves, as suited a long-time British colony. The remainder of the population included some 7,000 Blacks come north from the United States and 2,000 Aboriginal people. With these small aberrations, so they were considered at the time, the dominant frame of mind, as with the McQueens, was comfortably self-referential.

The years during which Jessie and Annie McQueen came of age treated Nova Scotians, and Pictonians, less gently than had the preceding ones. In 1867 the British colony joined the new Canadian Confederation alongside Ontario, Quebec, and New Brunswick. Attitudes to the union were mixed, not surprisingly so given that it was, historians Margaret Conrad, Alvin Finkel, and Cornelius Jaenen conclude, 'essentially a top-down exercise.'[1] Some favoured the change in status, arguing that the Dominion of Canada offered concrete advantages such as a network of railroads. Others were openly hostile, fearing that Nova Scotia would decline into nothing more than an economic backwater. Thereafter the relative prosperity that encouraged a stable way of life began to slip away, as the traditional exports of lumber, fish, coal, and foodstuffs lost their markets. The advent of steam and rail technology, which caused Catherine McQueen to exclaim in 1878 over 'the great iron horse puffing and whistling & crossing the bridge at S.R.,' hastened the demise of wooden ships driven by wind, and thereby of a principal export.[2]

Despite an initial spurt, Nova Scotia could not keep pace with industrial expansion in Ontario and Quebec, whose growth was facilitated by a National Policy put in place by the national government and benefiting the centre at the expense of peripheries like the Maritimes. The promised rail link to central Canada, instead of sending manufactures in that direction, siphoned off raw materials in exchange for goods carrying high protective tariffs which prevented the same items from being acquired more cheaply from the nearby United States. At best, Nova

Scotia was in a holding pattern; at the worst, depressed.[3] Widely shared nostalgia for a 'golden age' encouraged a sense of tradition that the McQueen sisters would take west with them.[4]

Sojourning was widespread throughout the Maritimes and more generally. Michael Katz quipped in his study of mid-nineteenth-century Hamilton, Ontario, that everyone, it seemed, 'was on the move.'[5] The gold rushes in California in 1849, Australia in the early 1850s, and British Columbia in 1858 each attracted away considerable numbers of young men, as did the rapidly industrializing American Northeast their female counterparts. Betsy Beattie has described how young women from the Maritimes worked for a time as servants or engaged in wage labour in a city like Boston before, very often, returning home to marry.[6] From the 1860s onward, more people departed the Maritimes than arrived from elsewhere. Randy Widdis has determined that, of Canadians migrating to the United States during the late nineteenth and early twentieth centuries, Maritimers were most likely to do so more than once, 'migration across the border being seen as a temporary but regular occurrence.'[7] Each time men and women left, they did so in anticipation of coming home again. It has been estimated that from a fifth to a half of young Nova Scotians, male and female, left the province during these years, at least for a time.[8]

To sojourn did not make persons any less good Nova Scotians or Maritimers, for their reasons for doing so were mainly economic. In Pictou County not only was land suitable for agriculture long since occupied, few farms produced more than a bare living. The number of farmers held constant at about 5,000 between 1871 and 1881. In the latter year, another 1,350 Pictonians described themselves as farmers' sons, even though most plots could sustain only a single son over the long term. Some offspring found work in Pictou County's coal mines or other industries, while others went further afield by choice or necessity. Halifax and adjacent Dartmouth, with a combined population of 40,000 by 1881, could not accommodate all of those who sought jobs there. The majority of sojourners headed to the United States, as had Catherine McQueen's sister Ann, who lived in Massachusetts, and Daniel McQueen's younger brother Duncan and son George.

As George McQueen's escapades testify, sojourning did not always accomplish its goals. An early Pictou County historian wrote a bit sourly about his itinerating counterparts that 'the majority by industry [are] attaining a competence, which they might have done at home, and many, alas, making a shipwreck of earthly prospects and even of conscience and a good name.'[9] An Olding cousin in the States only half joked at becoming 'a little Yankefyed' in a 'very wild place' where 'they don't regard Sabeth [sic] much here it is ther [sic] Pleasure Day.'[10] It was not just the personal pitfalls, but the money to be earned was not necessarily that great. Shortly after leaving home for Massachusetts, Daniel McQueen's brother Duncan had second thoughts. 'If you know of any more joiners proposing to come here, you can tell them they will find a mistake as soon as they come.' He tried Indiana, where he did not fare much better, and hence the long letter of 1870 when he implored Daniel not 'to pull up stakes' and do the same thing. Duncan had long since realized that, as he put it, 'it is a struggle for life wherever you go, and I don't know that it makes much difference where that struggle is made.' He stayed in the United States, unlike his younger brother Thomas, who soon returned home to Pictou County. Shortly before doing so, he waxed philosophical: 'I sometimes think there must be some better portion of the globe than Nova Scotia but after all I may be mistaken ... I shall leave and return a wiser man to old Nova Scotia.'[11]

The widespread acceptability of sojourning meant that Catherine McQueen, who ruled with a rod or iron, could not reject out of hand the offer made in 1887 to her youngest daughter. It was almost commonplace for persons of her age and gender to head off. According to historian Alan Brookes, the most likely sojourners were skilled Scots Presbyterian young women from rural areas.[12] Catherine was loathe to part with Nan, but three other factors made the offer too attractive to resist. There was British Columbia's reputation for having a healthy climate, the money to be earned, and, very importantly, the Presbyterian connection.

Health was a serious consideration. The McQueen family correspondence is replete with references to illness and death, which Catherine tended to turn into morality tales for right living. The cures were sometimes as ominous as the symptoms. Both Annie and Jessie were subject to bouts of neuralgia, which Eliza, married to a medical doctor, defined as being '"run down" in health' and remedied by taking iron tablets and pulling teeth. Thus Nan had 'a severe attack of neuralgia & tooth ache but got 3 or 4 teeth extracted & is better now.' Shortly after Jessie complained of the same symptoms, Catherine reported she was at 'the Dentist a short time ago and had 9 teeth or stumps extracted.' Annie's illness while at Truro is probably why Eliza's husband weighed into the debate over whether or not she should be allowed to head west. Eliza informed Catherine. 'Norm says to tell you he thinks Annie would be foolish not to accept the offer. He does not feel like advising too strongly in the matter but says the climate is certainly better than ours.' She and her husband's information about British Columbia came from a neighbour with a clergyman brother in Victoria, who told Eliza 'they have almost perpetual summer.'[13]

The money was just as important, if not more so. The wages to be got from teaching in British Columbia were bounteous compared with Nova Scotia. The Nova Scotia Department of Education was well aware that 'the average rates of teachers' salaries are lower than in some Provinces of the Dominion,' which it attributed to an excess of supply over demand.[14] Teachers were paid by the term, which equated to 110 to 120 days, or between five and six months, of instruction.[15] The agreed salary was reduced by days not taught, which depended on how soon in the term a teacher was hired and whether there were school closures. The older McQueens received between $45 and $75 per term, even when teaching, as Mary Belle did in the late 1870s, in Halifax. Jessie took home $14.99 for the 56 woeful days she taught at Lochaber, thereafter $45 to $55 a term at her various Pictou County positions, as did Annie. Jessie's year at the Provincial Normal School raised her pay to $60–5 a term.[16]

The salary in British Columbia was $50 to $60, but for a month instead of a term. It is not surprising that Jessie exclaimed shortly after arriving how 'it seems like a "soft snap" to get $60 a month for teaching such a school.' Even taking into consideration the $62.50 it cost for a second-class rail ticket across Canada, far more money could be brought into the McQueen family coffers by Annie and Jessie sojourning than their continuing to teach near home. As Eliza put it to Catherine, 'it does not do to disregard the latter [higher salary] because it may enable both girls to take a rest sooner than they otherwise could.'[17] The two youngest would, in other words, be freed sooner from daughterhood's obligations and able to marry.

The higher wages came at a cost, which also fed into the McQueen family's deliberations. Nova Scotia did not have to pay teachers as much because it had an oversupply, which related to the established character of the province compared to that of British Columbia. Nova Scotia possessed innumerable advantages, including long established churches, an array of voluntary associations, and comfortable routines of everyday life, whereas most of British Columbia was still a frontier. It had been through the efforts of many a Catherine McQueen that Nova Scotia, or, at the least, Pictou County, was domesticated. British Columbia still awaited such ministrations.

To families like the McQueens, British Columbia was an unknown place. As George put it about Annie's heading off to Kamloops, "'twould convey pretty nearly the same idea if she had said Kamskaletra.'[18] British Columbia's newcomer history set it apart from the rest of Canada. Both Nova Scotia and British Columbia had been somewhat reluctant entrants into Confederation, the latter in 1871, but little else joined the far distant provinces. Prior to the coming of the transcontinental railroad in the mid-1880s, British Columbia could be reached only through the United States or by sea. The first newcomers had been fur traders, who arrived during the late eighteenth and first half of the nineteenth centuries. The only Canadian influence among them consisted of labourers from Quebec. Their French language and culture set them apart from the mainly Scots fur trade officials and the handful of English bureaucrats who governed the British colony of Vancouver Island, established in 1849. The newcomer population did not exceed several hundred until gold was discovered on the nearby mainland in the spring of 1858, leading to the creation of a second British colony, British Columbia, on the mainland. Among the many thousands of men enticed by gold were a small but noisy lot of British North Americans, whose opionions carried less weight in the decision to enter Confederation than did other factors. Most important was the federal promise of a transcontinental railroad that, it was hoped, would restore good times. Gold fever had declined by the mid-1860s, leading to the union of the two colonies into a single colony of British Columbia and to depressed economic conditions. In 1871, when British Columbia joined Canada, it was home to about 25,000 Aboriginal people and just 10,000 others, of whom about 1,500 were from China. Newcomers were predominantly male, and any children born in British Columbia very possibly hybrids with Aboriginal mothers.

From 1871 to the completion of the rail link in the mid-1880s, the piece of land lying between the Pacific Ocean and the Rocky Mountains was part of Canada in name only. The nation had no meaning, other than as a vehicle on which to lay the blame for economic woes. The number of newcomers grew slowly, to 25,000 by 1881, of whom about 4,500 were from China, and then more rapidly, as rail construction got under way, to about 30,000 by mid-decade. Towns were few. The capital city of Victoria, which affected a British air harking back to its colonial days, had a population of 12,000 by 1885–6. The only other towns of any substance were coal-mining Nanaimo on central Vancouver Island and the market town of New Westminster in the province's southwestern tip, whose populations of several thousand each were modest and unassuming. Vancouver, originating as the terminus of the rail line, was still on the cusp of urbanity.

Most of the rest of British Columbia was a frontier. A harsh geography discouraged newcomer settlement, except for parts of Vancouver Island, smaller islands along the coast, the routes to the goldfields, and a handful of interior valleys adjoining the United States or along the rail line. One-time fur traders or miners, by themselves or with newcomer or Aboriginal wives, occupied the most fertile patches of land. Some of the Chinese-born who had come to find gold or build the rail line continued to mine, while others provided services ranging from foodstuffs to laundry to labour. Some Aboriginal people had been pushed onto reserves; others vied with newcomers for access to the key economic resources of land, fish, and trees.

As is characteristic of frontiers, colonial or otherwise, there was a sharp imbalance between the sexes in the newcomer population. Among adults, men predominated by a ratio of three to one.[19] As historian Adele Perry explains, they had perforce to perform 'domestic' tasks – cooking, washing, sewing, cleaning – that women usually did as a matter of course.[20] The unions some of them contracted with Aboriginal women were probably motivated in part by a desire to rid themselves of these tasks. This transfer was yet another of the ways in which newcomers imposed themselves on Indigenous peoples in a process we commonly term pioneering or colonization. The domestication of Aboriginal women could not, however, by the very meaning of that term, be complete. Indigenous women might keep their houses clean and neat, cook and sew to perfection, wear proper clothing, convert to Christianity, and learn English, but they were not the right colour. They were not 'white women,' as the rhetoric of the time phrased it. They did not, it was generally held among newcomers, possess the innate capacity for domesticity. Their apparent domestication was no more than a veneer, and in any crisis that veneer would crack and the savage show through.[21] Their hybrid offspring by newcomer men were equally, if not more, suspect as to their capacity to engage in right behaviour. It was up to newcomer women like the McQueens to effect change.

British Columbia was very different from anything known to the McQueen family. On the mainland, a single wagon road existed, connecting water navigation as far inland as Yale in the Fraser Canyon with the gold mines of the Cariboo. Elsewhere, goods had to be carried by horse or mule.[22] The postal service was sparse, not more than twice a week at the best. Schools and churches were notable for their rarity.

There was no training college or normal school for teachers, no theological school or seminary, no medical or law school. Professionals were either migrants trained outside the province or those who gained expertise in their field by apprenticeship or self-instruction. Having been in British Columbia half a year, Jessie lamented how 'we are in such an out of the way place' and mused how 'it would be nice to be in civilization once more.' It was, she reflected some months later, a 'great, lone land.'[23] Survival, be it for Aboriginal peoples, hybrid families originating in the fur trade and gold rush, or other newcomers, hinged on flexibility. Economic and social well-being on the frontier depended on a willingness to accommodate to the environment and to each other. Newcomers' self-confidence and material advantages presaged the inevitable outcome, but the process whereby frontier became settlement was in 1887 still ongoing across much of British Columbia.

The most important factor to move the frontier toward settlement was the completion of the Canadian Pacific Railway during 1885–6. Just as had occurred in Nova Scotia, it foretold a different future, and this more than any other factor probably caused Catherine McQueen to overlook the tremendous differences that existed between the two provinces and to focus on the advantages to be had from the much higher salaries. The newcomer population was already swelling along the rail line, be it Kamloops, to which Annie had been bid come, or other locations across the province's interior. Teachers were in demand, particularly for small frontier schools. The number needed doubled to 150 between the beginning of rail construction and the line's completion. It reached 200 by the time Annie was recruited. There was, moreover, no expectation of formal training. Educational supervision was limited to a superintendent of education and a couple of school inspectors, who mostly visited town schools. Aspiring teachers had only to pass a knowledge-based examination given annually in Victoria, good for a year or more depending on the standard reached. Moreover, the province readily issued temporary certificates good until the next summer's exam.[24] Women like Annie McQueen, who had attended a normal school, were at a premium.

The Presbyterian connection was as important as the climate or the money, perhaps more so, in swaying Catherine McQueen. It was not just the Rev. John Chisholm at Kamloops who tied the family to the church's work in British Columbia. His predecessor, the Rev. George Murray, had in 1875 emigrated from Scotland to the British Columbia interior in response to an appeal from newcomer families.[25] Within the year, he erected the area's first Presbyterian church on the west end of Nicola

Lake south of Kamloops. An early visitor described 'the handsome little white Church, and neatly fenced cemetery attached, situated at the center of the town plot,' where it remains virtually unchanged to the present day.[26] By 1878, the demands of the frontier became too much for Murray, and he accepted a call to a church in New Glasgow, where he got to know various members of the McQueen family. Annie attended high school in New Glasgow in the spring of 1882 and may have first heard of British Columbia from Murray's sermons.

The zeal underlying the Rev. John Chisholm's proposal reflected a larger change occurring among Presbyterians in Canada. Some adherents were moving away from the arbitrariness of predestination toward the softer concept of providence and even to the evangelical doctrine of free grace granted by God to those who would repent. Such a shift in interpretation made it possible, and even obligatory, for good Presbyterians to improve conditions on earth rather than sit back awaiting heavenly judgment. A key figure in this change in direction was George Monro Grant, born in Pictou County in 1835. Trained as a Presbyterian minister, in 1877 he was named principal of Presbyterian Queen's College in Kingston, Ontario, twelve years later becoming moderator, or head, of the Presbyterian Church in Canada. For Grant and others of similar disposition, the kingdom of God to be created on earth, in the form of Canada, rather resembled the devout, hard-working, self-denying society of Pictou County.[27]

Many Protestants, perhaps most of all Nova Scotian Presbyterians in the mould of George Monro Grant and the McQueens, were coming to believe that they had a mission to make Canada an emanation of themselves. 'Presbyterians who attended church with any regularity and read their denomination's publications could scarcely escape the conclusion that they had some responsibility for the quality of Canadian national life,' Margaret Prang explains. More than any other group in Canadian society, they had the means to do so. 'The churches constituted national networks that had considerable influence in shaping their members' vision of Canadian society and informing their opinions.'[28] Virtually everyone during these years accepted without question the primacy of organized religion, which in Canada equated with Christianity and, outside of Quebec, most often with Protestantism. Just as did the McQueens, they followed its principles not only on Sunday but every day of the week. The values and way of life of Scots Presbyterian families like the McQueens became perceived, historian John C. Moir argues, as being at the heart of Canada as a nation. Moir terms the generation who came of age in the decades after

Confederation, as did Annie and Jessie, 'a clerisy – an educational (in the broadest sense) family compact – and one of the most important exports of the Maritime provinces to the rest of Canada.'[29]

Pictou County's George Monro Grant was a central player in nation-building. Prang considers that, 'in the later nineteenth century, few Canadian leaders were listened to on national issues with more respect than Principal G.M. Grant of Queen's,' whose trip west at the time of British Columbia's entry into Confederation anticipated that of the McQueen sisters by a decade and a half.[30] His account, published as *Ocean to Ocean* in 1873, foresaw the transcontinental railroad, and its human cargo, as the means to link Canada east to west, Nova Scotia to British Columbia. Grant assumed an equation between piety and the emergence of a nation. 'A great future beckons us as a people forward. To reach it, God grant to us purity and faith ... Thank God we have a country.'[31] It was Grant's 'Canadianism,' Moir argues, 'that marked him out as the most influential and vocal of those Maritime Presbyterians who held a national rather than an Ontario vision of Canada's destiny.'[32]

Grant believed fervently that, as the West was opened up to settlement from within Canada, newcomers had to be made to 'feel that they are going away neither from their own country nor their own Church.' He might have been speaking directly to Catherine McQueen when he added that, 'in the interest of patriotism and religion it is desirable that all the forces that mould the character of a people to high issues should be brought to bear' on the process of settlement.[33] Grant influenced a generation of Canadians to act as he spoke, including fellow Pictonian Alfred Fitzpatrick. A Presbyterian of similar background and age to Jessie and Annie, Fitzpatrick was mentored by Grant while attending Queen's College. At first ministering to the spiritual needs of men in logging camps, Fitzpatrick came to realize that the best way to reach these mostly immigrant workers was through education and went on to found Frontier College with its double goal of literacy and 'Canadianiza-tion' for working men.[34] Education was, for Grant, the second great priority after the Church in what he saw as the increasingly urgent task of binding Canada together as a nation in the mould of Pictou county. It was as if he had Fitzpatrick and the McQueen sisters in mind when he fretted, just about the time the Rev. John Chisholm's letter arrived at Sutherland's River, how 'we are nearing that point in our history when we must assume the full responsibilities of nationhood, or abandon the experiment altogether.'[35]

Young women like the McQueen sisters had a special responsibility to make the Canada men like Grant advocated. Women, Prang comments, 'possessed less direct political influence than their fathers and husbands, but they were a significant part of the religious networks.'[36] Being, in Moir's words, 'products of a stable, rural society' and sharing in a 'rich heritage of Maritime culture' and a 'common faith in the superiority and covenanted responsibility of Presbyterianism,' women like the McQueens and men like Fitzpatrick were 'God's instrument to build a righteous and exalted nation.' By going west, Annie and Jessie would not just sojourn, they would further the larger cause of nation-building. Moir describes how 'the Maritime provinces exported their most important resource, namely leadership in the form of their talented offspring who carried with them a moral idealism that they popularized through public life, the classroom, literature, and music.'[37] Fellow historian Ian Manson emphasizes how, 'by stressing the virtues of becoming diligent and god-fearing, hard-working, and responsible citizens of Canada and the British Empire, the Presbyterian church helped foster these ideals in countless homes, work places and communities.'[38] It was, from Grant's perspective, 'a people resolute, intelligent, calm and religious' who headed west, in his view 'the cream of our Older Provinces' who did so.[39]

The public rhetoric of men like George Monro Grant almost certainly reached women like Catherine McQueen who read the Presbyterian press regularly. Sentiment was growing that an obligation existed to further the kingdom of God on earth as in heaven. The passion for domestication that Catherine exercised in her household acquired a second, parallel dimension, which was to nudge frontier provinces like British Columbia into Canada by moving them closer to outlooks and practices in place elsewhere in the nation of which they were nominally a part. Her daughters, Annie and then Jessie if she followed after, would not so much be leaving home as taking it with them. Theirs was a mission that, almost of itself, justified their departure.

All of these factors – the prevalence of sojourning, a healthier climate, higher salaries, Presbyterian zeal – meant that the debate taking place in the McQueen family in the spring of 1887 had a certain predestined quality about it. Sensing her own escape in the wings, Jessie made as many arguments as possible for letting Annie go to their sister Eliza who then retailed them to their mother. 'Apart from the pain of separation, it does seem to be a good thing for Annie, both as regards her health and financially.' Eliza pushed every advantage. 'The school hours are from half-past nine a.m. to three p.m., not nearly as long as they are in D[art]m[ou]th,' where she lived. There was never any expectation that the move would be permanent. Annie promised to 'be back in three years,' as would Jessie later.[40] In the end, Nan was able to accept because of the sense of obligation to obey God's will that Presbyterianism gave, which her mother simply could not refute. The invitation was providential.

Annie left for British Columbia in the middle of June 1887. For a decade, the train had run from Sutherland's River to Truro, then to Moncton, New Brunswick, and on to Montreal. Jessie travelled with Annie as far as Truro, where Annie picked up her normal school diploma and a letter from one of her instructors 'to the minister of education or whatever he is out there.' Their older sister Eliza travelled up from Dartmouth to spend a day with the pair, bringing some pills, courtesy of her doctor husband, 'to be used for constipation – I only hope the journey won't send her to the other extreme.' Jessie bought her own parting gifts for Annie, consisting of a Bible and some yarn for knitting. The three visited their sister Janie, then being institutionalized to keep her from wandering off, as she was wont to do. No accounts survive of Annie's trip west, apart from her having a very 'pleasant' journey.[41]

Back home in Sutherland's River, Jessie did not waver in her determination to follow Nan west. Sisterhood's bonds were strengthened by their separation. It sufficed that Annie wanted to have 'a big slice of home' at her side. 'Oh Nan when we get together won't our tongues wag? Whoops! I wish I had you within reach of my sisterly clutches.' Annie set her eyes on a nearby school for Jessie and reported in October 1887 that 'I think you can get it at New Year.' By then even the errant George was forced to accept that 'our hard-working patient brave little Jess is going away in the spring.' Eliza mused how 'Jessie has been talking of going to B.C. and I cannot blame her for going. It is not possible that she can keep on teaching, working and worrying.' Concerned over her own well-being, Dove equivocated. Like the other sisters, she had been freed of worrying about their parents because Jessie carried the burden. Now Dove fretted: 'I can hardly bear the idea of Jessie going out West. It means so much if things would not change.'[42]

In early 1888, Annie learned that the school next to hers would become vacant in mid-March. 'Oh, child, you must come.' The down side was, of course, as Annie acknowledged, Catherine and Daniel's loss of their last daughter, apart from Jane, who was intermittently at home. 'My heart aches when I think of mother and father's loneliness, after you go away, I could just cry for them.' Ever the realist, Annie added in her next breath how 'it will be just as hard in June as it is now.' Jessie might as well make the break now when 'she could get such a good school right beside me.' Annie would do what she could from the British Columbia end, but Jessie must, to ensure she was offered the job, 'send as many telegrams [to the superintendent of education in Victoria] as you think necessary.' The money beckoned, for, as Annie explained shortly after arriving, about her fellow teachers from Nova Scotia working in British Columbia, 'when one gets sixty dollars a month out here they don't feel like going back to sixty dollars for *six* months.'[43]

School secured, Jessie headed west in mid-March 1888. She did so with trepidation, as daughterhood's obligations vied with sisterhood's bonds. She, like Annie, planned to send money back during her three years away, so that her family would be better off financially by virtue of her going, but there was also the wrench of separation. Before leaving, Jessie did all she could to ensure that her parents did not suffer financially over the short run. Having given 'the number of days taught' to the local trustees, she directed that the $44 she calculated was owed her be forwarded to her parents as soon as possible. In the meantime, she fretted, 'will you be hard up?'[44]

As so amply suited her modest character, Jessie took a cousin with her as a travelling companion cum guardian. Ed Olding, whose father was Catherine's brother, was going on to Portland, Oregon, to look for work. To save money, 'we carried our own lunch right through, and had a regular picnic three times a day.' Perhaps because Jessie left amidst family anxiety over her going, she took great care to share every detail of the trip west with her family. Each aspect was pleasing, from 'the tin-teapot' through 'cutting delicate slices of tongue (an inch thick)' to a fellow passenger 'eating "jam" with his *scissors*!' Jessie quickly became caught up in a westward movement much larger than herself. Despite their second-class tickets, Jessie and her cousin Ed 'were granted first-class privileges to Quebec,' and, indicative of Jessie's new self-assurance, 'after that – we generally took them.'[45]

Snow blocked the tracks for virtually twenty-four hours at Rivière-du-Loup in eastern Quebec, and Jessie dashed off a postcard home: 'Riv du Loup 2 P.M. Wednesday. Have been here since 4 last ev. on acct of snow ahead blocking Quebec trains. Have had breakfast & dinner here at Co.'s expense.' Just over a day later, 'we got into Point Levis [Quebec] about one o'clock last night, went to a hotel and enjoyed the luxury of a bed, and plenty of *soap & water* (and it *is* a luxury).' The train 'had to hang around the Stn. until 11 o'clock, there were so many coming West. The Colonist sleeping cars as they call them are very comfortable – divided into two compartments, and we (the crowd from N.S. & thereabouts) have one almost to ourselves. There are families of Swedes, Germans &c in some of the others.'[46]

Suspension in time and space encouraged Jessie's self-confidence. Her message home from 'Sudbury Junction' exuded train talk in its reference to 'the everlasting delays.' She added: 'I do not think we can reach Winnipeg before Sat night at this rate, but our provisions are holding out finely, and we can share with our *nicest* companions.' The trip became one long picnic. 'We shared our "condensed coffee" with him [a young man from New Brunswick], and we help ourselves to apples & so we are mutually convenient.' The trip enraptured the usually shy Jessie. 'I am getting so used to it now that I can ride head first, feet first, back first, or whatever way comes handiest ... The travelling and its accompaniments are so exciting that I can hardly think steadily of anything.'[47]

All the same, the sabbath was the sabbath. Jessie and her cousin reached Fort William in northwestern Ontario in time to 'stop off for Sunday,' where they 'found the best hotel in the place and had a lovely restful day.' From Jessie's perspective, this equated with as much church as possible. 'After breakfast, we enquired for the Pres. Church.' Having found it, 'we had Bible class first, and in the afternoon we went back to hear him preach, and we all enjoyed it so much.' Back in the hotel, 'there was a grand piano in the hotel parlor, and we had lots of music.' The two young Nova Scotians got their first, valuable lesson in making a home away from home. 'Once I looked out into the hall when we were in full blast, and found it full of people. They seemed to be a pretty rough crowd – smokers and drinkers, but we made the parlor a sort of a sanctuary for ourselves.'[48]

Each change of scenery as the train sped across Canada occasioned its own response. 'The prairies were restful. I could read, knit, or sing or do nothing with the greatest ease, refreshing myself occasionally with a glance out over the boundless waste, and quite easy in the consciousness that I didn't miss anything when I *didn't* look out.' Then came the mountains. 'I just kept running from one side of the car to the other, and had my eyes nearly turned out of my head, in a vain attempt to see everything above & below, and on both sides, all at the same time.' Jessie became more adventurous. 'I think my nerves are improving – I stood out on the platform when the train was rushing down the steepest grade on the line – whizzing past rocks & ravines & torrents – and it was the *wind*, and *not* the scare that finally drove me in.' The experience overwhelmed. 'It was all fine, grand, sublime, terrific!!'[49]

The eight days suspended in time and space went by all too quickly for Jessie, just as they likely also had for Annie. Whipping off a postcard from Swift Current, Jessie was already reflective: 'I believe I will be sorry when the trip is done.' The next day: 'I will be sorry when this trip is done for I've enjoyed it all so much ... I am not a bit tired – could travel for weeks yet I think.' To her sister Mary Belle, she lamented: 'If I could only tell you about my trip! It was the best thing I ever experienced, and I'd like to be able to do it again.'[50] But the trip was over. Like Annie nine months earlier, Jessie too had made it from Nova Scotia to British Columbia.

Chapter Four

Sisterhood's Bonds

NICOLA LAKE
LOWER NICOLA

By the time Jessie joined Annie in March 1888, her younger sister had already encountered and, she considered, mastered the frontier. The freedom the frontier gave meant that social conventions, at least for the moment, could be set aside. Boundaries for interaction and behaviour were more fluid across much of British Columbia than in Nova Scotia. Expectations were different. Older sister Eliza pronounced not long after Annie's departure: 'No doubt any faithful Christian will find plenty to do in such a country. These stories of shooting and Indians show what the West is like.' Well aware of Annie's character, Eliza added: 'I guess Nan is by nature a kind of Westerner herself and understands the people. Jessie always said she managed boys so well.' George quipped from New York City, only half jokingly as Jessie prepared to follow Annie west, whether they 'would be cow girl maidens' and were 'going to buy revolvers like the small boys in the novels.'[1] In those heady months of being on her own for the first time in her life, Annie was far more interested in having new experiences than in making the unfamiliar familiar, although, of course, she did both. In turn, Jessie did much the same, in good part because Annie had gone before.

Nan was very bright, engaging, and outgoing by the standards of the day. All of this she had no compunction in acknowledging to her family even while highlighting in her letters the news she knew her mother would want to hear. Having been allowed to go in part for reasons of health, Annie repeatedly used its improvement to rationalize her multitudinous social activities. Shortly after arriving in British Columbia, she reported her weight as 106 ¼ pounds and took special pride that by the

autumn she had got up to '116 lbs. with my heavy wrap on.' She bragged:
'You would hardly know your little girl, Mother, I am so healthy and rosy.
I am not much fatter, but I am a great deal stronger.' Annie let her hair
grow as soon as she got to British Columbia, so that by the time Jessie
arrived nine months later, it was 'just long enough to screw up and tum-
ble down again half a dozen times a day.'[2]

Nan's first task, on arriving, was to qualify to teach in British Columbia. The written examination making it possible to do so was given each
summer in the capital city of Victoria. The subject areas to qualify at a
primary level comprised spelling, writing, geography, English history
and grammar, composition, and arithmetic. In content, the examination could almost as easily have been given in Nova Scotia as in British
Columbia. Apart from a handful of references to the province (spell Lil-
looet, describe the economic basis of the Cassiar and Texada, locate
principal inlets from Juan de Fuca to Queen Charlottes, outline British
Columbia river system), it was comfortingly familiar. The penmanship
exercise was to write out 'The Saviour at his sermon on the mount.'
Annie also had to describe 'each Mary mentioned in English history,'
sketch the reign of Edward VI, and so forth.[3]

Annie performed, be it in Pictou County or Victoria. In so doing, she
both reflected and marked out appropriate behaviour for newcomer
women. Annie tended to make an impression wherever she went, as she
well realized. 'In fact I have "took well."' Even Mr Pope himself grins
gleefully at me on all occasions, and Mr Fraser, the minister, thinks I am
a daisy.' The first was Ontarian Stephen D. Pope, appointed three years
earlier provincial superintendent of education; the second, Rev. Donald
Fraser, one of two Presbyterian ministers in Victoria. So far as Annie was
concerned, it was to be expected that the two men responded to her as
they did. But Annie was no fool, and so she continued: 'Mr Fraser & Mr
Pope are both good friends, if that would make any difference on the
license question, but I don't think it will. They are both examiners, you
know.'[4] Annie almost certainly passed the examination based on her
abilities, but she had no qualms in doing what she could to ensure she
got the desired result.

Annie was no stranger to gender talk. Since childhood, she had used
flirtation as a means of communication and a mechanism for acquiring
agency as a female person. Still in school, a friend 'wrote my name and
Jimmie Bowes's on her slate, stroked out the letters the same in both
names, put "Marriage" & "Love" opposite them & then held the slate up
and showed it to Jimmie.' Annie's mock indignation – 'I never felt so

cheap in my life' – could not disguise the pleasure she took in relating the incident. As she had done while at Truro Normal School, Nan used male conceptions of the opposite sex to get attention and, more importantly, to get her way. All the same, Annie was constrained in ways that may have been invisible to her. She bragged how the Teachers Institute held in Victoria on completion of the teachers' examination was 'not nearly so far advanced in the management of affairs as in the Convention at Truro.' Even so, it was a venue whose hierarchy she did not, despite her high spirits, challenge. 'They quarrel fearfully, and say hard things at each other, while we girls giggle joyfully.'[5] Gender mattered.

Just as Annie did not much worry about the teachers' examination, she had no qualms about changing schools, writing home, 'I have accepted Nicola Valley.'[6] The Pictou County connection was responsible for her doing so. The Rev. George Murray had returned from New Glasgow to his old haunts at Nicola Lake. The area around the church had during his absence 'become a "most business looking place."'[7] Nicola Lake, as the growing community was called, possessed a gristmill, sawmill, shingle operation, and general store, as well as private homes. Most newcomers came from elsewhere in Canada or from England, which may explain why in 1882 the Anglicans opened a private school nearby. All Saints School did not last very long, but it fuelled the community's desire for its own public school, which was spun off from one serving the entire Nicola Valley. The first teacher, Janie Douglas, came from Pictou County, very likely recruited through the good offices of the Presbyterian Church.[8] She had become engaged to marry a local Englishman cum rancher. Determined to secure the school once again for the Presbyterians, Murray lit on Nan. So it was that, at the very instant of Janie Douglas's resignation at the beginning of August 1887, 'Miss Annie McQueen has made application for the school.'[9] Murray promised her accommodation as soon as his family's new house was completed.

Annie was on familiar turf. Parents were comfortable with the Nova Scotian attributes that she embodied. Nan understood what it took to satisfy the educational hierarchy based in Victoria and also what she might expect from them. Within days of her appointment, Annie was letting the superintendent of education know in no uncertain terms what was needed to bring her school up to scratch. 'On examining the contents of the teacher's desk, I find that there are no blank forms of the monthly reports to be sent to the Superintendent, so I take the earliest opportunity of writing to ask you to send them to me.' Annie had no qualms about telling the superintendent just what she thought about the provincial regulations governing school construction, as was occurring at Nicola Lake. 'They are building a new schoolroom, which we expect to occupy some time next month. I am afraid that they do not intend to paint the interior of the building as it is "not in the specification." The arrangement of the windows, long and narrow, two at each side and two at the end, does not seem to me to be very excellent, but they are there now, and it cannot be helped.'[10]

Annie knew how to flatter as well as to harass, and she understood the need to interweave the two. She waxed enthusiastic about her twenty some pupils with a sophistication lacking in the letters of some of her fellow teachers. 'The school is small at present, but we will have more later on.' She possessed a gift for language, perhaps emanating from her normal school training. In November 1887 Annie was 'glad to be able to report everything going on favourably, with the pupils acquiring deeper interest in the studies day by day.' Nan considered her pupils superior, and herself also by inference as their teacher. 'It pleases me very much to find that they nearly all prefer school to a holiday at Thanksgiving.' In the same breath, she requested 'a set of wall cards for the school.'[11]

As well as drawing on Nova Scotian ways, Nan used gender expectations, in particular assumptions about female deference, to advantage. In communicating with the superintendent of education, she could be virtue itself: 'One of the children at my boarding house died last week, and I had been sitting up with her the greater part of the night, and assisted to dress the body. I felt quite unable to teach that day. The school was closed that day, also the day of the funeral. Shall I teach on Saturdays to fit in one or both those days?' She ended her letter: 'I fear that I trouble you too much by so many inquiries, but as you have been so kind to me in the past, it encourages me to trouble you further.' Another time: 'The school is doing *fairly* well, although some *will* persist in coming late, in spite of all my efforts in the opposite direction.' At year's close, Nan reminded the superintendent how 'I have tried hard to do all the necessary work as you would like to have it done.'[12]

Annie tended to get her way, be it with the superintendent or the local trustees, and wrote home in January 1888 with satisfaction how 'the new seats were put up in the schoolroom today, and look beautifully.' She added: 'Every little thing that is done about that place has to be bossed by your small daughter. The trustees came after me today to come & show them how the seats were to go.' Getting 'an awful whack of valentines this year' pleased Nan as much as it ever did. She noted a month later how the children had brought her some buttercups, and so 'today I taught them a lesson on the buttercup, to their great delight.'[13]

The school's appeal to Annie was linked to the pleasure she took with Nicola Lake. When she arrived, she reported, '[T]he carpenters are still at work fitting up this house for Mr. [Rev.] Murray.' For a time she lived elsewhere, but in January 1888 she could announce, 'I am now boarding at Mr Murray's and am very pleased over it. They just took me in like one of family.' Annie was, in essence, at home again. 'Mrs Murray has a splendid piano which I am at liberty to use as much as I wish. I am going to practice every day.' Annie delighted in the family, reflecting that the Rev. Murray 'is truly a father to me.'[14]

For all of Annie's desire for freedom, she could not escape Nova Scotian assumptions about the conduct of everyday life. The Church was at the heart of sociability, and Annie played her expected role, being variously active, including in the Blue Ribbon Club, which advocated temperance. The public Annie and the private Nan were not quite the same. Shortly after arriving, the wife of the secretary of the school trustees invited her 'to tea and to spend the evening' with 'about twelve to thirteen young folk altogether.' Nan wrote home: 'It was unique, that affair, I'll not describe, for I don't think it is fair to laugh at the poor souls. They have plenty of money, but as they have lived up here in the mountains for nearly twenty years, you may imagine what it's like.' Attending the funeral of 'one of the pioneers,' who had 'died of an over dose of whiskey,' Annie reported that many of the 'crowd of old pioneers' who had carried the body over thirty miles to the church were themselves 'very drunk indeed.' Referring to a 'governess whom Mr Murray brought out,' likely from Nova Scotia, Annie considered her like 'a green spot in the desert unto me.'[15]

Protected by her impeccable place of residence, Annie was able to explore widely. Despite the condescension in some of her letters home, Nan revelled in the freedom the frontier gave to newcomer women like herself. Nicola Lake was, from her perspective, a place where the social conventions associated with a settled society were not yet in place. Confident in her self and in her eventual return to Nova Scotian ways, she used the opportunity to act as she would. Annie learned to shoot, responding eagerly to a neighbour's invitation 'although I was scared to death.' She explained to Jessie, still back home in Pictou County: 'They put up a target one hundred yards off, threw up a plank on a saw-horse as a rest for the gun, and then ordered me along, I believe I would have backed out ignominiously, only Reid [who was working nearby as a tutor] came dashing behind me, and grabbed my shoulders saying "Let me support you, you are fainting!" It made me so mad that I boldly walked up and grabbed the gun, squinted along it after the most approved fashion, to make sure that I was aiming at the bulls eye and fired!!!' As usual, Annie responded well to a challenge. 'To my great surprise I didn't mind it a single bit, of course I didn't hit anything but the straw stack, anything as small as the bulls eye was beneath my notice.'[16]

Not only fellow newcomers, but the local Aboriginal people became part of Nan's frontier. By this time, their numbers across the province had fallen to about 25,000, as a result principally of epidemics of disease. Several hundred lived in the Nicola Valley, making them more of an everyday presence than had been the case in Pictou County. Communication was facilitated by virtually everyone across British Columbia speaking the trade jargon of Chinook with its limited vocabulary of 300–600 words. Annie bragged three months after arriving that 'I am getting into the way of learning Chinook pretty well now and find that, like the rest of the people here, I use lots of words in ordinary conversation without noticing that I do.' Annie was already becoming, in her own mind, a local. 'For instance the word "cultis" meaning "worthless" etc. I catch myself using very often, it is so expressive.'[17]

Invited by two newcomer men to 'a cultis pot-latch at the rancheree above Quilchena,' Anne responded: 'Well, of course, I said "Yes'r I'll go!"' Nan shared her newfound expertise in a letter home. 'Now as you are uninitiated I'll explain, a cultis pot-latch is an Indian festival, where the Indians gather from all directions to give each other gifts, make speeches and make fools of themselves generally. The rancheree is the Reserve where the Indians dwell.' As to the potlatch itself, Annie considered it not an aberration but rather 'picturesque enough for fairyland itself.' She explained: 'There were the tents with fires gleaming from the doorways all surrounding one enormous tent with two doorways and the roof open to the sky, a large fire reached almost from doorway to doorway and all around the tent was the Indians & Klootchmen.' The last was the Chinook word for Indian women, one that Annie used without feeling any need for translation. She was generally complimentary, referring to 'the comely brown faces, the bright dark eyes,' and describing how 'one young Siwash began to sing so softly and sweetly,' now using the Chinook word for Indian man. 'I thought I never heard anything prettier.'[18]

Annie had a pony that she used to get about. Her daring extended into riding, as she put it, 'Klootchman style.' She rode astride, even though 'a side-saddle' was available for her to use. 'So I climbed on Kootchman style and started off full tear with nothing but the halter to hold on by, presently owing to the tightness of my dress I found myself on my back on the ground but I held on tight by the halter and the pony danced the can can all around me but he didn't drag me any which shows he was a decent little beast.' To Annie it was all great fun. 'I sat there and laughed for about two minutes before I got up. I wasn't hurt a single speck.'[19]

Several months after arriving, Annie was approached about a teaching job at Kamloops, where she had originally intended to go, but did not follow up. As to her reason, 'I am freer here than I could be in Kamloops.' The more settled character of Kamloops meant that she would be under surveillance, whereas at Nicola Lake she could be her own person. All the same, Nan eagerly awaited her much less adventurous older sister, for whom she had found a school and accommodation. As she told her mother just as Jessie was beginning her journey across Canada, 'I am anxiously counting the days now until Jessie comes.'[20]

Travelling through the Rockies in March 1888, Jessie already realized that 'I'll have to pull myself together, and settle down to work once more.' She was met at Kamloops, where the train stopped for just ten minutes at midnight on its way to Vancouver, by the Rev. John Chisholm, revelling in having ensnared yet another Nova Scotian Presbyterian to teach in British Columbia. Annie gathered Jessie up from the manse on Saturday morning to take her to Nicola Lake for the weekend and from there on Monday morning to her new job about twenty kilometres away from her at Lower Nicola. Jessie's first impression of Lower Nicola was short and direct: 'It's only a little country place with a total population of 30 or thereabouts ... There are no more than twelve children of school age in the section and I've had 11 yesterday, which is as many as I can expect.'[21]

All was not so straightforward as it seemed at first glance. As soon as Jessie stepped into the classroom, she was enmeshed in a dozen years of frontier politics. The school at Lower Nicola, from which Annie's Nicola Lake school had spun off, went back a good dozen years. Travelling the new province to check out educational needs, British Columbia's first superintendent of education, John Jessop, visited the Nicola Valley in the spring of 1874. He found '21 children of school age, within a radius of 4 1/2 miles, so it is probable that a school district will be established there.' Classes began a year later after the first teacher, a young Ontarian named Archibald Irwin, arranged to have a stove and some books packed in by Indians across a mountain range from the gold rush town of Yale.[22]

The first three trustees, all parents of school-age children, reflected the Nicola Valley's two strands of early newcomer settlement, a distinction the first teacher institutionalized by dividing his days between two locations. Children were meant to travel not more than three miles, or five kilometres, each way to school, which was difficult to manage in areas of widespread ranching settlement such as was the Nicola Valley, particularly given that ten children of school age were needed for a public school to open. According to a long-time resident, 'there was a great deal of difference of opinion as to where the school-house should be placed ... on account of the distance some of the children would be obliged to travel, no matter what site was chosen, so a compromise was come to by building two school-houses six miles apart.' Each was 'built of squared logs, not much to look at, perhaps, but neat and comfortable and substantial, and easily warmed in winter.'[23]

One of the settlement strands and schools was personified by trustee Harvey Woodward, with whose family Annie had arranged for Jessie to board. He was the son of a Methodist Ontarian family that arrived in the Nicola Valley about the time British Columbia joined Canada. According to a descendant: 'The Thomas Woodwards came by covered wagon in 1871, crossing the United States to the west coast, then up the coast to Victoria. From Victoria, they travelled by stern wheeler to Yale; from Yale to Nicomen by the Cariboo wagon road; and from Nicomen to Lower Nicola via the Indian Trail. Thomas Woodward settled on land along with his family of three sons, Harvey, Marcus and Melvin, and one daughter, Christine.' Thomas Woodward's brother Henry joined them about the time the new school opened at what became known as Lower Nicola, where Marcus ran a general store, most of whose trade was with Aboriginal people. The Woodward clan contributed half a dozen children to the school that patriarch Thomas agreed to have built on his land. In his reports to the superintendent of education, Irwin took pains to note that all the children in attendance were 'white.'[24]

The second school, erected at the forks of the Nicola and Coldwater Rivers about halfway between Lower Nicola and Nicola Lake, responded to a quite different settlement strand whose origins harked back to the gold rush. A Methodist minister who arrived in 1875 to serve the Woodward clan encountered 'a strong race of men, those old miners and packers and pioneers of this country.' He fretted about how they had been long 'away from home and friends where a loose rein could be

given to lust and passion,' by which he meant consorting with Aboriginal women. The minister's strategy, undoubtedly consistent with the
Woodwards' thinking on the matter, was to force the men to choose,
whatever the practical consequences. 'Several white men who were living with native women have been induced either to get married to them
or give them up ... To see a man (from principle) breaking through
what has been considered a legitimate custom for years; not only so, but,
in a sense, breaking up his home, or else having to undertake the duties
of cook, laundry-maid, and housekeeper, in addition to the toils common to farming, is to us a far great proof of a man's sincerity than to
stand up in some powerful revival meetings.' It is testimony to the men
behind the Nicola Forks school, whose dozen or so students were, to use
the teacher's terminology, '*all half-breed,*' that not only did they resist
repeated attempts at such outside interference and stereotyping, they
were determined to secure their offsprings' education.[25]

Trustees Alexander Coutlie and William Voght, along with their
neighbours William Charters, Jesus Garcia, and Thomas Lindley, had
Aboriginal wives and hybrid children. Respectively from Quebec and
Germany, Coutlie and Voght had been enticed to British Columbia by
the gold rush. Soon Coutlie was operating a successful roadhouse cum
hotel and saloon at Boston Bar on the way to the goldfields, and Voght
was farming at nearby North Bend. In 1873 the two men moved with
their wives and children to the more remote forks of the Nicola and
Coldwater Rivers. They did so, at least in part, to shield their families
from the prejudice against persons of Aboriginal or part-Aboriginal
descent that was becoming commonplace among wholly newcomer families. Voght continued to farm, whereas Coutlie opened another multi-
purpose public establishment that included a general store. Among his
customers was Jesus Garcia, who had packed his way north from Mexico
during the gold rush, at first wintering his animals near the forks of the
Nicola and Coldwater Rivers and in 1872 settling down there. Not that
far away was Englishman William Charters, who had pre-empted land
along the Coldwater River in 1868 and later opened a store at what
became known as Quilchena. 'A poke full of gold dust' in hand, fellow
Englishman Thomas Lindley headed to the Okanagan Valley and then,
after several bad crops, pre-empted land on Nicola Lake in 1871.[26]
Clearly ambitious for his children, Lindley, who would later serve as
trustee of the Forks school, sent his children to both of the part-time
schools so that they could receive double tuition.

The twinned schools made overt the racial and status differences

between the two settlements. Lower Nicola essentially had its own
school, albeit on alternate days, without the requisite ten children
needed for one to operate in British Columbia. Irwin's willingness to
maintain this situation was linked to his courting of Henry Woodward's
daughter, whom he married at the close of his first year of teaching.
After spending a little over a year away, the couple returned to the Nicola
Valley to settle down. Back teaching, Irwin continued the practice of two
part-time schools to his inlaws' advantage at the expense of the hybrid
families in the Nicola Forks school, who had enough children to maintain their own full-time school. From his very first report, Irwin differen-
tiated between 'white' pupils attending the Woodwards' school at Lower
Nicola and the 'half-breeds' attending the Forks school. Despite the
pupils' roughly similar ages and attendance rates, Lower Nicola pupils
were taught 'Reading, Spelling, Writing, Arithmetic, Grammar and
Geography,' whereas those at the Forks were all only 'reading' in the
First Reader, excepting Sophia Voght, who was in the Second.[27]

Visiting in the spring of 1877, Superintendent Jessop followed Irwin's
lead, commenting that 'all of them did remarkably well, the white children particularly.' The next March, Irwin deplored 'the neglect of
home tuition' in hybrid families, not unexpectedly so given most fathers
had humble origins and Aboriginal mothers were illiterate in English.
'You doubtless are aware that a number of parents are unable, were they
willing, to assist much in this way.' Irwin repeatedly justified differentiat-
ing his pupils. 'When the schools were first started, few excepting those
now in the 3rd & 4th readers, could read any and several could not
speak or understand English. All of those attending the East End school
[at the Forks] are halfbreeds. Many of their fathers are unlearned. And
when we consider that there is only school five days in two weeks, it is
not surprising that progress should be slow.' The perceived deficiencies
were joined with assumptions about racial inheritance, as in a teacher's
report from May 1883: 'None of the pupils at the East branch could
undertake the written exam: they not being sufficiently familiar with the
English language, all of the children at this school being halfbreeds.'
The differences between the two groups of families, and schools, only
grew over time. A visitor of the early 1880s enthused: 'At the end of our
12 mile walk we found the "Woodward Settlement," and after a little rest
and refreshments at Mr. A. Irwin's we visited the homestead of Thos.
Woodward, Esq., where we, also, met his two sons, Marcus R. and Harvey, the latter with his family living a mile to the west ... An alternate
[days] school is convenient [for them].'[28]

The antipathy that existed among families like the Woodwards toward hybrids, or halfbreeds, became visible in the scandal that erupted at the Lower Nicola school in early 1882. Shortly after Irwin's departure for full-time farming, his wife's younger half-brothers Frank, Joseph, and Emerson Woodward, aged ten to fifteen, began misbehaving with their cousin Harvey Woodward's seven-year-old daughter Maggie. According to her trustee father, one of the brothers 'had Maggie in the watercloset and to use his own words said they got between her legs.' Another time 'the boys had thrown her down during the noon hour when the teacher went up the road to feed his horse.' The subsequent investigation revealed a pattern of such activity. The boys' father Henry Woodward desperately tried to put the blame on the hybrid sons of trustee Thomas Lindley, for daring to attend the school the Woodwards essentially considered their private fief, and on the new teacher. The Lindley boys simply had to be responsible, given their Aboriginal maternal inheritance. Whether or not they committed the acts was irrelevant; their presence had contaminated his own sons. It was simply impossible that they would have so acted on their own. Harvey Woodward's wife, Agnes, had originally raised the alarm over her daughter Maggie's 'disgrace,' but for naught. Race and gender were against her. Despite 'gross immorality' considered proven by the teacher, all of the male Woodwards closed ranks in a litany of denial rather than acknowledge any culpability. The events may have caused a long-term rift. Jessie, who got to know Agnes well while boarding with the family, observed how 'Uncle Henry's' are of a different stamp, & we don't have very much to do with them.'[29]

When the Nicola Lake school, at which Annie would teach, opened in 1885, the Nicola Forks school was absorbed into its Lower Nicola counterpart, which thereafter served both the Woodwards and hybrid families. It was not surprising that the Lower Nicola location should have prevailed, given its description by a visitor at about this time. 'Squire Woodward with his brother Henry, who occupies a valuable farm a little to the north, comes from near London, Ont., after some years in California, finally settled down in his present position; he and his family possess over a thousand acres, a large portion of it excellent land. Both grist mills and sawmills are upon the premises and also, a dairy.'[30] To the extent that Nicola Valley was being domesticated, the Woodward clan was in the forefront, along with teachers like Jessie.

Jessie not only inherited a school with a fractious history, but also the family at its core. Previous teachers had as a rule boarded with trustee Harvey Woodward. So did Jessie. Her first impressions had more to do with her own well-being than with the family as such. 'Mrs. Harvey W. is a Scotch woman – has six or seven children, I forget which, and seems to be nice & kind. I have a room up-stairs to myself – carpeted – with a closet for my clothes – table for my books &c ... I am to pay $18 per month – washing included – but I'll do my own ironing. It's a good price for a country place.' The room became her refuge. 'It is such a relief to escape to my own room, & shut out all the racket ... I can sit & read or write – with comfort at any time.'[31]

The counterpoint to Jessie's new place of residence was the school itself. She was not a passionate teacher and probably not an exceptional one. During her disastrous first term in the classroom in Nova Scotia, she described her defences: 'I put on a severe look when I get outside the door [of the classroom] and wear it till 3 o'clock at which time school closes.' All the same, she took pride that, just three days after stepping off the train, 'I am actually teaching in B.C. – a thing I scarcely believed would ever come to pass. But it is a solemn fact – dreadfully solemn when you begin to consider that I am between 50 and 70 miles [80–100 kilometres] from the Railway – 50 one way – 70 another and I drove (or was driven) every inch of the 70 miles from Kamloops.' From Jessie's perspective, she was now, like Annie, on the frontier, a transition marked by the distance she had to walk between where she boarded and the school, located on the land belonging to Harvey Woodward's father Thomas. 'It takes me a good half-hour to walk it, but some folk say it's not more than a mile.'[32]

Perhaps because Jessie found teaching more of an effort than did the exuberant Annie, she took it more seriously. When Annie could not understand the forms teachers were meant to fill out, she threw herself on the superintendent's goodwill rather than figure them out herself. 'I enclose the voucher for Sept. My sister tells me that I should fill in the number of the Vote, but I do not know the number of the Vote, and am sadly afraid that I do not even know what it means – and neither does anyone else in the village. I send only the September Voucher, in case I am wrong, which will save you the trouble of sending them all back.' Jessie admired Annie, whereas Annie admired herself, so she confided yet again to the superintendent: 'My school is doing finely, and I am very proud of it. Jessie thinks my schoolroom is one of the prettiest she ever saw.' Being informed by the superintendent that 'my average for Sept. was not up to the required standard,' Annie shot back: 'There is some mistake, my average was above the required standard. I think you intended this for Lower Nicola, but you addressed it to "A.L. McQueen," so of course I got it.' Cognizant that Jessie was the teacher at Lower Nicola, Nan added somewhat contritely: 'I am sorry to hear of this, and hope that the school will not be closed.'[33]

Jessie was, for her part, quietly persistent in attempting to improve attendance. Trustee Harvey Woodward's explanation for its dropping below the provincial minimum of ten provides insight into the relationship that existed on the frontier between schooling and the economy. 'I am sorry that the attendance at our School has been small, but probably when I explain that in the farming districts it often happens as it has in this instance when times are dull and help scarce that Farmers are almost compelled to keep their children that are large enough to help at harvesting at home a portion of the time to help gather crops etc. and I can assure you that it has not been from carelessness that the attendance has fallen so low and now harvesting & thrashing is about done the School will regain its normal condition & as there are several children about ready or old enough for school therefore we trust you will not be hasty in the matter but give us a time to recover.' Jessie's explanation was somewhat different, echoing the tensions of past years. 'I have been unfortunate enough to incur the hostility of some of the "natives," who are anxious to see the school closed. One child has been sent to my sister's school, at the Lake, but we still have eleven available children, and I shall use all lawful endeavors to have them attend regularly, now that harvesting is done.' At the end of October, Jessie reported triumphantly that attendance showed 'a marked increase.' She was optimistic. 'We had to "go out into the highways and hedges and *compel* them to come in," and we hope to have a still greater number during the months of Nov. and Dec.'[34]

For all that Jessie taught and boarded, it was proximity to her energetic younger sister that shaped her first months in British Columbia. Until Jessie stepped on the train, she had been largely enfolded in her mother's identity. Jessie was the dutiful daughter par excellence. Catherine still sought to exert her influence, causing Jessie to write apologetically in her first letter that, 'as to liking any place better than home (as lots say I will) that's all trash I never did & never will.'[35]

Of the ties that continued to bind Jessie to Nova Scotia, none was so ever present as the economic. Her salary as a teacher, which had never been hers alone in Pictou County, continued to be a family possession. The McQueens repeatedly tipped over into debt, to be rescued by their unwed daughters. In this sense, Annie and Jessie represented the extension of a Nova Scotian family economy westward to British Columbia. In

British Columbia a few short weeks, Jessie warned her mother, in respect to money, that it would likely be 'some weeks yet ... before I could have any to send you.' Just how much she and Annie sent home out of the $60/month salaries is difficult to determine, for the topic was discussed explicitly only on separate tiny pieces of paper. Marked 'Private,' these 'slips' were removed from letters prior to their circulation among the sisters back home in the Maritimes. One of the few that has survived reads: 'Private – I meant to have sent this X [in original] before so that you could renew all your subscriptions but its so hard to get any but B.C. bills ... Tell me if you need any more. Jessie.' British Columbia was still such a distant place that only some of the bills in use were accepted as legal tender as far away as Nova Scotia. Another time: 'I shall send what I can to [local shopkeeper] Geo. Douglass, and will tell him to give you whatever you want. You will need some you know, for that horse. Has father paid that man for Charlie? It was due in June, wasn't it?'[36]

All the same, a continent now separated mother and daughters, and it was the relationship between the sisters, both in their mid twenties, that took centre stage in their lives. Four weeks in British Columbia, a homesick Jessie fretted when Annie, ill with a cold, did not turn up on the weekend. 'My stars, but I was disappointed when last night passed and no Nan ... I kept squinting out towards the road all evening, till it got too dark to see, and then I could have wept with vexation & disappointment.' The sense of protection that Annie felt toward her shyer older sister is caught in a letter she wrote home shortly after Jessie's arrival. 'I hope she won't be lonely there [at Lower Nicola] ... I'll do my level best to help her, you may be sure.' Nan's litany of exploits undoubtedly eased Jessie into her new way of life. If far less gregarious, Jessie was soon taking a quiet pride in following Nan's example. Less than a week after her arrival, Jessie wrote to her mother about jam spilling on an apron. 'I washed it out all O.K.' She added in the very next sentence: ''Scuse my little slang mother, it's just so much more expressive than plain English.'[37]

The sisters quickly became as intimate as they ever had been at home. They took turns visiting each other on weekends, catching rides with whomever might be going in that direction. Other times, Annie rode her pony. 'I had quite a time of it, going down alone, the little pony tried to take advantage of my ignorance but I convinced him of my knowledge with a good stout switch.' As Jessie recalled about the same weekend: 'We never seem to get through with all our talking though we are at it every chance we get. Home and friends, past, present and future came in for a good share of discussion.' Jessie gradually became accustomed to the twenty kilometres separating them. She noted six months after her arrival: 'I don't mind the roads now, and the road between here and the Lake isn't really dangerous – at all – only a little inconvenient to pass at times, if you don't keep a look-out ahead.'[38]

Even though Jessie had always been 'scared' of horses, in mid-May, two months in British Columbia, she had her first ride. 'We only went about a mile and I went very cautiously and sustained no damage except a hole in my dress when I bobbed up & down on the saddle.' She took special pride that she did not feel 'stiff' the next day 'so I think I'll do finely.' A month later: 'I rode my own horse alone for two miles.' Jessie also took the great step of moving from side-saddle to astride: 'At the store the other night I got on an Indian cayuse Klootchman style! The Siwash who owned it, told us "halo buck" that is "no buck," and took his pack off to let me try. I had a good deal of faith in the Indian, but I didn't go very far on the thing in case he *might* of been mistaken.' Jessie even bragged about how she expected 'to cut quite a figure by the time I go home.' In August she expressed disappointment that, because of the harvesting, 'the horses are so busy now that I have no chance to ride, but "by and by" I'll make up for that.'[39]

Annie had taken pride in learning Chinook, and here too Jessie followed her example. Just a week in British Columbia: 'Mrs. C.[hisholm] had a Klootchman washing ... They laugh at me for saying "Klootchman *woman*." *Siwash* is the masculine noun – *Klootchman*, the feminine.' Two weeks later, Jessie retailed how she 'had my first "tell" to-day, from Annie, the Klootch who washed here.' The teacher boarding there before her, she was told, 'didn't like Siwash Klootchman, and always slammed the door shut between them.' The washerwoman considered Jessie treated her decently, so she explained in detail to her mother. 'She told Mrs. W. she had a "skookum tum-tum" for me, because I always spoke to her – said "hallo Annie" when I met her on the road one day &c &c. "Skookum" is *good* or something of the kind, and "tum-tum" is *idea* or *thought*, or *opinion*. "Hi-yu – lazy – tum-tum 'stop'" (very lazy – thinks he'll stop) was what she said about the horse one of the boys was riding today. Chinook does sound so comical.' Jessie made it a point to add Chinook words to her letters, with explanations such as 'tillicum' is 'Chinook for friend.' She described Annie's weekend visit as 'what the youngsters here call a "hi-yu" time' and added perkily, 'That's Chinook of course.' Another time she reassured Catherine how 'I am all "skookum" again, as they say here.' Later, Jessie wrote about having ordered a pair of shoes that did not fit, and so 'I shall have to sell them to some other Klootchman.'[40]

Jessie quickly became aware of a familiar Nova Scotian ethos. It seemed as if every second person she met had some link back home. There were the Reverends George Murray and John Chisholm, who had persuaded the McQueen sisters to come west in the first place, but that was not all. Annie's predecessor at the Nicola Lake school, similarly lured from Pictou County, had returned home to get together her trousseau before marrying a Nicola Lake rancher, William Pooley. Jessie's arrival coincided with much speculation as to exactly when she was returning west. 'Miss [Janie] Douglas hasn't come yet, so far as any one knows, but Pooley expects to go into Kamloops some time next week – probably on business!' Jessie shared in the general euphoria over how 'a bride at the Lake will make quite a sensation.' The couple were married by Chisholm in late April, and Jessie soon became as friendly with the newlyweds as was Annie. The sisters shared tidbits with their mother back home about their fellow Pictonian now tied to British Columbia by marriage. During harvest time: 'Mrs. Pooley is getting on very well with the housekeeping. She has four men to cook for besides her husband ... She has considerable pluck and perseverance.' In the autumn, her sister joined her from Pictou County. 'Mrs. Pooley's sister, Miss Douglas, has arrived safely. She is the prettiest of the three girls, and seems very nice too. Mrs. Murray, and Mr. Murray and I were down to see her.'[41]

Not only did the McQueen sisters engage in sociability that was for the most part familiar, they did so consciously. Nine months in British Columbia, Jessie took pride in how 'I have no use for any of "the natives" as intimate friends.' Spending a weekend with the Murrays, she confided how 'it must be because they are Nova Scotians that I like them so much better than any other family in the Valley.'[42] Pictou County ways of behaviour were preferred. The model of domesticity that Catherine McQueen worked so hard to maintain at Sutherland's River still guided her daughters in British Columbia. Jessie, in particular, but also Annie, sought to make their settings more homelike, to introduce into them and to sustain familiar values whence they came. For all of their adventures, the McQueen sisters more domesticated the frontier during their first months in British Columbia than they were changed by it.

Chapter Five

Taking a Chance on Love

NICOLA LAKE
LOWER NICOLA

Even as sisterhood's bonds were being reconnected in the Nicola Valley, the seeds had been sown for their sundering. Teaching was well and good for a time in the life cycle, but women were expected to marry. Jessie had already reached the optimum age by Pictou County standards, and Annie was on her way there. Not unexpectedly, given their personalities, it was Annie who first took a chance on love, and Jessie who followed in her wake.

The reasons for the McQueen sisters' change in direction are not difficult to fathom. To be a single woman, even as charmed a one as was Annie, did not count for very much. All women, whatever their occupation, lived in a state of dependency, expected if not also real. Annie's flirtatious ways and audacity were acceptable precisely because they did not challenge, but rather played into, the gender assumptions of the day, just as did Jessie's modesty.

For all that it gave access to the public realm, the schoolroom in and of itself gave scant prestige. It was precisely for that reason that the occupation attracted more women than it did men. Teaching's status paled before the far greater respectability of marriage. Teaching was for most women, as well as men, a means to an end rather than the end itself. For men that end was a better job; for women, the married state. Few locations offered more opportunities for a newcomer woman desirous of finding a husband than did British Columbia. Both the fur trade and the gold rush, the two impetuses to settlement prior to the railroad, were essentially male events. Across the province there were three adult newcomer men for every woman, proportions being far higher outside of the handful of towns and villages.

Annie was careful, in her letters home, to go only so far in describing her actual life. Early on, while still in Victoria taking the teachers' examination, she took pains to point out to Jessie, to be relayed to her mother, that, even though there were more eligible men than at home, she was not changing her behaviour. 'Mother will be glad to hear that I am considered very "straightlaced."' Even so, Annie could not resist imparting little nuggets. However small, they caused her mother to send worried letters to her other daughters, likely privy to much franker accounts, who then had to think up a judicious reply: 'Mother dear about Annie. I could shake her for giving you a moment's worry about her nonsense. She wrote me too and chaffed a good deal and then before she closed her letters says "Liz, don't repeat that *trash* about nos. 1, 2, & 3" ... She had just got back from Kamloops and described *three* of her would-be adorers ... Mother dear I could trust Annie *now* as fully as any sister I own in such a matter.'[1]

From the time of her arrival in British Columbia, Annie demonstrated an almost joyous interest in the opposite sex. 'Yes, all reports are true, gentlemen are very plentiful over here. Even I, if I wished, might have a string tagging at my heels but I don't.' Not only did Nan flirt with young and old alike, she observed carefully what she saw. British Columbia was quite different from Pictou County, and Annie was determined to experience it as fully as possible before making her choice. While in Victoria for the teachers' examination, Annie very much enjoyed 'the whole crowd' of young men where she boarded, who 'tease and fight for me in the same breath.' With her landlady, she visited the Victoria jail on Sundays to give uplift and even there used her charms. 'The room was well-filled with prisoners. I played the hymns, and they all sang like larks.' With Mr Davis, 'a middle-aged gentleman' who was 'a friend of one of my acquaintances,' Annie visited the 'joss-house, the Chinese place of worship,' and 'one of the Chinese stores, and when I wasn't looking, [he] bought me the cutest Chinese cup and saucer, and gave it to me after I got out.' With other newly made friends Annie 'went to see the Spiritualists, but the spirits wouldn't come until after we went away, so we didn't hear them.' Then there was the 'middle-aged minister,' who 'calls on me, and meets me on the street & stops to talk everlastingly, when he should be attending to his congregation in the country.'[2] Tales of admirers were calculated to amuse, but they were also something more.

Annie's flirtations with her 'dudes,' as she termed eligible men, represented strategic entryways into the mating game as opposed to random sociability. She had before her the model of her Pictou County predecessor, her contemporary in age, who had found herself a prosperous local rancher. As Janie Douglas had likely done, Annie scouted the field with some deliberation. In January 1888, even as Jessie was making final plans to leave for British Columbia, she wrote home in teasing fashion: 'Mother, what would you say if I told you that by-and-by I was going to marry a B.C. business man, one who is nice, steady, clever and wealthy in the bargain! Mind, I don't say that this is the case, but what would you say if it were?' Whether or not Jessie was so aware when she headed west in March 1888, the impetuous Annie had found herself a special 'dude,' as Jessie put it in a discrete letter to Mary Belle shortly after her arrival. She had, moreover, already won over the Rev. John Chisholm, who assured Annie, 'Since I last saw you I became more intimately acquainted with Mr. Gordon ... A sweeter disposition no man ever possessed. And for virtue, integrity and industry he is surpassed by none.' Perhaps Jessie first realized what was happening when Nan indicated, just as she was about to head west, that a 'Mr Gordon' might be driving them from Kamloops to the Nicola Valley.[3]

The process by which Annie found her 'Mr Gordon' and then manoeuvred her parents a continent away into his becoming their son-in-law provides a unique window into frontier sensibilities, as juxtaposed with those of Pictou County. Repeatedly, Nan, and also Jessie, relied on the differences that they attributed to their new setting to cajole, if not acceptance, then acquiescence. The ease with which the sisters, even the compliant Jessie, felt able to make the argument speaks to the freedom that the frontier gave, and did not give, to newcomer women. The entire episode set up Annie as exemplar, whose behaviour likely encouraged numerous others to follow in her stead.

Flirtation was inevitable, given Nan's character, but a serious beau did not sit well with the McQueen family back in Nova Scotia. Once Annie let slip her choice, Catherine went into action. She did not want Annie to settle down in British Columbia, nor had she even anticipated that Annie might do so. Her three married daughters had each wed in the parlour at home in Sutherland's River, and so should Annie. Catherine's opposition may also have been because Jim Gordon was a businessman rather than a clergyman or doctor, like two of her other sons-in-law, and possibly because he was raised a Methodist. Five years Annie's senior, he came from an Ontarian cabinet-making family. His parents lived in Goderich, an attractive town of about 5,000 on Lake Huron that counted a salt works among its several industries. Jim and his younger brother Marsh, who had bad asthma, went west for Marsh's health in their early twenties. Crossing the continent as outriders with a wagon train, they worked for a year in a furniture factory in Victoria before moving to Kamloops for its dry climate. Doing what they knew best and anticipating the rail line, in 1884 they opened Gordon Bros, a furniture store. Even as Jessie travelled west, Annie was defending herself against her mother's displeasure and essentially laying down the gauntlet. 'And mother, I don't think I am really as selfish as you think me. I try not to be, and your letters make me feel very badly. I hadn't any idea of "caring particularly" for Mr. Gordon until it was too late, and I couldn't say I didn't care for him when he asked me, but if you say you don't want me to marry him, I'll obey you, without a word.'[4]

Nan's beau shadowed the sisters' relationship. In her first long letter home, Jessie reported back to her mother without further comment about the trip from Nicola Lake, where Annie taught, to Jessie's new job at Lower Nicola. 'A Mr Gordon drove Annie & me down here last evening.' Jessie repeatedly fretted how they would have more time together 'if Nan weren't engaged.' Another of Jessie's letters, written while in Annie's company, closed: 'P.S. – well, I was just going to say she won't have time to write to-night, and she won't, sure enough, for here is Jim, & all is excitement. Here is one of her remarks, "say, Jim – I like you Jim" – same old Annie in spots, as she used to be.' Sisterhood's bonds meant that Jessie as well as Annie sought to normalize the relationship in their parents' eyes. Shortly after Jessie's arrival, Annie wrote almost in passing: 'Well, my boy was out here last week and I enjoyed his visit very much. Jessie likes him, and is satisfied over matters, I think. He is thoroughly good and honorable.' A month later, Annie sent home, without comment, 'a photo of Mr. Gordon, my betrothed.'[5]

At the beginning of August 1888, Annie raised the stakes. She informed her parents that she was pushing forward the proposed date of marriage. 'Jim is determined to be married at Xmas. I insisted on the 1st of July but he will not hear of it, so we will probably be married during the first week of January 1889.' Jim was not happy where he was boarding 'and is so anxious to have a home of his own.' Annie appealed to her mother's sense of obligation to male needs. 'I feel sure that you would advise me to do as I am doing, if you were here.' Nan reassured Catherine that 'I have perfect confidence in the man who is to be my husband, and am certain that my feeling for him is real love, for I care a great deal more for him than I do for myself.' Long familiar with straitened family finances, Annie added: 'we will be very comfortable and have more than enough for the necessaries of life.'[6]

Catherine McQueen did not take kindly to losing her influence over her youngest child, and Jessie became caught between daughterhood's obligations and sisterhood's bonds. She began a 'private' letter of mediation with the open question: 'Well, Mother dear, what do you think of Nan's intentions?' As to the proposed wedding date, 'I was in blissful ignorance until Sunday – quite sure that it wasn't to be until next summer.' Jessie acknowledged her own misgivings, particularly over the speed with which Annie intended to move from engagement to marriage. 'I'm so bothered by Nan's prospective change of plans, that I can't think or write decently. I don't see how she has the cheek to be married away out here, but I may as well give in and do what I can to help her.' Jessie was very conscious that Annie at age twenty-three, several years younger than when their sisters had wed, was flouting Nova Scotian norms about the right age for marriage. 'Poor child, she seems to be *too* young & inexperienced to undertake the cares of housekeeping.'[7]

The frontier helped Jessie to justify the accelerating set of circumstances in which she had become embroiled. She was willing to defend the truncated engagement on the grounds that such matters were perceived differently in British Columbia than in Nova Scotia. 'Everybody here, though, cries out against long engagements, and, as Jim is boarding, I daresay he is anxious to get settled as soon as possible.' Jessie also demonstrated in her letters the sense of predestination that still lingered in Presbyterianism. 'If it's got to be it will be I suppose, and I won't worry Nan by fretting over it.' In the event, Jessie's loyalty to her much loved sister, the baby of the McQueen family, took precedence over her own misgivings. She used all the diplomatic skills at her disposal to make the case for Annie. Jessie emphasized that 'they are a wonderfully sensible pair, and don't expect to find life *all* sugar & honey.'[8]

Jessie saw her principal role as one of mediation. 'Even if you don't approve of Nan's action, mother, dear, it may be best to say little about it. Things *hurt* far worse in letters than if they were *spoken*.' The suggestion unleashed a thunderbolt. Catherine vented her spleen on Jessie. Why had Annie not sent a proper photograph of her 'Mr. Gordon'? What about waiting until her health improved? And why was Annie not coming home first, likely so her parents could try to dissuade her in person? Jessie tackled the issues directly, throwing the gauntlet back to Catherine for spoiling her youngest child in her observation that 'she couldn't afford a trip home just now, for you know she doesn't know how to save.' Jessie used the bluntest language she ever would toward her mother. 'I was afraid you would feel badly about Annie, but please, mother dear, *don't* write to her as you wrote to me.' Jessie pointed out the detrimental effect of distance in shaping Catherine's reaction. 'Mother dear, the other girls were differently situated – they could *talk* to you about their affairs, and consult with you about them, but you know that letters take *so* long to go and come, and are so unsatisfactory besides.'[9]

Hoping to pre-empt her older sisters' likely objections to the marriage, Jessie recalled, quite rightly, how each also took 'unto herself a strange man,' and 'I don't see that it will do any good to "kick" about it.' Having made her point, Jessie scurried to patch up differences. 'And now for a word between ourselves, Mother dear, for I know there's lots of things you want to know. I like Mr. Gordon very much, but I wasn't broken up on him at first. Fact is, I didn't *want* to like him, and as he is a small man ... and rather quiet, he's not calculated to take people by storm. He "grows upon me," though, as I tell Annie, and I think he is a thoroughly fine fellow.' Jessie again turned to the language of predestination. 'So let's think it's for the best mother, and *make* the best of it anyhow.'[10]

For all of Catherine's objections, her youngest and always headstrong daughter had made up her mind. Come mid-September, Annie reminded her in no uncertain terms that 'we have decided to be married out here and have Mr. Murray perform the ceremony.' Seeking to mollify yet stand firm, Annie continued: 'Dear mother I know how you feel about it all, and I do not feel offended. I never was nor never can be offended at anything you say, for you are my mother and I know you love me.' The rest of the letter retailed, brusquely on a single page, the sequence of events that would surround the wedding. The very same day Annie reassured her oldest sister Jane, unsettled by the turmoil, that 'I haven't ceased to love you.' Concerned to make events explicable, Annie described somewhat idyllically for Jane how, once married: 'We are going to begin very quietly, begin on bread and cheese, for now, and work up to chicken, like the wise young couple we used to read about. I wonder what sort of housekeeper I will make. Washing and ironing will be done by the Chinamen. They do it very cheaply, so I won't have to do that. Cooking will be the worst, but I'll do my best.'[11]

At the beginning of November, Annie told the superintendent of education: 'So far I have escaped the *usual* fate of the Nicola school teachers, but I do not expect to go safely past New Year.' She took for granted the rightness of the generally held assumption that married women did not belong in the classroom as teachers. All the same, Annie, as ever, sought favour: 'Now I have a question to ask: it seems silly, but I am really in doubt about it, and would like you to settle the matter. It is this: – My resignation will be sent in dated December 1st, and it is desired that my marriage should take place on Christmas Day, but I cannot see that this would be right, as the thirty days will not have expired until after that date. Please tell me your opinion.' She added an enticement: 'I sincerely hope that you may be able to visit the schools in the Valley before I leave.'[12] The request was likely denied, for the wedding was within the week postponed to New Year's Day.

It was not until ten days after Annie officially resigned that Jim Gordon wrote formally – likely dared write – to Daniel McQueen for permission to wed. Historian Peter Ward found in his study of courtship and marriage in nineteenth-century English Canada that, 'almost invariably, by the time a suitor spoke to his intended's father or mother, the couple had agreed to marry.'[13] Even so, it was very late in the courtship that Jim Gordon acted. His letter was decidedly unconventional, as much an announcement as a request. 'You will not be surprised to hear from me for you must know by this time the relation your daughter Annie & I bear to one another. We are engaged to be married on New Year's Day, and though it may appear late Sir, in one sense, to ask for your daughter's hand, in another sense it is not, for I believe if you objected to our marriage that Annie would not hesitate to break the engagement, such is her sense of duty to you.' Jim went on to praise Nan in a fashion calculated to achieve the desired response: 'She loves her father & mother so much she would sacrifice anything to please them and do what is right. Annie McQueen is a treasure and I thank God I was fortunate enough to meet her ... I not only love her but she loves me.' He ensured an economic argument could not be used against him: 'I am in a good position to support a wife, my brother & I have a flourishing business here.' As to 'character,' he relied on the Nova Scotia connection. 'I can refer you to Mr Chisholm or any of your friends in this locality.'[14] Daniel McQueen's response, if there was one, does not survive.

The same day that Jim requested permission to wed Annie, she wrote her mother a long folksy letter, attempting to normalize herself within a British Columbia setting. She mentioned, in turn, the upcoming Sunday school concert where 'we are to sing one of your old favorites,' the beginning of deer hunting, a recent letter from a Truro friend now living in Vancouver, and a concert to pay off the church organ. Annie made clear that wedding events were going ahead, and this too was part of her new life. 'The boys here are getting up a Social before I leave, and everyone all over the Valley has been invited.' She closed on an exceptionally affectionate note: 'Dearest mother, I miss you more now than I ever did since I left home. If I could only be with you for even ten minutes, I wouldn't mind so much, but Jim will take me home as soon as possible.' Nan sought to integrate her new life with her old, in her mother's eyes, and was, at least to some extent, successful. Catherine began to come to grips with the situation and eventually wrote the letter that Jessie had cajoled her to pen. As Jessie gratefully reported back home about Annie, 'she was getting worried & nervous, but your letter and Aunt E's note too "soothered" [sic] her wonderfully.'[15]

Even as Annie's family back home in the Maritimes was being reconciled to the inevitable, plans went ahead for the wedding, and here the frontier gave way so far as possible to traditions familiar to longer settled societies. In effecting the transition, Annie domesticated with panache. Dresses were ordered from home, so Jessie informed one of her sisters: 'Did we tell you that Nan meant to send to N. Glasgow for dresses? I think I shall have one too for the occasion.' Nan's 'trunk' arrived in mid-December. 'The things are very nice. I'm sorry you hadn't seen them, but they look far nicer on her. In her black silk, black jacket, and black & white hat, she is just scrumptious, somewhat different from the "little Ann McQueen" though who used to fly round between the house & barn in short petticoats.'[16]

Responsibility for the requisite trousseau fell on Jessie. Having borrowed the Woodwards' much-used machine, she wrote a bit later how on Saturday 'I was running the sewing-machine for all I was worth.' October was largely taken up with sewing. 'I made two skirts for Nan like the enclosed sample, I sent to Victoria for it, & got it for 12 1/2¢. I made them double, so they will be very comfortable as well as pretty. There is a good deal of sewing to do yet, but I hope to overcome it all in good time.' Eventually Jessie completed her task. 'Did I tell you that I have her duds about done? Two nighties, two underskirts, two white-shirts, four pr. of drawers, three slip-waists, and Mrs. Harvey made the most of her two wrappers. Mary Belle sent the material for one, and I got the other. I have three more slip-waists that I want to do next week. I've put off making them, in the hope that the new machine would be on hand, but it hasn't come yet.'[17]

The wedding presents, like the dresses and trousseau, made familiar an otherwise frontier event. More than any other element, they spoke to their givers' and recipients' hopes for a settled society reflecting the ways of life whence they came. Given the meaning bestowed on them, the gifts merit attention here. 'Mr & Mrs Murray's present to me is a handsome silver butter-dish and butter knife. Miss Gillie's sister in Scotland sent me a lovely plush and satin shopping box. I was so surprised over that.' As to gifts from friends and acquaintances in the Nicola Valley, Jessie listed 'half a dozen dinner knives & half a doz. each of silver forks, dessert and tea spoons from Geo. Armstrong & Hugh Hunter, a plush covered dressing-case from Frank Parsons, two silver napkin rings with initials on each from Mr [William] and Mrs [Janie Douglas] Pooley, a morocco writing case from Tom Hall, a book "Poems of the Affections" from Harvey Woodward.' That was not all. 'Mrs [Maria Woodward] Clapperton gave her a beautiful quilt – red sateen, heavily lined with the best wool; and Mr [George] Clapperton gave a whisk & holder, decorated with crimson plush etc the holder in the shape of a snowshoe. Mrs [Mary Ann] Riley gave two pillows with slip & a pair of sheets, Mrs Caleb Woodward another pillow & pair of slips, Mrs Harvey [Woodward] half a dozen fine hem stitched handkerchiefs, Mr Harvey a linen table-cloth, and Mr and Mrs [A.E.] Howse a handsome oil-painting in a heavy gilt frame just a magnificent thing about 3 ft by 4 ft.' All of these, she emphasized, were only 'the Nicola gifts.' Gifts from Jim's friends in Kamloops included a silver cruet stand, two silver cake baskets, silver card receiver, clock with silver ornaments, and vases. Family presents added to the largesse. Jim's relatives in Ontario sent a silver stand and salad bottles, silver butter dish, family Bible, toilet bottles and cushion, and a cup & saucer. McQueen family members across the Maritimes came through with a brass crumb tray and brush, valise, night dresses, slippers, and household items. 'Oh I almost forgot *the* present of the whole lot. Jim bought her a dainty little gold watch & chain – a perfect beauty. The chain is new style – only about four in. long with a golden ball at the end – fob chain I guess they call it.'[18]

The gifts' supreme importance in affirming the respectability of the married state, hence domesticating the frontier, is attested by Annie's giving her mother a complete listing in the first letter written after the wedding. By comparison, her new status got the briefest mention. 'I am very well indeed.' No gift pleased Annie more than 'that dear little broach,' which her relenting mother had sent, but there were many others. As well as the Nicola Valley gifts already mentioned by Jessie, Annie added a lamp, pair of vases, shoe case, watch holder, vase mats, and a glass pitcher, glasses, and waiter. She ended her long list on a note of anticipation. 'I hear that there are some parcels yet to come.' Indeed, soon there was a third silver cake basket, a dressing case with silver mountings, and a Chinese tea set. Not long after, 'one of the Chinese merchants Chong Lee ... gave me the prettiest Chinese fan you ever saw.'[19]

Annie McQueen married James Gordon at the Rev. George Murray's church at Nicola Lake on New Year's Day, 1889, and Jessie took special care to describe the event as fully as possible for the family left out of events. At the centre was, of course, their errant daughter. 'Annie looked lovely – this is only for the family eye remember – the plain white dress and veil [arranged with white lilac blossoms and green leaves sent especially from Mary Belle in St John] set off her blushes and brown eyes to perfection.' Jessie's account emphasized community approval in a fashion intended, once again, to naturalize this far frontier. Jessie's landlord, Harvey Woodward, gave Annie away as 'the most suitable person for that position among the Valley folk.' Jessie repeated a local's assessment that 'it was the biggest congregation he ever saw in *that* church, and as we turned to come out the *rice* just showered down on us, and from the door to the gate the old shoes flew thick & fast. At the carriage some one shouted "three cheers for *Miss McQueen*" but they changed it to Mrs Gordon and gave them in full force, & off we went to the manse in fine style, one fellow was ringing the school bell – a big one on the roof – as hard as he could wag it.' If modified, social conventions still held: 'Well, we had dinner (or breakfast, I believe they call it in such a case) at two o'clock or thereabouts – the ceremony was at one.'[20]

Peter Ward argues that 'traditions of communal control over marriage' were in decline by the later nineteenth century.[21] It may have been the case in longer settled areas of Canada, but on the frontier the community's approval mattered. The relationship went two ways. The community, as much as the minister, consecrated the union, even as the marriage legitimized the community by virtue of occurring there. Annie's wedding got headline coverage in the Kamloops newspaper, for which the most ordinary comings and goings of teachers were considered newsworthy. Women teachers were one of the few categories of females whose activities could be made public without their being attached to a man. Not only that, but the groom was a local businessman. The account concluded: 'The *Sentinel*, in common with the many friends, desires to extend congratulations, and expresses the hope that for them the voyage down the stream of life may be pleasant, happy and prosperous.' The paper emphasized 'the esteem in which the bride is held by the young people.' As evidence of this, when the couple left the church at about 4 P.M., 'they unhitched the horses from the rig and drew the newly-married couple for over a mile on their way to Lower Nicola.' Jessie described the same happening in similarly enthusiastic terms, with even greater detail, as indicating how the frontier spirit took over. 'Then we all got ready for the start; Nan's trunk, valises, wraps etc and *ourselves* were safely stowed in the buggy by "the boys," who were there in full force to see us off ... When the last good-bye was said, we thought we were off, but before we could wink, the boys loosened the traces, and took the pole of the buggy themselves while some pushed behind and *then* off we went, Jimmie [Gillie]& his flag in front & Frank Parsons racing alongside with our two horses.' Even Jessie was caught up. 'I'm weak yet when I think of the look of us with Jimmie & his red flag careening madly in front.'[22]

The role of the community was not yet finished, so Jessie recounted in her letter home. 'Opposite the "store" they stopped while two "bombs" were let off ... And while we stopped for the bombs to explode the boys ranged themselves on the platform in front of the store and chorused "God Save the Queen."' Then, 'some more good-byes were said and then they buckled to again & took us to the "town limit" and then replaced our team & sent us off with a last long cheer.' Even that was not the end. 'At Coutlie's (The Forks) they had a banner arched across the road and in the fading light we were just able to make out the description thereon: "Nicola mourns your loss," and at that store too, there were waving hats & caps.' Jessie's summary underlines just how important was the role for the community. 'Dear me, it was a fine send-off and no mistake.' She could not resist closing her litany of events without another plea to her mother to let go of any lingering antipathies. 'Jim is a *fine* boy mother, quite a credit to the family, and the more I know him the better I like him.'[23]

Annie's teaching career was over, inevitably so given the assumption that married women did not belong in the classroom except in very unusual circumstances. The secretary of the Nicola Lake board of trustees informed the superintendent of education: 'Our late teacher Miss McQueen was married in the church here one Jan day and to show the high esteem in which she was held I may state that the young men unhitched the horses from the vehicles and drew them through the town amidst firing of booms, anvils, etc.' The letter concluded: 'Hope we are as fortunate in our present selection.'[24] Annie McQueen had moved on.

The newlyweds settled at Kamloops, and Jessie returned to her job at

Lower Nicola. The plan had been for Jessie to get a school at Kamloops in the new year and to board with Annie and Jim, but the job fell through. All the same, Jessie lived in expectation of her next visit to her beloved Nan, comforting herself that 'she doesn't seem so far away.' Then, without warning, sisterhood's bonds were even more fully tested. Anticipating her marriage, Annie had reflected how 'I cannot make up my mind to live here all my life, and am very glad that Mr. Gordon intends going back East to live before very many years.'[25]

The decision to do so was taken much sooner, even as Annie was still wallowing in her new respectability. In her house, she informed her mother with great pride, 'the bay window has lace curtains across it, and looks quite nicely.' That was not all. 'We have lace curtains up in the dining room too.' While the house was mostly furnished, she would 'have a smaller table in a day or two, to hold my silver.' Revelling in the married state, she could not resist adding how 'the set in our room is walnut, and is very handsome.' Annie had foretold to her sister Janie back home that she would have hired help, and she did. 'Today I have a Klootchman cleaning the stoves, and scrubbing the kitchen floor. She is a great old chatterbox, and I find my Chinook came in very handy.' Outdoors was also being taken care of. 'We have two Chinamen at work in the yard chopping wood.'[26]

Annie's joy in her newfound domesticity was short-lived. Despite 'a cosy little house' in Kamloops, Jim enthused 'at the thought of living at home again.' Less than two weeks after moving into their new home, it was no more. Annie got a rude awakening of what it meant to be a wife as opposed to a single woman. Jim's parents wrote inviting him to return home to Goderich, Ontario, and he agreed. Everything was simply let go, from possessions to his business partnership, sold out to his brother Marsh. 'We will take nothing back with us but our clothes and wedding presents, as freight is so dreadfully expensive on the C.P.R.' Annie seemed dazed. 'I can hardly realize that we are going to leave B.C. for good.'[27] Annie had sojourned in British Columbia for a year and a half, but it was almost as if she had never been there at all.

Jessie got lost in the shuffle. Just as Annie increasingly took her for granted once Jessie arrived in British Columbia, using her to accommodate their family to Jim, she had only the briefest qualms about abandoning her altogether. Annie's double departure from her life left Jessie to lament: 'No one knows how I miss her, not out of B.C. alone, but out of my whole life, she was always the biggest part of my plans, past, present & future.' To the extent that Jessie had family to comfort her, it was her cousin Jessie Olding who took over Annie's school at Nicola Lake. Jessie had been just a couple of months in British Columbia when the sister of her travelling companion, Ed Olding, began to make plans 'for going to B.C.' Jessie Olding was an experienced teacher of precisely the kind the Presbyterian element in British Columbia was seeking to attract. Jessie came west in June 1888 with another young woman from Pictou County. In Victoria for the teachers' examination, Jessie landed a job at Metchosin on southern Vancouver Island.[28]

Jessie Olding's transfer to Nicola Lake lays bare, once again, both the Presbyterian and the Nova Scotian influences on public education in British Columbia. Having decided that the marriage would go ahead, Annie got her cousin to apply for her job 'on account of our own Jessie.' The letter that the secretary of the Nicola Lake trustees sent to the superintendent of education announcing Annie's resignation requested permission to 'engage a teacher now for the ensuing year' since they had 'an application and the applicant wants an early reply so she may give notice of intention to leave in conformity with requirements.' The superintendent objected strongly to the trustees 'engaging a Successor to Miss McQueen from among teachers now employed' rather than hiring from the pool of unemployed teachers. Thereupon the Rev. George Murray weighed in. Writing from 'The Manse' at Nicola Lake, he explained that it was he who had 'urged the Trustees to engage Miss Olding.' As to the reason? 'I knew of her proficiency as a Scholar and efficiency as a teacher,' since 'she taught in the formal educational institutions of the Maritime Provinces and regret was expressed when she left.' Murray was very likely behind the board's manoeuvre whereby Jessie Olding officially resigned at Metchosin before 'she was aware that her application had been accepted by us.'[29]

No sooner had the strategy been effected, then the superintendent was beseeched by another Nova Scotian to have the Metchosin job. Her letter of request speaks to the widespread acceptance of the practice of sojourning. 'I have heard that Miss Olding has succeeded in getting the Nicola School. Now what about Metchosin?' The petitioner could not understand why she had not obtained a job already, since she had 'a Provincial License and good certificates,' and ended her letter with a very revealing plea. 'Mr. Pope really I hope I will get a school it seems to me as if fate was against me ever since I've been here and you have always done so much for all the other young ladies who came from Nova Scotia that I feel disheartened in my treatment.'[30]

Back in the Nicola Valley, Jessie McQueen expressed relief, for 'I don't think I *could* stand the Valley without some one to go and see now and then.' By this she meant someone from home or who, at the least, was homelike. 'If I hadn't Jessie O. to unburden myself to when Nan goes, I don't know what would become of me.'[31] Her cousin Jessie was, she emphasized, 'one of my own folks.'[32]

Annie also bequeathed her sister Jessie something more, and that was a new courage to consider her options for the rest of her life. Family letters hint at the conflicting pressures that had long swirled around Jessie as to whether or not she was free to marry. On the one hand there was the good-natured teasing urging her into intimacy. As Jessie was about to head west, her brother George admonished her: 'One word of advice don't marry a man unless he's three quarters Scotch & one quarter English and has been brought up a Scotch Presbyterian. It's the best mixture in the world and we says it who ought to know. Don't think little girl I don't feel your going away, but I can appreciate the motives and considerations that have led to your decision and I only hope the ranches and saw-mills and steamboat-men will duly appreciate the sterling qualities of our little Jess.' On the other there was the nagging sense of obligation to assist the family economy both financially and as the proverbial maiden aunt, particularly after Annie married out of turn. This strand comes through most clearly in a letter to Jessie from her sister Eliza: 'Beware for widdymen Jess dear. Have you patted mother down smooth again on the young man question? – You'd better wait and find your four-leafed clover growing by your own door-step Jess dear. You're the one ewe-lamb now and mother is going to tether you I 'spect – We'd all like to fasten our apron-string to you.'[33]

The frontier gave courage. Even while speeding across Canada, Jessie began her new adventure of being a single woman amidst many men. She reported to her mother from the Rocky Mountains that 'I'm the only "woman-lady" on this car & one of the men arranged a bed for me last night that was better than a pullman.' Jessie elaborated to her sister Eliza: 'During the last part of the journey I was the only lady on the first-class car, so I used to frequent the Pullman to get up my toilet.' Even in comparison with Nan, she was not doing badly, she confided to her father in June 1888. 'Annie does the most tearing around, for I am very new to the business yet, but I'm learning every week, and expect to be able to cut quite a figure by the time I go home.'[34]

Jessie's attitude toward men was ambivalent. Annie told her about 'the Kamloops braves' in the months before her arrival in British Columbia, and even on her first day there she 'saw a fair representation.' As reported back to Eliza, 'I wasn't particularly overcome.' Jessie went on to assess her attitude in a way which may have reflected her larger perspective or perhaps only her shyness and thereby reticence toward new experiences. 'I don't believe I like men - in the abstract.' Yet in another letter she requested Catherine, in respect to a male friend, to 'tell him that I haven't secured a rancher yet, but am living in hope.'[35]

The flurry of letters back and forth around Nan's 'dude' encouraged Jessie to think about herself. Responding to her mother's sending newspaper clippings about 'S.R. boys,' Jessie wrote in September 1888: 'Speaking of *boys*, reminds me that *I'm* not doing well at all in that line. It will be six months to-morrow since I left home, and I'm not married yet, nor even engaged! Isn't it simply disgraceful, but, never mind, leap-year isn't out yet and who knows what may happen in a few months!' Writing the same day to her sister Jane, Jessie was concerned that her words not be taken too seriously. Following a reference to Annie's 'dude,' still a bone of contention with her family back home, Jessie went on: 'Wait till you see mine! But I haven't seen him myself yet, so I had better crow low for a while perhaps.'[36] Jessie's attempts at banter hinted at something more, that she may already have been engaged in a mild flirtation and was laying the groundwork just in case it came to anything.

Among the experiences that caused Jessie to reflect on what sacrifices a woman should be willing to make to secure a husband was the marriage of a hybrid Voght daughter during her first fall in British Columbia. Jessie quite liked her, musing how 'Tina Voght is a half breed ... but she is clever & pleasant, and just like white folks.' Invited to Christina's wedding, Jessie confided to her mother: 'The girl is a half-breed ... and I think she is far too nice for the man she is getting. He is old enough to be her father, and had a Klootchman for a wife once, but she left him, and took her children with her.' Jessie was absolutely correct in her version of local gossip retailed home to her mother. The husband of twenty-year-old Christina Voght was a local farmer born in Germany in about 1840 and therefore almost thirty years her senior. Tom Schwartz had already fathered three children by an Aboriginal woman named Susan. The two oldest, Henry and Annie, attended the Forks school with Christina, which may explain how the pair met. Alternatively, Tina's father may have acted as matchmaker, given the two men's common Germanic origins. Jessie and her landlady, Agnes Woodward, called on the bride a couple of weeks after the wedding, and Jessie acknowledged that 'she has a very nice little house – kitchen, large dining room, pantry and two bedrooms, but no upstairs bit' and 'quantities of nice presents too – among others, a lovely sewing machine.' Still, Jessie was not convinced, adding in revealing fashion: 'In spite of nice house presents I don't envy her. I'd rather be the indigent-est kind of school ma'am than be in her shoes, but she seems contented so it is "all right."'[37]

Over time Jessie accommodated to the couple, so she reported three months later: 'We went visiting one evening this week to Tom Schwartz's – he who married Tina Voght (a half breed). They have a very nice house – nice furniture, organ and sewing-machine, about as nice a place as is in the Valley, and the old chap is as proud of his young wife as can be.' Time made Jessie wiser in the ways of the world. 'Dutch Henry, who is working at Harvey's now, says it is a shame to see *her* with such a house and furniture; but the matter of him is that he wanted Tena himself once, and she wouldn't have him, so it's a clear case of "sour grapes." The story goes that he threatened to shoot himself when she refused him, and Tena in her quiet voice said "very well, I will get you a *gun!*"'[38] Jessie almost envied Christina Voght Schwartz her nice house and her sewing machine, but not quite. Or did she?

For a moment in time, it seems, Jessie was tempted to take a chance. Not all of her letters survive from her first winter in British Columbia, perhaps because some were too intimate to do so. Alternatively, they were of such general import that they were passed around among so many of Jessie's sisters that they disintegrated or disappeared.

The man who caught Jessie's imagination was Thomas Hall, a native of Leicestershire in England who had lived in the Nicola Valley since his early twenties. Tom and Jessie met shortly after her arrival, and it may have been their age difference – he was twenty-five to her twenty-seven – which accounts for several comments made in passing in her letters home. Another of the young men in the area, Frank Parsons, 'had tea with us last Sat. evening said he could not decide which of us *was* Miss McQueen! Not bad for me when I'm almost five years older than Nan.' It was six weeks before her twenty-eighth birthday, and Jessie mused to her mother how it 'isn't very far away, so this "girl" had better crow low, lest folk ask how old she is.'[39]

At first Jessie did not take Tom Hall very seriously. Looking for work in New Westminster, he sent her a letter consisting in its entirety of Sir Walter Scott's poem 'The Lady of the Lake,' one of whose lines ran, 'The stag at eve had drunk his fill where danced the moon on Monan's rill.' Jessie and Annie are meant to have 'thought this quite hilarious!' Jessie came to realize the reason for the letter was that Tom did not have much schooling and so borrowed the words of others. She began to tutor him. Her respect grew when he turned out to be a good pupil, and she gave him a small Bible that he thereafter, according to family memory, carried in his shirt pocket next to his heart. In November 1888, as plans were going ahead for Annie's wedding, Jessie wrote her mother almost in passing: 'Hall sent me his photo last week – it is a very good one & Nan likes it fine, says she knows she'll like *him* fine too. He is a *pet* & no mistake, but don't be alarmed mother ... "I don't want any *boys to bring up!*" And I don't think Hall is looking for any one to adopt him just yet.' The events surrounding Annie and Jim's wedding, to which Tom Hall's present was 'a morocco writing case,' likely gave opportunities for encounter.[40]

With the flirtatious Annie married off, Jessie discovered, perhaps for the first time in her life, the pleasures of being sought after as a woman. Just as she used to visit Annie, she now spent weekends with her cousin Jessie Olding at Nicola Lake. The consequence was, so Jessie confided to her mother, that 'the Lake boys are a kind lot, but they do gossip most outrageously' about whomever gave her a ride. 'Armstrong drove me down twice I think, and it's not long since I heard, it was "all settled" between us!' Offered a ride on another weekend by a Jack Clarke, 'I told him he'd be sure to be "talked about" for driving with me.' Jessie was delighted by the flurry of attention, and likely it was about this time that she bought herself a fetching new cloak for winter wear. 'They make such mountains out of molehills. I daresay I sometimes forget myself, and don't act with the dignity befitting "Miss McQueen, from Lower Nicola," but I can't be on my dignity all the time.' Most importantly perhaps, Jessie confided to her mother, 'Hall drove me twice, and now, it's all about him.'[41]

Jessie took special pleasure over her growing 'friendship' with Tom Hall. She had repeatedly proclaimed her disgust at what she considered to be the public nature of intimacy on the frontier. 'Weddings, or engagements either, can't be done in a corner here, everybody knows all about everything about as soon as it happens – sometimes sooner – they are inveterate talkers, and what one knows everybody knows. I, myself, am learning to be very discreet & reticent.' At the end of February, she lamented to her mother, in reference to 'that story of my engagement,' how 'everybody out here knows every other body's business, & are not a bit shy about talking of it either.' Now it was Jessie herself who was contributing to the talk. 'By & by, I'm afraid they'll find out I'm not so quiet as I look & some of them will be so astonished, they'll not know what struck them.'[42]

Romance, real or anticipated, was on Jessie's mind. Writing at the end of March 1889, she told of a son in the family with whom she was boarding being asked 'where "Nanna's darling dude" was,' and of his replying by pointing at a young hybrid, Louis Lindley. 'There was a general roar, but I was ever so glad it was no worse – if it had been any white man I suppose I'd never hear the end of it.' Whether or not Tom Hall was urged on by the flurry of competition for Jessie's attention, she delighted in how they were 'getting really acquainted.' They went riding and they made plans to attend the 24th of May picnic at Nicola Lake celebrating Queen Victoria's birthday. In effect, they were courting. Jessie dared to think that her mother might approve, for he was 'a member of his own church, and a good, pure man, even after living four years in such a country as this.'[43] Jessie could, in other words, embrace the man without necessarily embracing the frontier.

What is remarkable is that Jessie acted thus despite her beloved Nan's disapproval. Removed to Ontario and almost immediately pregnant, Annie longed for her British Columbia 'dudes,' and did not want Jessie to usurp her place among them. Her warnings may have been, in part, intended for her shyer sister's own good, but they were also something more. Tom Hall had been among Annie's circle of admirers, and here he was abandoning her memory. 'Jess, I've been worrying about you since I got your last letter, do be careful, and don't give that crowd a chance to whet their tongues against you. Men are deceitful things (all except Jim), and don't you let Tommy make love to you, mind that now. It would do you both harm.'[44]

Then the unthinkable happened. 'On Wed. morning he walked to school with me from Mr. Harvey's, and the next Wednesday he was killed.' Jessie wrote her mother in a letter marked 'Private': 'I said goodbye so carelessly, and never dreamed that I would never see him again.' On Monday, 13 May 1889, Tom Hall began a new job in a 'steam sawmill, about 40 miles from here.' His task was to assist the sawyer by carrying away the edgings from the cut lumber.[45] While doing so, Tom crossed over the lumber on the carriage behind the saw and caught his foot. Tom Hall was essentially chopped into pieces. The Kamloops *Sentinel* newspaper reported: 'His right leg was severed below the knee and his body fell on the saw making a cut extending from the knee through the flesh part of the right leg at an angle across the abdomen and chest only ending at the left shoulder when the saw must have caught his clothing and threw him about sixteen feet.' According to the story passed down through Jessie's sister Eliza, 'as he lay screaming in agony on the ground, his companions pulled the Bible [Jessie had given him] out of his breast pocket and pressed it between his teeth for him to bite on.'[46]

The intimacy with which Jessie wrote about Tom Hall's death, so unlike her other letters, argues that she genuinely believed that her life would have been very different but for the accident. 'Mother dear, a week ago to-night (Wednesday), such sad news was brought to us. In my last letter [which has not survived] I spoke lightly of a young man being out riding with me. I meant to have written – a slip and told you who it was, as I have mentioned him often before, but was hurried at the last; and last Wednesday the word was brought from the [Nicola] Lake that he was dead. And just the Wednesday before that, we were together, and had such a pleasant evening, little dreaming that it was the last. And he was my only friend, mother, the only one I had made in the whole Valley, or ever wanted to make.'[47]

As for Annie's response, perhaps it gave comfort, perhaps not. She saw Tom Hall's death principally in terms of herself, being 'quite ill all the rest of the day' on hearing the news. It was her loss that grieved her. 'Dear, you know how often I have told you that I liked him, that he was to be trusted and a great many other things that I have not the heart to speak of now, for I dare not dwell on *the* subject. Last Sunday in church, the thought of him came to my mind so strongly that before I knew I was crying and almost unable to stop.' In good part to assure herself of her continuing place of pride among her 'dudes,' Annie affected the closer relationship with Tom Hall. 'You are mistaken in thinking that your influence on Tom was not for good. I am quite sure that he was a better man for having your friendship for he was greatly influenced by those he cared for. I like to think that I never had heard him talk lightly of any girl or try to make me think less of any of the boys.' Annie sought to convince the grieving Jessie she was over-reacting. 'And now, dear, don't mistake the feeling of strong friendship and comradeship for anything else, for I know you & I am certain that there was no *love* for him, such as I give my dear husband. The loss will be a great one, and I believe you will always have a keen regret for him, for I will too, and I believe that I liked him quite as much as you did, although I will not miss him as you do.'[48]

If other family members are to be believed, Jessie was convinced, at least in retrospect, that there had been much more between herself and Tom Hall than Annie's self-serving view would suggest. Jessie is said to have marked his grave with a tombstone and to carry the tooth-marked

Bible she had given him with her over the years. Jessie had been willing to meet the frontier part-way. Tom's death confirmed for her that such was not intended to be. She was predestined to serve her family and would in the future acquiesce to her fate, so she assured her mother was the lesson of Hall's death. He had died for a purpose. 'I hope I will never again be as selfish as I have been and I think the loss of this dear friend has taught me to think less of myself & more of others. I see life as I never did before, and perhaps this is part of God's "perfect plan."'[49]

In her turmoil, Jessie came to consider that she had defied her mother by insisting on going west, 'even for the money.' She berated herself. 'I sometimes think I was headstrong & self-willed about coming here.' Catherine's reply, which has not survived, did little to assuage Jessie's anguish, as indicated by her response to it. 'I know that "God meant it, and God sent it," but oh mother, I do seem to lose hold of all my comfort.' Catherine could not let go of the bone, and in her next letter reassured her daughter, in a fashion calculated to ensure her continued dependence: 'No Dear you were not headstrong about going out to B.C. You needed change & we never objected to you going & is it not probable you have been a means of good to some one who may bless your endeavor to aid.' Catherine's next letter took yet another tack, combining coercion with a play on guilt. 'Do you know I've been thinking if you don't feel like work, or don't feel in normal health, it would be better to give up the school & come home, what signifies money when your health & comfort is concerned.' Jessie berated herself all the more. 'I'm glad you didn't think I was headstrong about coming out here, and I wish I could think, or know, that I had ever helped anyone. I can keep trying to, anyhow.'[50]

The McQueen sisters each took a chance on love. Annie culminated her adventure in marriage, whereas Jessie's ended in tragedy. For Jessie it appeared to be a sign. Thereafter she should not resist daughterhood's obligations. God, through her mother, had intended a course for her life. In comparison with the previous year, Jessie's twenty-ninth birthday passed without self-reflection. Its only celebrant was a pupil born the same day who proudly proclaimed how 'the day before Christmas is my birthday and Miss McQueen's.'[51] Unlike her beloved younger sister, Jessie approached middle age all alone.

Chapter Six

Domesticating Everyday Life

LOWER NICOLA

The sad ending to Jessie's hopes for intimacy turned her inward on herself. In doing so, she drew on a part of her character that had always been present. From her very first days in British Columbia, Jessie lived a contradiction. However contagious Annie's enthusiasm, Jessie took comfort in Nova Scotian norms. She once wrote to her mother, 'there's no *daring* in me.'[1] As a sojourner, committed to a three-year exile to sustain the McQueen family economy, she had little impetus to move beyond the familiar any more than was absolutely necessary.

Jessie retreated, not through a single swoop but as a matter of accretion. It was easiest to stay put, and she did so for the two years following Tom Hall's death. In Victoria for the teachers' examination shortly after arriving in British Columbia, she had been enchanted. 'I never fell in love with a city before, but I *am* wildly in love with Victoria.' Vancouver intrigued her. 'I saw ever so many brick buildings in various stages of advancement.' Even so, Jessie made no attempt, as was commonplace among teachers, to change schools. She had neither the will nor the contacts to do so. Annie had observed cynically on hearing that her room-mate from the Truro teacher-training college had migrated to New Westminster, 'She expects to get one of the schools there, and as she has some influential friends, she'll be all right.'[2] Jessie also hung on to her modest Lower Nicola school for another reason, and that was the proximity of her cousin Jessie Olding as Annie's replacement at Nicola Lake.

To the extent Jessie acted, she did so in familiar ways. It was the re-creation of family and home, comfort in things Nova Scotian, religious observance, and her work as a teacher that sustained her. Jessie needed to feel, as she put it, 'useful to society.'[3] In each of these four aspects of her everyday life, Jessie, and for a time also Annie, domesticated.

Family and home lay at the heart of Jessie's upbringing and outlook. There was no expectation that she or Annie would be more than sojourners in British Columbia. Pregnant with her first child in small-town Ontario, Annie waxed nostalgic for what had already become a youthful adventure 'out West.' She assured a sorrowful Jessie how 'you'll look back to the B.C. days just as I do, miss.' Jessie did not adapt easily. Every aspect of the physical and human frontier could be cause for consternation. In Kamloops the day after her arrival: 'There seems to be a scarcity of paint, and the unpainted buildings don't turn a soft grey as they do at home, but are more the color of *toast* nicely done. A dismal tint I think.' Jessie wanted interiors, as well, to be exactly the same as at home, but, she reported, 'Mr. Chisholm's house and church [at Kamloops] are the only plastered buildings I've seen since I struck B.C.'[4]

Pictou County remained Jessie's point of reference. The Nicola Valley presented 'a very dark dry looking landscape,' as seen through her eyes. 'I can't get used to the dark hills and rocks – I don't know what it is I miss, but there seems to be such a lack of brightness somehow – perhaps it's the want of water that makes the difference – a sheet of water I mean, like the river & harbor at home.' A month later: 'You can hardly begin to imagine the amount of dust we have on the roads now. My shoes always look as though they belonged to some kind of tramp – they are so brown and dusty.' Time did little to soften the landscape's alien character. 'I don't know that I need to be so spiteful at the country, it has never done me any harm, and after all it is a part of "this Canada of ours," but not the *best* part, by a large jugful.' Even though Jessie identified both Nova Scotia and British Columbia with Canada, it was not easy for her to do so. 'It is emphatically "a country without grass," except where it is cultivated; but I am getting used to it, as one will get used to disagreeable things.' Her second summer in the Nicola Valley, Jessie compared the view from her window with the one she had at home. 'Oh the green grass & the trees & the river – so very different from this dusty dusty corner.'[5]

Jessie responded similarly to the family that took her in. The Woodward children were 'noisy, quarrelsome little beggars.' She went further. 'I'd like to cuff them soundly many a time.' Slowly Jessie accommodated, re-creating Harvey and Agnes Woodward and their children as her family, or at least the best that she could do for the interim. Having boarded for half a year, she considered that 'Mrs H. is just like an older sister to Nan & myself, and the place is getting wonderfully home-like, though I take spots of hating Nicola.' In Victoria her second summer for the teachers' exam, Jessie lamented that she had no 'word from my Nicola folk until Wed. & it does seem a long time since I left them.' It was not just that the Woodwards echoed many of the attributes of Jessie's own family, their farming round was familiar. She depicted it with admiration, for the results of their enterprise far surpassed anything she knew from her childhood in Pictou County. 'Mr. Harvey is better off this year than any one I know. Plenty of grain, potatoes and hay – about a dozen pigs (all for home consumption) and is still milking seven cows and making beautiful butter. Only the hens are not doing their duty, and before long eggs will be up to 50¢ a doz.'[6]

The Woodwards' seasonal round became Jessie's own. The spring of her arrival: 'The eldest boy is ploughing this morning with three horses gang-plow, I think it's called. They have another team harrowing, so they make quick work. They are milking two cows this week ... [they] say it pays better [to buy butter] than to feed the cows, and churn.' Jessie was thinking back to her family's endless butter making for the little cash it brought. The month of May three years later garnered a similar description. '"Seeding" is all done – grain fields green & trees in full leaf.' As spring became summer, the dry climate that caused Jessie so much consternation made ad hoc irrigation essential. 'The sound of the little brook that Mr W. brought down from the hills to water the garden is better than music. He has four or five little streams running through the currant bushes to-day and in a day or two he will turn them on to another strip of garden and so on.'[7]

The harvest was so very different from anything Jessie knew from home. A large grain field was 'dead ripe,' and 'folks are busy harvesting now.' The Woodwards were at the forefront in bringing agricultural machinery into the Nicola Valley, and Jessie admired the new technology. 'Mr Woodward has been away all week with the reaper [cutting grain on neighbouring farms]. It's a fine arrangement, leaves the grain *bound* in sheaves. They don't have to hurry in their grain here – the field opposite my window has been cut & bound for a week and may stay there for weeks yet.' Writing a week later, Jessie noted that 'the grain is all standing in "shocks" or "stooks," or whatever they are, and they expect to thresh it all as soon as they are done cutting.' Come the middle of September: 'We are having a busy time at our house this week, for threshing is being done. The grain is all stacked outside, is threshed and cleaned all at the same time, and the straw re-stacked, they never put any in the barn. They have eight horses on, and thirteen men.' The demands put on the household to feed the men were enormous. 'They began on Tuesday morning, will be done this evening (Thursday) and in that time have got away with three quarters of beef, three sacks of flour – (they never get it by the barrel here) and unlimited quantities of tea, sugar, and all sorts of vegetables.' By the end of the month: 'I had bread this week, made from the new flour, and it was quite as good as any of the Ontario flour we use at home. We have a mill in this settlement, though we haven't much else.' It was not just the magnitude of the harvest that overwhelmed Jessie. 'Mrs. Harvey's garden was late this year, but still there are quantities of cucumbers, onions, beets, cabbage etc. We haven't tried any of the corn yet, but I think it is about fit to use now.' By the beginning of October, the harvest was winding down. 'The grain & vegetables are all weighed – Their potatoes were late going in, but they had some pretty good bouncers. It seemed quite homelike to see two or three big Early Roses walking in for exhibition.'[8]

The winter had its own rhythm, one that took Jessie, at least momentarily, out of herself. She fretted about the animals, but 'Mr. Harvey says this bunchgrass won't freeze off – it will be there for the cattle right along.' The beginning of November: 'We have had hard hard frost the last two nights, & places where the sun didn't reach yesterday, remained frozen all day. The sky is bright & clear, & the air now is really bracing.' By the middle of the month, 'this night feels very wintry, but that is not surprising as the mountains all around are white with snow.' As was so often the case, Jessie could not resist a comparison with home. 'There are good big stacks of hay, bins of wheat, sacks of flour, a "root-house" full of potatoes, and between Saturday and Monday Mr. Harvey and Grandpa Woodward killed *fourteen hogs*. Grandpa took two of them, but the remaining dozen were all cut up here into hams, bacon, sausages, lard, potted head, and everything else that *pig* could be made into. We've had "spare rib," enough and to spare, and I don't like to say how many lbs. of soap are being made ... They are still milking one cow, so we haven't come down to condensed milk yet. I am patriotic to the backbone, but I prefer B.C. milk straight from the cow, to the best "Truro condensed milk." This is a very different country from N.S.'[9]

The new year was marked by weather. 'New Year's Day was about the coldest we had – it went down to 35° below zero, & in some places even worse than that ... It looks to-day as though we were in for a "January thaw" & if so it will be harder on the stock than steady cold. Mr Harvey lost another horse – cause unknown ... it is no fun for the stage-drivers, freighters.' In late February: 'The thermometer stood 35° below zero last night ... This last cold snap has lasted 12 days ... Several Siwashes & some white men too have found their horses on the mountains, fast in four or five feet of snow & starved.' By the beginning of April, spring was once again on its way. 'The snow is all gone on one side of us, but there is still plenty of it in the shady side of the mountain ... Mr Harvey starts his plough to-day, & expects to have his "garden" all in next week. The cattle are doing wonderfully for there was *green* grass under the snow all the time – the frost never got at it.'[10] The yearly round began anew.

The Woodwards were at the fore of the process by which the Nicola Valley was losing its frontier character, a shift Jessie accelerated by her boarding with them. The everyday business of living was not easy for women on their own, particularly where appearance counted, as with teaching. Most clothes were home-made, and hence the seemingly end-less interest in sewing. On the first weekend that Annie did not come to visit, 'I'd rather stay at home and read or sew, but Mrs. W. wants me to go' visiting with her. Jessie reported to her mother about a weekend visit to Annie that 'Nan was busy sewing – making a dress for herself – cheap white material and was making a pretty good job of it too.' In line with her character, Annie made the practicalities of dressing for the frontier into a game. Not long after she arrived, she wrote home how 'I have started to knit myself some stockings, for I am nearly bare-foot, and I am getting on famously, in spite of the fun.' Jessie also knit. 'I have almost finished one pair of stockings for myself, and am at the heel of one of a second pair. I keep that one in school, for work at noon, and it doesn't progress very fast.'[11]

Sewing was comfortingly familiar. Sometimes it was by hand, taken with when visiting, and other times, on a machine that was kept 'clicking most of the time.' The advent of sewing machines was a great boon, and Jessie took advantage of every invitation for their use. 'I may make up that seersucker in holidays, but it can wait.' She once explained how 'Mrs H. was away all day Sat. and when I wasn't hunting the young ones I was running the sewing-machine for all I was worth.' It was not just dresses that had to be constructed. 'I think I'll make a slip-waist for a change,' Jessie sighed with relief. Home in Nova Scotia, Jessie had slept with someone else in the same bed, and she noted during her first Brit-ish Columbia autumn, 'Have a flannel nightie partly made, as I have to be "brick" for my own toes this winter.' The seasonal nature of clothing added to the sewing tasks. Jessie reported in late August, a time of cold nights but warm days, that 'I had off my flannel garment for *two* days, but it's on again and will stay on. This B.C. weather isn't to be trusted no how.' In mid-October, 'Friday was so hot that I wished I hadn't had my flannels on.'[12]

The necessity for endless sewing bound Jessie to the Woodwards. 'Sewing for such a family is quite an item; but Maggie, the oldest girl, can take all charge of the baby, wash, dress & feeds him, and so leave her mother free to sew when she is home. She is only 13 I think, but can do almost any kind of house-work, but is dreadfully backward in school.' Jessie took a special interest in Maggie, the child who had earlier been maltreated in school by her Woodward cousins. Perhaps for that reason, she did not do well there, and was now forced to run much of the household. Jessie facilitated free time for Maggie, during which they likely shared views on right behaviour and other topics. 'Maggie Woodward & I rode to the [Nicola] Lake. She took "Lewis" & I took a big, quite old horse & we had a very pleasant ride, & not a bit tired after it either. We did the twelve miles (between Uncle Marcus' & the Lake) in about two hours. Not bad for greenhorns was it?'[13]

Much as Jessie had helped with the upbringing of her younger sister Annie, four and a half years her junior, she became involved with the younger Woodward children. Her favourite was 'little Fred,' whom Jessie nursed when ill, taking pleasure that 'he is just as contented with me as with his mother.' The family's economic self-confidence is indicated by their getting a medical doctor to attend their sick child, his bill equating to virtually a month of Jessie's pay. 'The Dr. called around last week (for his little bill of $50) and said it *was* bronchitis sure enough.'[14] Having boarded for a year, Jessie came to see Fred almost as her own child. 'This is morning now, the small Fred has just climbed on my lap. He often comes up to my room and enjoys himself with my brushes etc. ... He is as much my pet as ever, & sometimes refuses to go to his mama from me.' Six months later, Jessie took pride that Fred now called her 'Keen' [McQueen] and himself 'Keen's dood [dude] boy.' All the same, Jessie had her limits, noting at the beginning of her third autumn boarding at the Woodwards how 'eight children are a terrible houseful sometimes.'[15]

Jessie's association with the Woodwards' well-being served to consolidate the values that they and like families brought to British Columbia, in their case from Ontario. By virtue of the teacher identifying herself with their behaviour, it was normalized as the way to conduct everyday life. 'My circle of Woodward friends, which includes Grandpa's, Uncle Francis' and Uncle Marcus' families, are all as kind as can be, & I am equally at home in all their houses,' so Jessie wrote after almost three years on the British Columbia frontier.[16]

In re-creating family and home, Jessie both included and excluded. Over time acquaintances became friends, but only some acquaintances. A very significant aspect of Jessie's re-creation of family and home were the exclusions. Practices of which her mother would not have approved became grounds for dismissal. In dissociating herself from the 'big day' at Coutlie's stopping house to celebrate the 1st of July, she used as her reason the 'games of all sorts, ... racing, & lots of "drunks."' Persons who lived too long in British Columbia ran the risk of being contaminated by the frontier. Whatever their skills, they were less able to be incorporated into the nation as she conceived it. The local medical doctor 'has been thirty years in B.C. and any one who lives here that length of time is fit for anything I believe,' she confided to her mother.[17]

In signalling who was excluded, Jessie drew also on notions of the nation grounded in colonial practice. She divided persons by skin colour, much as had the twinned Nicola Valley schools not so many years earlier. She took for granted her privilege as a woman of the palest skin colour, as in lauding two young women as 'the prettiest girls in the Valley – very fair, and such lovely color nearly always.' Attending the May 24th celebration at Nicola Forks, Jessie mused on the hybrid Garcia and Voght families. They had a perfect right, in Jessie's view, to attend this public commemoration of Queen Victoria's birthday, which linked men and women of the frontier to their counterparts across Canada and also to the greater colonial and imperial enterprise. 'The Garcia girls, Tina & Tillie Voght & myself were the only girls there, but there were plenty of men "of the kind."' Still, persons 'of the kind' were not quite the same as she herself, so Jessie explained to her mother. 'There were four half-breed girls there belonging to one family – Kossuth or Garcia, they get both names, one is Spanish & the other English. They have attended school for years but in spite of that they still have the squaw looks & manners. Their father is a Mexican Spaniard ... so they came honestly by their black looks.' Hybridity gave the excuse for not taking others seriously or not naming them in their entirety, as in Jessie's reference to a chase across the border after 'a half-breed Anthony for horse-stealing.'[18]

Colour was a critical marker of the feasibility of domestication. Jessie continued in her letter home written after the May 24th celebration: 'I've been in [William] Voght's house once or twice. They have nice books & an organ, and altogether it's as nice as any house I've seen in the Valley. The mother is a pretty neat little thing but she keeps out of sight when there is company.' Jessie clearly approved that, as an Aboriginal woman, Klema Voght knew her limitations. Hybridity in and of itself was suspicious, be it the Voghts' married daughter Christina or others of mixed heritage she encountered. Jessie once returned to the Woodwards to find the mother, Agnes, ill and 'their only help ... is a half-breed girl both slow and stupid, though I suppose she does the best she can.' Given such an attitude, it is not surprising that the help left after a couple of weeks, despite 'promising to stay another month.'[19]

The numerous men from China who remained in the British Columbia interior following their employment in the construction of the transcontinental railway, and their counterparts who had come earlier with the gold rush, posed less of a threat to Jessie's re-creation of home. They were simply too alien to be even considered for inclusion. 'I saw my first Chinaman in [the Rev. John] Chisholm's yard [in Kamloops] – sawing wood – with his pig-tail twisted up round his head. This fellow was quite as dark as our Indians – but smaller featured, with bright black eyes.' If men from China were peculiar, women were even more so. 'There are heaps of Chinamen in K.[amloops] and some women too. The latter are desperately low – no character at all. I saw three of them wending their way to the photographers one day – got up regardless, of course. They just looked as if they stepped out of a picture book – with blouses, trousers, pig-tails &c so it's no use to describe them further. They each carried an ordinary umbrella (for sun) and walked like "well-bred ducks" – in a row – straight one behind the other.' Jessie acquired a certain appreciation of the role men from China played in the local economy. Writing from Victoria her first summer in British Columbia, she even sought to impress by her familiarity with Chinese ways. 'I like to peek in at the Chinese Laundries, they are so spry about their work. We pass them every day' on the way to the teachers' examination. Not having had letters recently, she rationalized that 'I suppose they'll come in a bunch "bime-by" as the Chinaman says.'[20]

The incorporation of men from China into the Woodward family economy caused little concern. Jessie's first spring: 'Mrs. W. got a Chinaman to-day – Sing by name – $20 a month ... he looks pleasant – had his pockets full of candy for the children when he came.' His stay having been of short duration, a successor arrived in mid-September through Nan's intervention. 'Annie secured a Chinaman for Mrs Harvey, and sent him down Monday. I don't think she could possibly have got along without him, for he does *all* the cooking and dish-washing, and that's no small amount, for it's dinner *three* times a day – meat & vegetables every time. When *John* (the Chinaman) wants to look stylish, he puts on the white shirt that he wears *outside* his pants ... and fastened to one side with brass buttons and loops of cord ... I don't like to be too inquisitive when he has it on. I saw several tiny fellows on the boat with fine cloth "shirts," and brocaded silk trousers.'[21] Jessie lacked any appreciation of these men beyond their exoticism and economic utility. They were irrelevant to the sociability, and to the work, of domestication, in which she and like-minded persons were engaged.

It was much the same with Aboriginal people. Initially, Jessie verged toward some sense of accommodation. She had had some contact with Mi'kmaq in Nova Scotia, with, as she once put it, 'our Indians.' All the same, she was unprepared for their far greater immediacy on the British Columbia frontier. She only had to climb 'the big hill behind the schoolhouse' to see 'up past the Indian reserve,' which lay between Lower Nicola and Nicola Forks. Initially she appreciated their role in the local economy. Jessie noted at the end of her first August that Agnes Woodward was 'about as well as usual, but has no help, hasn't even been able to get a washer-woman this time, for all the Klootchies are away gathering huckleberries. All except Annie who used to do the washing regularly; Billy her man is "hiyu sick" – got on a spree some time ago, and Siwash Drs. don't seem to be able to get him straightened out again, so she can't leave him.' Going to visit on the other side of the river, Jessie was stymied on discovering it 'was too high to ford, & no Indian was in sight to take us over in his canoe.' Another time 'the Indians brought word to-night that the thaw has made the roads very bad – almost impassable in places, with snow slides from the steep banks above.'[22]

Jessie's easy familiarity went only so far. As time passed, she picked up the language of ready dismissal of Aboriginal people commonplace across North America during these years. 'They are a dirty looking lot in the camps.' In the Nicola Valley a year, Jessie condoned the ridicule inflicted on an Aboriginal man by a newcomer 'who used to drive the stage [and] was going to the Ferry, so I got along with him.' She described what happened. 'We caught up to a Siwash, and he (Clarke) let out yelps, until the poor beggar's horse just pranced like a deer – a jump for every yell, just as if some one were prodding him with a sharp stick. I do think my sides were aching a little bit yet, from the effects of his nonsense.' Jessie's pleasure in young Fred Woodward's learning to call her 'Keen' caused her to overlook, perhaps to condone, what else he said. 'One morning in bed, Fred says "dirty Siwash." I said *who's* a dirty Siwash? "Keen!" I'm "Keen" now all the time.'[23]

Over time, as newcomer settlement grew in the Nicola Valley, as it did elsewhere across British Columbia, divisions based on skin colour, generalized into races, became more rigid. The distinctions were ever present, even where irrelevant to the situation. Each fall Jessie gave an admiring account of threshing on the Woodwards' farm. September 1888: 'They have eight horses on, and thirteen men, only three of whom are white men, one is a half-breed, and the others solid Injun – Siwashes, they call them.' The next fall, 'the thresher is here to-day with four whitemen and nine or ten Siwashes.'[24] In 1890, 'there were eight Siwashes and five or six white men.'[25] At the heart of the frontier's end is the closing of options for some of its members. Nowhere is this better demonstrated than with the Woodward clan's steady march into mechanized farming with Aboriginal people being pushed to the edge as seasonal labourers.

In re-creating family and home on the British Columbia frontier, things Nova Scotian were never far from Jessie's mind. Nova Scotian, and more particularly Pictou County, ways were the ways to which she turned as a matter of course and where she positioned herself. They were the domestic props that gave reassurance of the home that she had left behind. In British Columbia, Jessie remained an anomaly, or so she considered. The arrival of the Rev. George Murray's sister-in-law from New Glasgow for a visit caused Jessie to reflect to her mother how 'Miss McD & I are pretty fair examples of the "solitary" being "set in families," aren't we?'[26]

The Nova Scotia connection validated both things and persons. Their origin legitimized them, regardless of what might be their other characteristics. Ties to Pictou County were strengthened with the arrival of Murray's sister in the fall of 1888, and a year later Catherine wrote, 'I heard lately that a sister of Mrs Murray's is going out to B.C.' Laying eyes for the first time on Murray's sister-in-law, Maggie McDonald, Jessie mused, 'She seems very nice, but how could she help it when she is a *Nova Scotian* and a *Pictonian*?' Jessie was repeatedly soothed by making comparisons. Fresh milk might be better than the condensed milk used at home, the flour much the same, but most often things Nova Scotian triumphed. 'Mrs Murray and I are all one in our opinion of B.C. It may be good enough, but it doesn't come up to N.S. in any way.' She continued: 'As Mr Murray and I drove home last evening, some of the mountains looked *almost* beautiful in the sunset light, but it only made me think how much more beautiful home would be at the same time.' Politics prompted another comparison. 'It is election time here too, but they don't seem to make much fuss over it. The two parties here are not so definitely defined as at home, and so far as I can make out, are somewhat mixed as to opinions. The premier, John Robson, is really a Liberal, and the rest of the Government partly Conservative, but they are all down on the tariff, as their principal trade is with the Americans, so while they are "John A. men," they are minus John A.'s [National] policy.'[27] British Columbia lacked organized political parties in the model of Nova Scotia and elsewhere in Canada until the early twentieth century. By virtue of such comments, Jessie made some elements of frontier life more acceptable than others, because they seemed more Nova Scotian or, more generally, Canadian.

As well as the ongoing correspondence, which gave Jessie the opportunity to justify her views and be justified in them, one of the most enduring links to Nova Scotia was the financial obligation. However beloved Daniel McQueen might be as a father, he could never quite manage the family's finances. From the early 1880s, Daniel suffered from poor health, which worsened the situation. Jessie paid off a family debt of $200 to a nearby store and then an unspecified amount her parents had borrowed from their older daughter Eliza's husband. Most transactions occurred without having to be made explicit, and hence the asides. 'Mother, won't you let me know the state of the family finances? Is it "hard sleddin" or how?' Another time: 'You always say you'll tell me when you need anything, but you never do speak of any needs, & there must be some.' Sometimes a trace survives, as in Jessie's reassurance to her sister Jane. 'You must be wearing out some boots too, doing your share of the work and mine too. Get good strong ones, Janie, ones that will keep you comfortable in all sorts of weather, and I'll see that you'll have plenty to pay for them. I'm a reliable person you know, so get the boots, and I'll foot the damages, *sure.*' About the time Annie got married, Jessie wrote home how 'I meant to have paid up your subscriptions to all the papers, but couldn't get P.O. orders ... so it will have to wait until next time.'[28]

One of the strongest statements of Jessie's sense of daughterhood's obligations was her assurance to Jane after passing her teachers' examination in August 1888 that she would 'send home my "marks" so that you family may all know if I did my duty as a man and a brother.' By her actions, Jessie alienated her increasingly wayward brother. Dove tried to comfort Jessie in 1893: 'Why did [George] act so? He has crawled back into his shell ... I truly think the reason he did not write you before was that he feels that you have done what he has not – taken care of the home ones.' A few months later, Jessie assured her mother, likely at her behest, that she had tried once again. 'I have a letter ready to mail to George now – one more trial.'[29]

So far as making purchases was concerned, Jessie scrimped, unlike Annie while teaching in British Columbia. 'We have agreed to differ on that point for neither of us can convince or convert the other.' Prices for goods were in general higher in British Columbia. Nevertheless, Jessie explained about Nan: 'She didn't send for anything mother because she buys what she needs here unless it is too expensive altogether. She hasn't as much of the Chinaman in her as I have and doesn't think it fair to take all the money she can get here and spend it somewhere else.' Jessie was referring to the stereotypical view of Chinese men working in British Columbia as hoarding their money to send back to relatives at home, much as she did herself. Not only did Annie spend her money more freely, but she even, Jessie acknowledged, bought 'a nice little lace-covered parasol for me (to match that muslin dress [sister] Liz gave me).' Jessie accepted the gift, but noted how 'I felt real mean to think of letting her spend money for me when I wouldn't spend it for myself.' Jessie once described herself as 'mean' with her money and repeatedly referred to herself and others like her as 'we "North American Chinamen."'[30]

By getting virtually everything that she needed, including dress material, from home, Jessie reinforced her ties to Nova Scotia and made Maritimes products appear to be the norm in British Columbia. In August 1888: 'I may want to order some more foot-gear for Nan & myself.' The next spring, Jessie sent 'for a couple of summer undershirts [that] only cost about 35 cents apiece, including postage, duty, and all.' Her sister Eliza queried from her home in Dartmouth, 'You haven't written me for any summer things – Won't you need a cool dress?' As was her refrain, Jessie wrote gratefully about one parcel: 'The contents give entire satisfaction, and I'm ever so much obliged for all the trouble I've been to the family.' Having sent for 'dress material,' Jessie rejoiced how 'Belle got such nice material & trimming, much nicer than anything I see in Kamloops, & fits my purse better too.'[31]

It was not just goods and dollars that sped back and forth. Reading material from the Maritimes not only gave comfort, but it also served to accustom British Columbians to Canadian ways. Virtually all of the older sisters, as well as Catherine, passed on used newspapers and magazines, which were then recycled to friends and acquaintances across the Nicola Valley. Catherine sent the local newspaper so that her daughters could read the 'Town news,' and also the '*Witnesses & Messengers*,' which Jessie considered were 'good everywhere.' In a typical response, Jessie thanked her mother for 'the last bundle of papers – Witnesses, Chron's, and Maritime and Children's Record.'[32] The *Presbyterian Witness*, which functioned as the Church's unofficial voice, and the Baptist *Christian Messenger* were two of the principal religious newspapers being published in Nova Scotia during these years. According to historian John C. Moir, the *Witness* reflected its long-time editor's commitment to the creation of a Christian Canada, one which readers like Jessie then fostered through the schools. Moir describes the *Witness* as 'the Maritime voice of the new national vision' being fostered under the banner of Presbyterianism.[33]

Stories in the *Presbyterian Witness* and other papers were intended to effect change in and of themselves. Jessie wrote to her mother how she had 'saved the piece of poetry you marked; it is very good.' Another time: 'I saw the piece of poetry you spoke of in the Montreal Witness ... Isn't "Pansy's" story in the Witness a nice one?'[34] Jessie was referring to one of some 150 'Pansy' books written between 1865 and 1931, a series commonly known by the pseudonym of their author, an American Presbyterian minister's wife named Isabella Alden. Directed primarily toward young people, the books gave lessons for living that centred on doing good works in the church. Among them was advocacy of temperance, as much a part of the American as the Canadian ethos during these years. Consciously intended by their author to 'win souls for Jesus Christ,' the Pansy books sold some 100,000 copies a year at this, their height of popularity.[35] Such stories were, literary critic Elizabeth Langland points out, 'not simply fictional representations but the interacting texts through which a culture represents itself.'[36] The Pansy stories encouraged women like Jessie, whose actual circumstances might be isolated, toward similar dispositions and practices.

The various publications sometimes took on a life of their own, as when Agnes Woodward came across one of them while in a depressed state. 'Hardly knowing what she did she went into the front room & began to sort some books & papers, when she noticed pencil marks on one – a Messenger the piece was "Comforted," and she said she read it all through with the tears dropping, but by the time she was done, she was singing the hymns & was indeed comforted. That was what you marked for me mother dear, & it has done so much good already. Mrs. W. has that paper yet, and says it will have a message for some one else.' Other times it was simply that 'we all enjoyed the papers.'[37] Through such everyday intermediaries as Jessie McQueen, the press in nineteenth-century Canada instilled in persons who never knew each other similar dispositions. The different papers published by the Protestant denominations in Canada did not all have the same perspective, but they did share certain broad assumptions about right behaviour and, for the most part, took the existence of Canada as a nation for granted.

What may be termed chain sojourning played a critical role in bringing British Columbia into Canada. Just as Annie facilitated Jessie's arrival, she then encouraged their cousin Jessie Olding to come. The Rev. George Murray's wife had not only a sister but two brothers in the Kamloops area. Visiting Nan's predecessor at the Nicola Lake school, now married to local rancher William Pooley, Jessie reflected how 'it's nice to see some Pictou folks out here – their houses are more like home than any others.' Janie Pooley's unmarried sister no sooner came for a visit, than she wed a Kamloops businessman, causing Catherine to sputter: 'You never mentioned Miss Douglas' marriage. Is it owing to the climate that people when they go to B.C. are so ready to fall in love and get married in such a short time? Is it really Love or convenience or position the ruling motive?' Even older McQueen sister Eliza, long married to a medical doctor, mused wistfully: 'Annie gives such an account of the *need* of a doctor out there that I believe [husband] Norm would take a trip to spy out the land if we had not rooted ourselves so strongly here by building this house.'[38]

Jessie's letters are filled with references, many brief and in passing, to chance meetings with fellow Nova Scotians and Maritimers that inevitably cheered her. From Victoria her first summer: 'it's nice to find so many friends where one expected to meet only strangers.' Visiting New Westminster: 'This Mrs. McNab is from Antigonish, & there are ever so many from N.S. and N.B.' At Spence's Bridge on her way back to the Nicola Valley: 'His name is Aitken, & he seems to know all the New Glasgow folk.'

Jessie seemed to run across ministers with Maritimes ties every time she turned around. When she and her cousin stopped off at Fort William 'for Sunday' on their way west, the minister came up to them after morning service at the church they attended to say he 'knew me as one of the McQueen tribe.' She was delighted when 'he said he knew my face.' It turned out he and his brother had attended the local school with Jessie's brother George. He arranged for his brother, living in Brandon, to be 'waiting with open arms' when the westward train made a stop there. Returning to Kamloops by train in August 1888, 'a gentleman spoke to me about exams in Victoria or something of the kind, and in a very few minutes I found that he was the Rev. Mr. McLeod who was minister in Knox Church about seventeen years ago.' For all of her habitual shyness, the two struck up an acquaintance. 'He made us go & have supper with him at North Bend and when I thanked him afterward, he said – "don't say a word – many a tea I have had at your *home*."' A few weeks later, Mary Belle 'sent a parcel out to Annie [by] a Methodist clergyman, who is taking his family to B.C.' Another time: 'Did I speak of a new Dr. when I wrote last? ... He is a son of Rev. Jas. McLean of Shubenacadie – a connection of the McLeans at Springville, & that's all I know about him.' Jessie grew increasingly blasé about transplanted Nova Scotian clerics, as with her reference to a visiting Methodist minister 'from Nova Scotia somewhere but has been in B.C. a good many years now.' All the same, after meeting him, Jessie told her mother excitedly how 'he knew Mr. Brown in Merigomish & H.M.D. Scott and John McBain's folk, so we are quite chummy.'[39]

From their first days in British Columbia, the sisters corresponded regularly with Nova Scotian friends and gave support to fellow teachers wanting to come west. Annie enquired of the superintendent of education her first autumn in British Columbia about a job for 'a friend of mine, a B.A. graduate of Dalhousie College,' who 'is not strong' and wants 'to come out to B.C.' for that reason, but whose 'educational career has been remarkably brilliant.' The next fall, Annie reported how 'little Emma Hay with whom I used to board in Truro [Normal School], is now out in Vancouver keeping house for her father.' Taking the teachers' examination in Victoria with her newly arrived cousin Jessie Olding, Jessie told her mother how 'an old Normal school friend of Jessie's, Miss Jennings, always walks back and forth with us.'[40]

It was not that Jessie and Annie indiscriminately enticed Nova Scotians to British Columbia. In a moment of discouragement, Jessie wrote about herself and her cousin Jessie: 'From our own experience, we would not advise any one to come – even for the money.' About the same time, Jessie wrote home how 'Bessie Warner talks of coming out too – perhaps only for a visit, but she isn't decided.' To this her mother tartly responded, 'how is it B.W. is going out to B.C. when you would not advise any friends to go there.' Catherine's letter went on to talk about how a neighbour couple 'talks of going to Vancouver to mining work, he has a brother there & she has one too out there.' Chain sojourning built on individual decisions and, more generally, on the familiarity which women like Catherine, who would herself never cross the continent, could now profess by virtue of having daughters gone west. Jessie might assert all she wanted that 'I never did, never will, try to induce any one to come West.'[41] Her actions spoke far louder than did her advice, which could easily be interpreted as not wanting to share British Columbia's largesse.

The comfort Jessie took in things Nova Scotian related closely to her piety. Chain sojourning and the missionary impetus were linked. However much Annie and then Jessie might have considered they were their own persons in heading off to British Columbia, they were also instruments of the missionary impulse. Annie was able to go west only because of the intervention of the Rev. John Chisholm and perhaps also of the Rev. George Murray. When the McQueen family debated via correspondence whether Annie should be allowed to depart, numerous acquaintances, and acquaintances of acquaintances, were mustered from across the Maritimes who had already gone west and could assist on her arrival. Presbyterian ministers seemingly abounded, each with their own tales of the advantages to be had, including Eliza's friend's brother enjoying the 'almost perpetual summer' to be had in Victoria.[42]

Annie was boarding with the Murrays at the time Jessie arrived, and Jessie continued to visit them frequently after her sister's marriage. The Nova Scotia connection was reinforced each time she did so. The Murrays eased Jessie's transition to British Columbia, just as they had Nan's. 'Mrs Murray is going to give a little party [Easter] Monday evening on Jessie's account, she wants her to get acquainted with all the young folk around.' On another occasion, Jessie reported home: 'Nan was just going to bed when I arrived, and Mrs. Murray came upstairs in her night-dress, and we had a grand pow-wow together. Mrs. M says the sight of me always makes her homesick.' A warm friendship grew up between the two – 'I like Mrs Murray better every time I see her' – based on an affinity to things Nova Scotian. In the Nicola Valley a year, Jessie was as excited as ever about a visit to the Murrays: 'We are all Nova Scotians there, and "hale-fellows," so we had a cosy time.' The Murray clan remained firmly Nova Scotian. Speaking at the end-of-term closing of Jessie Olding's Nicola Lake school in June 1890, which his own children attended, the Rev. George Murray 'made an elegant speech eulogizing Pictou Co. in general & Pictou Co. teachers in particular.' Such public statements encouraged Jessie's piety as well as her and others' identification with things Nova Scotian.[43]

The piety into which Jessie was born was rather like a web that enmeshed her wherever she went. 'I often think of all the neighbors, especially on Sundays, when they will be all gathering to the church. Sundays here are so different, such a handful of people when there is service. They are lazy too, to turn out in such hot weather.' It simply went without question that Jessie, as had Annie, would exercise her piety. Annie taught Sunday school at Nicola Lake, and Jessie quickly became a mainstay of the Presbyterian congregation at Lower Nicola.[44]

The extent to which the Nicola Valley was still a frontier comes through clearly in the matter of organized religion. There were simply not enough parishioners for regular services. Two months in British Columbia, Jessie lamented to her father: 'How I did wish I could go to prayer-meeting last night. The handful that used to gather there would seem to be a crowd now. I think it's more than a month since I heard a sermon.' She was hopeful of a Sunday visit by the Rev. George Murray, who 'hasn't preached in this school-house since I came.' Even his services in the church at Nicola Lake were not necessarily that well attended, Jessie remarking, on a Sunday when she made it there, that 'there was quite a congregation – about *twenty-one* or *two*!' A year later at a Murray sermon at the Forks: 'There were only *nine* present. People are so very careless.'[45]

Sparse numbers, combined with great distances to be covered, caused the Presbyterians and Methodists to work in tandem. Back in 1875, an early Methodist missionary three months in the Nicola Valley reported in some detail on the arrival of Murray, whom he saw as an ally. 'A Presbyterian minister, sent out from Scotland, came upon the scene, necessitating a readjustment of my plans and the embracing of a wider field so that I might not come into collision with one who, though called by a different name, was serving the same Master and working for the same end. Had he not come, Nicola Valley and Kamloops would have been as much as I could have attended to; but now I am able to extend my labours to parts which otherwise I most likely would not have visited.' Fifteen years later, the Methodist hierarchy in Toronto reminded the two denominations of the benefits to be got by working in concert across the 'alert, wide-awake' province that British Columbia had become since the transcontinental railway's completion.[46]

This circumstance encouraged Jessie gradually to move beyond the Presbyterianism in which she had grown up. When Annie made boarding arrangements for Jessie, she felt compelled, in her letters home, to downplay the Woodwards' adherence to Methodism in favour of the advantages: 'Jessie will not have to pay as much for her board in Lower Nicola as I will have to pay in Nicola Lake ... They are nearly all

Methodists down there, some of them really good people, some of them regular shams.' Increasingly, Jessie opted for a double dose. Reflecting the resilience that the frontier gave, by the late spring of her first year she accepted that her piety might encompass Methodism. Thus she anticipated rather than lamented that 'the Meth. Conference has appointed a Mr. Winslow to this district.' The promise did not immediately materialize, much to Jessie's distress. 'I wish that other man would come. It's awful to be so long without preaching.' When he did, all was not well. In Jessie's view, ministers should be hearty folk. Annie 'has seen the new minister and his wife (for Nicola) and that they are both delicate-looking. I pity the poor souls.' As if that were not enough, 'the last time Mr. Winslow was there ... after waiting half an hour, no one came.'[47]

The Rev. J.W. Winslow was equally frustrated, he reported back to the Methodist Conference in Ontario, which had charge of British Columbia. His mandate was to serve the entire Nicola Valley, almost a hundred kilometres in length, and nowhere did he find the reception he considered his due. After being there a good year: 'I cannot help mourning the littleness of the apparent good accomplished, and the not very encouraging prospect ahead.' He put the population of 'this valley (i.e. whites)' at 191, nearly four-fifths of whom were 'by birth or membership adherents of other denominations,' so that his conversions were limited to 'a young husband and wife from Ontario.' Winslow went further and, in doing so, pointed to an important distinction with some other denominations, one that equally troubled Jessie. 'Sabbath-breaking, drinking and card-playing are common, and dancing has the support and countenance of the members of other churches.' He put the blame on the character of the newcomer population. 'The generality of them are here, to a great extent, because they have gold and popular freedom from moral and religious restraints far above more noble "goods" that are to be found in the homes left behind in the places from whence they have come.' In his view, there were far too many 'heads of families whose religious principles are elastic.'[48] From his perspective, the Nicola Valley was indeed a frontier where newcomers were able to think for themselves and to make their own choices.

Jessie was in a better position than the Rev. J.W. Winslow to adapt to the pragmatics of the frontier. Piety in a broad sense soon took precedence over denominationalism. She confided to her father that, 'when I go to Victoria, I must take in all the sermons and prayer meetings I can, to last me through the fall and winter.' There for the teachers' examination with her cousin Jessie Olding, Jessie in effect shopped around in order to get enough religion. 'We (Jessie and I) went to hear Mr Fraser (Pres) last Sunday morning, and to the Meth. Church with McMillans in the evening. Next Sunday, we will hear the other Pres. Minister Dr. McLeod and the Baptist minister too.' The next summer Jessie did much the same, as if recovering from a drought. 'We went to the Pres. Church in the morning & Sabbath-school in the afternoon ... We went to the Meth. Church at night.' Once Jessie even pondered attending the service held by a visiting Anglican minister to the Nicola Valley, but that was going too far, even for her. She reported back to her mother how one of the persons who did go felt compelled to remind the cleric afterwards that 'we didn't belong to his flock – but were "very good people nevertheless."' As for Jessie's reasons for staying away, 'some C. of E. people look on all outside of their church as veritable outsiders – heretics.'[49]

Over time, Jessie became more accommodating in her ways, although there were always lines to be drawn. Chatting with a Nova Scotian newcomer in the summer of 1889, Jessie agreed that 'Victoria is a pretty city, but very wicked – fruit & liquor stores etc. all open Sunday.' She had discovered shortly after arriving in Lower Nicola that 'they have the "Sunday at home" here & plenty of good books and with them and my own good Book, I spent a very pleasant Sabbath.' Lent an uplifting book, Jessie enthused, 'I am so glad to have it for Sundays.' She was willing to visit the elder Woodwards because 'the poor old folks are so lonely,' but 'I don't believe in going other places on Sunday.'[50] It was simply assumed that Sunday would be kept in British Columbia, so far as possible, as it was in Nova Scotia, and the attitudes of women like Jessie McQueen encouraged it to be so. The message from the pulpit was reinforced in school by a corps of teachers imbued with the same religious and social outlook. The everyday familiarity that grew up between preachers and teachers helped the Presbyterian and Methodist churches to consolidate their hold in British Columbia.

The re-creation of family and home, comfort in things Nova Scotian, and piety were all bound up with the fourth aspect of Jessie's life as a sojourner, and that was her work as a teacher. As she put it shortly after Tom Hall's death, 'I am so thankful for my work too, and that I have time & strength and money to help others a little.' Jessie went west to teach, and the classroom gave, just as it had for Annie, the rhythm to her life. Jessie's school at Lower Nicola never got much beyond a dozen, and she acknowledged that 'my position is what all teachers are popularly supposed to have – "a very soft snap."'[51] Teaching gave Jessie a prime opportunity for inculcating right behaviour. Hers was the responsibility to socialize the next generation into the way of life she considered most suitable for them.

The absence of a normal school in British Columbia until the turn of the century put the emphasis on the knowledge and understandings that teachers brought with them from elsewhere. Several times Jessie wrote home for textbooks. 'Now that I think of it, will some of you look for a "physiology Primer," that used to be in the little table in my bedroom upstairs? Please send it by the mail, as I want to book up my young ones before Xmas exam.'[52] The prescribed texts, to the extent Jessie had access to them, were little different from those she had used in Nova Scotia. Gage & Company of Toronto was a major publisher of textbooks adopted across Canada. Gage's *First Primer* assumed an agricultural setting. Farm animals were front and centre in its simple phrases and sentences, as with Lesson 5:

> The cow is whisk-ing her tail,
> The maid is hold-ing her pail.
> We'll spend the day
> In making hay.

The other basic motif, equally familiar to Jessie, was religion, as with 'When the morning has begun / Think the Lord is nigh,' and 'When you work and when you play, / Think the Lord is near.'[53]

Other texts were similar. Gage's *Practical Speller*, authorized for use in New Brunswick, Ontario, Quebec, and Manitoba, as well as British Columbia, put the emphasis on 'words in common use in daily life.' The assumptions were those of settled society, the home having a bathroom and veranda; the parlour within it, a lounge, piano, and ottoman; and the dining room containing silver and a sideboard. Words suggested to describe boys included dull, wise, manly, witty, steadfast, ingenious; girls were shy, silly, giddy, sedate, kindly, gentle, simpering, impulsive, frivolous, and nonsensical. Gage's *Canadian Readers*, which spanned the primary grades, combined fairy tales and short stories with morality lessons ('Alcohol and Its Effects,' 'About Strong Drink'), snippets of Canadian history ('The Death of Wolfe,' 'Canada's Progress'), and scriptural readings ('The Gospel Preached to the Gentiles').[54]

Textbooks counted certainly, but much more important was the example that teachers like Jessie McQueen presented day after day, week after week. From the beginning, Jessie made comparisons with her earlier positions. Her Lower Nicola school she diminished as a 'little log cabin.' She lamented that, were it not 'for one or two clever steady little chaps,' she would despair. 'I suppose S.R. School spoiled me for others ... What wouldn't I give now, if I could transplant any one of them right over among this crowd.' Jessie had no doubt as to which experience counted for more. 'I'm afraid I'll not know how to teach a decent school again after this.'[55] In her letters, Jessie did not write a lot about the routine of school life, likely because it was so little changed from Nova Scotian practice.

Jessie encouraged children to stay in school and thereby to be co-opted as fully as possible into the settlement society forming itself across British Columbia. She despaired whenever children were kept at home to help and when others did not go to school at all. 'Larger children are kept out now for help, the parents, owing to "hard times," being unable to hire help as usual.' Jessie visited a family 'across the river two or three miles from here, and over a piece of the roughest road you could imagine.' Previously they had lived closer to the Lower Nicola school. Then 'two of the children attended school, but since they moved to this new house of theirs they are too far away, and the river can't be crossed in high water, so the six little children haven't much prospect of an education before them.' The next autumn, Jessie lamented the loss of another family, whose half dozen children 'are not able to come, because they lost the only horse that was fit for them to ride.'[56]

In Jessie's work as a teacher, her greatest challenge was her pupils' hybridity. She was in the classroom at Lower Nicola just a matter of weeks when she realized the basic distinction that existed among her pupils, going back a decade and more to the twinned schools. In no way did Jessie more domesticate than in her incorporation of these children into the school on a basis of rough equity, more so than had occurred earlier. At first she equivocated, much as she did with hybrid adults like Tina Voght. As the new teacher, it was part of Jessie's responsibility to visit pupils' homes, and some were easier to enter than others, so she confided to her mother. 'I've been to all the houses in this section but one, a Lindley's, where the lady of the house is a Klootchman.' Jessie gave distance as her excuse – 'its more than 2 miles away, so I'll not go until I'm driven' – but there was something more. 'Two of the children come to school – Sarah & John [Lindley] – they have the Indian features and voices, but are good, and fully as clever as any of the others, and I like them.'[57] Perhaps there was just a little bit of fear. Having met their mother, she mused whether she might like the children less thereafter.

Jessie continued to wrestle with the implications of hybridity and, more generally, fret over the margins of her responsibility as a teacher. She explained to her mother during her first winter at Lower Nicola how 'I had fourteen in school one day this week, six of them are half-breeds.' She retailed the response of a visitor who 'said when he was in on Friday that it made him think of an advertisement he had seen, with a lot of babies – here a black one, and there a white one!' One of her pupils, Johnny Florens, Jessie described as 'my *purest* half-breed, if there is such a thing.' She added protectively, 'he has very good English though his accent is odd.' Jessie repeatedly pondered how far her role stretched. 'Another half-breed who started in this week is a great big fellow, eighteen years old.' Six weeks later, she confided: 'I think I told you of a big half-breed coming one day, but he only came the one solitary day, for he took sick after it (I don't know whether I sickened him or not) and there's too much work to be done. So long as we have plenty without him, I'd just as soon he didn't come, for he's a great big fellow – about 18 or 19, and I don't very well know what to do with him.' One of Jessie's great strengths was her perseverance in conditions that alienated many teachers of the day.[58]

Part of the reason Jessie coped had to do with the proximity Lower Nicola gave to her cousin Jessie Olding now teaching at Nicola Lake. 'I don't think now though that I'll leave this school until I leave B.C. – unless Jessie – "ups and dusts," same as Nan did.' It was almost inevitable that Jessie's cousin should, in time, find herself a beau. As with Annie, Jessie Olding chose strategically, in her case a young Englishman who had just secured a job as 'police constable, recorder and I don't know what all.' As Jessie noted in August 1889, Hugh Hunter 'came home from Victoria this week in high glee. No more pitching sheaves for *him* – he'd got his position, and was going to lead a *gentleman's* life!' By the spring of 1890, the courting was serious, and Jessie Olding confided 'how glad I was when Hugh told me that there was nothing to hinder him from being a Christian and that he meant to try to live as a Christian.' Within the month, the couple was engaged to be married a year hence. Hugh was gold commissioner in the remote mining boom town of Granite Creek, located about a hundred kilometres or three days by trail on horseback south of the Nicola Valley.[59] The distance meant that the two Jessies could, in the interim before the marriage, continue to spend weekends together.

For all of her work of domestication, the most important reason that Jessie stayed put at Lower Nicola in the months and years following

Annie's marriage and Tom Hall's death had, of course, to do with the money, the reason for her being there in the first place. So long as she remained an unwed daughter, she was expected to sustain the family economy. Approaching her thirtieth birthday in the spring of 1890, she mused: 'I wish B.C. and N.S. were a little nearer, but I must be thankful for all my "benefits" ... I am learning to "work and wait."' As the three years to which Jessie had committed herself to be away from home came to an end a year later, she considered she was free to return to Pictou County. Jessie did so a few months later. To the extent the train trip east matched its glorious predecessor, its charm lay in 'a new kind of car on the route now – "the tourist car" furnished just like the Pullman only with leather instead of plush, & with a range whereon the "tourist" may boil his tea-kettle &c &c.' What's more it cost $20 less than a Pullman car, that is, if tickets were got from Victoria and the trip begun there, which Jessie and her cousin did.[60]

The two Jessies, McQueen and Olding, travelled east together as soon as the school term came to an end in the Nicola Valley in June 1891. Jessie Olding went to prepare her trousseau for her October wedding.[61] Jessie McQueen had no such happy event to anticipate, but she did have the pleasure of renewing sisterhood's bonds. She stopped along the way to see Annie in Ontario and visited with her older, married sisters across the Maritimes. Most important, she returned to Pictou County, where her sister Jane, parents, and the family farm awaited her. Three years away, the sojourner was home again.

Chapter Seven

Daughterhood's Obligations

NICOLA LAKE

When Jessie went west to British Columbia in March 1888, she had intended to stay, as did Annie, for three years and then return home to Pictou County. She did so, but there was a complication. Her family simply could not survive without her financial support, and she knew it. Daughterhood's obligations entrapped her.

So the long anticipated return home in the summer of 1891 was, in the months before Jessie's departure east, refashioned into a visit. In March she shared with the superintendent of education her 'natural longing to see that home (in Nova Scotia) once more, but do not wish to give up my position just yet.' A month or so later, she queried Catherine: 'Well, mother, what do you say to a three months "furlough" to see & help you all, & then back to get my money's worth.' The decision to stick with British Columbia was not taken lightly, nor was it by desire. 'Oh if only I could find a $60 school near home!'[1] Nonetheless, it had to be taken.

Two months after heading east in the summer of 1891, the dutiful daughter returned to British Columbia. There were some differences. Having entered her thirties, Jessie had come to realize that, if she did not take control of her circumstances, no one else was going to do it for her. The first time around, Annie was there to smooth over the rough spots. Thereafter she had drifted. This time some things would be different. In the sense that they became so, Jessie now domesticated more consciously than merely by the example of a Nova Scotian woman happening to live in British Columbia.

Given the demands put upon her finances and thereby on her way of life, Jessie went west in September 1891 with a heavy heart compared with that first joyous trip a little more than three years earlier. Then, for a moment in time, all seemed possible. She was just reaching the age when her older sisters had felt free to marry. Annie was hinting in her letters at the prospects for intimacy that lay on the British Columbia frontier. The carefree character of those eight days were recalled in a letter from her travelling companion, Ed Olding, now working on a sugar plantation in Hawaii. 'It seems such a long time ago since we travelled to-gether and took in the wild west ... they will forever be a bright spot in my memory.'[2]

Providence appeared to have doomed Jessie to another kind of existence. While she accepted her destiny and took pride that she was not 'travelling in the "Colonist," or emigrant car,' filled with 'a most miserably dirty lot' of people, she could not help, from time to time, feeling a bit sorry for herself. Having 'nearly 4 hours to wait' between trains in Montreal, she wanted to have a look around, but 'I won't go far, you may be sure,' for, 'being alone, I'm *shy*.' Sending a postcard from Owen Sound in Ontario, Jessie described herself in the waiting room, just as she had earlier from the Nicola Valley, as 'another example of the "solitary" being "set in families."' Thinking back to her earlier trip, she mused, 'At Moosejaw Ed & I bought a loaf, & in order to make history repeat itself – I did need one too – I got out there & made a similar purchase.' Jessie had another pang in evoking the '"sleeper" passengers, somewhat above the rest of us in the social scale, & therefore people whom we merely beheld from afar.' Some of them, she sighed, 'stayed off at Banff – it is world renowned now for its curative springs.'[3]

Back home in Pictou County, Catherine McQueen rationalized Jessie's second exile. 'I think Jess can be more contented there than I once thought she could.' At the same time, she sought to ensure her eventual return. As Jessie's married sister Eliza warned her, 'You're the one ewe-lamb now and mother is going to tether you I 'spect.' Just a month after Jessie's return to British Columbia, Catherine informed her that, despite 'a good offer,' she had refused to 'sell the young Pony' Jessie admired on her visit home. 'I said no, that is Jessie's Pony ... & you may if spared drive her yet.'[4]

The plan, when Jessie returned west in 1891, was for her to sojourn another three years in British Columbia and then return permanently to Nova Scotia. In the interim, her wages would continue to sustain the family economy back home, and Catherine became increasingly explicit as to how this might occur. Jessie sent home $10 shortly after her return to British Columbia. Of this her mother spent $8.15, including '25¢ for church,' but 'I can't mind where the rest went, but used it as careful as I could, now I don't know if you sent any since or not I hope not as none came here.' Jessie responded, perhaps in a pique, very unusual for her: 'Please don't bother telling me what you do with anything I send. All I want is to know that you don't let yourselves be in want of anything for your comfort.'[5]

As always, Catherine played on her daughter's sense of obligation. 'You want us to get a waggon well My Dear girl that would need new harness & would be nice to have, but we can get along without that & there are things that is needed just now.' Twenty dollars in debts were separately enumerated, but that was not all. 'The Collector of tax may come any day & coal would be better if got now, we all need foot gear for winter now I am telling this to let you see tis no use thinking of a waggon, we may have to get a sleigh or pung. We seem farther back this year than usual, have no beast to sell ... may have some butter later on to help keep the pot boiling.' In one of her bluntest statements ever, Catherine summed up: 'I feel sorry to worry you with these things & I'm afraid I've said too much. If things were better managed long ago I would not need to be drawing on you so often, but the past can't be recalled.'[6]

Requests for financial assistance became more frequent and more open during Jessie's second sojourn in British Columbia. Once Catherine wrote only, 'Ashamed to be asking you for money.' During a visit to Sutherland's River by Jessie's older sister Eliza: 'E & I were saying you would be worn out with long teaching, & we have had so much from you that I feel ashamed to be asking you for money.' Again Jessie responded with her customary goodwill. 'I'm sorry it has been such a bad year, but you mustn't skimp yourselves, and you mustn't keep worrying over the little help that I can give. Who else have I to share with anyhow?' Another time: 'Please hand father the enclosure with my love.'[7]

From time to time, Jessie was cajoled not just to support the family at home but also to assist her married sisters. In reference to Mary Belle's husband: 'I did not intend to ask you to give so much to Free but no doubt the poor man will find use for it, he has to pay out so much & not too good economy at home or abroad in many things. Free is his name no doubt. I sometimes fear your income is too hugely taxed & you are being worn out with teaching it does wear & oh Jess Dear if you feel it is telling on you drop it & come home tho that is not easy.' Eighteen months later: 'If you have a *dollar* to share send a little to Dove she said in one letter that money was scarce round there this year. I would send her some myself if the butter was sold.'[8]

Jessie's web of familial obligations was sharply gendered. As the sole self-supporting unmarried daughter, she was expected, as a matter of course, to give assistance. From her mother's perspective, she existed apart from her married sisters, whose first responsibilities were toward their own families, and also from her brother George. The proverbial prodigal son, he lived up to his obligations merely by deigning to write home from time to time. Catherine prodded all her daughters to write him, even though receiving no responses, and from time to time enquired pathetically of them: 'I suppose if you get word from George you'll let me know. Is it not strange he don't write.' Even as she should have been rejoicing over Jessie's return for her holiday visit in 1891, Catherine fretted over George's silence. 'Isn't it a wonder George never writes or comes home I know it worries Pa more than he ever dreams of.'[9]

Jessie was repeatedly reminded that, for all she did, George was the beloved only son. 'Dull times in the States, numbers are coming home, why don't George come, Pa worried over his silence & absence.' Catherine still conceived of George as a sojourner. It was only rarely, following repeated requests to write just once more, that Jessie rebelled, as she did following her return to British Columbia. 'No mother, I haven't written to George – it seems such a hopeless performance. It is more than three years since he wrote me a single word and I've written many times since, but all in vain.' Following George's short defensive letter stating that his return home 'cannot be for some little time,' Catherine was all hopes again. 'In return I told him, we were too glad to scold him ... when I showed it to Pa he said oh I was almost sick [with worry] last night thinking of him &c.' Then, as the months once more passed without any contact whatsoever, 'Is it not strange that he won't come home & see us, he surely is not our George that he used to be.'[10]

The next Christmas, George informed his sister closest in age to him, Dove, but no other family members, that he had just wed an English widow. The marriage certificate, dated 1 December 1892, gave George and Isabella Chase, eight years his senior, as living at the same address. Dove dispatched the letter to her mother with a no-nonsense comment that underlined Jessie's plight. 'Well, dearly as I love him I am sorry to have to say that if he had borne the yoke of self denial in early youth our only boy would not have been such a willow the wisp [sic] ... Jessie is after all the best boy you have.' Dove consoled Jessie, after her the nearest to George in age, that the reason he had not written her was that 'he feels that you have done what he has not – taken care of the home ones.' Catherine was not yet out of excuses for her errant son, telling

Jessie 'a false pride I think keeps him silent. Oh, if he only saw his true position, we need to pray more earnestly for him.' The only other reference to George's wife is a document five years later in which she released him from any further obligations in exchange for the lump sum of $150.[11]

Pictou County's dutiful daughter made one significant change to her life. Before she went home, in anticipation of having to return, Jessie changed schools. Her previous year at Lower Nicola saw her caught in a Woodward family drama not unlike its predecessor of a decade earlier. She was, at least in spirit, pressured out of the school where she had taught for a good three years. The protagonist was her landlord's uncle Henry Woodward, whose sons had been implicated by her landlady, Agnes Woodward, over their actions a decade earlier toward her daughter Maggie. Henry was, to quote from one of Jessie's letters home, likely one of the 'two disaffected persons [who] have been anxious to secure a *male* teacher.' The other was probably Henry's son-in-law, former Nicola Valley teacher Archibald Irwin, whose younger brother Joseph, also a teacher, was married to another of Henry's daughters and had his eye on Jessie's job. Jessie's landlord, long-time trustee Harvey Woodward, reported to the superintendent on persons 'wishing to have the Teacher discharged by circulating damaging reports about her ability to teach, especially boys.'[12] It was a year later that Jessie resigned.

Jessie had an out. With her cousin Jessie Olding's upcoming marriage, the school at Nicola Lake became vacant, and Jessie secured it before returning to Pictou County for her summer visit. 'Well, I've given up this school, other Lake people want me there – some of them ... it's a good school & has many advantages not to be had here, & when I teach, I must teach in B.C. I hate going among strangers, & that, with other reasons, makes me wish to take the Lake school.' The trustees even found a substitute for the first month of the new term, which she would miss by virtue of going home. The hardly surprising postscript to the little frontier drama is that, on Jessie's departure from Lower Nicola, Archibald Irwin replaced his cousin-by-marriage Harvey Woodward as secretary of the board of trustees and immediately engaged his brother Joseph as Jessie's replacement.[13]

In the four years since Annie taught there, Nicola Lake had grown steadily. It was now the government and commercial centre of the Nicola Valley. As well as the sawmill, general store, and churches of Annie's day, there were a blacksmith, hotel, and two wheelwrights. The larger community meant more pupils, which pleased Jessie: 'Had twenty one in school to-day, & that number of B.C. children is a handful I assure you. This school is not quite such "baby work" as the Lower one, & I suppose I'm all the better for that.' For the first time she merited a visit from the school inspector. A month into her new position, Jessie reflected how 'time never drags in school hours,' and she hoped to 'like it very well.' She now had more to do. 'I find school-hours now too short for school work, but that's better than finding them too long.'[14]

Jessie valued good teaching and much preferred a challenge. Thus in January: 'I've had the smallest lot yet, owing to cold. Just six children every day! They happen to belong to four different classes though, so it's not quite so tedious as it might be, & I tell you, I teach them real hard.' Six weeks later: 'School is not large, but is large enough for comfort – thirteen or fourteen every day, and they are improving.' By the spring: 'Oh school is a fine spot when you can get the children to pull with you instead of against you & I am sincerely thankful for the small measure of success I seem to be having at present.' Her new school grew on Jessie. 'I am getting to like these children better & better. There doesn't seem to be nearly so much of the "ugly" in them now, but maybe it's only sleeping. Long may it be so.'[15]

Jessie continued to combine British Columbia and Nova Scotia learning materials and thereby align her pupils with Canada as a nation. She was pleased when the superintendent of education mailed each school 'a map of B.C.,' but also drew on familiar textbooks got from home. 'Mother, will you please take a look among the books in the front room for an old school reader – No. 6 not the *old* No. 6 but the one in use in my day. It is not very thick, & has a brown cover I think, & either Annie's name or mine will be on it. And if you find it, please mail to me.' Jessie's teaching reflected schooling's growing interest of these years in the natural world. Given 'a silver leaf geranium with a scarlet blossom,' she mused in early spring: 'I think I'll bring it to school. All I have in the school windows so far is a small dish of *peas*, planted for botanical purposes. The children go fairly wild over botany – went wandering off at noon to-day, & fairly filled my table with bits of fir, maple & various weeds and flowers ... My small [magnifying] glass brings out many new beauties before their wondering eyes.'[16]

Nicola Lake was less of a frontier school. 'There is about 100 per cent more beauty & comfort in this school-house than in the one at Lower Nicola.' There were still parents for whom the family economy took precedence – 'they kept him to "dig 'tatoes"' – but overall the school was more reflective of newcomer settlement in the Canadian tradition.[17]

The backgrounds of children were more homogenous, hybrid families tending overall during these years to hug the frontier, where they were less liable to encounter the racial discrimination animating most newcomer British Columbians and Canadians.

It was not just Jessie's job that changed. Everyday life 'at the "hub," which is the Lake,' was far more social than in rural Lower Nicola. It is a measure of Jessie's resilience, of her willingness to accommodate to the British Columbia frontier, that she felt herself up to the challenge. Perhaps she considered that the efforts of herself and others like her had effected sufficient change that she was now more comfortable living there. Shortly after her cousin's engagement, perhaps in anticipation of securing the larger school, Jessie had mused how 'there are ever so many people at the Lake that I don't know – the millwrights, carpenters and some of them are very decent-looking.'[18]

In the event, Jessie never much accommodated to Nicola Lake. Three factors held her back. The first was a paucity of persons with whom she felt comfortable socializing. In this sense her situation was the classic plight of the single woman on the frontier. Newcomers with whom she had developed a friendship while visiting Annie and then her cousin Jessie either had, or were getting, married. By the time Jessie returned from Nova Scotia, the Rev. George Murray's sister-in-law, who had come out in 1889, was back home in New Glasgow preparing to wed a Nicola Valley man who travelled there for the occasion. Jessie must have felt a touch of envy as she noted how, prior to Edwin Dalley's September departure, 'he himself has been painting and papering, and putting [his house] in apple-pie order.' She wrote wistfully to her mother: 'Mr. D. is a bachelor man, soon to be something else though. He leaves tomorrow for N.S. and if you watch the papers, you will probably see a marriage notice some of these days, Maggie McDonald of New Glasgow to Edwin Dalley of Nicola, B.C.' Shortly after the newlyweds returned, so did Jessie Olding to marry Hugh Hunter at Nicola Lake. Again, it was very much a frontier wedding. 'The boys made a great hullaballo with guns and tin pans etc.' Among the bride's wedding gifts was a saddle-horse, 'very useful,' Jessie commented, 'as she will have to ride to her new home' at Granite Creek.[19]

As a single woman in a newcomer community premised on single men, couples, and families – 'I don't care to visit much where there are children' – Jessie was, even in larger Nicola Lake, somewhat of an outsider. Much of sociability was premised on visiting back and forth, and Jessie's sense of the proprieties restricted her, for she would not enter a residence unless another woman was with her or guaranteed to be present. Planning for the annual May 24th celebrations in honour of Queen Victoria's birthday, Jessie explained to her mother how 'we are to have a "potato paring bee" the night before at Jas. Gillie's bachelor quarters, with Mrs [Maggie] Dalley as "chaperone."' However well Jessie might know the occupant, a house with only 'a bachelor man' she considered off limits. The consequence of the restrictions that Jessie put on herself, as well as her actual circumstances, was that, she reflected sadly, 'I don't care to visit now, half as much as when Jessie was with me.' Responding to her daughter's plaint that 'I have no chums,' Catherine noted aptly at the end of 1891 that 'Jessie is lonesome since J.O. got married.' Jessie reflected after eight months at Nicola Lake how 'it does seem strange not to be able to find one intimate female friend, but that is how the case stands at present, & is likely to remain so.'[20]

To the extent that Jessie did socialize, Nova Scotian ties still counted the most. She took special pleasure in a visit by the wife of a settler family 'living at Stump Lake – nearly 30 miles from here' who were 'from Abercrombie Point, & know all the people about Pictou & New Glasgow pretty well.' Mrs. Murray's newly married sister gave comfort, even though, as Jessie was well aware, her principal allegiance was to her husband. 'I've just come in from calling on Mrs. Dalley, who seems quite at home in her new sphere.' Jessie played '"Logomachy," the same game that [we] used to have at home,' with the Dalleys. 'We had a good old-fashioned game of "Logomachy" though to me, it hasn't half the charm it used to have when you helped us make "sweeps,"' she reassured Catherine lest she think her dutiful daughter was enjoying herself too much. Jessie also continued to see Janie Pooley, Annie's predecessor at the Nicola Lake school now married to a local rancher, musing how 'she is more like company than any of the rest.' A third Douglas sister came out from Pictou County in 1891, and the two single women, Jessie and Grace, spent time together. 'Miss D. stayed two nights with me since Jessie [Olding] left [to get married], & I was very glad to have her. She is a nice bright, lively girl, brimful of health and spirits, & very good company.' Such encounters, however, only convinced Jessie that she was becoming, as she put it, 'a bashful old maid.'[21]

The second factor that kept Jessie from accommodating to Nicola Lake was her living arrangement. Just as had her cousin Jessie Olding, she rented a room in a boarding house run by a versatile Nicola Lake family, the Rileys. 'I pay my $20 regularly,' which included 'my washing & ironing.' Arrived from Ontario in the late 1870s, William Riley drove the

stage coach and was also the local blacksmith, while his wife Mary Ann
was a nurse and midwife. 'They came rapping for Mrs Riley at 2 in the
morning & she went down to do what she could till they got the Dr.'
Another time, 'Mrs Riley has been away for a week, nursing Mrs Blair, at
the Forks.'[22]

Although Jessie's boarding arrangement gave a certain routine to her
day – 'must go & help entertain the company, then comes dinner, &
then the mail' – no longer did she have free run of a house or, as the
weather grew cold, even of a room of her own. It was approaching mid-
November when 'Mrs Riley gave me blankets to-day to put on instead of
sheets, & if it keeps getting colder, I guess they'll put a stove in room.
That's what I'll like – not that I am an unsociable creature, but I do like
to be able to stay ten or fifteen minutes in my room without stiffening
up ... I feel perfectly lost somehow.' Jessie was not without resources.
'Last Saturday I made some flannel garments for myself – "both long
and wide" and expect to suffer some comfort in them.' She assured her
mother, 'I wear nothing but flannel in winter – only pocket handkerchiefs, & I don't think I'm in danger of taking cold through them.'[23]

The Rileys did their best. 'My room has new lace curtains at windows
this week, & what with my window-garden & four bouquets besides, it is
quite a bower of beauty.' As had Annie and her cousin Jessie before her,
Jessie grew fond of the Rileys' four daughters, and they in turn did their
best to accommodate to her needs. Although Jessie and the youngest
Riley, Letitia or Tish, sometimes sang or went riding by 'horse & rig'
together in the evenings, a fifteen-year age difference separated them.[24]

The third, and perhaps most important, reason Jessie never made
Nicola Lake her home was the hold exercised over her by the Woodwards. Almost every weekend and for holidays, one of them, as Jessie put
it, 'fetched and carried' her to Lower Nicola, where she was passed
among the various households to give succour and assistance. Some
members of the family recognized, as one of them acknowledged to her,
'that perhaps they made too free with my services.' Jessie needed to be
wanted, and the Woodwards offered her that privilege, if at the price of
serving their needs. Hence her response: 'I assured her that it was no
such thing. I was always glad to be around to fill a gap, and my help was
more often *moral,* than *physical.*' Jessie made the weekly trip even in bad
weather when the twenty kilometres took 'nearly three hours' each way
because, so she mused on one occasion, 'Mrs. Harvey seemed to want
me – thought I'd cheer "father" up, and so I went.' The Woodwards
became, more than ever, Jessie's surrogate family, and it was to them she

referred on writing: 'Oh I can't be thankful enough for so many friends in this far away country, though I still miss my "very own."'[25]

If weekends were taken up by the Woodwards, Jessie still had to fill in the weekdays. To counter a paucity of sociability and her boarding circumstances, she created two other 'homes' for herself during her first months at Nicola Lake.

Jessie's first new home was the school itself. 'I am writing in the school-house again,' she told her mother just a month after beginning to teach at Nicola Lake. As the weather turned cold, more and more she took shelter there. 'The school house is very comfortable, & one of the boys lights the fire every morning about eight. I usually go over about half-past eight, & as school doesn't go in until 9.30, the room is in fine condition then.' As the temperature fell to 30° F below zero after Christmas, it was the school that comforted Jessie. 'This is such a comfortable, airy school-room ... and now the days have turned, I have a whole hour & a half of daylight after school closes, & it is much nicer to spend it in the school-room than anywhere else.' The next spring: 'Folk wonder why I stay so long in school, but there is solid comfort in being alone & quiet for resting or reading, & I just revel in it. Only for the lack of things, I'd willingly come back after supper, & finish out the day here, but I daresay I'm getting myself into a bad old maidish habit.' Jessie entertained there. 'She called on me in my own house last week – the school house – and we had about two hours there, all to ourselves. It's very nice to have a private reception room now and then. People who come there, come solely for the purpose of having a quiet, friendly visit with me, the formal calls are made at the boarding house.' Another time, Jessie explained to her mother how 'I had a visitor just as I started to write – about 3.30, and we had so much to talk about that we never left the school-house till 6 o'clock.' There were exceptions. 'Lady visitors of course can come into my bedroom.'[26]

Jessie's other home during her first year at Nicola Lake was the church. Her piety continued to override denominational specifics. Settled in Nicola Lake a few short weeks, she carefully explained to Catherine, after describing 'a Bible class in the parsonage every Wed.,' how 'the *parsonage* is Methodist, & the *manse* is Presbyterian.' The next spring Jessie admitted: 'You mustn't be surprised to hear that I have "a strong leaning to the Methodists" ... For a small place, there are many petty divisions & strifes, & I can't say I am altogether proud of the actions of my fellow Presbyterians. I believe in "live & let live" & less of this everlasting fault-finding & carping.'[27]

Much more than at Lower Nicola, Jessie could participate in organized activities even though, she grumbled, numbers were less than they
should be. 'There were a good many out – for Nicola – *but* there were
plenty who never stopped work at all.' The Wednesday night Bible class
led by the local Methodist minister, the Rev. James Calvert, gave Jessie a
welcome rhythm to her week. 'It is our regular Bible class night, and I
believe I haven't missed a night since I came. There are seldom more
than half a dozen there ... A subject is chosen for each night, and each
one comes prepared with verses.' When classes were 'suspended for the
time being' because the minister and his wife went off to visit England
in the spring of 1892, Jessie was 'left rather forlorn & homeless, so to
speak.'[28]

Jessie's piety had its limits. Reflecting the prejudices of her age that
even the frontier did not make it possible to overcome, she had nothing
to do with Catholicism and could not resist taking swipes at the Anglicans, even though she now attended a service from time to time. 'An
English Church clergyman preached, and everybody liked him well. The
Church service is fine, and he didn't gabble over it, as so many do. No
one could listen to him without knowing him to be a single-minded earnest Christian. A teetotaler too – a rare thing among that class of clergy-
men. Most of them take a little "for their stomach's sake" – or their
own.' Jessie returned, this time to hear a service so different from the
Canadian ethos of Presbyterian and Methodist sermons that she felt
compelled to detail it to her mother. 'Spoke first of the three kinds of
ships, in the Royal Navy, viz. line of battle-ships, the solitary cruiser, &
lastly the small, but deadly torpedo boats. Similarly the Christian's
defence lay in the *three* kinds of prayer – public, private, and what he
said he would call, for lack of a better word – ejaculatory prayer.'[29]

Just three months at Nicola Lake, Jessie became caught up in the temperance movement, which gave women across Canada an unequalled
opportunity to act. One of the principal vehicles for doing so was the
Grand Lodge of Good Templars, a fraternal organization strongly supported by the churches. The lodge of Jessie's childhood had been firmly
Presbyterian. At Nicola Lake its backing came from the Methodist
Church. Favouring total abstinence and government prohibition, members were encouraged to sign a pledge promising not only personal
abstinence but, so Jessie phrased it, not to 'furnish or cause [liquor] to
be furnished to others.' For the retiring Jessie, the decision to commit
to the Lodge was not taken easily. 'Tuesday night I joined Lodge – took
a sudden notion to make the plunge, my grandson [her pet name for

one of the younger Woodwards] had been talking strongly about temperance people not throwing all their influence on the right side, but for a long time I felt too lazy to make the effort. It's a long time since I belonged to a Lodge before – not since Lorne Lodge used to meet in Merigomish.' Membership in the lodge, which met every other week in the 'court house,' encouraged Jessie to move into the public realm as she otherwise would never have done.[30]

In January 1892, Jessie went on the offensive. Taking her courage in her hands, she decided to read at a Lodge meeting a chapter 'about bringing up boys & girls' from *My Opinions and Betsy Bobbet's* by Marietta Holley, an American who wrote under the pen-name of Mrs Josiah Allen. Jessie was a vociferous reader, not just of newspapers dispatched from the Maritimes and those printed in British Columbia, but of current novels passed on to her by family members and British Columbia acquaintances. She continued to enjoy the Pansy books, sending her mother for her birthday the 'sequel to "Chrissy's Endeavor" that was published in the Montreal Witness a few years ago.' Mark Twain and Louisa May Alcott, as well as numerous long forgotten authors, were among her reading fare.[31] Generally, these were private experiences, and she left no record of her responses to particular authors.

This time Jessie took a stand. In her view, Marietta Holley's heroine Samantha Allen 'has acres of common good sense, and her remarks on women's rights, free love & divorce, &c &c are just solidly good.' Jessie's decision to identify herself with Samantha, and to read one of Holley's books aloud to others, gives one of the few clues that we have to her inner self. *My Opinions and Betsy Bobbet's*, published in 1873 and reprinted in 1891, was the first of some twenty homespun books by Marietta Holley that became immensely popular across North America in the years up to the First World War. In them, Holley used the character of Methodist Samantha to voice strong opinions that were acceptable Lodge fare because they were pro-temperance, even though they were also pro-women's rights and moderately feminist. Holley managed a subtle balance. Samantha considered that 'the talk about wimmen havin' to fight, and men wash dishes, if wimmen vote, is all shear nonsense.' As for differences between the sexes: 'It is enough to make anybody's blood bile in their veins to think how different sin is looked upon in a man and woman. I say sin is sin, and you can't make goodness out of it by parsin' it in the masculine gender, no more'n you can by parsin' it in the feminine or neutral.'[32]

Jessie must have taken special comfort in Samantha's strongly held view that 'marryin' aint's the only theme to lay holt of ... No women can feel honorable and reverential toward themselves, when they are [only] waiting for some man, no matter who, to marry 'em and support 'em.'[33] Marietta Holley never married, which may explain her willingness to put forth a position so sympathetic to single women like Jessie. For Jessie, the opportunity to share books of which she approved was particularly important. 'I just ache sometimes to be with folk who read & like the same books that I do. A book is worth twice as much to me when I read it with some one, or at least talk it over afterward, & that doesn't happen here very often.'[34]

Jessie's commitment to temperance made her much more of a public person, even though, she acknowledged, 'I am bashful as ever.' She ago-nized over an essay she had to write for a Lodge meeting. 'I'm not at all in love with the task, but I suppose it's for the public good.' There was also direct action, considered acceptable for its end result of persuading persons to give up liquor. Assisted by Tish Riley, also a Lodge mem-ber,'we captured one fellow last week [who] was in at Riley's, and two or three of us got "argerin" ... He acknowledged at last that we were work-ing at a good cause, & then we clinched him with "He that knoweth to do good, and doeth it not, to him it is sin."' In the spring of 1892, Jessie was 'elected Chief Templar for next quarter, that is the presiding officer you know, & I'd much rather be out of it, but if it's for the public good & under the circumstances I suppose it is I won't kick a single kick, but shall take hold & do the best I can.' Come the end of her term, 'glad I am to subside into the Treasurer's place.' Very soon, Jessie agreed to take on the Lodge's newspaper, selecting from contributions submitted which ones to print.[35]

Jessie's common sense and her passion for liquor reform sometimes clashed. Publicly she stood firm, but within her self she wavered. She considered that 'the hotel in this place is doing mischief.' On the other hand, 'it's the only place for the young men to gather, & as nearly every one is away from home, they must have *some* place where they can meet and have a good time.' Much as numerous other social reformers believed, Jessie's ideal was 'a cosy room for the boys to meet for recre-ation and improvement,' although, she was forced to admit, 'some of them would take the recreation fast enough, but the "improvement" school might whistle.' She acknowledged that, despite a visiting lecturer advocating temperance 'pretty well' filling the local hall, 'not one of the grown-ups felt inclined to act on the good advice.'[36]

For all that she might desire Nicola Lake residents to come together 'in one concentrated effort for good, irrespective of creeds or classes,' Jessie was well aware that 'it is a very much divided community.' The only new members recruited by the Lodge were 'two of my scholars,' one of whose fathers was 'a ne'er-do-well, who gets drunk when he can get anything to get drunk on.' Jessie acknowledged privately, 'One is for temperance, but prohibition will never be an accomplished fact, and the Lodge does more harm than good – coaxing people to sign the pledge, who we know won't keep it & so they perjure themselves etc. etc.'[37] All the same, there were some lesser victories, as when in 1891 provincial legislation closed all places selling liquor on Sundays.

As Jessie began her second year of teaching at Nicola Lake in the late summer of 1892, the courage that she took from the Lodge extended into other aspects of her life. She got her nerve, at least to some extent. As she put it, 'I have a livelier interest in the place, now that I know some of the people, and the *geography* of it pretty well.' The drawbacks of spending virtually every weekend supporting the Woodwards became apparent. 'Mrs Harvey's nine children fill her house very full indeed when I go down there now, the noise seems dreadful – I think I made the change just in time – at any rate I don't believe I could stand so many around now.' Writing from Ontario, Annie agreed, for she had wanted Jessie for some time to 'be rid of the Woodward tribe, who are growing too numerous for comfort.'[38]

The Woodwards' influence waned. Jessie let them know in November 1892 that 'I do not think I can go anymore until holidays – there is so much to do getting ready for the open Lodge meeting on 14 Dec., and the Pres. Social on the 23rd not to mention my exam on the 22nd.' Increasingly, Sundays were spent at Nicola Lake, which allowed Jessie to give full rein to her piety. 'We had service here yesterday, at 11, by Mr. Murray, and again at 7.30 by Mr. McDuff [Anglican]. Sunday-school, as usual at 2.30, so the day was pretty well filled up.' Other opportunities built on the Maritime connection. 'I am asked to Mrs. Dalley's right after school with Miss Murray and Mrs. Pooley – Nova Scotians you know, are always clannish.'[39]

Among the forms of sociability that took the Woodwards' place was the Ouija board craze, in no way seen as antithetical to Jessie's religious faith. 'There were half a dozen or so gathered to "make the table move." We laid our hands on the top of the table – just letting them touch each other, & before very long, the electricity developed in the circle, made the table walk off around the room, moving round & round, sometimes just about as fast as we could keep up with it. It was comical, & I believe was electricity, fair & square, though some of the on-lookers said we *pushed the table*.' Jessie's openness to new experiences was evident to Annie, whose husband commented how Jessie 'likes BC better than ever.'[40]

However Jessie behaved, she did so not only as a single woman but as the teacher at Nicola Lake. With each choice made, Jessie domesticated. Her very public alignment with the Woodwards had confirmed both to long-established residents and to newcomers the status of this prominent Ontarian family and of the values that they embodied. So did her continued attachment to Nova Scotian acquaintances. In similar fashion, Jessie's devotion to the Church enhanced its respectability. So did everyday occurrences, as with her decision not to attend a party at the house of Christina Voght Schwartz, whose marriage caused Jessie so much turmoil some three years earlier. 'I was invited, but I don't often indulge, particularly when I have no kindred spirits there.' Part of the reason for not doing so lay in Jessie's attitudes toward suitable marital partnering, but it also reflected her continuing ambivalence toward the hybridity that Tina embodied. Much as her mother would have, Jessie saw as a morality tale Jessie Olding Hunter's husband passing through Nicola Lake 'with two prisoners – a Siwash for being drunk & trying to shoot another, & a half bred for supplying the liquor.' The second, a son of Alexander Coutlie who kept 'a saloon' at the Forks, 'got six months with hard labor,' and Jessie considered he 'should have had it long ago.' In line with her temperance sentiments, she took pleasure that 'Coutlie is likely to lose his license.'[41]

Jessie could not escape the racist assumptions of the day, writing unconsciously about one of the young Woodwards that she 'isn't quite as much of a Siwash as she looks! She is really a pretty child.'[42] At the same time, Jessie treated with a degree of respect hybrid persons she got to know as individuals. If well aware of their racial inheritance, Jessie did not wholly stereotype them, which is about the best that anyone could have done during these years. Hybrid pupils from her Lower Nicola years continued to see Jessie as their support, indicating that, whatever her private misgivings, she had treated them equitably. In the first autumn that Jessie was no longer teaching there, she was told how 'Mrs. Lindley – a Klootchman – regretted my leaving there.' Jessie explained: 'When I was there, she said, we read in the book [Bible] every morning & "wa-wa, soghalie Tyee," that is "spoke to the Father" [prayed], & the children would get their books every night [to take home], & read, & ask each other questions &c &c, & in short I guess she thinks those were good old times, gone now, never to return. I understand that the new teacher, a man, is hard on the Lindley children & that none of them attend now. It's too bad, for two of them are nice bright children, & fond of study.'[43]

Jessie's successor, Henry Woodward's son-in-law Joseph Irwin, also managed to disenchant Woodward family members, one of whom reported how 'Cousin Joseph scares her, he shouts so loud.' About the same time that Jessie turned down the invitation to Tina Voght Schwartz's party, she took pride in the maintenance of connections with her former hybrid pupils, so she acknowledged to her mother. 'Oh I must enclose a letter I got some time ago from one of my former scholars in Lower Nicola – she is a half breed, but a very good, intelligent child.'[44] In the classroom, so it appears, Jessie did not visibly play favourites.

Jessie got her nerve in other ways, as well. On the British Columbia frontier during these years, just as was happening more generally across North America, the role of teacher was increasingly perceived to extend outward from the classroom into the community. By her actions, the teacher indicated appropriate behaviour for others. So it was with Jessie's new commitment to regular physical activity, a variant of the organized sports that, as Eric Hobsbawm has pointed out, encouraged a sense of community conducive to nationhood.[45] Initiated on 'Dr.'s orders' but also consistent with her mother's maxim from her childhood that 'a healthy body helps to make a vigorous mind,' Jessie began to take a daily walk. 'Don't you worry about me mother, my health is always good, it's only when I take a small spell of nerves that I don't sleep, but a good brisk walk will generally set me up all right.' Jessie wrote contentedly in late autumn: 'Came home and did up two or three weeks ironing for myself, and after that, had my constitutional, between the lights. Fancy being able to walk out dry-shod, almost anywhere, after all the frost we've had ... one could walk in slippers.' Other times the walk became her consolation. 'I had a long walk last Saturday – was out nearly two hours, but walking, simply for the sake of walking isn't very enjoyable. It was better all round, than staying in the house though.' Even at 30° F below zero, Jessie kept to her routine. 'My evening walk is quite enjoyable & bracing – the air is so clear & cold and the road so solid & smooth.'[46]

Whatever the weather, Jessie walked. Her second winter at Nicola Lake: 'My chief regret is that the walking is so bad, but I can generally find some decent spot.' As spring came, 'the walking keeps much decent, for which I am grateful. I was out Saturday morning – and back again before 7 – before breakfast, of course. It was beautiful, so bright and bracing, though a little keen too.' Even during spring break-up, Jessie persevered. 'Oh, I went out for a walk the other evening, & before I knew where I was I got into the mud with both feet, stuck fast, lost my rubber, stuck fast again, & had all I could do to pull myself out. You never saw such a spectacle as I was – boots mud all over, & rubbers the same, inside & out.' Only rarely did she have a companion. 'None of them seem to care much for walking, though occasionally I get Tish [Riley] (the youngest of the grown-ups) to try it with me.'[47]

The image of the tiny teacher, her cloak wrapped around her for warmth, trotting briskly along day after day, week after week, season after season – 'they think I'm a "terrible one to walk" but it's just the life of me' – modelled a form of behaviour more to do with settled society than with the frontier, where most newcomer activity had to do with the work world. 'Nearly 5:30 now, & I must go for my walk before tea. In bad weather or bad roads I must get my walk in daylight or I'm not liable to get it at all.' Jessie demonstrated not just the phenomenon, but healthy use of leisure. As time passed, she became zealous to encourage others at Nicola Lake to follow her example, assuring them that, if they 'would only take a leaf out of my book, they'd feel the better of it.'[48]

Jessie also became an exemplar by beginning to wear spectacles as the passage of time took its toll. Her eyes had long caused her trouble, but in late 1891, at the age of thirty-one, her sight deteriorated. 'I had a little trouble getting through your letter, but I managed it all, by dint of resting my eyes now and then by closing them.' She had always gobbled up newspapers and magazines as soon as they arrived in the mail, but now acknowledged, 'Got the papers to-night too, but don't think I can read them.' A bit later, 'my eyes are not at their best yet, so I have to take care of them.' Jessie's world began to close in on her, so she noted in January 1892 on receiving a letter: 'I couldn't read the note at all by lamplight.' She had to pace herself. 'My eyes get quite well when I give them a good rest, but a few papers and letters are about all I can manage.' A month later: 'I should read more than I do, but newspapers are hard on my eyes.' The next April: 'I don't think it's anything but old age that ails my eyes for if I rest them for a whole week, & then use them steadily for two or three hours, they are as useless as if I had been using them right along.' The Methodist minister's wife had 'a pair of blue glasses' known as 'Preservers,' and in the spring of 1892 she promised to 'try & match them' for Jessie the next time she went to Victoria. A month later, Jessie got her glasses, very plain with steel shanks, '& they are quite a comfort.'

They became so essential that, a year or so later, when she inadvertently left them behind, she had to borrow a pair 'or I'd be reduced to the sole diversion of knitting after lamplight – I don't have much use for them during the day.'[49]

For all that age was taking its toll, the renewed Jessie once again dared hope that intimacy might come her way. She retook pride in her physical self, as indicated by her response to a pupil's compliment. 'I actually blushed in school to-day. A small boy aged *seven* had been told to make sentences about things in the school-room, & one of them was "Miss McQueen is pretty"! It was either the suddenness of the remark, or astonishment at the nature thereof that upset me, but I was a fury glowing red for about two minutes.' Jessie was similarly flattered on being teased by one of the senior Woodwards, following the marriage of a young family member, that 'there may be a chance for me now.' As to the reason given her, 'she used to go for every fellow there was, so that the rest of the girls had no show.' Drawn in, Jessie followed up. 'When I wanted him to tell me why one couldn't be an old maid in peace, he said old maids were all right for a while, but when they got old & wore glasses and got into corners, and had faces – *so* long & thin - why then, they weren't respectable!'[50]

The best evidence that Jessie had not wholly given up on intimacy was the conviction that her every action was being so appraised. She disliked checking for letters on the mail's arrival twice weekly at the Nicola Lake general store because of 'such a crowd of men sitting around the store mail nights.' The Methodist minister offered to take any letters to the parsonage for her to pick up there, a system that worked well until a single 'young Meth. preacher' came to visit for a couple of weeks from the Fraser Valley for his health. Jessie's choices gave her a certain tingle. 'Now, I'll either have to brave the brigade of men again, or run my chances of going to the parsonage "to see the new minister" for that's what they're seen to say, in this hotbed of gossip. A bashful old maid gets into tight places, sometimes, doesn't she?'[51]

At the same time, Jessie continued to have grave reservations about the nature of intimacy on the British Columbia frontier. Her Nova Scotian assumptions as to the proprieties of courting and marriage continued to hold. 'One of the girls at the Lake is to be married to-night, & go off on the stage to-morrow. Her husband (to-be) is much older than she, and it is said that he has been a hard drinker. If so, she is very much to be pitied. He was one of the new employees on the construction of the Roller Mill.' Despite her outward support for the Woodward family in all of its manifestations, Jessie wrote privately, likely well aware of his past misbehaviour toward Maggie: 'Emerson Woodward (Uncle Henry's son) is to be married at Spence's Bridge to-day. He is a kind of a "blow hard," very unpopular with everybody, & Mrs Calvert [wife of the Methodist minister] says she doesn't think she would envy the girl "even if" she "*were single.*"' Then there was the enigmatic 'Miss Emma,' thrice engaged during Jessie's first four years in the Nicola Valley. The second time around, Emma was 'so deeply in love that she said it would "kill her" if he proved untrue.' Just three days later, 'a stranger appeared on the scene, *looking for a wife,*' whereupon the fiancé 'got his dismissal without any apology or excuse only that she thinks he "is not able to support" a wife!' Drawing Presbyterian virtue around her, Jessie waxed indignant. 'That's young B.C. for you, but she's a disgrace to any country.'[52]

Jessie's interest, almost despite herself, in such marital shenanigans may have been linked to a new possibility for intimacy, one that was star-crossed from the beginning and in the end came to naught. Shortly after arriving in British Columbia, Jessie described for her mother how 'Frank Parsons is said to be like a coyote (pronounced coy-o-ta) ... and now that I've seen Parsons I guess I'll recognize the original animal when he appears. And still I'm not taken with or by any of them strange to say.' Frank, who was one of Annie's 'Lake dudes,' would sometimes ride with her when she went to visit Jessie at Lower Nicola, and led the high jinks that accompanied her wedding. Just a couple of weeks after the accident that killed Tom Hall in May 1889, Frank Parsons was seriously injured when 'his horse reared & fell on him bruising his leg badly.' Hospitalized in Kamloops, he recovered sufficiently, though still lame, to take Jessie riding the next August, just as he had Nan the previous year. Then, in October, he had another accident. 'Do you remember me telling you of Frank Parsons who was in the hospital so long? He was here Sat. night, and when going away it was so dark that he stumbled and fell bruising both his legs, and the one that was hurt before swelled up hard.' The doctor did not know what to do, and Parsons was eventually discharged from the Kamloops hospital at the beginning of 1890 on crutches, unable 'to do anything.' Even though he had a married brother and a sister residing nearby, 'Frank Parsons left the Valley.'[53]

When Jessie came to teach at Nicola Lake a year and a half later, she discovered that Frank's unmarried sister was 'sewing in the village.' Perhaps nostalgic for him, Jessie commented hopefully, 'she seems to be about my age, and I think I would like her.' Matters came to a head at Christmas 1891. 'I had a photo of Frank Parsons to-day, sent through his sister. I like to have it, but I suppose he'll want one of mine in return, & that I don't like to do.' What happened? Had Frank recovered enough to dare to think he could support a wife? Was a courtship ritual under way? If so, Jessie clearly spurned the advance, for he disappeared out of her letters.[54]

Part of the reason Jessie did so lay in her continued perception of herself as a sojourner. For all of the direction that Jessie sought to give to her solitary life at Nicola Lake, it was daughterhood's obligations that counted the most. Her first responsibility was to her family. 'I'm afraid it would be hard scratching for us if I were at home just now. When I do go, I want to be able to take hold & make things comfortable for you all, & that I can't do as yet.' Depressed economic circumstances added to her worries. 'Everybody seems to think too, that salaries will go down before very many years, and they are so good now that I suppose I am greedy & want to grab all I can.' Jessie developed a certain ambivalence about going home at the end of the promised three years, musing to her mother in the spring of 1892, 'Old as I am I'd like to go to Normal school again, & study for the first B [level] so as to have a life certificate.' When Catherine urged her to do so, she shot back 'that doesn't say I want to spend my life time in B.C.' Jessie reminded her mother: 'I never settled on any definite time for return. Of course there are friends here I would miss, but they are very few, and anyhow, they occupy their own places, not the places of my own old home friends.'[55]

All the same, it was during Jessie's years there that the frontier receded from Nicola Lake, as it became more like the home she had left behind. She mused, in respect to a newly arrived dressmaker, how 'the folk are just as anxious for *style* as though they lived in a fashionable corner of the world, instead of away up among the mountains.' Law and order arrived. 'We have had a permanent constable appointed in the village, at a salary of $69 per month.' Social amenities grew. Toward the end of 1891 a 'Medical Club' was started. Jessie explained how it operated. 'Yearly subscriptions for heads of families are $10, for single persons $5 and all who subscribe are entitled to the reduced prices as set forth in the paper, varying, of course, according to the distance the Dr. has to travel.' Jessie joined on the grounds that 'it's better to be sure than sorry.' She came to consider that 'on the whole there are worse places in the world than Nicola.' The spring of 1893, Jessie enthused how 'the place is full of strangers, & wonderfully stirring.' She was invited to play croquet, ended up 'sitting on the grass,' and mused: 'Never had a chance to do such a thing at Nicola Lake before. You could hardly believe how much grass adds to the appearance of a country!'[56]

Even as some frontiers receded, others came into being. The work of domestication did not cease. Upon her marriage in October 1891, Jessie Olding Hunter went to live at Granite Creek, accessible by trail from the Nicola Valley. The cousins corresponded, and Jessie McQueen became convinced that 'she is a power for good among those rough miners, so far from all other good influences, & I suppose that is one of the reasons why she was permitted to get married & go to bury herself in that out of the way corner.' The stories Jessie Hunter would pass on to her daughter are similar. 'Mother's new home was a large log cabin set in a townsite containing many saloons and houses of "night entertainment."' The small organ Hugh Hunter gave his wife for a wedding present 'was the focus for the rare church services and many sing-songs which were appreciated by everyone, especially the lonely bachelors.' In the summer of 1892, after sitting for the teachers' examination at the newly established site of Kamloops, Jessie took her courage in her hands and went to visit her cousin. She assured Catherine: 'Don't fret about me riding to Granite mother. We're to have a tent along, camp out & take three days to [do] the trip, so it will be a continuous picnic.' Back in Nicola Lake, Jessie more than ever appreciated Granite Creek's isolation and thereby of her cousin's work in domesticating this new British Columbia frontier.[57]

So Jessie stayed, at least for the time being. Daughterhood's obligations still counted the most, but she had begun, just a little, to make a life for herself at Nicola Lake more on her own terms than she could have done at Lower Nicola. Her pleasures were small, but they were pleasures nonetheless. British Columbia effected some change in her, most of all perhaps in her understanding of hybridity, but overall she remained a sojourner. Five years in British Columbia, she was in no way British Columbian. Nova Scotia, and more particularly Pictou County, remained her principal point of reference, and its ways of everyday life those that she sought so far as possible to retain for herself and to share with others.

Migration within Canada was, as Jessie's half decade demonstrates, a far more complex undertaking than change in residence. The sets of values and understandings that sojourners like the McQueen sisters brought with them were fundamental to how they responded to their new settings. British Columbia's absorption into Canada in the years following the completion of the transcontinental railroad derived far more from inconspicuous women like Jessie and Annie McQueen than it did from the public pronouncements of fellow Nova Scotians like George Monro Grant.

Chapter Eight

Enduring Bonds of Sisterhood

KAMLOOPS
CAMPBELL CREEK
SALMON ARM

In settling down, in modest fashion, at Nicola Lake, Jessie assumed that she would continue to sojourn in British Columbia on her own. Annie had long since left her behind without much thought, and her cousin Jessie Olding Hunter was installed at remote Granite Creek. Jessie's solitary state was not to continue. When the newly wed Annie abandoned British Columbia in the beginning of 1889, she was firmly convinced that it would be 'for good.'[1] Thereafter the sisters corresponded, but it seemed as if they had gone their separate ways. Then, four years into Annie's marriage, they came together again in British Columbia. The enduring bonds of sisterhood again took hold.

The years during which Jessie engaged quietly but persistently in the work of domestication in the Nicola Valley passed very differently for Annie and Jim Gordon. By virtue of entering the married state, and in part as a result of her character, Annie easily sloughed off both daughterhood's obligations and sisterhood's bonds. The circumstances of the wedding signalled the priority that Annie gave to her desires over her family back home. The newlyweds' departure for Ontario just six weeks into their marriage underlined Jessie's relative unimportance once she had played her role as mediator. She was left behind, literally and figuratively.

Even though the couple headed east at the behest of Jim's parents in Goderich, Annie could not abide sharing her newly-wed husband, much less giving up that ultimate symbol of marital respectability, her own home. Two months after arriving in Ontario, Annie wrote Jessie delightedly that 'I'm on the move again ... And best of all I'll have Jim to myself once more.' From 'the slowest old snail of a place' that was Goderich for

Annie, the couple moved to St Thomas, where 'one of the leading furniture manufacturers has given Jim this position, as manager and partner in a retail furniture store.' Set in the rich farming country of southwestern Ontario, the village of St Thomas had been transformed into a city on becoming a railway centre during the 1870s. Its population of about 11,000 supported at least three furniture makers. The company that hired Jim advertised itself as being 'well stocked with a large and handsome selection of house and office furniture of all descriptions, and in different woods, embracing parlor, bedroom and dining room sets in very handsome and modern designs.' St Thomas was large enough to give pleasures not to be had in British Columbia, as with Annie sitting 'at an upper window above Jim's shop ... to see Barnum's menagerie pass.'[2]

Again in their own home, the Gordons' first child was born in late September 1890, just ten months into their marriage. She was named 'Jessie McQueen, by Jim's desire,' after her aunt. Delighted by this renewed emotional contact with her beloved sister now so far away, Jessie affected modesty in querying her mother: 'What do *you* think of the name for her baby?' Ever energetic, Annie soon persuaded her husband 'to join the [local Methodist] church,' where they 'commenced family worship.'[3] A second child, named Daniel Marshall after Annie's father and Jim's brother at Kamloops, came along in October 1891.

For a time, it seemed as if Annie would, like George, drift away from the other McQueens. After a year or two, Jim opened his own furniture store on St Thomas's main street, adjacent to a dry goods store, dressmaker, and stationer. The Gordons appeared to have settled down. Annie visited Pictou County with baby Jessie in the summer of 1890, but the trip was brief. Her short and infrequent letters were taken up with the minutiae of family life. 'I know I ought to have written before, but I have been so tired when night came and the children got to sleep, that I felt more like going to bed myself.' Annie was ill, one or more of the children did not feel well, the hired girl had quit or was incompetent – there was always an excuse. Jim sometimes sent short notes to family members apologizing for Nan's silence. 'Annie is so busy today that she cannot write, so she requested me to do it for her.' Responding to Catherine's anxious queries, he sought to assure her that 'your baby is quite well,' in some cases in teasing fashion. 'I saw her dancing a jig in the kitchen last night and I think that is a very good indication as far as the body is concerned and as to the soul, well, she has Presbyterian feet & we will excuse her this time.'[4]

Then came another move. Weighed down by the demands of a young family, still in her mid-twenties, Annie fantasized about the freedom the frontier gave, even though, she acknowledged, 'Jim is wildly in love with Ontario.' It was not the same with her. 'I have such a longing to go back to the Valley once more,' and 'I would rather have B.C. by a long way.' Following the birth of her second child, she mused about returning to Kamloops, where Jim now had two brothers, but nothing came of it, for 'business continues very good with Jim, and he is quite content to stay in St. Thomas.' Then came the depression that hit around much of the world during the early 1890s. As times turned 'dull,' Annie again talked about leaving Ontario. 'Mother, I feel further from home here than in B.C. ... Anyway if we stay here, we could never afford to go [home], so *I* think we had better get out. We'll see about it. Time will tell.'[5]

Rumours of a move began to circulate around the family in early 1893, and both Jim and Annie assured her parents and sisters they would make every effort to visit the Maritimes before heading west. Jim had yet to meet his inlaws. The McQueens were kept on tenterhooks, not even being informed when 'Nan's taking the Grip' in Montreal caused the Gordons to go straight to British Columbia with their two young children. Still anticipating their arrival, Dove fretted that 'we won't know each other by and by I'll be looking for an impulsive little Nan who has probably fled forever.' In explaining the last-minute change of plans to her mother after their arrival in Kamloops, Annie saw it primarily in terms of the effect on her. 'It was a great disappointment to me, as it was to you too ... Oh, mother, I can't tell you how badly I feel that I didn't get down home. I have had a more decided fit of homesickness ever since, than I ever had in all my life before.' Jessie agreed with her mother that 'it was cruel of Annie to leave you so long in suspense ... I see you day after day, waiting and looking for the stragglers.' Catherine reluctantly acknowledged that 'self is a prominent object with poor Nan.'[6]

It was not just daughterhood's obligations but also sisterhood's bonds that, initially, got short shrift. The McQueen sisters' encounter in British Columbia was very different the second time around. They had gone their separate ways and were no longer the same persons who had greeted each other so joyously in Kamloops five years earlier. Indeed, the Gordons' return reached Jessie only through third parties, which miffed her. 'I'm not so young and so excitable as I used to be – have learned to sit on myself a little bit.' Arriving in Kamloops in early March 1893, the Gordons did not even bother to let Jessie know. She got the news from one of her landlady's daughters, who called on Annie while passing through Kamloops and reported that she 'was alone, & dreadfully busy & had no writing materials at hand.' Working as a salesman on commission 'for two or three furniture firms,' Jim travelled as far east as Winnipeg and west to the coast. His job meant Annie was on her own for weeks at a time in 'my little collar box of a house' with young Jessie and Marsh, who could, in her view, be 'very troublesome.' She told her mother: 'I have worked and toiled and done my very best to straighten things with him [Marsh] in my arms, and Jessie at my skirts, and now I feel too tired almost to *breathe*.' Conciliatory by nature, Jessie eventually took the initiative with her sister. 'I wrote her a short letter on Thursday ... so I suppose it will be all right soon.' Only at the end of the month, she explained, did Annie and Jim send her a message through an intermediary that 'they'd be out to see me perhaps after a few weeks.' Annie used as an excuse, perhaps with good justification, that 'her hands were so crippled up with rheumatism that she could hardly hold the pen.'[7]

Almost a hundred kilometres separated Nicola Lake from Kamloops, but the distance did not prevent Jessie from again being drawn, irresistibly, into Annie's orbit. Nan's first letter informed her somewhat peremptorily that 'the Kamloops school would be vacant in July,' and she should apply for it and live with them. Annie had used her connections, talking to the husband of the Pictou County Douglas sister settled in Kamloops, and he thought he could swing it. Jessie did not want to move, likely anticipating that she would end up doing Annie's will around the house. It was not just that salaries in Nicola Lake and the larger Kamloops school were the same, she confided to her mother. 'I have a horror of changing around, and by the time I'd get that school broken in, it would be time to go home [after the promised three years away], and I'd be all used up, instead of being fresh and able to tackle anything, as I want to be when I go back to you.'[8]

Initially Jessie had the strength of character to resist, which annoyed Annie no end. 'I am very much disappointed that Jessie is not coming to Kamloops. She is always growling about Nicola and the folk there, so I thought she would jump at the chance.' Annie persuaded Jessie by diminishing the very same Nicola Lake that had once so entranced her. 'The school is not a hard one, but they are very troublous people to live among.' Even as Jessie proclaimed her intention 'to stay here another year,' she kept being got at by her younger sister, who professed to 'need' her. Jessie agonized: 'I'm afraid she'll be disappointed – it gives myself some range, but I've always had the disappointments before, and after all, I don't suppose I'm essential to her comfort or happiness. And as to my *duty* – somehow I don't know, that's a question that puzzles me many times.'[9]

Sisterhood's bonds won out. Shortly after going to visit the Gordons in Kamloops at end of term, Jessie was persuaded to give up the Nicola Lake school in anticipation of securing Kamloops. The promise of family life was pivotal. 'After living such a long time in a boarding-house it is good to be with one's own folks again, & I don't mind the children nearly as much as I did at first ... It is a graded school, he [Kamloops principal Stuart Woods] says I only need to try it, to appreciate the difference between it & a miscellaneous one, such as I have always had.'[10]

Spending part of her summer with her cousin at Granite Creek, Jessie returned in mid-August to Kamloops in anticipation of settling into her new school. There she was quickly absorbed into a daily routine that also included Jim's brothers Lynn and Marsh. 'Annie and I enjoy ourselves finely - we are busy most of the time – the children make so much work, and take up time too, but it's pleasant all rough and real good for us too.' By then, however, Annie's plan to incorporate her dutiful sister into her household was turning into a disaster, one that only the Presbyterian concept of providence made it possible to accept. 'The best laid schemes have gone astray again – a letter from Jim informs me that the trustees have engaged a male teacher. We had all been so sure of being together this winter, that it is quite a disappointment, but it doesn't do to dwell on the dark side of things. It must be all for the best, however it is, and I am very glad to be able to look at it so.' Jim's lament to his mother-in-law underlines how much Jessie's anticipated presence meant to the Gordons. 'We were building so much on having her here with us that it has dropped us down pretty hard and we are feeling a little sore.'[11]

Much to Jessie's credit, she rebounded. She applied for the vacant Lower Nicola school, but parents keen for her return lost out to those who wanted 'a *man*.' She then requested from the superintendent of education any situation where she would retain her previous salary. 'So far, my salary has been $60 per month, & I would not care to take a school for less.' While waiting to hear, Jessie became interim 'housekeeper' for one of the Woodward clan at Lower Nicola while his wife was away visiting her aged mother. The situation was fraught with irony. 'The teacher boards here – a rather unpleasant-looking boy, to me. I don't think I'll like him at all.' By so doing, Jessie made a statement about her future relationship with Nan, so she wrote home: 'Annie didn't approve of it ... but she didn't really *need* me.'[12]

The school that Jessie got in mid-September 1893 opened up a very different teaching and domesticating experience from that of her previous five and a half years in British Columbia, first at rural Lower Nicola and then in the village of Nicola Lake. She was now in 'the Wild West life,' no holds barred, she confided to a Pictou County friend. Reluctantly agreeing to a $10 salary cut, Jessie accepted 'the school at Mr. L. Campbell's, Campbell Creek,' located twenty kilometres east of Kamloops along the Thompson River.[13]

The Campbell Creek school reflected the will of a single self-made man of the frontier. An American who had driven cattle north during the gold rush, Lewis Campbell soon partnered with a former Hudson's Bay fur trader from the Orkneys, John Lennard, who was settled on the south side of the Thompson River east of Kamloops. Not only did Campbell benefit from local expertise as to the best ranchland to acquire, he got a wife in the bargain. Lennard had a marriageable daughter, Mary, by an Aboriginal woman with whom he had lived while stationed at the Hudson's Bay post of Fort Alexandria in the central interior. Lewis Campbell and Mary Lennard's first child was born in 1865, followed by seven more over the next two decades. Campbell pre-empted land north of the Thompson River in 1869. He gradually added to it, including land acquired from his father-in-law, until he owned almost a thousand acres on which to run stock and grow hay through the use of irrigation ditches dug and tended by 'Chinamen.'[14]

Jessie was enormously intrigued by her first extended encounter with ranch life. 'Mr. C. owns over 1300 head [of cattle], that is no light task.' There were turkeys, as well. Two grown Campbell sons assisted together with a hired man who 'gets $30 a month, & there has been an Indian ploughing all fall, besides one or two others helping the boys hunt cattle.' Over the winter, three hired men fed the cattle, left outdoors on different parts of the ranch. 'The older boys seem to be on the go all the time, driving the cattle, and hunting out "strays."' Everything interested Jessie, down to chaps. 'Do you know what they are? I don't think I ever heard the word at home, but they are leather overalls, or rather *legs* of overalls, hitched together at the top by a belt, which the cowboys wear when riding. The Campbell boys got new ones last week, at $30 a pair. The pants are goat skin with the hair left on, so they are rather ferocious looking things – both boys and chaps.'[15]

Jessie appreciated the hard work that had got the family to where they were. 'Mrs Campbell told me ... that when they first came here, she & Mr C. lived in a tent, & there their first child was born, & that if they were comfortable now they had to work for it all. She herself ploughed and fenced & did all sorts of hard work.' Success came at a price, Jessie learned. 'Her health is badly broken now, she seldom does anything but the family sewing.' Not only that, 'Mr Campbell himself is in very poor health this winter – seems to be breaking down completely and he is not an old man either. He spends most of his time in the house, goes out for a walk now every day, but isn't able to do anything.' Lewis and Mary Campbell, respectively in their early sixties and late forties, oversaw on the ranch 'a family of fourteen,' including a widowed daughter and grandchildren.[16]

The Campbell offspring huddled on the edge of respectability. For all of their father's material success, their mother's heritage doomed them to hybridity. They were 'quarter breeds,' in the language of the day. To the extent physical appearance did not give them away, they were tainted by proximity to their mother's three younger half-brothers. Mary Campbell's father, John Lennard, had a second family with a Shuswap woman from the Kamloops area. Following his accidental death, John, Joe, and Louis Lennard were 'brought up in the Kamloops Band as Indians' and continued to make their lives there as Shuswap. A visitor to Kamloops – described the half-brothers' home. 'Across the river, in the corner of land washed by the two rivers, was the Reservation for the Kamloops Indians, with their dirty little town of miserable huts, and behind this a steep, barren, and tireless mountain.'[17]

Campbell employed various strategies to manoeuvre his children's acceptability into the edges of settler society. Shortly after the birth of their third child in 1872, Campbell married their mother in a Catholic ceremony, ensuring that subsequent offspring would be baptized as 'legitimate' rather than 'natural' or 'illegitimate.' In 1886 Campbell built a house in Kamloops, and briefly ran a meat market there, so that the children could attend its newly opened public school. Whether it was economics or racial prejudice that drove them out, Campbell soon took his family back to the ranch. In 1892 he got permission to open a school there, with 'Mr. Lewis Campbell providing the building, furniture, etc.,' and no public money being expended except for the teacher and incidentals. Campbell later recollected how, to attain the minimum number of ten needed to keep a school open, 'I have also at my own expense, kept these orphan children who would otherwise be denied any opportunity of learning those simple things which are necessary in the present struggle with the world.'[18]

The school's location put Campbell in conflict with his neighbour

George Martin, a member of the provincial legislature ranching ten kilometres away at Duck's. Jessie had just begun teaching when she became aware of the tension. 'Mr. C. is afraid the people at Duck's Station are trying to make trouble for him in regard to the school. You see he provided the school-room, fixings &c himself, and last winter he boarded three or four children for nothing – for the sake of keeping the school open. They won't take the trouble to send them here, & want to build a new school at the Station & compel Mr. C to send his seven all that distance. He says he told [Superintendent of Education] Pope this summer how he was situated, & Pope said he would allow him a *Monitor's* salary, that is ten dollars a month less than it was before, but he understands these people are kicking again, & wants me to write to Pope when I send in my report this month. It seems too bad if the man can't have his school for his children when he does so much, & is so anxious to have them learn.' The dispute was resolved, Jessie explained in a later letter home, by the promise of 'another school at Duck's Station' and also by an interim solution. 'Mr. Martin, member for this district, was here last week, & is to send one of his children to Mr Campbell's right away – expect her to-day.'[19]

In her routine correspondence with the superintendent of education, Jessie gave strong support to Lewis Campbell's efforts. She pointed out at the end of September that, although attendance was small at seven, the children came every day. 'Mr. Campbell says that as this is a Monitor school, there will probably be more leniency shown us, but I should very much like to know if we can go on with less than the required average, as I do not wish to be thrown on the cold world "again, without due warning."' Her tenuous position gave added fervour to Jessie's descriptions. 'Mr. Campbell is most anxious to have educational advantages for his children, & last year, he boarded three or four from the [Ducks] station – *free* – in order that the required number might be maintained.' The Superintendent must have expressed concern for Jessie's well-being, for she responded, 'in reply to your enquiry, I would say that I like my new situation very much though I should be glad of a larger class.' She took pains to be positive. 'The children are working hard and may yet do credit to my efforts.' Jessie noted four months into the job that 'the children seem to be learning well, & we are all pleased over it.' Unlike Lower Nicola, where a small number of children had caused her boredom, this time a similar situation gave pleasure. 'When there are so few you see, I can make every single chap work up to his best level all the time.'[20]

Approaching her thirty-third birthday, Jessie was thrown into a new, third mode, not just of teaching but of living typical of the frontier. Lewis Campbell's determination to secure his children's education was so great that he constructed separate accommodation for a teacher right on the ranch. Jessie's salary was $10 less than the year before, but she did not have to pay for room and board. In her first letter home since taking the job, Jessie assured her mother that 'I feel quite "set-up" as folks say.' She praised her circumstances. 'Mr. C says he wants to do what's right by me, & I told him that many a one might do what's right & still not do one-sixteenth that he does. However, he says I'm not getting the salary I might, & he wants to make it as easy as he can for me.' To the superintendent of education, Jessie explained: 'He has fitted a very comfortable, well ventilated & well lighted school-room in his own house. He supplies food & all necessities besides accommodating the teacher with a two-roomed, furnished house, as well as farm produce, in order to eke out the $50 salary. In fact, he does everything in his power for the sake of the school.'[21]

Jessie was now 'housekeeping' for herself in a cozy 'mahogany hut,' whose logs were rechinked for her in late November by the hired man. It was probably the first time in her life she enjoyed such freedom, certainly in British Columbia. 'I have lots of wood, & can keep my cabin good & warm. The little stove heats very quickly too, which is quite a consideration ... I can have a good fire & dinner in ten minutes.' The family provided the essentials of domesticity, down to a 'a granite-ware tea kettle & bread pan.' There six months, Jessie rejoiced how 'on this ranch they don't know what bed bugs are,' compared with 'many other places I've been.'[22]

Jessie cooked for herself. She got basics like flour and fresh beef at cost from the Campbells and other foodstuffs, such as salmon, venison, and eggs, as gifts from time to time. 'The family sent in a prairie chicken & some doughnuts for my supper, so I fared sumptuously,' she wrote home one evening. 'Oil, flour, meat & a few groceries will be the only outlay for me.' Jessie had the run of the family garden. 'I go out & gather ripe tomatoes by the lap-ful.' Whatever the Campbells could do for her welfare, they did. 'They milk one cow, & only churn once in a long time, so I am told to go & help myself – never mind asking – just get it.' Jessie took particular pleasure, less than two weeks after arriving, that 'I made my first batch of bread this morning.'[23]

Jessie soon added a cat to her 'bachelor quarters,' she reported home proudly. 'I've succeeded in taming a cat, so that she'll come & overhaul the mice for me occasionally, & when she stops overnight she is wonderful company.' Jessie was still taken up a month later. 'That miserable kitten of mine is a perfect nuisance – see where he snared the letters at the top, & he's got my hands all scratched up too. It's just his play, but he won't let me read or write in peace half the time.' Named 'Christopher,' he 'shares all my meals, takes a snack of whatever is going, even *beans & rice.*' Over time, Jessie came to value her living situation. 'It's a very free independent sort of life & so long as I keep myself busy, I'm all right.'[24]

Jessie had rallied in what must have been difficult circumstances. Her letters home were upbeat, filled with gratitude for how 'the [Campbell] parents do so much for me.' She enthused: 'The latest is a nice hand sewing machine in fine order, & it is to stay right in my house as long as I want it.' Thinking back to her years with the Woodward clan, Jessie added: 'That's a long way better than having permission to go and use theirs in their house.' Catherine McQueen's responses were telling. For the first time, her daughter had, in her view, overstepped the boundaries of acceptable behaviour. From a Pictou County perspective, she was too much caught up in an alien frontier. Catherine's letters are also interesting as indicating her growing religious zeal. 'Well Jessie Dear tis too bad you have to meet such hard times trying to help us, sometimes I could wish you had never gone to B.C. but perhaps you had a work to do there besides school and as I thought of your loneliness now the thought comes perhaps as tis a new place & likely little chance of preaching or religious teaching perhaps Jessie may help some one to start in the Christian life or help some poor dead one to revive. There are mysteries we cannot understand.' Catherine's very next lines made clear the family's dependence on Jessie's earnings. 'Now don't scrimp yourself trying to save, we have plenty of milk & butter.'[25]

The best part about Campbell Creek was its proximity to Kamloops, which may explain why Jessie accepted the school in the first place. There only a week or so, she already appreciated 'the advantage of getting a horse whenever I want to go down, & being told to put him in Mr Campbell's own stable there' in Kamloops. She was already planning, on the upcoming Friday afternoon, 'to ride down to Kamloops – twelve miles will be nothing to me, who have done my thirty & even forty miles a day.' Having made the trip, she reported, 'I took fully two hours & a half to [do] the twelve miles, so I wasn't at all hard on the horse, but the wind was high & I have enjoyed rides more in my day.' A couple of months there, 'I daresay I spend a good deal of time trotting down to Kamloops, but that's what keeps the life in me – keeps my heart up.'[26]

By spring, Jessie had worn out the riding habit ordered from Nova Scotia shortly after she arrived in British Columbia.

Jessie also improvised by catching rides to Kamloops with family members, one Saturday morning in February with one of the 'revellers' who had come for a 'big dance here on Friday night – forty or more at it.' Another time, when only 'a strange cayuse,' a horse that had been allowed to run wild, was available, she decided not to take a chance and walked the distance. 'I didn't take four hours, & you may be sure I didn't hurry.' Jessie often returned to Campbell Creek on Monday morning 'with the Section men on the hand-car,' whose job was to maintain the rail tracks. She took pleasure in March that 'the men begin to know me now' and, despite not being meant to go so far, 'come right to my crossing' to drop her off.[27]

When in Kamloops, Jessie not only visited with 'my own folks,' as she referred to the Gordons, she also satisfied her piety. 'We were all out to Methodist service this A.M. and will go to my church this evening. For this is Sunday, and I thought it would be much wickeder to leave you without a letter than it would be to write.' Jessie had learned to accommodate to whichever Protestant faith might be about, but one weekend discovered to her dismay that her namesake niece was not quite so understanding. 'She was crying in bed one night, and I went in to quiet her. "Just wait till to-morrow night" I said "there is to be a big Xmas tree in the Pres. church," but was interrupted by a melancholy howl "but I ain't a Presbyterian!" I retired, utterly vanquished by the unapproachable logic of the four year old.'[28]

Jessie's location meant that she could be surprised on an autumnal Friday afternoon not only by 'Anne and the babies,' but by their newly arrived cousin Liz Olding, all come to take her to Kamloops for the weekend. Liz, just off the train from Nova Scotia on her way to recuperate with her sister Jessie at Granite Creek, had talked about going west for some time, and finally made up her mind to do so after a serious illness. Chain sojourning was alive and well. As Annie told the story, 'we got a double rig, and all went out to Jessie's little house & she never saw us until we got to the door, and then – you ought to have seen her face, and heard her yell at Liz.' Another weekend when the Gordons visited, 'Jim made shelves for my books out of pieces of a packing box, & you could hardly believe how much "furnishing" they make in my bed room.' In the days and weeks when Jessie was not in Kamloops or Annie did not visit, she kept them very much in mind by sewing 'a snug little pinny for Jessie,' knitting mittens and stockings for Marshie, and so on.

'That sewing machine is the best company I have. I only wish Ann had given me some more sewing.'[29] Jessie became as dutiful an aunt as she ever was a daughter and sister.

For all that Jessie used the school as a launching point for weekends with the Gordons, she also domesticated. Her influence on the Campbell family went far beyond the hours spent in the classroom. The close knowledge of ranch life that she retailed home suggests many chats with various members. During a ride to Kamloops with a Campbell son, Jessie 'got lots of information about ranching, pieces of hay &c &c if I can only remember it all.' She learned the proprieties of ranch life, telling her mother: 'I usually lock my house when I go any distance, & leave the key at Mr C's. The other teacher used to lock up when she went to school, & they rather resented that as an insinuation to themselves.' Jessie's presence gave the Campbell men practice in the gendered behaviour expected at that time. 'Mr Campbell has two grown-up sons, but I see very little of them. They never pass me anywhere, without touching their hats most respectfully, & seem very decent, civil young fellows.'[30]

Despite her hybridity, Lewis Campbell's wife quickly became 'Mary' in Jessie's letters home, and it is clear that the two women saw each other often. 'Mary & I went in the canoe with the boys.'[31] About fifteen years Jessie's senior, Mary was literate with English as her first language. Her father had been transferred from remote Fort Alexandria, her mother's home, to Fort Kamloops when Mary was ten or eleven. She likely attended school there even as her father began his second family. Mary walked a difficult path between two cultures, having a large family by an ambitious newcomer husband, but also three half-brothers on the Kamloops Reserve who identified themselves as Shuswap.[32]

Like others of her time, Jessie inevitably drew a line. She never referred to Mary's hybridity in her letters, likely because they had early on developed a personal relationship that overrode the alien quality causing newcomers to discriminate on the basis of physical appearance and skin colour. Jessie's line became visible, not in reference to Mary Campbell or to the Campbell children, but rather to the wife of their ranching neighbour, George Martin of Duck's, whose daughter was added to her classroom several weeks after she began the job. Agreeing to take her on, Jessie was a bit miffed at not being told the entire story. '*Mrs. Martin* is a delate [acknowledged] Klootchman; Mr. M. didn't tell me that, but he did tell me that his girl would be the stupidest I ever had in my school.' Introduced half a year later to Martin's wife, Jessie was even more indignant about the menage. 'I met the wife of the M.P. [i.e.,

MLA] for this district this week. She is a "delate" squaw – doesn't even understand English, but may be too good for him nevertheless. And his father was an English admiral!'[33]

It was the social distance between the couple that most agitated Jessie. As for the specifics, Jessie got it almost right, for Martin, educated at the prestigious English 'public' school of Cheltenham, was the son of a Royal Navy commander and grandson of an English MP and of an admiral. A typical nineteenth-century adventurer, Martin had stints in the Royal Navy and with the East India Company behind him when he was, like so many others, caught up in the British Columbia gold rush. What Jessie did not appreciate was that Martin's wife was no ordinary Aboriginal woman, but a daughter of Jean Baptiste Lolo St Paul, a powerful fur trade intermediary whom Martin encountered while employed by the Hudson's Bay Company at Fort Kamloops.[34] Lolo's origins were obscure. According to one account, he was the son of an Iroquois who came west from Quebec with the fur trade and of an unknown Aboriginal woman which whom he partnered somewhere along the way. The tremendous respect Lolo commanded from all elements of the fur trade was lost on Jessie. In her view, Anne Martin was just another Indian who did not conform to her expectations for domesticity. In part because Jessie did not get to know her, she lay beyond the boundaries of consideration. That Anne Martin ever could have acquired any kind of acceptability from Jessie's perspective is highly doubtful, given the assumptions about race embedded in colonialism.

In contrast, Jessie shared in the social life instigated by Lewis and Mary Campbell, thereby validating it. She even put in an appearance at a dance held at their ranch on a Friday evening in mid-December. 'There is to be a big dance – a very big one, at Mr Campbell's to-morrow night ... I shall have to grace the dance with my bodily presence for a few hours – they would be mortally offended if I didn't, although they know I don't dance. I'm hoping to be able to slip off to my own cabin at an early hour, the house will be so full that one won't be missed.' Discreetly not commenting on the nature of her participation, Jessie noted in a subsequent letter about 'the great party at "Lew Campbells"' that 'they danced all night till 'twas daylight, literally, broke up finally at 10 A.M.'[35]

Jessie was far more supportive of the Campbells than she ever was critical. She was well aware that 'boys who have been used to tearing over the hills on horseback from daylight to dusk, find it hard work sitting still four or five hours a day.' In this sense, her riding served multiple purposes. As well as giving Jessie access to Kamloops, it accommodated her pupils to her, 'for the Campbell boys are riding every day.' In turn, the young Campbells worked hard to look after their teacher. After Jessie had hung out her washing one evening, 'it blew a perfect gale ... & the boys were picking up my clean clothes all over the ranch this morning.' Jessie became quite defensive of her charges. 'It is a fact that they are not bright, any of them, but then they've had little or no chance so far, & they are good tempered & obedient, so I enjoy working with them.' She took real pride in how, at the Christmas examination, 'the children were quite a credit to me, though I say it.' She was also well aware that they had to work as well as study. 'The boys are ploughing & harrowing this week,' she noted at the end of March.[36]

Jessie's contact with her charges went far beyond school hours. Her first letter home from Campbell Creek began, 'Dearest Mother, I got out paper &c an hour ago, to write to you, but the children came in.' The young Campbells became frequent visitors to Jessie's cabin. She commented to her mother on a winter evening: 'Well, I've just said good-night to the last of the *Campbellites,* poor young ones. I *could* dispense with their company many a time, but I haven't the heart to pack them off.' Jessie continued her exercise routine, mostly after school and 'sometimes it's after 6 before I come in from my walk & light the lamp.' One or more of the children often went with her on her daily constitutionals. 'I went for another long walk with two of the little girls. Two of the boys joined us down the road a bit, so it wasn't at all a lonely walk.' Another time 'I went off "up the canyon" with the children, & clambered up & down till I was good & tired.'[37]

Jessie wanted to be wanted, but perhaps not quite so much. 'I'm afraid I'm *too* popular with the young ones at times. Since beginning this letter I've had the same two small boys in to see me for more than an hour, & me just aching to get my letters written, but the chaps seem to like to come & I try not to begrudge the time they take. The boys seldom come in except in the evening, but the girls may drop in at any hour of the day.' Sometimes it was just too much for Jessie. 'Once or twice, when I spied them coming at a very inconvenient hour I've just snibbed my door & said nothing, leaving them to infer that I was asleep or out, or anything they pleased. It's possible to have too much of a good thing you know, but I suppose it's a trial of my patience. I generally keep a little stocking on hand to knit up my aggravation when I have to entertain.' It is likely that Mary Campbell realized her children might be overstepping the boundaries, for she dispatched little treats from time to time as symbols of her gratitude. 'I've had great hunks of *cake* sent down to me lately.' Jessie's Presbyterian ethic was unbalanced. 'I'd never bother making cake or any such frivolity for myself, but when it comes that way it makes a very good "snack" when I feel like "snacking."'[38]

Of the eight Campbell children, Ulysses, who was one of Jessie's oldest pupils 'somewhere between fifteen or sixteen,' developed the closest bond with her. He first turns up in her letters following a day's trip on horseback to Kamloops. 'After my twenty-four mile ride last Saturday, I went out salmon fishing at night. Ulyss. had got a new canoe, & made all preparations, so when Miss McQueen was invited, she saw it would be a big disappointment if she didn't go. We weren't very lucky though, only caught three salmon while we stayed, but it was rather enjoyable, out on the still, dark river, with the big torch gleaming over the water, & half stifled shrieks of "there's one, Ulyss," every few minutes.' Ulysses began looking for reasons to spend time out of school with his teacher. He gave Jessie a ride to Kamloops with him one weekend in 'the big sleigh.' A couple of days later: 'Ulyss. doesn't often come in, but to-night I turned him loose among some magazines & papers, & I really began to think I'd have to help him to get started home at last. Four times he said he must go, & still he sat ... & *couldn't* move. Maybe I haven't made it clear to you who Ullyss. is, but he's only one of my school-boys, & a comical one at that.'[39]

When Jessie returned in January 1894 by train from her Christmas holidays in Kamloops, she was genuinely touched by her reception. 'They all seem kind of glad to see me back, & when the train bell rang that night the children all flew out of the house like a flock of partridges. Even my big boy Ulyss was at the gate as soon as anyone, & they had me & my traps collected in no time. If some of them do hate school & study, by their own confession, there's still room for encouragement so long as they don't hate the teacher.' Classes began again, and Jessie took special pleasure how Ulysses 'never liked school, but seems to endure it with better grace this winter than ever before.' In making the assessment, she was well aware that the obligations of Ulysses and his brothers went far beyond the classroom. 'Ulyss. helps him [the hired man looking after the stock on the nearest part of the ranch] feed, mornings & evenings.'[40]

The materials Jessie encouraged Ulysses and the other Campbells to read reflected her interest in temperance. Not only were there newspapers espousing that point of view, but Jessie also continued to enjoy the adventures of Marietta Holley's Samantha, of which twenty-one volumes would appear up to 1914. She eagerly awaited each new book in the series, writing her mother in December 1893: 'I saw that "Samantha" has another book out – "Samantha at the Fair" – & I expect it will be a rattler. How do you like the one you have? Annie sent me two at different times.' Only with rare exceptions did Jessie have the same opportunity, as at Nicola Lake, to engage in group advocacy. One time she was able to do so at her employer's initiative. 'Lew Campbell drove me down on Thursday after school & as that was Lodge night I attended it, & thought it the best I had been at in Kamloops. Rev. Mr Lee was Chief, & the subject of Prohibition was discussed in solid sensible fashion.' Jessie took an interest in current events, writing home in a postscript in April 1894, 'I am ever so proud of my country's showing for prohibition, but that John T. has given the temperance people rather a set-back by refusing to promise any help.'[41]

The contact between teacher and young man did not end with Jessie's departure at the end of the school year. Shortly before she left, Jessie reported excitedly: 'My boy Ulyss. has promised me to leave drink alone, & if you knew his situation &c you would know how glad I am to get that promise. He won't tell me any fibs *because I always trust him* – but you can't begin to think how the moral sense in general is lacking. I seem to have better hold on him than on any of the rest, & I think his example & influence may do a great deal for the other little ones.' She was enthusiastic. 'No teacher ever had a better pupil than he has been all through, & I wish he had better surroundings. I see a big difference in him since I went there, & he really does try to do right, as far as he knows how. He says if he ever has money enough, he shall come to N.S. to see me, so that will show you how much he thinks of his old teacher.' The two kept in close correspondence and, as Jessie noted the next January, 'he is doing well in school and "keeping his promises," poor little lad.'[42]

Jessie once termed her year at Campbell Creek 'my "lull in life."' Perhaps it was the time for reflection that encouraged her decision, made by the end of March 1894, to return to Nova Scotia at the end of her promised three years. She assured her mother how she intended to 'save my good clothes till I start for home.' Her decision to leave British Columbia caused Jessie to resign from the school, as opposed to the nature of the job encouraging her to leave. Indeed, she was invited in December to apply for a job in New Westminster, where one of the trustees was a fellow Nova Scotian, but did not do so. As well as wanting to stay near 'my own folk,' she considered that 'I'm getting along very well' at Campbell Creek. On learning in January that the teacher at nearby Shuswap wanted her Campbell Creek position for her sister, Jessie

retorted that 'she had better wait till I *am* through.' By late May, Jessie
was both anticipating her release from 'my little old log cabin' and wax-
ing nostalgic. 'While I'll be glad to be free, I'll be a little sorry too to give
up the children, for some of them have taken quite a strong hold upon
my affections.'[43]

The special role that Jessie played in the lives of the Campbell clan
contrasts sharply with the family's experience with her successor two
years later. The young teacher, by the name of Winifred Swan, could not
cope with the isolation and began physically disciplining the younger
students very severely. 'The place is very lonely.' As for Lewis Campbell,
according to the school inspector, 'He is much dissatisfied with Miss
Swan, says she teaches nothing – eats nothing – and burns no wood! In
fact the girl seems utterly wretched all alone in a house by herself.'
Campbell fretted that 'Miss Swan has become a victim of hysteria in an
aggravated form.'[44]

It was the teacher's Kamloops cousin, a CPR official, who escalated this
little frontier drama. He claimed to the superintendent of education
that, among other offences, 'one of the largest boys after drinking about
half a pitcher of water deliberately threw the balance in her face [which]
is, as you must confess, very hard to stand from a lot of half breeds.' Not
only was the school closed, the charges against Campbell and his family
were sensationalized in the press and even discussed in the provincial
legislature. Campbell was particularly upset over the assertion that 'the
treatment Miss Swan received from the scholars was very hard to stand
from a lot of halfbreeds.' He countered: 'There is not a halfbreed in the
school but even if there were their rights are as much to be respected as
another person's and such slurs are unbecoming to the form of even the
Supt. of the Canadian Pacific telegraph lines in B.C.'[45] Jessie had been,
in comparison, a far more resilient and caring teacher.

Before heading home, Jessie spent some time during the summer of
1894 with Annie, but in a far different venue than would have been the
case a few months earlier. The Gordons were never satisfied in Kamloops. Their four-room rented house, for which they paid $15/month,
barely sufficed, and Annie did not relish being on her own for much of
the time while Jim travelled. When he was home, he did double duty,
helping out in his brother Marsh's furniture business for $15/week. Jim
suffered stomach problems, a reoccurrence of an affliction already
treated in various fashions. About to leave St Thomas for British Columbia, Annie had described how 'Jim is trying K.D.C. for his dyspepsia and
is finding it does him a great deal of good.'[46]

For the Gordons there was always another dream to be had just around the corner. In the fall of 1893, even as Jessie was settling into Campbell Creek, the coast was talked about. 'We think of moving to Vancouver in the spring; in fact we would move now, if it were not for Jessie. It is a great deal less expensive living there, and right in the heart of Jim's business too.' Nothing came of it, for another adventure soon loomed larger. The Gordons turned to the land. 'Jim is taking up a ranch and intends to build and move us on to it as soon as Spring comes. He will continue his present business and work on the ranch between times. It is nearly all bush, so he is going to have a sweet time clearing it. It is excellent land.' Annie confided to her mother that 'I don't exactly like the idea of it, for I don't feel strong this winter, and I feel as if the hard work would be too much for me, and the loneliness when Jim is away will be the death of me.' Even the ever supportive Jessie was hard pressed, admitting to her mother how 'I hoped it would be only talk.'[47]

In the event, Jessie became intimately caught up in events, for Jim's enthusiasm outstripped his resources. He was determined that the family should move as early as possible in the spring of 1894 so that they could put in sufficient vegetables to tide them over the next winter. The Gordons gave up their rented Kamloops home at the end of March, but there was a catch. 'He has been felling trees – some of them three ft. thick, making a road, & building a bridge, the latter 80 ft. long, & the best on the river he says.' Their house still to be built, Annie and the two children bunked with Jessie at Campbell Creek. Their departure after a month left Jessie, for whom the bonds of sisterhood were so important, distraught and alone. 'I wasn't a bit ready to let her go even then, & when I came back into my empty hut, I think I might have wept.'[48]

It is revealing of the sisters' different personalities that the prime advantage Jessie, now well into her thirties, saw in the move to the ranch Annie, still in her twenties and always the more sociable of the two, lamented as a loss. 'Nan will be rid of the everlasting swarm of callers who deluge her in Kamloops, & won't be under the necessity of toeing the mark so exactly in regard to children's dress & general appearance.' As for Annie: 'I feel kind of divided in my mind about it. For my own part I would rather live in town ... it is a harder pull than any one would think for me to leave Kamloops.'[49]

Annie already had a good sense of what a frontier life entailed, having recently lost an argument as to the most suitable present for her church in Kamloops to give a newly-wed couple 'going to live in a log house on a ranch.' Annie was thwarted. 'I wanted to have them get her a sewing machine, but the majority thought differently, so a [silver] tea service it is.' It is very possible Annie was thinking back to her own wealth of wedding presents, most utterly unsuitable for the frontier. The best Annie could do was to rationalize Jim's decision. The railway was only a few kilometres away, the nearest neighbours less than a kilometre. 'It is a good chance, and a ranch is something certain to fall back on, and will be there for the children when we are gone, and I think that maybe the outdoor work might do me good.'[50]

As a dutiful wife, Annie had little real choice. She became, at the age of thirty, a classic frontier wife. Jim's ranch was sited, according to Annie, in a valley 'sixty miles from Kamloops by rail and about four miles from the station at Salmon Arm.'[51] Salmon Arm, located east of Kamloops and north of the Okanagan Valley at the southern edge of an arm of the Shuswap Lakes, was a recent creation, its post office just three years old when the site caught Jim Gordon's fancy. At about this point in time, Kamloop's *Inland Sentinel* newspaper lauded a new wagon road being constructed in the ranch's direction and 'a large tract of the best land yet to be settled.' Another advantage was sufficient rainfall, unlike the Kamloops area, which meant there was no need for irrigation.[52]

This ranch's appeal may have had as much to do with social attributes as with agricultural potential. Then a toddler, Marsh later described it, based on common knowledge within the family, as 'a bush farm' in 'a howling wilderness thinly populated and heavily forested.' The *Inland Sentinel* pointed to the presence of a resident Methodist minister who holds service 'twice each Sunday in the valley' at locations that 'are nicely warmed and lighted and bibles and hymn books provided.' In a similar spirit, Annie wrote home enthusiastically: 'It is a great Methodist settlement, no liquor allowed, about seventy five families in the valley which is ten miles long ... All the people are Methodist with the exception of three, one an atheist, another Catholic and a third English Church, but he goes to the church with the others and is nightly in the Bible class. They are a very good class of people, and the land is among the best in B.C.'[53]

The Gordons' first house, in a deep wood amidst firs and spruces, was a single room with walls of rough logs and a ladder to the second floor, which held makeshift sleeping accommodation for the children. 'It makes more work too, having bedroom, sitting room, kitchen and dining room all in one, but it is cheerful.' Annie later recollected how Jim 'sawed the flooring,' but she 'laid it.' Most important was the matter of making a living. The *Inland Sentinel* article reported that 'the principal interest is the raising of vegetables, for which there is an excellent market,' which explains Jim's hope of planting 'three acres of vegetables' in the early spring of their first year on the ranch.[54]

The family first planted potatoes, which were washed away, along with Jim's newly built bridge, in the great 'flood of 1894,' when 'the water came within a foot of our door.' The spring flood was widespread across British Columbia, causing rivers to rise in disastrous fashion. The family no sooner regrouped than they were almost burned out. Annie wrote home in June 1894 how 'we had to fight a bush fire one day, and got it put out all right. Marshy Dan fell into the water one day, and was nearly drowned, we got a terrible fright.' A decade later, Marsh vividly recalled 'the flood of '94 which came right up to the doorstep, the too frequent appearance of inquisitive bears which were extremely numerous in the cedar swamps, the forest fire which threatened our house and would have destroyed it but for the sudden changing of the wind.'[55]

The Gordons again recovered. 'We have a garden planted with peas, beans, corns, beets, carrots, lettuce and parsnips & radishes.' They replanted 'an acre of potatoes,' which produced 'half a ton,' and Annie also grew tomatoes, peppers, and cucumbers. The property contained several acres of hazelnut bushes, which cheered Annie. 'We have a cow and a very fine calf, also a horse and a dog which is the whole of our live stock at present.' Most importantly, 'the land is very rich, and there is not a stone on it.' For all of Annie's brave face, it was back-breaking work, she acknowledged. 'I have been at work from six in the morning until nine at night ever since I came here.' It was also a lonely business, particularly when Jim was away. 'I haven't set eyes on a woman for weeks, but day before yesterday two of them came.'[56]

Jessie promised her sister that she would spend a month on the ranch before heading home to Pictou County, but as the end of term neared at Campbell Creek she debated with herself over the best course of action. As always, the money factor loomed large, and she pondered whether she should 'teach again for a couple of months – it would help my pocket quite a bit.' Leaving Campbell Creek at the beginning of July, Jessie stopped off in Kamloops, where, after some initial hesitation, she took the teachers' examination to renew her British Columbia credentials just in case. Making it to the ranch, Jessie was not impressed by what she described as 'the backwoods, for backwoods it certainly is, more so than any place I ever was before.' Annie's new house was 'of a comfortable size but it is surrounded by such big trees that it really looks tiny & the children, as I got my first glimpse of them, looked like little fair-haired sprites.' Even though Jessie considered that 'I should find it rather inconvenient somehow,' the sisters' time together stretched into six weeks. 'It's hard to tear myself away from here.' The visit was the most satisfactory they'd had since Annie's marriage, for Jim was away much of the time and they had each other very much like their previous years together. They hunted for 'raspberries, black currants (wild) and gooseberries' with the children, or the more adventurous Annie went out on her own while Jessie cared for them at home. 'I tell Annie she won't have a whole dud left by the time she gets her supply of jam put up.'[57]

Over time Jessie was caught up in Annie's optimism. 'The ranch seems to agree with every one, & they all like it so much better than Kamloops ... I believe the life will suit Annie.' Part of the reason was pure economics. 'It doesn't cost them much more than a quarter to live here, of what it did in Kamloops, and they take great delight in having a place of their own.' The religious factor helped to change Jessie's mind, for the resident Methodist minister was none other than the Rev. James Calvert, whom she knew from Nicola Lake. As Jessie noted with interest, 'they too are living in a little log house, & as it is Mrs C's' first experience in such a life I guess she finds it trying enough.' It was during Jessie's time on the ranch that the Gordons arranged for Calvert 'to have service in our house here every second Sunday.' The work of domestication was under way. Jessie reflected as she prepared to leave the ranch in late August: 'They are a contented lot – those Salmon Armers, & have great faith in the future of their Valley.'[58]

Jessie left for home in September 1894 content that she and her beloved Nan had renewed sisterhood's bonds. It is unclear what were Jessie's intentions as she headed east. She had just taken the teachers' examination, and this suggests she intended to return to British Columbia. However, as she prepared to leave Annie, she assured Catherine: 'Don't you begin to fret yourself mother as to the possibility of my finding the old home lonely – I, who have lived "my lee lone" – & stood it too. No ma'am, not a bit of it – it may take me a while to fit into my old *place* again quite smoothly, but I'll get there in time, you'll see, & glad enough of it too.' Jessie did not contradict her young nephew Marshie when he wailed at her departure, 'I'll never see auntie again.' On the way home, she renewed sisterhood's bonds by stopping in Saint John to visit her sister Mary Belle, who considered her just back from the frontier. When Jessie's brother-in-law teased her that she '*didn't* look very wild!' she was tempted to 'pretend to have a six-shooter under my pillow.'[59]

The McQueen family home, constructed in 1852 at Sutherland's River, as it appeared in 2001

Jessie and Annie McQueen's parents, Daniel and Catherine McQueen

Jessie and Annie's older brother, George, taken while at Dalhousie College, 1878

Jessie at Truro Normal School, 1885

Annie at Truro Normal School, 1887

Annie with her pupils at Nicola Lake school during 1887–8

Annie McQueen and Jim Gordon's wedding photo, taken in Goderich, Ontario, in 1889

Mary Campbell of Campbell Creek, where Jessie taught during 1893–4, with her youngest daughter, Henrietta

The Gordon family on their Salmon Arm ranch c.1894

Rowena Phillipps of Tobacco Plains, where the Gordons lived from 1898 to 1902, with her son Michael, or Nessie, and daughter-in-law Mary Paul Luke Palook

Dal Gordon peeking behind Rowena Phillipps's brother Paul David at Tobacco
Plains, 1898

Jim and Annie Gordon with their children, Marsh, Jessie, and Dal, during the family's visit to Goderich, Ontario, in 1902

Catherine McQueen as a widow

Annie Gordon as a widow and social reformer

Marsh, Jessie, and Dal Gordon as young adults in front of the family home in Victoria

Jessie McQueen with her nephew Dal Gordon during her visit to Oxford University in 1920

Then disaster intervened. During her year at Campbell Creek, Jessie had repeatedly expressed concern over her parents' situation at Sutherland's River. 'I can't help thinking & wondering if you are having it cold at home, & if you have plenty of coal in and everything comfortable. Won't you have some one this winter to tend the barn – it isn't fit for any of you folk. Father mustn't wear himself out cutting wood – coal is cheap, & fathers are scarce & dear, *very scarce* & *very dear* in my part of the country.' She did what she could at a distance. 'I'm going to put in a few stamps, to save you extra trips to the Post Office.' It was not enough. Daniel McQueen died of a stroke on 3 October 1894, just three days after Jessie arrived back in Sutherland's River.[60]

What should have been a joyous homecoming became a time of mourning. Of all the family members, it was Annie in faraway British Columbia who was most affected. 'It's the first time death has ever touched us, Jessie ... I never felt the distance from home or my own poverty as much as I do know ... I am very lonely for my own kin.' Jessie had no time to comfort her beloved younger sister, for it was her mother and older sister Janie who demanded all of her attention. As Annie noted aptly four months after Daniel McQueen's death, 'you folks at home have in some ways the easier, and in other ways the hardest of the trouble to bear.' The pressures on Jessie to stay home, at least for a time, to help her mother were enormous. Jim counselled Jessie to 'be good to her [Catherine], Jessie, and you will have your own load lightened in so doing.'[61] Jessie's acquiescence means virtually no letters have survived about what transpired, apart from her rare visits away from Sutherland's River.

Even more than might otherwise have been the case, Jessie resumed daughterhood's obligations. Visiting her sisters Eliza in Dartmouth and Dove near Wolfville, Nova Scotia, early in 1895, she felt obliged to account for every cent spent. Catherine, Jane, and Jessie lived a frugal lifestyle in which needed cash came, as it had all along, from selling butter. Such other necessities as straw and wood often arrived in the form of donations from 'neighbors mindful of us.' With Jessie back in Sutherland's River, the link between the two youngest McQueen sisters was sustained by her role as aunt to her namesake and to Marsh, who kept waiting for their 'really truly Auntie' to come back. Annie noted wryly, 'I only wish B.C. could be moved a little nearer to N.S.'[62]

Sisterhood's bonds could not compete with daughterhood's obligations. Returned to Pictou County, Jessie's half dozen years in British Columbia seemed never to have existed, for she was back into exactly the same set of circumstances as before she had headed west six years earlier. Then, in 1888, she was a young woman, of prime marriageable age by Pictou County norms and still capable of dreaming. Now, in 1894, she was entering her mid-thirties and seemingly fixed in place as a dutiful daughter.

Chapter Nine

Annie on the Frontier

SALMON ARM
TRAIL
CROW'S NEST LANDING
TOBACCO PLAINS
GATEWAY

When Jessie departed British Columbia for Nova Scotia at the end of August 1894, she left Annie behind just as Annie had abandoned her almost six years earlier upon getting married and moving east to Ontario. Once again the sisters' lives diverged. Annie engaged the frontier at Salmon Arm, whereas Jessie returned to her earlier status as, in a literal sense, the dutiful daughter of Pictou County.

The long months Jessie sought to sustain domesticity on the McQueen family farm at Sutherland's River saw her sister Annie do much the same at Salmon Arm. Annie wrote home more often than usual, both because of her loneliness and of the need to comfort her widowed mother. Annie was remarkably honest about the back-breaking nature of frontier life. With Jessie's departure came great bouts of loneliness, making her grateful that 'I have to work so hard that I am utterly exhausted by the time I get to bed, for then I go to sleep at once.'[1]

Part of the demands put on Annie were inevitable, but the other part grew out of the need for Jim to maintain his furniture sales job, and also assist his brother in his Kamloops store, in order to make ends meet. He did so even as the couple sought to create a viable agricultural enterprise. The year before the Gordons' arrival, a nearby settler put in five thousand tomato plants, whose produce he successfully shipped that fall. Their second spring the Gordons planted tomatoes with mixed results. 'We gathered nearly all our tomatoes yesterday, for the heavy frosts were threatening them, and have about twelve hundred pounds of green tomatoes. The Ponderosas were something enormous, and were very productive too, but a large number were imperfect. The Optimus plants produced perfectly adapted fruits, but they were not large.'[2]

Amidst ups and downs, the homestead slowly took shape 'Our log house is quite spruce now with its new ceiling and boarded walls, covered with cotton.' Jim added a barn in the late fall of 1894. When it was dry enough but not so windy that the buildings were in danger of catching fire, trees were cut and their stumps and brush burned. Annie was hopeful that, 'if we get a good burn on, they will all burn up.' A couple of months later: 'I am longing for warm weather, so we can get the slashing burned ... The land is thoroughly cleaned and safe from one hundred and fifty to two hundred feet around the buildings, so when we have a favorable wind, all will be safe.'[3]

Left alone most of the time with two young children, sometimes a hired man, and a collie intended as a guard dog, Annie shouldered all of the demands of the frontier. 'The calf has led me the life of a dog ever since Jim left. I have to lead him back and forth to the slough and corral, and he hauls me over headfirst into the mud two or three times every trip, and if snags catch my clothes, there is no time to loose them, tear they go.' As was usual in such ventures, poultry were women's work, and Annie enthused: 'My new chicken house is nice and warm, and I am very much pleased with it ... Now the place really begins to look like a farm.' As Jim headed back to Kamloops shortly after their first Salmon Arm Christmas, she waxed philosophical. 'I will have so much slopping around outside to do, but it cannot be helped.'[4]

Much as for Jessie at Lower Nicola a half decade earlier, each season had its own imperatives. Winter proved the most difficult. 'The upstairs will be too cold for anyone to sleep in through the winter, but Jim will make a hatch to cover up the opening for the ladder.' Water for washing had to be carried up from the river or, when it was high enough, from a slough nearer to the house, and Annie fretted as cold weather approached. 'I will have so much to do, for there will be men working here most of the time [clearing the land of trees sold to a nearby lumber mill for needed cash], and the washing will be a nasty job in the cold weather.' Several months later, Annie rejoiced at having found a neighbour, who for $1.25 assisted in 'a big washing,' the first 'for over two weeks, for the slough was pretty frozen to the bottom.' The chickens required special care as the temperature dropped, Annie realized their first January. 'My hens have begun to lay. We put up a little box stove in the chicken house, and it seems to be what is needed. I feed them hot feed in the morning, and they rustle food for themselves the rest of the day.' Annie hoped to 'get some eggs to sell, but this family of mine gobbles them as fast as they arrive.' Whatever the season, Annie economized so far as possible. Together with farm produce, they ate deer meat. 'A parcel from Eaton's' arrived in the spring of 1895 'containing flannelette, ticking for a petticoat for me, pins, garters, pillow cases, boot buttons, overalls & smock for Jim, gingham for a working dress for me.' That was not the only sewing the parcel entailed, for 'the flannelette is for drawers for the children and myself.'[5] Jim's absences had their compensation, as with his once bringing back a box of oranges.

Even as the work of ranching proceeded, so did the work of domestication. A steady stream of visitors from among nearby settlers meant Annie baked 'twice a week, five loaves and a pan of buns each time.' Despite her protestations that 'I see so few women that when they come in a bunch like that, they frighten me,' and 'I have no intimate friends, and don't want them,' Annie remained very much a social being. Going to visit 'an English woman, formerly a governess,' she was flattered that 'she had all the family plate out in honor of my visit,' even though 'it did look out of place in that rough log shack.' Annie dispensed first aid to her neighbours, as with her doing 'up a finger,' which gave another conduit to encouraging appropriate standards of behaviour.[6]

Such sociability kept Annie in touch with larger events, so that she was able to retail to Jessie back home at Sutherland's River each little morality tale as it unfolded. Annie had briefly boarded with the Riley family, with whom Jessie stayed and got to know while teaching at Nicola Lake. This meant that when someone 'brought word' that a family member was implicated, the story was told even more deliciously than usual. 'Tishy Riley has a baby, and very nearly lost her life. The foolish child was out at the rink, skating, the night before the baby was born. The doctor had to be called through the night, and when he came, she told him that she "just had cramps." He answered rather sternly that she was in labor, and she flared up and denied it, saying that she had only been married two months. When he came to examine her, he found that her sides were black from being laced so tightly to conceal her condition, and the interior organs displaced from the same cause. Another doctor had to be sent for and even then they did not think it possible to save her, but she managed to get through, but the doctor's opinion is that she will never know health again.'[7] The tone of the letter makes absolutely clear that, while the frontier had its exigencies, boundaries for right behaviour still held. Annie added, for good measure, that the Rev. James Calvert knew the entire story. The freedom the frontier gave existed only so long as it did not infringe on the values that newcomer women, and men, brought with them whence they came.

Annie encouraged right behaviour. Sometimes it was just a word or a nod, as with Annie's support for one of the workmen on the ranch whose 'hymns are displacing the rough songs.' She explained to Jessie how 'he has a hearty, sonorous voice, and he knows lots of those ringing, catchy tunes, so he's roped the boys in.' Another time, when a neighbouring rancher opposed the choice of teacher 'on account of her religion,' which was Methodism, Annie felt no qualms in rejoicing that 'our influence counts far more than his.' The Gordons aligned themselves closely with the Rev. James Calvert and his wife, whose presence was influential in their settling at Salmon Arm in the first place. Annie noted proudly in February 1895 how the Sunday services held in their house had the 'biggest crowd yet, every available seat full, one sitting on the bed.' Something more was afoot. 'Tomorrow evening there is to be a congregational meeting in our house. We are going to build a log church, hewn logs, and they are going to meet to talk it over.' A few months later: 'The new church is not to be finished now until after seeding. Everyone is too busy.'[8]

For all of the back-breaking work that Annie, and Jim when at home, put into the ranch, it became clear from quite early on that it was not enough. Even though Jim did double duty, money was always in short supply. Annie pretended optimism her first Christmas: 'At present the family finances are rather low. We cannot say we feel poor however, for we have plenty of food for stock and ourselves, all paid for, and everything about the place paid for, and our buildings so comfortable and substantial if they aren't beautiful.'[9]

Much of the difficulty lay in the cost of getting to market the vegetables and other items that the Gordons and their neighbours produced. During their second year on the ranch, the man who ran the local sawmill announced he was 'going to run a steamer from here down to Savona this summer, so we will have cheaper freight than on the C.P.R.' The ploy was not enough, and Annie groused her second autumn, 'I am afraid we will be rank protectionists if we stay on the farm, for the American farmers are swamping the Coast and Kootenay with cheap farm truck, and consequently we are left lamenting. However, cows, chickens and fruit are still profitable, so we will not despair.'[10] The tendency for Annie, and others, to lay blame on the United States served to nurture a sense of common identity among the Gordons and their neighbours as British Columbians and Canadians.

How close the Gordons walked the edge of financial ruin is indicated by Annie's unusually frank reflection at the end of her second season on the ranch. 'I felt a little anxious for fear we wouldn't have money enough to meet all expenses this winter, but things are looking a little better now. Of course we have to be very careful, and do no unnecessary spending, but I think we will be all right. The daily bread and butter come to quite a lot in this expensive country, and sickness of any kind is the most expensive luxury one can indulge in.' Annie worried about how her husband was being affected. 'I think Jim felt a good deal discouraged over the little we had to show for all our hard summer's work, chickens gone and potatoes turning out so poorly, and then he wasn't allowed to go on his Eastern trip until a month after he ought to have gone, and lost a great deal of business by it.' It must be God's will. 'We decided not to give way to discouragement, and to do the very best we could, and leave the rest to a higher hand.'[11]

All the same, Annie acknowledged, life was very difficult over the short run. Alone and pregnant with her third child during the Gordons' second fall on the ranch, she grew less sanguine about being 'shut up here in the woods.' It became harder for her to cope. 'I am alone here [and] doubly lonely when he is away.' The pregnancy brought new demands, both literally and figuratively. 'I felt guilty in getting even the cheap dress goods I did get, but I had only one old wrapper that I could get on, and it will soon be too small for me. I am getting so very large all over especially my shoulders and hips ... The weight is almost unbearable at times even now.' The Gordons' third child came along without 'the aid of doctor or nurse' on 14 February 1896, being christened on account of the day of his birth Eric Valentine and known in the family as Dal.[12]

As the Gordons' venture tumbled down on itself, it was Jessie who came to the rescue. After twenty months at home, she headed west for the third time, in May of 1896. Her obligations to others caused her to leave Sutherland's River for British Columbia once again. Annie wanted her sister by her side, to give material assistance and to share in her loneliness. When the local school at Upper Salmon Arm became vacant at the end of March, she encouraged Jessie to apply. The ploy was successful because, for the McQueen trio back at Sutherland's River, something had to be done in any case. Even Catherine agreed 'that perhaps it was best to go West when there was the chance of a school.' Money played the central role it had always done. The three women huddled together on the family homestead had virtually no means of support. Catherine was approaching her mid-seventies, and Jane, whose prognosis was always uncertain, was never more than a helper around the farm. It was not just Jessie's widowed mother and sister Jane who needed to be sustained, but also Mary Belle, whose husband was 'only earning enough to pay house-rent.'[13]

In making the decision, Jessie felt herself caught between daughter-hood's obligations and sisterhood's bonds. 'If you think it best though mother for me to stay, just say the word – I want to do what is best for all of us – and my very heart is weak within me at times when I think of going away from you ... I can wire a refusal at any time, & *will* if you wish it.' At the same time, 'the money is not to be despised, & Annie at the end of the line is a pull – but there's a pull at this end too, & it's not easy to pull up stakes [for] I'm a bigger coward than I was eight years ago.' A third factor played a role. As it had earlier with Annie and later with Liz Olding, a common perception existed that health improved in British Columbia. Jessie's doctor brother-in-law, who always considered that she was not as well as she should be, advised Catherine that 'it will be better for Jessie's health to go West for a while, hard as it seems to let her go.'[14]

Even as Catherine acquiesced to her daughter's departure, she ensured that Jessie knew at what cost she went. Among the tasks she took up, almost as if to chide her daughter for having abandoned her, was to put a headstone on the grave of Daniel McQueen, some twenty months dead. Jessie may have still been on the train west when Catherine wrote, in a letter chock-a-block with religious platitudes, about how 'I would like his children & grandchildren would know where he was laid.' A visiting salesman had talked her into a headstone, even though she considered 'tis not right' to make a display 'while many are in need bodies & soul.' As to paying for it, 'I sold the big cow for [$]25 & that will pay to within 5 dollars of cost ... send a slip next time & let me know what you & Annie think of the matter.' Any 'slip' sent in response would have been removed before the letter made its usual round through the family and eventually into an archive. Catherine took care to remind Jessie how busy she was now that her daughter was gone. 'There is so many little things to look to that I have to do, hens, calves & things about the barn, and I have not felt any too strong lately.' Another time, 'thought you were more tardy than usual, but take all the sunny time you can get & I'll wait till you get time to write.'[15] Guilt-making almost became an art at times.

On Jessie's third trip west in May 1896, she was buttressed by family gifts for the Gordons and a 'lunch basket' put together by Mary Belle when she stopped on the way in Saint John. 'I've got dish towels, pudding dish, and a hat for Annie – hat something like my own. Also maple sugar & a small set of garden tools for the children, besides other little things. Spade, hoe & rake cost 19 cents & can be strapped in my umbrella. For my lunch I have a glass of rhubarb, a small loaf ... sandwiches, horseradish, crackers, cheese, hard boiled eggs, cream & a small glass of honey ... Belle has a 2 x 9 loaf in the oven for me now, so I'll live high, but I wish there were some one to share up.'[16] Jessie never forgot that first glorious trip west with her cousin Ed Olding.

Nor had Jessie forgot her earlier ambivalence toward the Gordons' ranch. Just as it was two years earlier, 'that five-mile drive in was *awfully* rough' and the mosquitoes were a bother. All the same, the bonds of sisterhood still held, captured in Mary Belle's last line in her first letter to Jessie again in British Columbia. 'Love to all Nan's family, which now includes yourself.' Jessie took pride that her niece and older nephew 'seem to remember me perfectly – talk over lots of things we used to do, & Jessie even remembered my old sailor hat.' She assured her mother, 'Annie fears I'll be lonely here, but I haven't the slightest desire to go anywhere, or see anything.' The Gordons had a hired man who did the outdoor chores in Jim's absence, and Jessie enjoyed 'the daily three-cornered squabbles that enliven us. It's a wordy war, of course, & all the better fun on that account.'[17]

Jessie was in the classroom by the end of May 1896, a week after her arrival. The next day she reported to Superintendent of Education S.D. Pope that 'there are 12 in attendance and 2 more to arrive.' Despite half a dozen years' teaching in British Columbia, her basis of comparison still lay firmly in Pictou County. 'But as I always said about B.C. children, that means as much work as twice the number of others.' The Upper Salmon Arm school was opposite the newly built Methodist church about two kilometres from the Gordons' ranch. As described by Jessie, the schoolhouse was 'fairly large but not much luxury about it – bench seats with no backs, & daylight to be seen through the many cracks.'[18]

Jessie walked to school each morning with her namesake niece, who was six and a half, and sometimes also with Marshie, not yet five and fast becoming a typical frontier child. 'I usually leave about a quarter of eight. Marshie went three days this week, & as he has to measure every tree with his eyes, from top to butt, our progress is rather slow. He knows all the trees, cedar, fir, pine, popular, alder, and it's comical to see him run his eye up them, & remark on the "tallness" and "very big butt" of some.' She took note how 'they go barefoot most of the time, and many a "snub" the poor little toes get in its roots & snags in the way.' Jessie was less sanguine about the walk home. 'I suppose I'll get used to it. The lunch-basket on one hand, & one of the little people in the other, most of the way, drags me a bit, for it's a full mile and a half, but I suppose it's little enough to do for $60 a month.' The school having been vacant for some time, Jessie worried that her pupils 'would weary of the confinement after running wild all day long, but they do very well indeed.' Two boys were 'inclined to be troublesome, at first,' for they 'expected to have a jolly good time with the new teacher, seeing she was a *woman*, but these same jolly times seem to have turned up missing.' Jessie acknowledged, perhaps for the first time, that she rather enjoyed being a teacher. 'I like all the school-work – enjoy fitting myself into the harness once more, and the scholars are beginning to act as though they liked the work too.'[19]

Jessie's arrival coincided with – perhaps made possible – yet another move on Jim's part. In her first letter home, Jessie wrote a bit disingenuously how 'Jim is going to Rossland for a while so it is rather fortunate that I happened along when I did.' Located almost three hundred kilometres south of Salmon Arm and eight kilometres north of the border with the United States, Rossland was a hard-rock mining boomtown high in a mountain range. It had sprung up out of nowhere in just the last few years, and there were fortunes to be made. Home just a day and a half, Jim was off again. 'He has gone to Rossland for the summer – some position there, I think. Annie has spoken of his being wanted for it, several times before.' Whatever else Jim was doing, he continued to sell furniture. Communication with him was cut to a weekly letter he and Annie exchanged and to third parties, such as a Salmon Arm neighbour who 'brought samples of the famous ore from Jim.'[20]

Jessie spent her six-week summer holiday with Annie on the ranch, planning to return to the Upper Salmon Arm school in mid-August. She was prevented from doing so by a series of incidents exemplifying the problematic character of frontier life. A neighbour who was the father of one or two school children drowned 'helping the men drive logs down the river.' A second neighbour, an Englishwoman who 'drinks when she gets the chance' and 'the mother of three of my scholars,' left her husband while he was away at work in the railroad yard in Kamloops for another man. After another neighbour disappeared in early August while out hunting, Jessie threw up her hands. 'This tragedy may affect us all as to our plans & intentions, for it will probably mean the loss of three children to the school, & that, as it is so small a one, will close it.' Attempting to explain what 'no one could have foreseen,' Jessie resorted to providence. 'It must be all right, though we can't exactly understand it.'[21]

Jessie's dilemma had consequences for both sisters' lives. 'If I have to leave here, Annie won't stay alone, & Jim can't afford to stay at home, with markets at their present low rate.' The uncertainty was compounded by the idiosyncratic nature of the frontier. Mink made off with some forty of the ducks Annie was raising, whereupon, Jessie wrote home, 'Annie sold ten of her young ducks @ 50¢ each. Thought that better than making mink pie of them ... the woods are full of these critters.' A month later, Annie lamented how a skunk 'got my last two ducks, little fellows.'[22] The ranch seemed to be collapsing down upon the Gordons.

Once again it was Jessie who took the initiative. The only commodity she had to sell was her labour in the form of a teaching credential. Few locations were better in which to market it than booming Rossland, where Jim was spending so much of his time. Although he 'was delighted with the place – so much go ahead in it,' and even bought a house in anticipation of the family's move there, initially Jessie was not impressed. 'It makes me tired to think of living in such a whirl of business as they do there. Salmon Arm is good enough for me.'[23]

Nonetheless, Jessie applied to teach in Rossland, in the interim reopening the Upper Salmon Arm school. Having taught the first three days of September, Annie informed their mother, 'a telegram came from Rossland for Jessie, and she is off.' As for justifying her actions to Superintendent Pope, Jessie explained how she had 'received a telegram from Rossland on Sept 3rd notifying me of my appointment as teacher of the third department, duties to commence Monday 7th.' She had no compunction about not 'giving the required notice' before leaving the Upper Salmon Arm school, for the average attendance in August was only 8.75 and yet another family was about to leave. Two of the three trustees had resigned a few weeks earlier, and the third was away looking for work. Even so, she got their 'full & free consent' to close the school. Jessie left the schoolhouse key with a responsible person in anticipation that, when 'times improve generally ... we may again have a flourishing school.' She ended her letter astutely. 'I did my best to keep that school together, and only when it was in imminent danger of leaving me, did I leave it.'[24]

The die was cast. As Annie explained to her mother, 'it seemed a special act of Providence when that school turned up.' She made plans to follow Jessie and Jim to Rossland with their three young children. 'We are all to go down as soon as we can get ready, and I assure you I am both lonely and busy,' Annie told Catherine. She had no second thoughts. 'It has been a long time for Jim to be separated from his family, but we would not have gone unless Jessie could go too.' For three seasons, the Gordons had tried to make a go of their Salmon Arm ranch, and all they had to show for it was Jim in worse health than ever, for very soon, if not already, he developed an ulcer. In no way was the Gordons' experience unique, for the area was, Jessie reflected on her departure, awash with 'forsaken homesteads.' When the Upper Salmon Arm school began in August 1895, twenty-three pupils were enrolled, a total that shrunk to nine and was heading downward even further upon Jessie's departure a year later. Annie pondered as she packed up their home, 'I wonder sometimes if I ever will look back to this as a happy time.' Among the few material possessions that continued to remind the Gordons of this episode in their life was what Marsh lovingly described a decade later in a school essay as 'a large photograph of our house and neighborhood.'[25]

In the event, Annie did not move to Rossland to be with Jessie. Rather, she began a peregrination that would send the Gordons, over the next decade, to the farthest edges of the frontier that was being created by the hard-rock mining boom. Jim realized that he could not support a family by farming alone. Selling furniture was uncertain. So he looked to the rapidly expanding public sector of southeastern British Columbia. The mining frenzy compelled the federal government to establish customs offices at the various locations where, from the early 1890s, mining equipment was being brought in from the United States and ore shipped out. At Rossland in the summer of 1896, Jim may have been working on a temporary basis for the Canadian customs post established there on July 1st. In any case, in the middle of October, he was officially appointed a sub-collector of customs, to be stationed at nearby Trail.[26] Ten kilometres distant, Trail was like Rossland a creature of the Kootenays mining boom. A narrow gauge rail line had just been completed between the two towns, and a smelter to receive Rossland's ore was approaching completion there.

The appointment meant that Annie and the children headed to Trail rather than to Jessie at Rossland. For the time being, the Gordons held on to the ranch at Salmon Arm, but it never became more than a holiday destination. Jessie visited them at Christmas, and perhaps once or twice at other times of the year she saw Jim when he came to Rossland on business, but that was about it. The sisters once again went their separate ways. The best description of the Gordons' life in Trail comes from a school essay Marsh wrote a decade later. He recalled the town as 'in a

very flourishing condition' with its smelter 'running full blast.' Aged six
at the time he lived in Trail, Marsh was most taken by the rail trip from
Trail to Rossland. 'The trainmen literally used to "let 'er rip" coming
down and as a certain engineer graphically expressed it, "It takes us two
hours to go up and about two minutes to come down."' With a touch of
bravado, Marsh added that 'passengers for the first time used to hold
their breaths but grew callous after a few trips.' The Gordons lived fru-
gally and saved their money, but they did not much like the place. Jim's
health problems flared up, and 'the Dr says his stomach is ulcerated.' It
was for this reason, Marsh explained, that Jim requested a transfer. 'The
constant fumes of the smelter proved too much for my father's health
and on this account we were forced to leave after a year's stay in the
town.'[27]

Jim Gordon was transferred, in the summer of 1897, to the less hectic
customs post of Crow's Nest Landing. According to Marsh, the post was
'created by the construction of the Crows Nest Railway, which had
begun.' Sited in the southeast corner of British Columbia, about two
hundred kilometres east of Trail at the mouth of the Elk River, the
post's purpose was to monitor goods crossing the border through two
means. The first was by steamboat on the Kootenay River, and the second was by 'a wagon road in fair condition.' Both routes linked the rail
construction, as well as the agricultural and mining settlement of Fort
Steele, with the Great Northern Railroad running west from St Paul,
Minnesota, across Montana. Marsh recalled how 'three steamboats running from American towns passed daily for awhile and many dozens of
loaded wagons from the same places all carrying supplies for the construction camps which were obliged to obtain everything from that
direction until the line should be completed through the Crows Nest
Pass.' They all had 'to be examined' by Jim, Annie explained.[28]

The job was less onerous than it had been in Trail. Jim bragged,
'there is *very* little office work & *I am* outside nearly all the time. Chop
the wood, catch the fish & hunt the deer but no catchee.' Annie was particularly pleased since, three months there, 'Jim has been steadily getting better for a long time now with only occasional back turns.' The
Gordons once again looked to settling down. 'We have been turned
upside down nearly ever since we came here fixing up the house &c. We
have a kitchen built on 12 x 20 and hope to be quite comfortable this
winter. I like the country very much. Annie says it's the prettiest she has
ever seen – much the same as Kamloops district & fine for ranching.'[29]

Wiser by virtue of their Salmon Arm experience, the Gordons eyed 'a ranch, across the river from us, without any heavy trees on it, about eight acres is meadow, without even a bush on it, twenty more acres have scrubby little willow and alders on, and the remainder is bench land with bunch grass on it.' Jim particularly liked how 'all kinds of vegetables & fruit grow nicely & all in all it is an ideal country.' Four months after arriving, the Gordons pre-empted 160 acres of the coveted land, for which they had to pay a $2 recording fee, $200 to the man who had it before them for his rights, and $50 for the surveyor's fee. As Annie explained to her mother, they were obliged 'to put a certain amount of improvements on it, also a respectable house,' and after two years to pay $1/acre to the government. Christmas 1897, the Gordons could afford to send $15 to Catherine, and the children 'a dollar of their money for Aunty Jane to buy herself a present, as there are no shops here.' Annie explained how 'they have earned it mudding up the cracks between the logs, and pulling wood in the yard for papa.'[30]

Hopeful of staying put, Annie took stock of her new frontier. Some neighbours she deemed acceptable, others not. It was no small matter that the customs collector and his wife favoured some persons over others. At Crow's Nest Landing two months, she lamented that, apart from a family who kept a saloon and stopping house, 'we haven't many neighbors.' A couple of months later, Annie reiterated her point. 'As for society, there is none.' Overall, the pluses outweighed the minuses. 'We are not awfully in love with the folks here, but they might be worse, and Jim's health is improving right along.'[31]

The one bright spot was, not unexpectedly, a Nova Scotian connection. Jim reported in September that 'the teacher here is a Miss Lyons from Truro who was attending Normal school same time as Annie did.' The two became such fast friends that they 'think of going back to N.S. next summer.' If so, Jim had no compunction about expecting his unmarried sister-in-law Jessie to assume Annie's role while she was away. 'If they do you'll have to come & keep house for me after you come from Victoria [taking the teachers' examination], don't you do any kicking now you've got to do it.' Unfortunately for the Gordons, Stella Lyons, at age twenty-seven, was highly marriageable by Nova Scotian standards. She was pursued by three different local men, described by Annie as a forty-year-old from 'a good old Southern family' who had 'led a pretty rapid life,' a member of the Provincial Police, and 'an ex-cowboy and former member of Buffalo Bill's gang.'[32] The year was barely out but that Stella Lyons selected out, and married, her southern gentleman.

However remote the locale, organized religion continued to function

as a prime means of domestication. There was only one Protestant clergyman, according to Annie, in all of the East Kootenays, and at least
once, and likely more often, she snared him. Annie took special pleasure in telling her mother that 'we have a real live Presbyterian preacher
in the house tonight, and had service in the schoolhouse at which nearly
all the Landing were present.' A Catholic neighbour 'lent her organ and
even played the hymns for us, and brought all her family out to service.'[33] As in the Nicola Valley, religion had to be got wherever and in
whatever form available.

In the event, the ranch at Crow's Nest Landing became yet another
byway for the Gordons. Annie realized early on that 'we have no surety
of being left in peace.' Marsh described what happened. 'After construction, all trade fell off almost completely. The steamboats ceased running
and the long lines of freighters with their loaded wagons appeared no
more. As there was no longer anything to keep the place alive everyone
began to move away and soon the place was almost deserted.' Annie and
Jim might like the peace and quiet, but from the perspective of Canada
Customs the post lost its purpose. 'The government accordingly moved
us to a place some twenty miles away.'[34]

The relocated customs post was on Tobacco Plains, a valley ten to fifteen kilometres wide and fifty kilometres long crossing from the extreme
southeastern corner of British Columbia into Montana. 'The chances
are that we will be moved to the Boundary Line this fall. ... I will be glad
to be settled somewhere. However, we won't know for certain what is to
be for some time yet. I am tired of moving.' Annie got her wish in the
sense that the move, at the end of September 1898, less than a year after
arriving at Crow's Nest Landing, would hold for several years. 'We are
within six miles of the Tobacco post office [in Montana] now ... The
Boundary line between the U.S. and Canada is only a few minutes walk
from our door.' Their mailing address was 'Canadian Customs, Tobacco,
Montana, U.S.' From there, twice weekly mail service operated to Kal-
ispell, on the Great Northern Railway running across the northern
United States. This reliance on the United States caused Annie to assert
her national biases. 'I don't think much of some of our Montana neighbors. They are a lawless lot, but they are as meek as mice when they come
over here, for Canadian law is to be respected.'[35]

As a 'preventative officer,' James Gordon was the enforcer of that law
from the perspective of goods moving across the border. He recorded
mainly animals and settlers' effects, and collected duty on them. Jim also
had to keep his eyes out for smugglers, in particular, according to the

stories he told, Americans attempting to take horses illegally out of Canada. Jim's job was at the bottom of the Department of Customs salary scale at $900/year. Men designated collectors or sub-collectors received substantially higher salaries, especially if stationed at major entry points into Canada.[36] Jim's position was particularly important for helping to bring into the orbit of Canada a part of British Columbia which, prior to the mining boom, had been left to its own devices.

Once again the Gordons settled down. 'We are buying two acres [for $25/acre], which will gives us plenty of room for our buildings and for a nice garden ... Our new home has large cheerful rooms with good high ceilings. I feel as if I cannot be thankful enough for the pleasant change. Jim has built a chicken-house and a wood-shed since we came here.' As before, the family hoped to make money from growing vegetables. Just arrived, Annie enthused how 'potatoes sold for ten cents a pound' and a few months later 'sent for our seeds.' By the next August: 'We have already shipped over six hundred pounds of early cabbage, and a crate of cauliflower besides beets and a few green onions. We have arranged to sell our whole crop of cabbage at 2 1/2 cents a pound, and we will have at least three tons. We will have tons of onions too, but onions will be pretty cheap, only about $25 to $30 a ton ... Our great hope is our celery. We have fifteen hundred plants out and hope to sell them at a good figure ... Jim is chinking up the root house today to have it ready in good season for storing the crop. We will have turnips, potatoes, cabbage, carrots, parsnips, beets, onions, pumpkins and celery to store. We will have plenty for ourselves and some to sell.'[37]

In practice it was never quite so easy. The second year, competition began to take its toll. The garden was 'still paying its way,' so Annie reported home. 'We harvested our onion crop [and] we are pretty tired, as there was about fifteen hundred pounds of them. We had already disposed of a thousand pounds, which makes our onion crop a ton and a quarter.' Quantity did not equate with a profit. 'Prices are poor for onions this season as the Okanagan district has filled the market with them.' The Gordons persevered. A year later, in 1901, 'we have something in the neighbourhood of two thousand cabbage plants set out, which has kept us hard at work. Onions are doing well. Beets and turnips growing like weeds.'[38]

Annie again raised chickens. 'Chickens are a dollar apiece this year, and scarce at that. If I am spared I'll have a hundred to sell next fall.' These were not just any chickens, for Annie 'sent for some thoroughbred fowls, Brown Leghorns.' The next August, she was optimistic. 'I have orders for three of my young thoroughbred roosters at three dollars a piece. I have only four more to sell, and can so do that. We lost a lot of chickens this summer through neglect. I had not time to attend to so many, but I have over sixty very fine ones, nearly all thoroughbred.' Soon Annie lost faith in chickens and pinned her hopes on turkeys. 'My experience is that they are easier to raise than chickens. The whole thing is to keep them dry and feed them well, and they will eat anything you choose to give them, and are especially fond of porridge scraps.'[39] The Gordons puttered along, but they never made the profits so eagerly anticipated when they first arrived on Tobacco Plains.

All of this activity was insufficient to satisfy Annie. Tobacco Plains was, if anything, more remote than either Salmon Arm or Crow's Nest Landing, and she did not take well to the loneliness inherent for newcomer women. Annie lamented to her sister Eliza, the fall of her arrival, how 'I never write to, or get a letter from any of you without crying my eyes out – however, my pen is running away with me, and I need not inflict my woes on you.' Three months later it was Janie at Sutherland's River who received the brunt of her despair. 'Jane, this is the loneliest country I ever saw in my life. It is enough to give *anyone* the blues.' It was to Catherine that Annie complained the next summer. 'Dear mother, I haven't much that is cheerful to say have I?'[40]

One of the dreams that sustained Annie was a visit home to the Maritimes, but even this hope receded as time passed. Her first autumn on Tobacco Plains, she assured her mother: 'We are coming home next year, sure mother, if Providence permits ... I am getting so old and thin and anxious-eyed scratching for money to go home, that you and Jane will hardly know me when I get there.' To her sister Mary Belle, Annie was more open. 'I feel as if I must have dropped out of your lives, all of you, when I hear from you so seldom ... and I am very lonely for my own kin, in spite of having my husband and children for company. Sometimes I think I will die of the longing to see you all, but I guess I'm made tough, for I have gone through a lot, and I ain't dead yet.' That winter Annie's honesty extended to her mother. 'I think I will die outright with homesickness if I don't get home next year.' The practical kept intervening. 'Our railway fare alone will be over three hundred dollars, besides clothes and meals and berths, and other expenses. We will have to call at Ontario to see Grandma Gordon and the aunties.' The trip did not pan out, forcing Annie to look another year ahead. 'Next June, God willing, will see me at Sutherland's River again. I am so lonely and tired out that it seems very far away.'[41]

More traumatic for Annie was the realization that with each passing year the Pictou County she knew was slipping away. By the turn of the century, it was a decade since Annie had been in the Maritimes, and time was taking its toll. 'Received your bunch of papers safely. It makes me feel what a stranger I am in Pictou Co. when I read of so many names in the papers who are total strangers to me.' The symbols of her remembered childhood took on new meaning. 'Oh dear me! I do want to see you all so much, and apple blossom time will be along very shortly now, would that I could see it.' Unable to afford a trip home, Annie, who had always looked to others to do her bidding, cajoled her mother: 'I only wish you and Jane would come out here with me for a year. Couldn't you rent the farm for awhile and come out?' The next summer, Annie held out another enticement. 'I wish Jane could see our fine garden and chickens. I would have great pride in showing her around the place.' Catherine was wise to her youngest daughter's ways, so she shared with Jessie. 'Do you remember how Annie used to like to get away among strangers, poor child she has had more than enough of it.'[42]

Part of Annie's loneliness and self-pity stemmed from the very real demands put on her, as on virtually any frontier wife. In caring for home, family, and farm, she had to rely largely on her own resources. 'There is a lot of sewing before me when I get able for it. I feel it my duty to make over all the old clothes I can ... I have a good machine, and boys' clothes never do take very long.' The children were encouraged to improvise. 'Marshall and Dal are building forts and trenches in the hill beside the root house.' If that was not enough, there was also a husband who needed cosseting. Jim's health was an up-and-down affair. 'Jim has had a poorly spell, but seems better again.' Annie's first autumn on Tobacco Plains: 'Jim's stomach troubles him considerably, he has been around the house so much lately and that never suits him.' A week later, Annie was once again cautiously hopeful: 'Jim is much better, I am thankful to say, and I hope it may be permanent, but unless he gets something to *cure* this catarrh of the stomach, he will die in one of those dreadful attacks.'[43]

Annie's discontents were exacerbated by her own intermittent health problems, which also had no easy remedies on the frontier. 'I have been sick for the last three weeks, first had neuralgia and my cheek swelled up, boiled and broke. I was nearly wild with the pain, got no sleep for a week. Then just as I was beginning to crawl around once more, the grippe took me.' To her sister Jane, Annie confided: 'I am trying to take Pink Pills to build me up, but half the time I forget them, so if I don't get any good of them, it is not entirely their fault.' Her menstrual periods were irregular, causing her to rejoice whenever 'I went my full *four* weeks this month instead of three weeks or even less as I've been doing for some time past.' Annie had long had piles and a couple of years later: 'I am not well at present (usual thing!) and must cut my letter short, and rest my most miserable back and head.' The same summer, Annie had such 'a bad spell of rheumatism' that Jim had to fetch the doctor from the American side of the border. The doctor assured her that he could 'operate on the piles shortly, not the old cruel hot iron method, but by a new and simple one, which requires no anaesthetic, the pain is no more than a pin prick.'[44]

Annie's faltering self-image was linked to physical appearance. Well into her thirties, she was aging, and she knew it. Hoping to get home soon, she confided to Mary Belle: 'When we go, I am going straight through in my shabby clothes, for if we outfit here it would cost more than the trip home.' Later in the letter, she waxed philosophical. 'It is very exasperating, but I will have to bear my wrinkles and loss of teeth patiently.' The next summer, she lamented how 'my eyes won't stand either work or writing at night as once they would.' A year later, 'my hair was getting grayer than ever.' In 1901, as she approached her thirty-sixth birthday: 'It seems to me that I live nearly altogether in the past, like an old person. I guess I am old, in everything except actual years.' From time to time, Annie took herself in hand. In recent years, she had not ridden much, but it became one of the few pleasures open to her. 'I have not yet forgotten how to ride, a horse, I mean. Jim and I went for two rides lately, and I enjoyed it very much, though it did churn my innards most desperately. Jim was quite vain of my performance.'[45]

Annie considered the income from chickens to be hers alone, and it more than anything else boosted her self-confidence. 'I'm going to take my fowl money, and get myself some clothes. I haven't had a new dress for so long that I have forgotten what it feels like. Not that I needed any here. I could wear my old wrappers from one year's end to the other, if it wasn't just for my own self-respect.' Even such a decision embodied an element of regret. 'I am getting myself a new fall and winter dress, ordering it from Eaton's, and it bothers me very badly. I have samples, but I do not like any of them. I don't supposed I'll ever see a store for ages to choose for myself.' Next year's order was larger, including, among other items, a 'homespun walking skirt ($3.75).' Annie explained: 'I had to get myself a regular fit-out, almost, for I had been wearing old things so long, and nearly everything was worn to shreds. I got shoes, stockings, underwaists, shirtwaists, a comb, two ribbons for ties (the first I bought myself for ten years) and a skirt.' Again, it was chicken money that made the purchases possible. 'The blessed hens paid for everything, and for the Outlook and Youth's Companion too.'[46] The first was likely *Missionary Outlook*, a monthly publication of the Methodist Church of Canada; the second, a popular American monthly with a Protestant ethos.[47]

There was only so much that determination could effect. 'There is nothing out here to make life pleasant, not a service, or a lecture, nor a Sunday School, for my children are the only Protestants. Not a meeting of any kind ... oh dear! life is so monotonous. I feel sometimes as if I couldn't stand it. No one will ever know how *hard* it is unless they have lived in the wilderness like this.' If that were not enough, soon after the Gordons' arrival a hotel was built 'a few hundred yards away from us.' Annie could muse how 'I do not like the idea of liquor being sold so near to us,' but there was nothing much to be done.[48]

Organized religion was almost wholly absent. Previously, Annie had been able to inveigle a preacher to hold services from time to time; now she simply despaired. 'No church, no Sunday School, day school very shaky, always afraid it may be closed up ... Nothing of any interest ever going on and more than half the time our mail goes astray.' In August 1899 she got a respite, if from the dreadful United States. 'A Methodist minister from Kalispel, Montana, was up to see us a few weeks ago. He is going to have services at the Plains once a month, and will send us word so we can attend.' Annie was ambivalent, although, to her credit, she realized why so. 'I did not like the look of the man, but he may be better than he looks, and I may be prejudiced against him because he comes from Montana, for truly I have yet to see any one very nice from that country.'[49]

No aspect of everyday life more frustrated Annie than did the Gordons' immediate neighbour. 'I don't like the people there,' she fretted in anticipation of the move south to Tobacco Plains. There a few months: 'No one within hundreds of miles that a persons *wants* to see.'[50] Annie's difficulty lay in an aspect of difference that had so far passed her by, even while intimate to Jessie's frontier experience. The relative ease with which Jessie accommodated to hybridity in the classroom contrasted sharply with Annie's boundary-making, particularly in terms of her own children.

Michael Phillipps, from whom the Gordons bought their property on Tobacco Plains, was the well-born son of an Anglican clergyman. Out from England to work for the Hudson's Bay Company, he was dispatched to the East Kootenays in 1865 and eight years later pre-empted land just north of the border. By the time of the Gordons' arrival, he had served as justice of the peace and Indian agent for the Dominion government. Subscribing to several newspapers, he was highly literate and even learned. Michael Phillipps was, in other words, too important a personage for the Gordons to ignore even though he had, in their view, a fundamental flaw. Phillipps had used his half dozen years in the fur trade to integrate himself, too much so from Annie's perspective, with local people. Learning the Ktunaxa language, he began a family that would reach a dozen children with Rowena, daughter of Chief David of the Tobacco Plains band. At the time of the Gordons' arrival, the family had become a clan, almost all the children living at home, including a son married to a local Kootenay woman.[51]

More than any other factor, it was Phillipps's ease with his family's hybridity that caused consternation. Tommy Norbury was a young English gentleman who, through the intervention of Phillipp's married sister in England, visited the Phillippses' menage a decade earlier to learn how to farm. He told how, on his way there, a fellow traveller confided that 'it was a pity he [Phillipps] had married a squaw.' Phillipps felt no need to enlighten his guest. 'When we came into the house, she was sitting down and the only introduction I had was from P. "Here's the woman" and that's all I know about it.' According to a local historian who spoke with descendants, 'Michael visited England twice but at no time succumbed to family pressure to take an English wife. He always returned to his North American family.' The story is told that, on his return from collecting the books and heirlooms left him in his mother's will, Rowena met him at the Canadian Pacific Railway stop at Golden, a good 350 kilometres to the north. She made the trip with two or three packhorses, and their youngest child in a papoose carrier.[52]

The Phillipps family lived between cultures. Young Norbury reported how the sons, the eldest of whom, William, was at 'age 20, a great hunter ... all dress like white men but have long black hair behind and they are only very little darker in colour.' The women were also distinctive. 'Nelly [Phillipps's sister] wants to know how Mrs. P. & fam (girls I suppose) dress.' Norbury did his best to oblige. 'I am told ... that 5 yrds of stuff makes a squaw a dress, so you may imagine there aren't many flounces etc. The stuff is generally a brilliant coloured cotton, quite thin, & I am told ... but of *course* I don't know, that they wear *nothing underneath*, it must be rather chilly 40° below zero. They have a gaudy pocket handkerchief tied around the head gipsy fashion and always wear a blanket over their shoulders. They of course all ride straddle legged with a blanket arranged in front of them to hide any little frills which might be there.' Norbury's discovery that, when he arrived in 1887, 'none of them can speak a single syllable of English' made for improvisation on his part. 'The boys often come out shooting with me and we get on capitally. I manage to make them understand anything I want with the aid of my Dictionary and signs.'[53]

The language situation had changed by the time the Gordons arrived. Phillipps, like Lewis Campbell at Campbell Creek, had taken the initiative to start a local school. As one of its teachers explained, 'he wanted them to be educated so he persuaded the Education officials to open a school at Tobacco Plains.' However, this teacher added, 'when Michael Philips would return to England to visit his family (parents) there, his wife would take all the children and go back to the reserve, so there would really be no school until he returned.' Within the family, everyday communication went on in the Ktunaxa language out of respect to Rowena, who 'lived in the background, not speaking English.'[54]

It was not that Rowena was in and of herself unsatisfactory. Young Norbury ended up, almost despite himself, impressed by how well such a woman suited frontier life. 'She is not bad looking but rather fat now and dresses in a sort of cotton frock and a turban, very clean, and well mannered and makes a capital wife, working well in the garden and house.' So long as Annie held the initiative, she too was willing to be sociable. 'I went over one day to his house, and Mrs Phillipps came in to see me, and a nice looking old body she was. I was quite surprised to see how nice and tidy she looked.' Still, Annie could not quite accept what she saw and had to find an external explanation, which she did in the Phillipps children. 'I guess the little girls had been fixing her up.'[55]

As well as the immediate Phillipps family, there were Aboriginal in-laws. Someone who knew Phillipps well recalled, 'I never knew of any friction with them, in fact they all respected and admired him.' Phillipps confided to the Gordons that it had not always been so. 'Three of them came to old man Phillipps as he was hoeing potatoes in the field, and told him that they were going to kill him and throw his body out on the range, so people would think his horse had thrown him. But Phillipps laid about him with the hoe handle so fiercely that one fellow lay insensible from a crack on the skull, the second man howling with a broken arm, and the third fled for his life.' As to their identity, 'the *first* was his wife's *father*, the others were her brothers.' By the time the Gordons moved nearby, the situation had been transformed. 'Mr Phillipps is king over them all right and I, for one, am glad of it.'[56]

In a general sense Annie was comfortable. 'Our Indian neighbors never give us any trouble.' Even Phillipps's brother-in-law, whose arm he had once broken, 'is quite a respectable citizen now.' The Gordons' handyman was Paul David, one of Rowena's brothers and successor to their father as chief of the Tobacco band. Annie dispensed medicines to local Kootenay. 'You must know I am physician in general to them all.' She told her mother how their handyman's 'old wife came in a few days ago to get me to doctor up her eye and a big bump on her head.' Another time 'one of our Indian neighbors' died, and Annie fretted how 'I'll have to rustle up some clothes for Joe's children before winter or they will freeze.'[57]

Annie could be sympathetic. Early in 1898 one of the Phillipps' sons was accused of contributing to a neighbour's accidental death. The official statement ran: 'Edward Bawlf, employed on railway construction Elk River was hit on left temple with revolver by half breed Philips Saturday night.' Tommy Norbury, now settled nearby, was upset by the Phillipps family plight. 'Whatever the boy did do was done in self defense – Old P. has asked me to go down and give evidence as to the boy's character and antecedents.' Despite Norbury's testimony, a trial date was set. Annie wrote home in November. 'Poor man! He has so much trouble. The trial of that poor boy of his has been again put off much to his disappointment.' A month later, the situation had not got any better. 'Poor Mr. Phillipps is still in trouble over his boy. The prosecuting attorney has been working against the bail being accepted, and the boy is still in jail. The bail papers were not even sent in to Victoria, the last time the old gentleman went to [Fort] Steele.' The charge was not substantiated.[58]

Annie's ambivalence came out in both big and small ways. At Tobacco Plains a matter of months, she described Phillipps's ranch as 'one of the finest in Canada' and then added, 'he hasn't done much to it.' To her sister Mary Belle, Annie was more brutal. 'It is a pretty spot, to look at, and dreary enough to live in.' It was in terms of her own children that Annie's attitude became most overt. She simply could not countenance them being schooled alongside hybrids. She had always considered she knew best. Back at Salmon Arm, when little Jessie was four, her aunt Mary Belle had sent her for Christmas 'a beautiful big doll, with kid body, shoes & stockings, dress and underclothing all complete, her own work,' whereupon Annie responded, 'it is far too good for a child her age.' At Tobacco Plains a few short months, Annie was already 'hoping to be able to give up and go back East, in five years time, to educate the children.' In the interim, she did everything she could to isolate them.

Jessie was nine and a particular worry to Annie, she explained to her sister Jane. 'I do wish there were some little white girls here for her to play with. I daren't let her go to play with the half breeds for they are liable to pull her hair out by root, and beat the life nearly out of her, as they did once shortly after we came down here.'[59]

Annie's consolation was the local teacher. August 1898 saw the arrival of Dora Fowler, an Ontarian Anglican in her mid-twenties whose resiliency makes her endearing. Dora's mother had died when she was two, and the Fowlers moved to a remote area of Manitoba, where her stepmother expected Dora, to quote her daughter, 'to do a large share of the work.' Dora escaped to a married sister in Brandon, where she attended a normal school, then to a brother in Winnipeg, where she got her teaching certificate. Dora taught in several small Prairie schools, but again her family put pressure on her, this time to marry a courting Presbyterian minister. To quote her daughter, Dora 'was by now, they considered, practically an old maid.' She escaped to Tobacco Plains. Dora Fowler's daughter remembers how Annie gave sustenance. 'There were also 2 children from the family of the Customs Officer where Mother boarded for a while.'[60]

Annie's personal relationship with the teacher was not sufficient to compensate for what she considered to be the poor state of the school. Even when Phillipps was around to chivy his family, the school was intermittently attended, as recalled by Dora Fowler's daughter. 'Attendance at the school was very erratic and spasmodic.' The school inspector visited in October 1898 and found eleven children enrolled but just eight in attendance. Annie confided to her sister Jane: 'I only hope we may get in some more families here next summer to keep up the school. A good deal will depend on Mr Phillipps' attitude, and we will have to see what that will be.'[61] Michael Phillipps was in charge of the local school board and, while Jim Gordon soon joined it, the school was his purview, both in terms of exercising authority and of providing the mass of the children necessary for it to stay open. To Annie's dismay, Dora Fowler moved, after a year at Tobacco Plains, to the larger community of Elko, about thirty kilometres to the north.

Dora Fowler's successor also gave comfort. Mary Dunlop, just turned twenty, was also an Ontarian, and Annie confided to her sister Mary Belle in the fall of 1899: 'We have a good looking young teacher here from the outer world, and I enjoy her company very much. She is very cheerful, but I can see that the isolation of the place is kind of wearing into her.' As with Dora Fowler, Mary Dunlop was privy to a sociability that eluded Annie. 'The new teacher at Elko is a schoolmate of hers, and they anticipate spending Xmas together.'[62]

When this teacher similarly left at the end of the year, as was almost inevitable at such remote locations, Annie reported, 'we miss Miss Dunlop dreadfully, and I rather believe the boys around miss her still more.' By then Jim was secretary of the school board, so that, when her successor arrived, Annie had even greater aspirations for sociability. 'Our new teacher seems to be an excellent one, and I only hope she will stay with us. She gets on very well with all the children.' The school inspector was less impressed. 'Work backward but improving,' he recorded. By the next June, Minnie McCain, an Ontarian in her mid-twenties, was just another memory. 'Miss McCain is going back to Ontario for the holidays, and doesn't think she will return ... we will not be likely to get the like of her again.' Despite Minnie McCain's departure she remained for Annie a critical link to the outside world, warming her heart the next Christmas with 'a dainty little volume of selections from Browning.'[63]

As school began again in August of 1901 with yet another teacher in charge, Annie was once more in turmoil on her children's behalf. 'The school is very disappointing. That poor miserable teacher is absolutely *scared* of those brats, and they know it. There isn't one there but could be managed very easily, if she had any earthly wit about her. I read the riot act myself. I was so angry at the way Jess and Marsh are getting along.'[64] As a one-time teacher, Annie considered she knew how to run a school and did not have a lot of patience with persons who, by her standards, were unable to take charge, particularly of children like those of the Phillippses.

If busy wrestling year after year with her aspirations for her family, Annie was comforted by the frontier's withdrawal. A way of life took hold that, in its essentials, reflected the perspective of settlers like the Gordons. Rumours of a rail extension north from the Great Northern began in 1899. 'There is some talk of a railroad coming through here next summer.' Mineral speculation meant 'we have been having such a lot of millionaires lately around the place, as thick as hairs on a dog's back, to speak vulgarly.' The Gordons got caught up, Annie reporting how Jim was 'going out on the hills prospecting.' After several years of effort, Tobacco Plains acquired its own post office, dubbed Phillipps to distinguish it from its Montana counterpart. Initially, Annie was to be named postmaster, but Michael Phillipps somehow got the contract to provide service at the rate of $150 a year. When the office opened in the fall of 1899, it was in the Gordons' home with Phillipps officially in charge. 'The Post Office is here now at our house and a great big nuisance too, but there was no other place for it.' A few months later, Annie complained how 'us having the P.O. makes a lot more work and people back and forth and such mud as they bring in on their feet!' By the summer of 1901, Annie might have been in any of numerous settlements across British Columbia. 'Well, the railroad is going on, grading has begun, and the C.P.R. is fighting it tooth and nail on this side of the line. The [steam]boats, three of them, are running from Jennings [Montana, about eighty kilometres south on the Great Northern rail line] to Tobacco Plains.'[65]

The change was two-edged. Annie groused how 'railway construction brings lots of drunkenness and rough times.' Saloons proliferated. 'The Canadians are granting licenses as thick as autumn leaves. Every Tom Dick and Harry who asks for one gets it.' The economic gains offset the negative. A new market opened up for the Gordons' vegetables. As for turnips, 'we have about five tons of them, and two tons are already sold to railway contractors.' Onions were an even better bet. 'We could have sold far more than we have got. There were over thirty men camped in the big corral at the gate.' It is an indication of the frontier's retreat that Annie now grew not just vegetables for sale but also such luxury items as flowers. 'The garden is lovelier than ever. After the rains, we have poppies, mignonette and stocks in bloom, and a few sweet peas. The stocks have a lovely spicy perfume, very much like the clove pink. Jim has the sweet peas trained up on wire netting, and it gives quite an air to the place.'[66]

Even as Tobacco Plains became less of a frontier, the Gordons were on the move again. In 1901 the Great Northern Railway began to construct a branch line north from Montana along the Kootenay River to exploit coalfields in the Crow's Nest Pass. A boom town sprang up at the point on the Kootenay River where the line crossed the border. 'It is a very "shacky" town, but has one good store,' Annie reported to her mother. According to Marsh, 'there was quite a "boom" town on the American side though, owing to the obstinacy and jealousy of the C.P.R. which owned the adjoining land, none on the Canadian side.' The community was located about eight kilometres west of Tobacco Plains and appropriately named Gateway for its cross-border function. It was inevitable that the customs post was transferred there.[67]

The family knew by the summer of 1901 that they would have to relocate. The weather during the next winter made it imperative that they do so. 'We have just arrived home from the Christmas Tree at Gateway, and a fearsome time we had, coming in the dark, road slightly icy, and our horses slipshod. I will not permit myself and children to travel the road *any* more after dark! Hear me!!' The Gordons set to building themselves a house about a quarter of a mile from the new railway station. Marsh recalled how 'we could not even procure a lot for building on [from the CPR] and would have been badly off had not the Great Northern given us permission to build on their right of way which was about two hundred feet wide on each side of the track for about half a mile on each side of the boundary line.'[68]

The Gordons settled into Gateway in the spring of 1902 even as their house was still being completed. 'Jim is lining the sitting room with heavy cream coloured building paper. It is put on with tacks, and looks very well.' The outside was also being finished. 'Jim has been building a W.C. today, to my great relief, for if there is one disagreeable thing it is taking to the bush as we had had to do since we came down.' Annie's chickens also made the trip. 'The fowls have a great time here. They roam over the whole country and even go up on the grade to come down shrieking in a fearful rush when the train comes in sight.'[69]

In late summer, the family finally made the long promised visit back to their families in Ontario and the Maritimes. To get the money for the two-month trip, according to Marsh, his parents sold the ranch at Salmon Arm. It was a memorable time for the boy of twelve, 'travelling by way of St. Paul, Chicago, Port Huron and Montreal, thence to St. John N.B. and various Nova Scotian towns.'[70] The most visible legacy of the trip was a carefully posed family photograph taken in Jim's hometown of Goderich. The Gordons shed every intimation of their decade on the frontier; it was as if they had never left Ontario, apart perhaps from Jim's weary look.

Annie was generally pleased. 'The work will be easier here when the house is finished than in any house I've had for many a day.' Not only did Annie take another step away from the frontier on moving to Gateway, she escaped hybridity in the persons of the Phillipps family. 'I will be so glad and thankful to get away from the place here, from the loneliness, isolation and most of all – the neighbours.' If feigning modesty, Annie eagerly awaited 'lady visitors' as well as the usual 'lots of men.' She prevaricated: 'You needn't think I am rushing to get acquainted here, for I am not, my ideas have changed a little since you last saw me, and the fact is I am not anxious to make the acquaintance of any of them.' The most visible symbol of settlement was, of course, the new rail line. 'It is very cheery to see the trains passing, and the children still rush out to see every one that passes. Whichever one sees it coming first yells "train, train!" and then the others run too.' Annie did not wholly escape the uncertainty characteristic of the frontier, she cautioned her mother. 'I do not think for a moment that I have left all troubles behind. On the contrary, I am always nervous about both river and railroad for the children, and keep them under my eye pretty closely.'[71]

One of the ways in which the frontier still impinged on Annie's life was male sociability. Although 'the American town' was more than a kilometre south of the Gordons' home, she was very aware of 'all the houses of prostitution and saloons and dance-halls in Gateway, Montana,' over which she doubly had no control by virtue of being a woman and being Canadian. Annie could only express indignant relief that, by the time she moved to Gateway, 'the construction boom is over, and the dance hall girls have gone, the prostitutes have nearly all gone, and there are *only* four saloons there now.' Moreover, the comfort that organized religion gave was closer at hand. 'We have no services anywhere near here, but Mr. Dunn of Elko spoke to me some time ago of the possibility of his coming down once in a while to preach here.' Annie did not necessarily approve of what she got. 'Last night we went to service, a young lad about nineteen or twenty preached, and really I felt as if I did not want to go again. I felt as if he was meddling with things too great and sacred for him.'[72]

By virtue of moving to Gateway, Annie also acquired one of the most important statuses a married woman could have in the transition from frontier to settlement. In November 1903, Gateway officially replaced Phillipps as post office for the southeastern corner of British Columbia. Whereas Annie had previously acted on Michael Phillipps's behalf, she officially became postmistress in her own right. She later recalled how the money came 'in handy' and 'the work is light.'[73]

Where Annie remained most dissatisfied was on her children's behalf. If away from the Phillipps family, the local school she considered inadequate, in part because 'the Montana teachers are fairly tumbling over themselves' to teach in it. She continued to see herself as a teacher par excellence and recalled many years later how 'the only luxury we allowed ourselves in those days was books and good magazines; and it has certainly proved our salvation.' Annie improvised. 'Marshall drew a map of United States putting in all the states, then cut them all out, and Dal has learned to put them all together correctly, and is very proud of the feat.' She found a music teacher for Jessie, and Dal got a bugle. While still at Tobacco Plains, she began to teach the children herself at home and continued to do so for the most part. Writing home, Annie lamented how 'I am pegging away at Latin myself, even in the holidays and I find it very hard work with housework.' She was so involved that she did not 'have time for sewing when lessons begin.'[74]

Annie's disquiet came to a head in the summer of 1905 when Jessie was sixteen, Marsh fourteen, and Dal nine. She pondered getting 'a governess from the Coast, but I don't like the idea of a stranger.' Through Jessie's intercession, their sister Eliza's daughter Muriel, aged twenty-one, was persuaded 'to come out to teach the children,' even though the Gordons could only afford 'twenty five a month (three hundred a year).' The reason for wanting to secure a niece from the Maritimes had to do with academics but also with boundary-making. 'I would be so glad to have Muriel for a companion for Jessie, she is a nice child, if I do say it myself, and the girls here are inclined to talk about "boys" all the time, and to think themselves grown up. They need someone like M. among them to stir them up a trifle.' Even that was not enough so far as the eldest son was concerned. Marsh held a special place in his parents' heart, so much so that after two 'most unsatisfactory' years at the school on the American side of the border, they 'decided that I should go away to school and sent me to attend the Vancouver High School.' The Gordons thereby completed the process by which their children were hived off, first from the Phillipps and now from the others in 'the village.' A quarter of a century later, Annie still took pride how 'she kept her family from "going Indian," as so many of the pioneer settlers did.'[75]

By this time, the Gordons had been living for a good decade at the edge of the edge. For all of the change that Annie wrought, it was inadequate, from her perspective, to protect her own children. The older they got, the more she fretted over their frontier upbringing. The family's stature made it all the more important that her children be kept apart from the locals at Gateway, not to mention the hybrid Phillipps clan at Tobacco Plains. At the time the Gordons moved between the two, Annie's sister Eliza reflected on the dangers to be had on the British Columbia frontier: 'Go where they will they will find evil – it was around them at "Phillipps" and I suppose he [Jim Gordon] must go where his office goes.'[76] As did Eliza from her distant vantage point of Dartmouth, Nova Scotia, Annie lacked the flexibility of their sister Jessie, who had long since come to terms with hybridity in the classroom and sought to domesticate its human legacy into British Columbia. There was, of course, a very important difference. Jessie dealt with others' children and so could afford to test the boundaries of colonialism. There were no personal consequences, unlike for Annie, who was gatekeeping on behalf of her own children.

Chapter Ten

Jessie in Charge

ROSSLAND

When the McQueen sisters came together at Salmon Arm in the spring of 1896, it had been Jessie who made the running. Jessie sought to resolve the Gordons' woes by getting a teaching job in Rossland. Even though loosened by circumstances of sisterhood's bonds, she stayed four years in Rossland. Much of the reason Jessie did so was that for the first time in her life she understood what it meant to take charge, and she did so.

Jessie's departure from Pictou County for British Columbia in May 1896 differed from March 1888 and August 1891. The passage of time reduced Jessie's direct contact with things Nova Scotian. She became less of a sojourner. As she herself acknowledged, she no longer recognized names in letters or faces in pictures. In conversation she found herself sticking up for British Columbia. 'The Dr. was summing up the miseries of existence in B.C. one day, but I took up the cudgels, & proved beyond a doubt that it's not a bad sort of country after all.'[1]

Jessie's links to Nova Scotia were also diminished by changes in her family there. Her sisters, scattered across the Maritimes, were far more interested in their own doings than in hers. In her correspondence, and likely also person to person, Catherine increasingly resorted to religious clichés instead of measured responses that reinforced her daughter's Pictou County ways. When Jessie wrote about cases of illness near to where she was teaching, her mother replied, 'There is a physician that can exceed all our Drs.' Twenty months back home renewed ties with the Maritimes, but increasingly Jessie lived nowhere. A Dartmouth niece very perceptively asked her parents, shortly after Jessie returned to Nova Scotia in 1894, 'Where *is Aunt Jessie's home?*'[2]

In her mid-thirties, Jessie finally became her own person, relying on her own resources. She went west a third time, in part to rescue Annie trapped at Salmon Arm, and then, when that option was stymied, made the leap to Rossland. Jessie did so despite Catherine's very real displeasure at the family having any connection to what she saw as an immoral enterprise. Having read a newspaper article lambasting Rossland's saloons, Catherine lectured Annie on what she considered to be her husband's inappropriate association with the mining town. Her mother's tirade was such as to cause Annie, who had not written home for some time, to fire off a testy reply. 'You seem to think that Jim is "rushing" after gold, nothing could be farther from the facts of the case. He has been unable to make one cent off the ranch and has been obliged, much against his will, to leave home to make enough for us to live on.'[3]

Jessie's teaching life in Rossland was very different from anything she had known before. She was part of an urban school and, moreover, one in flux. The best-known of the early hard-rock mines responsible for Rossland's existence was the Le Roi, staked in 1890 and brought into production a couple of years later by Spokane businessmen. By the beginning of 1895, Rossland's hilly streets contained some fifty buildings, cabins, and shacks housing a few hundred people. The success of the Le Roi and other mines attracted the adventurous and ambitious. 'They get the gold fever as soon as they arrive here, and all are intent on becoming rich,' reported the *Rossland Miner*, which began publishing in March 1895.[4] By the end of the year, Rossland's population had ballooned to 3,000. Increasingly, people came with families in tow, not to speculate but for a better life as merchants, service providers, or miners.

The *Rossland Miner* boasted in its first issue that 'there are more than enough children to start a school.' The first school opened at the end of September 1895 in the newly constructed Methodist church, whose founding minister functioned as teacher to about fifty pupils. Wooden boards hinged to the back of the pews served as desks. Enrolments doubled by the end of the year, when a second teacher was hired and a large canvas sheet put up to divide the church's interior into two classrooms. Jessie became the third in September 1896. A schoolhouse was completed just before her arrival, but its two rooms were already overfull and she got the church. 'I accepted at once, and opened the school today with fifty-eight pupils enrolled,' Jessie reported to Superintendent of Education Pope on 7 September 1896. For this extraordinarily demanding job, which included 'janitor work,' her salary was $50 a month.[5]

The large number of students reflected Rossland's boom-town character. The school inspector, who visited shortly after Jessie's arrival, considered that 'Rossland is a lively place, and begins to wear quite a city air.' An experienced teacher in diverse settings, Jessie responded well to the challenge this new frontier gave. Her two fellow teachers were junior to her, at least in age. David Birks, in his mid-twenties, had been a student assistant to the Methodist mssion begun in the nearby West Kootenays boom-town of Nelson in 1892 before, newly ordained, being dispatched in the summer of 1895 to bring Methodism to Rossland. An assured salary of $60/month as a teacher proved more attractive than the ministry. While Birks continued to encourage Methodism, he essentially traded in one job for another. The other teacher when Jessie arrived was eighteen-year-old Maud Moffatt, an Irish Presbyterian who, born in New Brunswick, hailed from New Westminster. Like Jessie, she was hired at $50 a month. As with Birks, Rossland was her first teaching job. The school inspector considered that 'Miss McQueen is doing good work with the primary pupils.' As for how she coped with such large numbers being a self-described 'scrap' in size, 'when I get among my sixty infants, *then* I pile up dignity & responsibility & all the rest.'[6]

One part of Jessie was overwhelmed by her new circumstances. 'Rossland terrifies me with its rush and noise, and streets modeled after the fashion of a tobaggan-slide.' There was none of the solitude of country schools. 'Oh, it's so hard to be in a place like this, where one can't be alone ... There are people everywhere, and I haven't a corner to myself.' Another part of Jessie was, almost despite herself, entranced. 'One can just see this town growing every day, buildings of all shapes & sizes going up in every direction, & as I came from school last night, I heard a man say too, that an extra big crowd came in on the train last night.' A visitor at about this time described, much as Jessie, how 'the streets are crowded from morning to night with miners, prospectors and others.' Everybody came from somewhere else and had a story, real or imagined, to tell. In Rossland two weeks, Jessie was entertained in the boarding house where she was staying by a visitor who 'had been *five* times around the world – was a very interesting talker.' The completion of a rail link to Rossland a few months after Jessie's arrival fuelled the speculation. Even faraway Ontario became caught up. The Toronto *Globe* newspaper devoted a special edition to Rossland, so great was the excitement across Canada. 'Three years ago the site of Rossland was as remote from civilization as any spot on the globe'; now it has a population of some 5,000 and even 'streets at right angles.'[7] The provision of the public utilities of water and electricity added to the urban air.

The excitement rebounded on the classroom. Reflecting the transient nature of the mining frontier across North America, many newcomer children had not previously been in school. 'There is considerable variety of attainment among the pupils,' wrote the school inspector. Jessie, somewhat sympathetically, described 'one little beggar' who 'is like a Jack-in-the-box, out on the floor – under the benches, standing on one foot, whistling, punching his neighbors fore & aft, & every mischief you can imagine.' She lamented how 'some are rather ready with their fists, & it takes me all my time settling rows between them at noon & recess.'[8]

A continuous flow of newcomers translated into ever greater numbers of children. The secretary of the trustees reported four months after Jessie's arrival: 'Miss McQueen's room is altogether too overcrowded and we are in absolute need of a fourth teacher. She has an attendance of nearly 70 pupils and has all the inconvenience possible to accrue to teaching in a church where there are some kind of services almost every night necessitating the removal of the forms outdoors.' About this time, Jessie wrote home that 'I've had lots of new scholars, & have now 100 enrolled, though 50 is the usual attendance.' A month later: 'I have such a full school – sixty & upwards every day now – 68 yesterday & 69 today.'[9] In other words, about half to two-thirds of the children on the books actually attended on any given day, likely a quite different mix from day to day. It was not just the numbers, but also their diversity of ages. Jessie's primary class had children aged between six and nine, with a handful ten or eleven.

Yet others were not in school at all. 'There are scores of children not attending schools for their parents knowing the glutted state of things in our accommodation at school refuse to send them believing they cannot get justice done them.' Jessie described in November how two rooms were added to the rear of St. Andrew's Presbyterian Church to accommodate the overflow. She noted with relief the next February that a fourth teacher had been hired, who 'will open up first Monday in the Pres. church with two classes – the younger ones probably from my room.' In turn, 'I shall have one class from Miss Moffatt's which will give us all about 40 or 50 to start with.'[10] Rossland was incorporated as a city in March 1897, which gave the community, now approaching 7,000, authority to borrow money, seek provincial funding, and levy and collect taxes. The advent of self-government made it possible to plan for a much-needed new school, as well as provide fire protection, street improvements, and a sewer system.

In the interim, Jessie remained caught in a spiral of growth. Her second fall in Rossland, 1897, she and fellow teacher Maud Moffatt were relegated to the Presbyterian church. Its newly arrived unwed minister lived in the building, and 'the walls are not overly thick either, & I'm afraid he can frequently hear my dulcet tones raised as I guide & direct my infants along the pathway of knowledge.' Hers were no ordinary pupils. 'Some of them do take a terrible amount of training! If he were a nervous man, it would be worse for him than for me, but he says we never disturb him, & I believe I have the reputation of being slightly quieter than *some* of our staff, whose commands can be heard over a whole block.' Even though 'I never worked harder with any school that this one,' there were rewards. 'I often get a word of appreciation from one & another ... The children seem fond of me, & the last new class I got in, is a great pleasure, if it is a lot of work.'[11]

Other times, Jessie felt overwhelmed. 'Here are Miss Moffatt & myself – the pioneer teachers on the staff – and the two that have the very worst accommodations – rickety old benches that hold eight or nine, & that's far too many infants to have in close contact. You may get two good enough to sit together, but *nine* – never. The other female teachers hold forth in halls & *bar rooms* (intended-to-be) and have patent desks, & don't have to gather up slates & books every night & distribute them every morning. With upwards to fifty that takes a bit of time.' The change to shorter school hours as winter approached, a usual practice in schools at this time, annoyed rather than comforted. 'Short hours are on now – 9.30 to 3, but I could wish the long ones were left instead – I can hardly ever get caught up with myself from the time school opens till it closes again.' That was not all. If now provided with janitors to start fires each morning, 'most of us teachers will have it cold enough this winter, for the new school house isn't in sight yet.' By the time a contract was let for construction at the end of 1897, Rossland contained some 500 children of school age, and two male and five female teachers.[12]

Jessie eagerly awaited the new building's completion. 'School was so worrisome the first week [after the 1897 Christmas holidays] that I couldn't read, write, study, or do anything else when I got home.' Again she rallied. 'It seems to be better now – the youngsters are getting into my ways, or else I'm getting more patience.' The usual winter incidence of illnesses proved a mixed blessing. 'School has been pretty heavy, but a good many are out this week with colds – some have whooping cough, & I am

interviewed on every corner by mothers who tell me that Beatrice or Maggie, or Ethel &c &c have *such* a cough that they *had* to keep them home.'
The school inspector spent three and a half days at Rossland in the middle
of January 1898. He found 56 pupils enrolled and 46 present in Jessie's
class, a total surpassed only by Maud Moffatt with 58 and 53 respectively.
His report stated that reading was Jessie's strongest subject and her work
was 'thorough.' Back four months later, the inspector found the enrolment had climbed to 63, daily attendance 53; all the same, he considered
her 'work careful' and students' 'reading improved.'[13]

Large classes made squabbles inevitable. Jessie's lengthy description
of the discipline she employed gives a unique insight into the power
relationship assumed to exist between student and teacher. 'I had a
scene with a child last week – a regular bad 'un she is – was disobedient
& "sassy" & I had to take the strap to her. Of course I did it after school,
but she fought like a little tiger, & threw herself down on the floor, &
kicked up her heels. If she did, I saw just where the strap could do most
effective work & laid it on accordingly. Didn't she yell? Roared out that
she'd get the policeman after me, but when I got through & put her
right side up with care on the bench & sat down to talk to her, she astonished me with "I can't help it, Miss McQueen, my temper gets away with
me!" We had a good deal of talk, & she left in a very decent frame of
mind apparently. Emma Le Boeuf (pronounced *Le beff*) is her name.'[14]

The tension that came with having great numbers of students in close
proximity was broken by the completion of the new school in May 1898,
by which time 'I have over 70 in school every day I think I have about
enough to do.' Central School was a frame two-storey building containing eight rooms. 'We go into the new school to-morrow,' when Jessie
anticipated that her class would be 'thinned' out to about sixty pupils.
She was impressed. 'It is just fine, bright, clean, airy & so convenient,
with all the black-board space one could possibly wish for ... my work is
comparatively light now.' The one drawback was a lack of heating,
meaning 'I still wear all my winter clothing, & with my fur cape around
my shoulders, I've got along very fairly well.' The absence was deliber-
ate, for the trustees hoped to install a furnace, which they managed to
do by the next winter, and realized that, if they improvised, stoves would
become the status quo. In the fall of 1898, Jessie was 'promoted' to first
assistant to the principal, and her salary upped to $60 a month. Her
tasks included supervision of the grounds during recess. 'I have just had
my week, & took some fun out of watching the boys at football and mar-
bles, & the girls at skipping.'[15]

Rossland was acquiring an air of permanence. Jessie mused in the spring of 1898: 'Society – of course there is – all sorts and sizes, and churches, Pres. Baptist Meth. Episcopal & Catholic – besides S. Army.' A year later: 'There are several very nice houses being built – a big improvement on the shacks that used to grow up like mushrooms.' Indicative of the shift to a settled society was Jessie's comment about how 'the school children bring donations of sweet peas & pansies &c to school.' By the end of 1898, according to a boastful resident, 'the mining camp on the steep slopes is becoming a dangerous rival ... to the coast cities of Victoria and Vancouver.'[16]

With the advent of the new school, Jessie wrote far less about teaching in her letters. It had become ordinary. Next fall the inspector found 40 or so children enrolled and about 37 present in a classroom he described as 'good.' A year later, the beginning of her fourth year in Rossland, Central School's eight classrooms and the two in the old school were filled to overflowing, and everyone agreed that at least four more classrooms were desperately needed. Class size ranged from 36 to 56 pupils, Jessie enrolling 42 at the start of term.[17]

It was not only Jessie's present pupils who exercised her during her Rossland years. Catherine wondered shortly after her daughter's arrival there, 'Have you forgotten Ullysis Campbell I often thought you might give that poor Boy a helping hand and the right way when he had no encouragement at home & allowed just to grow without any advise in the right way.' After a hiatus, Jessie got another letter from Ulysses in the spring of 1898, which may have given more pleasure to Catherine than to Jessie, if for different reasons. 'Do you know I was thinking lately of Ulysis Campbell & thinking of saying to you, tis a pity you ceased corresponding with him you don't know how a little seed dropped for the Master might grow and it gave me a thrill of pleasure to hear you had word from him it may be the Lord intends you to be helpful to him.'[18] Religious piety had become her stock in trade.

When Jessie visited Kamloops that summer, Ulysses came twice to see her. 'He is quite grown up, but has a good deal of the child about him nevertheless. Things have evidently not changed much since I left – on the Campbell ranch I mean. I very much doubt if poor Ulyss ever gets a chance to make anything of himself, but he is so much in advance of the rest that he will not drink, anyhow.' Ulysses Campbell would stay in the locality, making his living as a farm labourer. His death certificate of 1965 described him as 'white,' suggesting that is how he represented himself as an adult, a possible legacy of his youthful encounter with

Jessie McQueen.[19] She likely did not much affect his economic status, but she may have given him more of a sense of belonging to Canada, hence to the skin colour of the dominant society, than would otherwise have been the case.

Jessie did not just teach in Rossland, she lived there. Historian Jeremy Mouat has detailed how, during these years, 'Rossland gradually became a settled community, self-consciously part of Canada.'[20] It was not only the transformation of the economy through growing Canadian investment and infrastructure that effected the change. Teachers like Jessie McQueen were equally critical to the process by which Rossland and its inhabitants were domesticated into Canada. She acted as a teacher but also as a woman.

Jessie quickly fell into a new independent way of life. It was one responding to the exigencies of the mining frontier, but also to her growing self-assurance. Jessie was comfortable doing so because, while Rossland shared in some of the openness characteristic of mining booms, the town never got out of control. As one resident put it a year after Jessie's arrival, 'rowdyism of all kinds has been frowned down.' About half of the miners were required by their employers to stay at company boarding houses, which gave the rest of Rossland a more settled air than might otherwise have been the case. There were prostitutes to service men on their own and numerous bars, but, as a visitor about the time of Jessie's arrival pointed out, 'not a dance hall or rowdy place in the whole town.' He continued: 'There are some disreputable women in the place but evidently they know enough to behave themselves and seldom show their faces on the street. Saloons are plentiful; ... but all these places are kept in a most orderly manner. Yes, Rossland is a wonder as a law abiding place.' A visiting American Catholic priest got a similar impression. 'What struck me most was the good order I found everywhere. All respect the laws, judges, and especially the police officers of British Columbia ... Rossland has two policemen for about 5,000 inhabitants ... but they have such authority that ... their appearance fills all the hobos and toughs with awe and respect.' Rossland's first judge similarly recalled: 'There never was a more orderly mining camp on the face of the earth than Rossland during those boom days. Law and order were observed as strictly as in any British town. The tramp of the people sounded far into the morning hours but good fellowship and kindliness seemed to prevail universally.'[21] In other words, it was quite possible for single women like Jessie to feel at home in Rossland.

Mouat argues, based on a close reading of the Rossland press, that such views are sanguine. However, during her years there, Jessie never wrote home anxious over public order or her own safety. Rather, she relished the freedom that this new frontier gave. Persons like her in their young or middle years were in the preponderance, with males outnumbering females by three to one.[22]

Jessie's first year in Rossland may have been the best of her lifetime. The mining frenzy gave her a freedom as a single woman that so far she had not sought but was now forced upon her. For the first time in her life, she took charge of her living arrangements. Rossland's boom-town character meant that she could not, on her salary of $50 a month, afford the usual teacher practice of boarding. 'I have been unable to get board under $10 per week,' she lamented to the superintendent of education shortly after her arrival.[23] The house her brother-in-law Jim Gordon had bought in anticipation of his family moving there was not an option, as it was rented out. So Jessie built herself a home of her own. Realizing that her 'monthly stipend will not be much more than what the miners are pleased to call "grubstake,"' Jessie determined 'to take up housekeeping for myself.' 'Shacks' erected in a hurry were a Rossland staple, and she followed suit. In just three weeks, she had her house built. Jessie once described how 'the majority of the houses' in Rossland 'are cheap & temporary,' and she may well have included hers in that number. Located on what an acquaintance affectionately termed 'our Nickle Plate Flat,' the house was sited next door to a train stop on the side of a steep hill.[24]

Jessie's new home was much more than what one contemporary described as the common Rossland '"shack" built of rough boards, à la packing-case, usually containing one room, and that room, if it be an orthodox Rossland shack, must not measure more than 10 feet by 12 feet.' Jessie's shack included, per her specifications, 'a little study,' indoor 'bath & fixtures,' and 'water heating.' As to where she got the money to do so, family correspondence suggests that before leaving British Columbia in 1894, she had made a loan to Jim Gordon to help buy the Salmon Arm ranch. He now repaid enough for her to acquire the land and have the house built. Jessie made the interior her own. On 17 October 1896 'Miss McQueen' purchased from Campbell Bros. of Rossland a kitchen chair, rocker, dresser, pair of curtains and rods, and paper rack, for a total of $16.90. She transformed 'a single cot-bed with woven under-wire spring, covered with excelsior & ticking,' into a lounge by topping it with 'a big gray blanket.'[25] At the age of thirty-six, Jessie was furnishing her first very own home.

Jessie was able to afford her new, very own house by taking in board-
ers, another very acceptable practice available to women on a mining
frontier. Two other single women, whom she familiarly termed 'Moffatt'
and 'Mackay,' came to live with her. Maud Moffatt was her fellow
teacher, a Maritimer like Jessie and almost two decades her junior. 'Miss
Mackay,' who may have been from Seattle, was employed, possibly as a
bookkeeper, in the firm of Bennison & Co. The enigmatic Mackay,
whose first name Jessie never revealed in her letters home, brought to
the menage not only herself but also part of the furnishings. When her
employer moved offices, 'they had a pair of dark red chenille curtains,
for which there was no place.' One of the firm told Mackay to 'take
them home & see if *we* could find use for them, & so we did.' The red
curtains replaced the gray blanket on the improvised lounge. 'They are
faded hopelessly on one side, but the other is very pretty, & they add
another cosy touch to our shack.'[26]

Jessie's letters indicate a very congenial way of life, what she termed a
'home feeling.' 'We get along very harmoniously & feel more at home
in our shack every week ... It's a good thing for all three of us that we
have combined forces – we have peace & comfort, & not a little enjoy-
ment together.' The housemates grew close, at least from Jessie's perspective. Writing to Catherine one evening, she explained: 'The other
girls are tired to-night, & both asleep already, so far as I can judge,
though it is only half-past eight ... Poor Mackay has had several sleepless
nights, or almost so, & is about used up, but I am rejoiced to *hear* her
sleeping at the present moment, on the lounge with my big shawl over
her, & her feet to the fire.' Referring another time to Mackay, 'she's lots
of fun, when she's feeling well, & I tell you, when she doesn't feel well,
we don't either.' The three looked after each other when one of them
became ill. Maud 'had a pretty hard time with a cold & cough,' so Jessie
took charge. 'I doctored her to the best of my knowledge & ability – with
hot water, steam, quinine, vaseline & turpentine rubbed in good & hot,
& hot flannels, & made her stay in bed Sunday.' Another time: 'Nearly
every man, woman & child in Rossland has a cold – us folk not excepted.
I'm doctoring Maud to-night, & if I need it by to-morrow night, she will
attend to me. The cold attacks her chest, & the surest & safest cure is
cold cloths on her chest and hot ones between her shoulder blades.'[27]

The trio shared household tasks. 'I made brown bread & currant loaf
last week – great successes both. That brown loaf of mine got so much
praise from those who tested it that I am in danger of getting the "big
head" over it.' Jessie closed her letter: 'And now, I must set the family

bread & get to bed.' A load of wood arrived. 'Moffatt & I pitched it into the woodshed with much rejoicing. We split it ourselves as we need it, & are getting to be adepts.' All the same, a break from the routine proved welcome. 'A friend of Miss Moffatt's – A Mrs Bart came to town this week, & as we have a spare bed now Miss Mackay is away [in Seattle], she is stopping with us.' The visitor took care to make herself useful. 'It's a change to get home from school, & find the house in apple-pie order, lamps trimmed & all, instead of having to rustle & do it for ourselves. She had *pie* for us to-night, & by to-morrow night there will be home-made bread!'[28]

The three were all working women, which in Jessie's view gave them rights that might not be considered acceptable in other settings. 'You can imagine how pleasant these evenings are to us all. We work hard enough each day to make the evening's rest very welcome, & so far, have no carking cares or worries.' Jessie's new home became a centre of sociability. 'We are not allowed to suffer from lack of company & indeed we never do that, even when we are alone,' Jessie assured Catherine in what was, if anything, an understatement. 'We have a good many visitors – very seldom spend an evening alone, so between that, & the schools & housework, our time is pretty well taken up.' Because everyone in Ross-land was a newcomer, or virtually so, the boundaries that existed in longer-settled societies had not yet grown up. 'We've had company the last two evenings.'[29]

The housemates often amused each other and friends by taking turns reading aloud. 'The company wanted to hear the story.' Another time: 'Last week I think I spent one or two evenings reading to the girls, from "Kate Carnegie" & "The bonnie brier-bush."'[30] Jessie had lit on another enormously popular author in the tradition of Pansy and of Marietta Holley and her humorously virtuous Samantha books. Written by Scot-tish Presbyterian minister John Watson under the pen-name of Ian Maclaren, *Kate Carnegie* and *Beside the Bonnie Brier Bush* were idylls of Scottish rural life laced with humour admidst prescriptions for right conduct.[31] As well as books, the trio read stories from *McClure's* maga-zine. The monthly had begun publishing in 1893, reflecting a larger shift whereby the kinds of stories Jessie had up to now read in books and newspapers became more broadly available. *McClure's* was first sent to Jessie by her sister Eliza in Dartmouth, but she later subscribed.[32]

Heavy snowfalls made winter sports a popular entertainment in Ross-land, and a house on a hill made it only necessary to step outside the door to go 'coasting.' Such adventures gave a levelling quality to sociability. About this time, one resident explained how 'society, in the general sense of the word – the society that is always spelt with a capital S – is an unknown quantity in Rossland.' Women and men went sliding together, as did pupils and their teachers. 'That hard-headed business man was hardly recognizable as he steered the sled down hill & finally landed us in a heap at the foot. We only went *three* at a time, & when I was in the middle, I was almost flattened. It does us all good, & we are careful too, mother. We select the hill that leads down from our door – fairly steep, but no danger about it – there is never anyone but ourselves on it after night, & when we *do* spill off, there is any amount of snow to spill into. I think we quit about 11, & came in to cool off. I think that was the night we started talking about creeds ... After he [the businessman friend] left, we girls toasted marshmallows & still talked in that line ... You can imagine how pleasant these evenings are to us all.'[33]

There were sleigh rides. 'About a week ago, a dozen of us went for a sleigh drive – just a few miles out of town – till we got room to turn & came back. We got rather chilly, & "Johnny," Moffatt & I left the crowd at the last railway crossing & *walked* in, about a quarter of a mile. The railway grade was easier than climbing the hill, & the walk restored our circulation in no time. And when we came in sight of the sleigh, a couple of hundred feet or so below us, we hollered & waved, Moffatt & I, our caps, but Johnny, he picked me up, & waved *me*.'[34]

Perhaps most enjoyable of all was skating on an improvised rink not far from where the housemates lived. 'I've tried skating again, & took heaps of good out of it. The rink is just a bit of level ground – Base-ball Flat, fenced in & flooded, so there is no dampness about it ... Miss Moffatt & I went two different evenings. I was clumsy enough the first time, but on the second occasion I seemed to get my sea legs somewhat better, & we stayed at it for nearly two hours.' Having also gone coasting, Jessie considered it 'a pretty fair allowance for one week's exercise,' but she had not stopped yet. 'If it's fair to-morrow, a crowd of us, old & young, are going skating, so Moffatt & we'll have to move around lively to get our Saturday's work done.'[35]

Spontaneity in sociability became acceptable in and of itself. One afternoon, Jessie and Maud Moffatt, having spent two hours skating, returned home to find 'unexpected company arrived, too, but they came loaded with bread & meat, oranges & candy, so *our* outlay wasn't much, & we had a very pleasant evening.'[36] Just arrived in Rossland and friends of friends, the two men invited themselves to a home-cooked dinner, a form of improvisation clearly acceptable on a mining frontier.

Friends begot friends. 'As the trains stop at our door,' the women got to know one of the customs officers. 'He asked tonight if he might bring up a friend some evening and of course we had to give him permission. "An awfully nice fellow" he says – a dentist from Victoria. I forgot his name but he has only lately come, hasn't brought his family yet, & is suffering comfort in one of the hotels, I suppose.' Newfound friends reciprocated by taking the housemates out to eat. '"Johnny" had us go & take dinner down town just before he left.' Another time, their fellow teacher Wesley Blair 'very kindly invited Miss Moffatt & me to take dinner with him.' When the school inspector turned up at Rossland, Jessie invited him home to lunch. 'We had corn soup (made of canned corn, milk, butter & seasoning), muffins, bread & butter & jam – yes and fried potatoes & pigs' feet – not bad, when we had to get it up, eat it, & be back to school inside of an hour.'[37]

Many newcomers to Rossland became caught up by, as one resident put it in 1897, 'the loneliness of it, and the feeling that you "belong nowhere."' Time and again, the housemates succoured lonely souls of both genders, as indicated by participants' reflections. 'Do you know, Jessie, that in that little shack I spent some of the very pleasantest hours of my life. Oh me, so often I cry for the yesterdays. Goodby my dear, dear, friend.' Writing a few months later, in December 1897 from Boston, the same man imagined Christmas with 'you and Maud ... sitting comfortably at home with your books, and each other to talk to.' He was hoping for two weeks holiday when 'I'll come up to supper every time you ask me, I'll haunt the little old shack – kick around under your feet until you frantically scream, Scat!'[38]

A second man, now caught up in Klondike gold fever, sent books he thought would interest Jessie and the other readers, including 'Mark Twain's new book,' and 'Quo Vadis,' 'altho' some parts of it are a little rapid.' He clearly knew Jessie well, as indicated by his next line: 'You can hide your blushes behind the Organ and read serenely. You won't have to "burn no rag" as it's not of the Tolstoi order.' Reflecting the language of nineteenth-century gold rushes, he concluded on a wry note. 'I try not to be good and am not so very lonesome, altho' I've wished many times that you were all here so that I could take you to see ... the "Elephant", – I have a speaking acquaintance with him.' Writing at the beginning of December 1897 from Seattle, he was 'still living in hopes of having you spend your Xmas vacation in the metropolis of the North West.' For her part, Jessie was not attracted to this new boom. 'I never can see any bright side to the Klondike picture – hardship, misery & death seem to be the portion of the greater number who go there.' It was not just that, but their absent companion 'hates the snow – couldn't stand Rossland on that account, so I'm wondering how he will flourish.'[39]

The idyllic circumstances of Jessie's first year in Rossland were too good to last. Even at the time, she was aware that it was a special moment in her life. Writing to Catherine during her first winter, she reflected a bit guiltily: 'I often wonder if it's selfish of me to enjoy life so much here, while you folk have so much of the hardness.' Her very next sentence made clear she had no intention of desisting. 'I suppose my being miserable wouldn't help you any though.'[40]

The transient nature of boom towns made change inevitable, and it came. Early in 1897, the elusive Mackay headed off to the United States and, unsuccessfully, cajoled Jessie to do the same. 'She wishes I could get some better place, & seems to think I might get near her some time. But it seems to me that our ways lie apart now – I miss her very much but "Yankee land" offers no temptation to me.' Like Annie, Jessie possessed a sense of Canada distinct from, and superior to, the United States to the south. Mackay's replacement in the shack was Maud's sister Veen, who worked at the telephone office. Sometime thereafter a third Moffatt sister, Bess, moved in. The preponderance of Moffatts began to grate on Jessie. Household tasks became more prescribed, as a kind of 'we' and 'they' grew up. 'It's my chore, you know, to get the breakfast – they get the other meals.' Saturday still meant housekeeping. 'All yesterday morning (Saturday) was housework – wood & water, washing, baking, scouring &c &c – a little of each.'[41]

It was not just Jessie's living arrangements that altered. She had less time for recreation. In the fall of 1897, virtually all of Rossland's teachers, including Jessie and Maud, decided to renew or upgrade their credentials. Jessie reflected on the advantages of getting a 1st B certificate, 'so as to have it for life,' as opposed to a 2nd A, good for five years. She was shifting her sense of self from being a Nova Scotian sojourner to becoming a British Columbian. 'The sooner I get 1st B, the better, for the rust will fairly grow on one in a school like this.' The housemates studied together with Principal Wesley Blair, an Ontarian Presbyterian in his late twenties who was sweet on Maud. 'It's to our mutual interest & benefit to study together, & we realize that fact, & act accordingly. Between his desire to study with me, & his admiration for Miss Moffatt, we see a good deal of him, but I'm not particularly fond of him ... [Saturday] we worked away for about an hour & a half – then he & Miss Moffatt went for a walk ... We all went to the Rink at 8.30 but I found I couldn't make my short legs go very well, so I "snuk" home again at 9.30.' A month later: 'Blair brought in a small "battery" yesterday (we are studying electricity) and we had several "shocks" all round.'[42]

It always took Jessie time to accommodate to change, and her second winter in Rossland was no different. Initially she fretted that 'we have no intimate friends at all, this winter, & it's better for us, I suppose – gives more time for work.' Very soon the sociability of winter sports was more than she could resist. 'On Nov. 8 we had our first coast – rather against my will, for I wanted to study, but I went for an hour, so as to keep peace in the family, & I guess it didn't do me any harm.' Only illness, such as a cold, could deter her. 'We haven't had a skate for three or four days, & we miss it too, but we'd rather be sure than sorry ... We have only gone to the rink once or twice after night. It seems to do more good just after school, & there are not so many on there, and such appetites as we do come home with! I don't know when I enjoyed anything so much.' Jessie became as content as she had ever been. 'We make our "home" radiate as much of the home atmosphere as possible, to all our friends.'[43]

Part of the reason for Jessie's renewed sense of satisfaction was that she had lowered her sights for the teachers' examination to a 2nd A certificate. She was a timid scholar, and, as her repeated comments in passing in her letters home indicate, she lacked self-confidence and perhaps ability. Much to her disappointment, Blair, who like her had a decade of experience in the classroom and attended normal school, in his case in Toronto, got a 2nd A, whereas she ended up with only a 2nd B, good for three years.[44]

Jessie's third year in Rossland brought more changes. It was not only the Moffatts but also Jessie's extended family that was attracted to Rossland. Two sisters of her namesake cousin Jessie Olding Hunter, long resident at Granite Creek, arrived in the spring of 1898 hoping, like other family members, to teach. The Nova Scotia link was at work. Liz Olding, who had thought about coming west as early as 1889 and did so once before when Jessie was in Campbell Creek, was in her mid-twenties, and her sister Harriet, turning twenty. They were, in other words, similar in age to Jessie and Annie when they first headed west a decade earlier.[45]

While Harriet Olding went directly to Granite Creek, Liz opted for Rossland, much to Jessie's delight. 'She is helpful morally & physically, & I hope she may find enough to do here to encourage her to remain.' Jessie fretted that Liz might be a bit bored, but a month after her arrival one of the teachers became ill '& Liz is substituting for him.' When school began again in August 1898, Liz taught vocal music on an ad hoc basis. 'All the teachers wanted it, but there was no appropriation so we asked the children to bring 20c a month each – those who wished to take singing lessons. It would work all right if they only had better memories, & of course there are always a few balky ones.' In the fall of 1899, Liz Olding got a regular teaching job, her class enrolling 56 pupils.[46]

After two years at Rossland, Jessie traded houses, although not housemates. In doing so, she was responding to changing times, another Rossland resident explaining how 'people who have "made their little pile" are building more substantial and ambitious houses, with four, five, and even seven rooms, and "all the modern conveniences."' As he put it, 'the reign of the "shack" is nearly over.' Selling 'the shack,' Jessie moved up to a larger dwelling place able to accommodate the five of them – herself, her cousin Liz, and the three Moffatts. Of wood construction, the new houses's walls and ceiling were 'boards with cotton tacked on & paper over that.' There was more space than in the shack. 'Miss Moffatt means to buy a piano – we have to get a new kitchen stove, and a carpet for the sitting room, but these are the biggest expenses.' The stove took six loaves of bread at a time, which Jessie considered 'a great labor saver.'[47]

Jessie explained the new house's financing to her mother: 'I have only paid $360 on the house as yet ... The total cost will be nearly $800 ... The girls will pay me rent, $3 a month each, & that of course, with what I can scrape & save each month, must go to pay up.' As was so often the case, the Nova Scotian connection clicked into place, for the wife of the man from whom Jessie bought the house, and who was now their neighbour, was from Truro. Jessie's newfound resourcefulness came to the fore when she discovered, the next spring, that he had not, as she had been led to believe, registered the deed. Taking the initiative, she managed to redeem the property by paying the back taxes.[48]

Domestic arrangements held. 'One week Liz & I do the work, next week the girls take their turn. Usually each set does the necessary buying for their own week. Then the bills come in at the end of the month – grocer, butcher, baker, Chinaman, wood & water, scavenger (who attends to the W.C. every month), rent [from her housemates], and any other incidentals that may be. We find the total, and each one pays one fifth. If we want to get things in quantities – butter or wood, we've got to tax ourselves a little extra.' The housemates ate together; 'then there's clearing up, & gossip over the day's doings (with wood & kindling to get) ... & it's bedtime before we know it. And there's when we lose time. We begin to get ready, & one reads or tells a scrap of news, & we stand or sit around, & discuss things up & down & all around, and by & by it's not so early as it was when we set out for bed.'[49]

Then came more changes. In early 1899, Veen Moffatt traded her telephone operator job in Rossland for a similar position in Greenwood, 'a new city south of this.' Jessie mused: 'She will find it different there – will have to depend on herself, & pay more for her keep too. She's a very trying person to live & work with, but we are all that way more or less I suppose. We'll miss her a good deal, & mourn her – a little.' When a male friend also headed off to Greenwood, Jessie realized what was happening. 'This Greenwood seems to be the boomtown of the Boundary country just now.' About eighty kilometres from Rossland, Greenwood had been growing rapidly since its foundation in 1895. Jessie became even more aware of its appeal when Bess Moffatt followed her sister there a month later. 'She has had little or nothing to do, this last month, and had a position offered at Greenwood, at $30 a month, & other work in sight too, so it seemed the best thing to be done.'[50]

The Moffatt sisters' departure proved fortuitous, for shortly thereafter the Bart family, whom Jessie had visited the previous summer in Seattle, returned with their young daughter Fay. Rossland's only photographer 'has offered Bart a half interest in his business, & if so, he will do all right.' The family filled the vacancies in Jessie's house, to her delight. 'Mrs Bart just came in the nick of time – work & school & study was getting to be too much, but now she takes full charge, & if we are all suited at the end of this month, we'll try it again next month. Beyond that we haven't made any plans. We will share expenses – we are all so glad to have the work taken off our shoulders – it seems a good thing for both parties. Yessum, I think we know Mrs Bart well enough to risk living with her – if she will risk living with us.' Jessie was almost ecstatic. 'It's a new thing not to have wood to split or kindlings to bring in – Liz & I have always had more than our share of the *rough* work – scouring – stove-cleaning &c, but we have none of it now, & it's great bliss ... Mrs Bart is very careful too, a good cook, & a good manager – wastes nothing, & always has the table looking so nice & fresh.'[51] A sign of settlement, the housemates planted nasturtiums, candytuft, mignonette, and sweet peas.

Each season retained its rhythm. The third winter, Jessie was only a little less enthusiastic about winter sports. 'I don't seem to be half as strong for the skating as last winter – not in any way. I went for a little while last night, but my legs wouldn't do their duty ... Last winter, I'm sure I've been skating nearly every day, for a little while at least, but I don't think I've been at it more than six or seven times at all.' The joys of skating reasserted themselves on an invitation 'to a "skating party" to-night, & of course we must all go.' Jessie took pleasure anticipating what she described as 'to-night's dissipation.' She explained its form. 'We'll meet at the rink – have an hour or so of skating, & then adjourn to Miss A.'s for coffee & cake.' Spring continued to be the most trying season of the year, for Rossland's rapid expansion outstripped public amenities. 'Spring seems to be with us now, sure, & the streets are bad, very bad, but I have no distance to travel to my work, so don't mind it.'[52]

In the spring of 1899, Jessie became caught up in a great new craze. Recreational cycling was another of the shared practices encouraging a sense of community across Canada. While men had ridden for several decades on machines with much higher front than rear wheels, historian Glen Norcliffe explains, women only joined them in the early 1890s, thanks to a safer, more flexible model with equal-sized wheels, gears, and inflated tires.[53] Cycling made it possible for women to move about publicly without being accompanied by a man or another woman. Its tremendous popularity contributed to the image of the 'new woman,' who sought independence and individuality on a number of levels.

Early in the decade, Jessie had been mildly amused at how one of the local men at Nicola Lake 'has a bicycle, and affords no end of amusement to those who see him being held up by someone, while he tries to "learn the critter."' Her first February in Rossland, Jessie observed with interest that 'no wheels out yet,' but it would be another couple of years before she dared try one out. Women like Jessie were encouraged to take to the 'wheel,' as it was popularly known, by Frances Willard, the middle-aged head of the principal women's temperance group, who deemed cycling to be healthy, virtuous, and Christian. Jessie had been becoming more independent ever since moving to Rossland, and now she nonchalantly wrote home: 'Don't be afraid about me & my wheel, mother. I'll never be a reckless rider – have only had it out once as yet, but I see dozens of them about town now – the streets are improved so much.' Come the summer, Jessie was still wildly excited by this opportunity to have fun and yet act uprightly. 'After dinner I thought I'd try my wheel for exercise to warm me up. By the time I had dragged it up two hills I was some warmer, but I didn't ride very long. It was too near dark, & as I won't go down our Rossland hills at all, I hadn't much room, so to speak. But it did me good – set my blood a-moving.'[54]

As Rossland became what Jessie termed a 'metropolis,' opportunities for sociability expanded. 'They have had a kinetescope here – I think that is the name. It makes pictures look like real things. Maud went one night, & said she saw a train come in – conductors & brakemen running back & forth &c &c with all the usual noise & bustle ... There is something of this kind going on all the time.' The kinetescope was the earliest motion picture viewer, foretelling a revolution in popular entertainment. The more passive, once loved practice of reading to each other fell into disuse. 'Oh, I could not read "Mrs. Solomon Smith" or anything else aloud. There's very little of that done nowadays. The other girls don't care to listen, & don't admire the books we do either.'[55] Jessie's tastes continued in a familiar vein. First published in 1882, *Mrs. Solomon Smith Looking On* was another of the Pansy books that she had enjoyed for so long.[56]

Sometimes with her cousin Liz Olding for company, Jessie spent more of her free time, it seems, in other's houses, often the parents of her students. 'When it's my week off in housework, I usually visit some of the folk when I feel able.' A favourite destination was their next-door neighbour whose wife hailed from Truro. It was not that so many people were from the Maritimes, but rather that the link opened up sociability in and of itself. 'Liz & I had tea with them last Saturday night, & think they will be very nice neighbors.' The tie promised familiar behaviour. 'I think Mrs. C. is a very fine person – one whose influence will always be on the side of right.' The toings-and-froings became more frequent. 'Mrs. C. has a nice new sewing-machine, & we are at liberty to bring over our sewing at any time.' More generally, 'we can drop in whenever we feel like it, & that's what's comfortable.'[57]

There were now nine teachers, which opened up another form of female sociability. Jessie took a particular shine to Edith MacFarlane, a Scots Presbyterian from Ontario in her mid-twenties who was already an experienced teacher in British Columbia before arriving in Rossland in the fall of 1898. 'Miss McF ... is a hearty, healthy invigorating sort of person. She has a class in Sunday-school ... & is a general all round good, helpful sort of a person.' Jessie spent a night with Edith MacFarlane and two female companions. There she got to know Alice Noble, an English Methodist from Ontario in her late twenties who had attended Normal Shool in Manitoba and, like Jessie, taught around British Columbia before landing in Rossland. 'Miss Noble, another teacher, was there too, & we had a pleasant, quiet time. The girls dosed me up for my cold before going to bed.'[58]

Jessie retook the teachers' examination in the summer of 1899, this time in the relative comfort of Vancouver, where she stayed with Edith

MacFarlane's family. Jessie finally got her 2nd A qualification, as did Maud Moffatt. That was not all Jessie did in Vancouver. She was so entranced with her new bicycle, she took it with her. 'I brought my wheel along, but didn't know, until starting, that I had to pay "excess baggage" on it.' The bicycle gave Jessie opportunities for adventure in the bustling metropolis of some 25,000 people. 'Have only been out twice on the wheel, & am so canny & cautious, that it won't ever be my fault if there's an accident. Mrs. MacF cautioned me yesterday to be careful of the [street]cars, but I'm that, all right – you can't get me any nearer to them than the other side of the street, when I'm on a wheel.' The MacFarlanes' cousin took her on a ride through Stanley Park, the green peninsula of winding trails amidst majestic trees that gave Vancouver much of its distinctive personality. 'So we went, and had the road to ourselves most of the way. We went to the Park, around by the beach, where the bathers were having glorious times in the surf.' Jessie was impressed. 'I can't begin to tell you just how lovely it is in that Park. We got off our wheels at one place, & went away down a shady path, to see some of the famous *big* trees, then down to the edge of the cliff where the breezes from the Gulf [of Georgia] could reach us. It was perfectly lovely.' Just as Jessie had done for several years in Rossland, she was now participating in a Vancouver way of life only recently accessible to women. A contemporary who lived in Stanley Park as a manager's wife recalled how, 'when the first two women rode a bicycle, it was not considered very respectable, just a little bold, but people got used to it, and after a time there were more women riding, until it got to be quite "the thing."'[59]

Jessie changed her living arrangements once more on returning to Rossland for her fourth year of teaching there. Mrs Bart was giving such good service in lieu of rent that she and Liz Olding decided, in the fall of 1899, to 'board with her' in Jessie's house. Fed up with the remaining Moffatt sister, their fellow teacher Maud, Jessie turfed her out. 'We didn't have a quarrel at all. She just said she thought it was pretty "cool," & I told her she might have known that changes would be made, even if Mrs. Bart hadn't come – and that was all.' Maud Moffatt's replacement was Liz Olding's sister, who had got work in Rossland. She had some private music students, as well as the promise of substituting as needed in school, and was leading the choir in the local Baptist church, to which the Olding sisters belonged. The Nova Scotia tie surfaced when a local man who 'used to take lessons from her in Sydney' turned up in Rossland. 'He has been in a couple of evenings, & is glad to find any friendly

faces in this strange place.' By October 1899, Jessie had paid off all but
$30 on her house. About that time, the Barts departed, which meant
Jessie and her two Olding cousins were forced to take on household
tasks again, while also prospecting for another housemate. 'We'll be
extremely careful in choosing – we'd all much rather be by ourselves,
than take in any who might be uncongenial.'[60]

The freedom to live as she would that Jessie embraced in Rossland in
no way diminished the domesticating function that she had exercised
since first coming to British Columbia a decade earlier. She continued
to do so in and out of the classroom. She acted or did not act in certain
ways; she held particular views about others and their behaviour; and
she made choices that modelled appropriate ways of behaviour. The
angst that Jessie expressed to her mother – 'I often wonder if it's selfish
of me to enjoy life so much here' – illuminates the full extent to which
she continued, even in her most halcyon moments, to live her upbringing. As she learned from her earliest days in Pictou County, she should
not find pleasure unless she acted out of duty and obligation. Jessie's
need to present herself to her mother as maintaining a suitably Presbyterian parsimoniousness is evident in her description of entertaining
friends for 'coffee & bread & butter.' She explained: 'We're not extrava-
gant but when folk come in after skating we usually have "somethin'
hot." One of the boys said he got a regular going over one night for the
way he walked into the refreshments – was told it wasn't polite – to take
three cups of coffee & *seven* slices of bread & butter – wasn't expected to
make a meal &c &c.'[61]

It was Jessie's integration of self into the mining frontier that gave her
the very great power she exercised in the work of domestication. By virtue of belonging, she was better able to effect change than had she
remained an outsider or observer, much as occurred in the Nicola Valley. The model that she and her housemates presented was extraordinarily tempting, as indicated by the endless stream of visitors making
their way to their door. Once inside, they were presented with a version
of domesticity that they could not help but envy, and very likely then
adopt, if they could, at some later point along the way. Jessie and her
housemates might lovingly term their first home a 'shack,' a popular
term in frontier Rossland, but it was well ordered, neat, and clean, and
had a strong uplifting element underlying the outward joviality. Many of
the books that they read aloud and discussed – Ian Maclaren's Scottish
idylls, the Pansy and Samantha books – have been almost wholly ignored
by literary critics, even though their prescriptions influenced a genera-

tion and more of everyday women, and men, who like Jessie found fulfil-
ment in the work of domestication.

The housemates demonstrated no fear in the frontier boom town that
was Rossland. The closest they came to a frightening encounter, as
reported in Jessie's surviving letters home, was in the autumn of 1897.
'We had such a scare last night. Maud & I were in our night dresses, &
Veen had gone to the woodshed (right beside the kitchen) when she
darted back, looking fairly gasping. "There's a man lying right at our
door, I almost fell over him."' The fright was short lived, for 'he was
drunk as a piper, but when Veen saw that that was all that ailed him, she
went out & tried to start him off.' Unsuccessful, Veen ran across the
street to get help from a neighbour, 'as it was rather cold for a fellow to
make his bed on an old pine stump in the open air.'[62] It turned out the
man had tripped over the stump and fallen.

The world was opening up for women in various ways. Among them
was the opportunity to exercise the franchise at the local level. Jessie
appreciated the opportunity to '*vote*,' so she underlined in a letter home
at the beginning of 1899. 'I've done that for the first time in a municipal
election! And our candidate was elected too. The new mayor – Mr. Gordon – is a member of our church, & I have two of his children in my
room. He & one of his men were around all that day, I suppose – anyhow they came to the school house just at noon, & I had a drive to the
polls & back – the first this winter.'[63] Jessie did not just vote, she
reflected on her choice and recognized the informal factors that influenced her decision.

Jessie and her companions modelled social activism, which was beginning to agitate more and more people as Protestant churches in Canada
became determined to implement the kingdom of God on earth. 'We
made up a bundle last week for a poor family – not the only one in town
either, they say. The father has been out of work for a long time, & at
present he gets *washing* to do, from the mines at the Le Roi. Between
Miss Mackay's old things & our own, we made up a pretty comfortable
bundle for them.' Another time, a man 'came & asked for something to
eat, & was quite ready to take the ax – "hatchet" he called it – till his supper was ready,' and so Jessie got the wood split even while doing good.
She evoked his circumstances with considerable sympathy. 'Had been
working in the mines in Montana, but they had shut down, owing to the
[Boer] war, & he had come here looking for work, but unsuccessfully so
far. His family is in the "home country" – Austria – and his English is not
very good, but he looks honest, & I can believe him when he says he

drinks only beer.' Jessie had carefully vetted her 'poor beggar' before she made him an offer. 'We promised him 50c to come to-morrow & split all our wood, & he seemed very grateful.'[64]

Sometimes the housemates could only stand back and watch as the mining economy that was Rossland took its toll. 'A home just across from us was sadly broken up last week. Mr. Kane was killed in the "Sunset Mine" – went down too soon after a blast, found the air bad & started to come out but fell from the ladder, & as the machinery was out of order, no one got down in time to do any good. Another (unmarried man) was killed. Poor Mrs Kane sold off her few things – packed up & was off for her home near Montreal before the end of the week. They had just one little boy; it was a terrible shock to us all – to see him leave home so well & strong, & be brought back again, within a few hours.' On another occasion, when a man with a wife and four young children died after two operations, the future seemed to hold a ray of hope. 'For the present, they will stay here. Mrs. B. says the B.A.C. people (large mine-owners here, for whom Mr. B worked) have been very kind, & that they will probably put her in the way of earning something.' Jessie was pleasantly surprised, even if she felt helpless to assist. 'I used to think they would be destitute, but it seems not – she said she would not wait till she spent *all* her money, but would save enough to take her east, if she found living here too expensive. Poor body, she is as brave & strong as can be, but the outlook is very lonely.'[65]

The women made judgments even while appearing to be very open. Their response to the marriage in early 1897 of the Methodist minister who had been Rossland's first teacher is indicative. 'Birks, our former principal, is away on his wedding tour. He has married a widow & is now stepfather to two grown-up children while he himself is only twenty-eight. Miss Mackay says "to think of his acting like this, after us having him up here, & *feeding him too*."' Amidst all of the supposed openness, respectability still had to be observed. Describing a visiting cartoonist, Jessie wrote home: 'It was *good clean* entertainment, & all the entertainments in Rossland are *not* so, unfortunately.'[66]

Other times, Jessie found herself in disagreement with her housemates. Her sense of social obligation was repeatedly tried by the Moffatts. Maud refused to donate to the new Presbyterian church in favour of buying herself a fur cape for $30 and the piano in their new house, paid for on instalments of $10–15 a month. 'I don't know when Maud vexed me as much ... I didn't say anything for a while – I was too angry, but asked her later on what her stand-point was, to think & speak as she did. They go night after night – enjoy the comfortable [church] building, & – expect others to pay the expenses. I think it down-right mean ... they don't know the first thing about giving as a *right* & think Liz & me fools to give at all.' Another time the tension had to do with visiting the sick. Liz willingly accompanied Jessie on her rounds, but their housemates 'seem to hold themselves so aloof, & to pay such visits only because it's *expected* of them.'[67]

Jessie also continued to be an exemplar in traditional ways. Religious observance remained important to her, although she was likely turned off by her mother's excesses and, more particularly, by Catherine's strident desire that she convert not just Ulysses Campbell but her housemates. 'You spoke once of Miss Moffatt not being of any decided religion. It will be good for her & intended if she takes a decided stand for the right in religion & will never regret it & I hope you will be helpful to her in this matter, don't be too backward where a soul is at stake let your influence be always on the right side.' In the event Jessie compromised. While accepting that her housemates did not believe in similar fashion to herself, she wanted them to understand her piety. After an evening of coasting when the conversation turned to 'creeds,' 'I asked them if they would listen to the 15th of Cor.[orinthians] which they did – Catholic, Presbyterian & the one of no belief.'[68]

In Rossland, so one resident described in 1897, 'we don't keep the Sabbath here with the Sabbatarian strictness with which it is observed in most of the Eastern cities, but six or seven religious bodies have places of worship, with large and attentive congregations.' Jessie quickly fell into this attitude toward religious observance. Rather than piety being distinct from other aspects of her life, she fitted it into her social round. 'Moffatt & I had a two-hours' walk Sunday after church.' Religion, rather than being an end itself as at Nicola Lake, was now combined with other activities. 'You should have seen us coasting the other *night* after I came from prayer meeting.' Even when 'too much school work' loomed, Jessie was dutiful. 'I manage to get to Wed. evening prayer meeting with tight squeezing.' Another time: 'I stayed in the church till 6, studying after my school work was done – back to prayer-meeting at 8, then four or five of us trotted off to the rink – some to skate & some to look on.' Jessie closed a letter home, written on a Sunday evening, 'The first bell (belonging to the Meth. Church) is ringing, so I must up & get ready for church.'[69] Historian Lynne Marks describes for small-town Ontario during these years how growing interest in leisure activities diminished Protestantism's hold.[70] While Jessie was determined to maintain the two aspects of her life in tandem, she was in fact increasingly accommodating the church to leisure as opposed to the other way around.

Both the Presbyterian and Methodist ministers were incorporated into Jessie's social round. The Nova Scotia connection operated, for Methodist minister Charles Ladner, whom Jessie heard preach when he was at Kamloops and who became resident in Rossland in the summer of 1896, had a brother preaching in Halifax acquainted with Jessie's mother. 'Give my kind regards to Mr. Ladner's family & say I'm glad you are with Friends,' Catherine commanded. Ladner was no ordinary minister. Every Sunday he walked seven miles downhill to Trail for morning services, returning uphill to Rossland for evening worship. He enlarged the Rossland church, painted and papered, got wooden benches, and opened a basement reading room as an alternative to men spending their free time in saloons.[71]

Jessie signalled her support for Ladner's initiatives by her highly visible friendship with his family. She borrowed skates from a Ladner daughter, and their son who worked at the post office pick up her mail, which she then collected from their house. Jessie joked to her mother: 'No danger of them bringing mail from the office on Sunday, & Miss Ladner would be sure to "round me up" if she saw me doing anything out of the way.' Although Jessie was in her heart of hearts a Presbyterian, she was nurtured by the Ladners. 'I did spend one Saturday in the hills, with Ethel & Will Ladner & a friend of theirs – I threw up everything, books, & work (even the baking) and went. It was good for one's health to be abroad on such a day.' The next spring: 'I have been spending my nights at Ladner's since Monday last, when Mr. L. went to District meeting, & get good long sleeps. They are so good and kind.'[72] Jessie also renewed bonds with the Rev. James Calvert, who had been so much a part of her life in the Nicola Valley and then of Annie's at Salmon Arm. In May 1897 he became Methodist pastor at Trail. Jessie took a church group with her in early 1899 to see her old friends.

Jessie's fuller embrace of Presbyterianism was linked directly to a new minister who arrived in September 1897, having only recently been ordained after studying in Ontario. A month later, she explained to her mother how 'I used to go to the Methodist church some Sunday nights, but now I hate to miss my own church service, and the girls nearly always come with me at night.' The reason she gave was that 'Mr. Gandier is a fine preacher – a strong, earnest, fearless man.' Again, the Nova Scotia connection whipped into place, per Catherine's response. 'I'm glad you like the new minister, I've heard his brother [Rev. Alfred Gandier] from

Halifax, heard him give a lecture at Trenton on Foreign Missions ... & I heard him too at our W.F.M. convention at N.G. by your remarks they are alike earnest, firm & fearless.'[73]

Something more was going on. Rev. D. McG. Gandier was single and so was Jessie. She was in her mid-thirties, past the usual age of marriage but certainly not unmarriageable. The number of single, as well as married, men with whom the housemates socialized was considerable, and they did so with an unsupervised intimacy that would have been suspect in more settled locations. Jessie remained ambivalent about her attraction to the opposite sex. When her old housemate Mackay wrote tempting her to the United States, she resisted on the grounds that 'I have to find my pleasure in my work, or do without it.' On the other hand, when one of her Olding cousins' brothers teased them, Jessie was flattered. 'He supposed it would be a race between us two now, as to who would first catch a man! N.B. The race isn't on yet ... & I am not conscious of any yearning desire to take upon myself any further responsibility.'[74]

The Presbyterian minister turned up far more often in Jessie's letters home than would have been the case had there been no attraction on her part. Her worry that her pupils might disturb him when she taught in the same building in which he lived was more than mere courtesy. She took pleasure that he gave rather more assistance with her class than might be expected. 'Mr. Gandier was so hoarse yesterday he could barely speak, but he came out & split wood, & built up a roaring fire (in school / the janitor is either lazy or stupid – at any rate, he seldom has a decent fire in, & Mr G. has come to the rescue more than once).' Jessie observed, and reported, his activities in minute detail. 'Veen says he was skating yesterday afternoon – getting up his circulation, I suppose.'[75]

Jessie sought out opportunities to encounter the Presbyterian minister. Reading a story in 'The Witness,' among her mother's regular parcel of newspapers, Jessie made a point to 'show it to Mr. Gandier some time.' In part because of the Nova Scotia link, she shared his news with her mother on a regular basis. 'As you will see by the papers I am sending, he is likely to have a new church, & I a new schoolroom before long. Myself & my 60 children must be a trial to him many a day.' When Jessie strapped Emma Le Boeuf for being 'disobedient & "sassy,"' she did so well aware that the minister was at home. 'Mr. Gandier was in his rooms all the time, & heard every sound! I knew it, but duty had to be done just the same. Won't I be glad to get into the new school?' Jessie became a bit proprietorial in describing how he went skating with the housemates after prayer meeting. 'Mr. Gandier came too – first skate he's had in three weeks. I like to skate with him – he's a tall man & a good skater, & a person of my size doesn't seem to be much trouble to him to tow around. We fetched him home with us & treated him decent – to coffee & bread & butter.'[76]

With her cousin Liz Olding's arrival and the teasing given them about looking for men, Jessie became more open. 'As for Mr. Gandier – my much respected pastor – I muchly fear my daily drill to the 60 "twigs" must have "spiked my guns" in that direction. That "excellent thing in women, a voice, gentle and low," is not always mine, & the thinness of the walls compels him to hear me when I speak – "which I do ever." He even heard me when I snapped at Miss Moffatt & Blair the other evening, when they came in & interrupted me in the middle of my work ... I did well to be angry – at the time – sorry enough afterwards though.' A month later: 'Had to take Mr. Gandier's class in Sunday school to-day, and next Sunday too – he is in Victoria at Synod or whatever it is. I would not do it for anyone else, but he is very good & I couldn't refuse to oblige him in this.' Jessie's succour did not end there. 'Mr. Gandier came home from the coast with a very bad cold, but he managed to preach twice yesterday, & we brought him home with us last night & gave him hot lemonade.' Jessie's next line was enticing. 'We want to treat him decent, so's *Mrs* Gandier will open her doors to us when she comes.' Shortly after Jessie traded houses, she wrote home: 'Mr. Gandier was in last night after church – his first call since we've been settled. We had a nice hot cup of cocoa all around, & some of Lizabeth's good cake. It's nice to have a sort of home, & make things comfortable for others.'[77]

By the spring of 1899, Jessie had her 'wheel' for getting around and told her mother how, one evening in late August, after riding, 'I got back in time to get ready for prayer meeting.' The Rev. D. McG. Gandier was part of why she did so. 'Mr. Gandier was wanting exercise too, so after prayer meeting he walked down to our house, but first, we went to the Meth. church, & got the tail end of a concert there. Some one had sent him two tickets, & it was real good of him to share up. "This didn't cost me anything" he said, "but if you'll allow me, I'll take you to the band concert next week"!' Jessie was delighted. 'You may be sure I said "yes thank you" with all my heart. He always says that church people should patronize the *really good* things that come to town, & practises what he preaches.' Such deeds may well have boosted her expectations for the relationship. 'Wasn't it nice of him to ask me? It's not so very often now that I get anything in that line unless I myself foot the bills.' The fall of

1899, a cartoonist came to town and drew several sketches, one of which Jessie relayed home in considerable detail. 'Mr. Gandier, whom he referred to as "the *high* church party," ... was represented in conversation with a very plump body who was speaking thusly, "oh, minister, if you only had a wife!"'[78]

As the nineteenth century gave way to the twentieth, Jessie likely took more pleasure in life than she had ever previously done. She had found herself in Rossland. Not only was she happy in her school work, she had gained a British Columbia teaching certificate which gave her security for another four years. She owned a home of her own, and the house was virtually paid off. She had dared to take to the 'wheel,' and, while not a 'new woman' in every sense of the term, she enjoyed a mobility and independence she likely would previously have not thought possible. Just how the Rev. D. McG. Gandier viewed her we cannot tell, but he was one of a circle of friends whose company gave her pleasure. Daughterhood's obligations were still part of her character, but, as the new century beckoned, she had reason to be optimistic.

Chapter Eleven

Sisters Full Circle

VICTORIA
SALT SPRING ISLAND

In the final years of the nineteenth century, the McQueen sisters seemed, once again, to have gone separate ways. Jessie was settled in the boom town of Rossland, content and quite prosperous. Mother to three children, Annie was living on the frontier, discontented with her lot and isolated from the way of life familiar to her from Pictou County. The dynamic between the two sisters had shifted. Previously, Annie served as Jessie's protector in venturing into the larger world. In return, Jessie was quick to respond, as she had done at Kamloops in 1893 and Salmon Arm in 1896, when Annie called on her for assistance. Annie always considered herself to be the adventurous, free spirit with a compliant elder sister. Now Jessie had found a way of life she liked and gained her self-confidence. Not needing to be shielded by her younger sister, she did not feel the same obligation to her. As their older sister Eliza's reaction on learning about Jessie's new position in Rossland revealed, nobody had anticipated such a shift. 'It was a great surprise to me to find "Rossland" up in the corner [of the envelope]. I was just thinking that Nan would enjoy the change more than you because you never liked having your routine disturbed.'[1]

The critical shift in the relationship between the sisters came when Annie, instead of settling in Rossland, where Jessie had got her job, went to Trail, forcing Jessie to fend for herself. Since Jim had a rail pass between the two towns, he saw Jessie from time to time. She spent her first Christmas with the Gordons. Her attention was fixed, however, not on Annie's doings but on her own life in Rossland and her new housemates. 'They came to meet me when I came back from Trail, & acted real glad to see me again. It was the pleasantest return to work that I've had in many a year.' During Christmas 1897, Jessie went to see her sister at her new home at Crow's Nest Landing, but, to Nan's chagrin, invited some of her Rossland friends along for part of the time. When their fellow Nova Scotian teacher at Crow's Nest Landing, Stella Lyons, quit her job to get married, Jim Gordon tried to get Jessie to apply for the post. Writing to her mother, Jessie prevaricated about an appeal that previously she would have accepted as her duty. 'I guess I could have it, but – there any many "buts" in the way, & I think it better to stay where I am – just when they are pushing on with the new school too.'[2] Jessie was no longer there to do her sister's bidding.

Deprived of the possibility of a summer visit home to Nova Scotia with Stella Lyons, Annie tried to cajole her older sister into going with her as a travelling companion. Jessie's plans to take the teaching examinations with her Rossland friends killed the proposal. As a compromise, Annie wanted Jessie to spend part of her summer holidays at Crow's Nest Landing, but once again Jessie found excuses which she retailed to her mother. 'I'd love to, but there won't be much time after exams & it takes quite a while to get there.' Cost may have been a factor. Annie admitted to Catherine that until the promised rail line to Rossland was completed, she herself could not afford to visit for 'it would cost forty dollars to get there.' Catherine intervened, employing Presbyterian guilt. 'Hope you will be spared to see Annie & all the Friends take this letter & let Annie see it. Would not Jessie & Marshie like to see you too. May the Lord preserve them all & I hope we may yet all meet here if not hereafter.'[3]

Lonely and alone, Annie did not warm to Jessie's newfound independence. The previous summer Jessie had taken a 'cruise to Spokane' and planned to do so again in 1898 after the teachers' examination. This time Annie went along, a trip that only further widened the gap between the sisters. Letting Annie return alone to Canada, Jessie continued on to Seattle by herself to visit with Mrs Bart, who had stayed with the housemates in Rossland. Annie remained miffed several months later. 'I am still feeling a little sore over the way she used me in Spokane this summer and had better not say any more.' Another source of alienation was Jessie's housemates, who may also have gone along on the cruise, for Annie added sourly: 'She should have cut loose from those Moffatt's long ago. I did not, and do not like the people she has made friends of there.'[4] From Annie's perspective, it was – to her unhappiness – not herself, as she would have liked, who was taking advantage of the

new freedom of action being accorded women, but Jessie, who had up
to then trailed in her wake.

All the same, as Christmas 1898 approached, Annie hoped 'Jessie will
be able to come down here at Xmas, if it doesn't cost too much.'[5] Jessie
had other ideas, particularly now that their cousin Liz Olding was living
with her. 'This time we'll not go anywhere, or do anything, but just rest
all over, & be glad of the chance.' Jessie did send Annie a gift, which
more reflected her new lifestyle than it did her sister's immediate needs.
For that very reason, the present gave special pleasure. 'Jessie sent me a
bottle of perfume, the only article that wasn't a necessity that I've had
for many a day.' The next summer, Annie groused, once again, how
Jessie was not coming, 'but I did not expect her.' As had become usual
in her letters home, she had a little plaint at her older sister's expense.
'She seems to be always chasing a good time, and does not seem to get it
when all is said and done.'[6] Any search for entertainment, being inher-
ently reprehensible, could not for that reason be successful.

Annie's suggestion in her letter of August 1899 that her elder sister
was giving priority to pleasure over duty to the family had some justification. Since Daniel McQueen's death in the fall of 1894, Catherine had
struggled to hold together the family farm at Sutherland's River,
assisted only by her eldest daughter, Jane. She depended for her comfort on her daughters' letters and visits. However, the always dependable
Jessie was for the first time growing away from her family. Letters
became more a listing of recent events than an exchange of views. Asked
by her mother whether she wanted to renew a newspaper subscription,
Jessie declined, since 'I would never get time to read the paper, and am
not exactly yearning for information about places.' Catherine persisted
in sending her daughter the local papers. Reading about yet another
Pictou County death, Jessie could only murmur, 'Changes, changes all
the time.'[7]

At one point, late in 1897, Jessie was forced to admit, 'Somehow or
other, I have mislaid your last letter,' to which Catherine responded a
bit caustically, 'No I was not anxious, but thought you were more tardy
than usual, but take all the sunny time you can get & I'll wait till you get
time to write.' Viewing existence, as she always had done, through a religious lens, she added, 'Don't overdo yourself, rest & sleep all you can, &
don't forget Peter's advice 1st P- 5-7.' Jessie even forgot her mother's
birthday, so Catherine reminded her with her usual tact. 'You will see by
the above date that yesterday was my birthday & even I would have forgot it untill [sic] I looked at the Calander [sic] with the verses for every

day.' Jessie continued to send money – 'Jane says to tell you she got good strong boots, & says thankee' – but less often. Near the end of 1898, she queried Catherine in a 'Private' note: 'How are your finances? I feel ashamed that I have sent you nothing for such a long time. Don't be in need – you must have it, if some one else has to wait.' Enclosed in the letter were 'a few stamps for your convenience.'[8]

Twice before, in 1891 and in 1894, Jessie had returned to the farm-house at Sutherland's River after a three-year stint in the West to which she had committed herself. Part of Jessie felt obliged to do so again. 'Oh, I must try & get home some time within the year, but worrying about it won't make it any easier.' As her latest three-year sojourn came to an end in the spring of 1899, she sought to avoid leaving Rossland. She proposed 'sending means to M. Belle to come home instead.' Catherine was outraged and, strategically, responded how 'Jane said oh nonsense, she did not want you to put off coming.' This manoeuvre elic-ited from Jessie expressions of remorse but no promises. 'It made me feel worse than ever, after reading your letter, to think that you had expected us & would be disappointed.' The use of the word 'us' was a diversionary tactic, committing Jessie to nothing more than the visit home that Catherine had long desired Annie to make. Jessie ascribed her own and Annie's inability to make any such visit in the immediate future to finances, an explanation which was true, at least in part. 'If we will only be spared to each other a little longer, next year will surely see us in easier circumstances. My house *was* a big undertaking, but it will surely pay, in the end.' Similarly, Annie told her sister Mary Belle later in 1899, 'we are scratching our ducats together to make the last payment on our house, three hundred dollars, after that we will begin to save again to go home.'[9]

In the end, Jessie did put daughterhood's obligations above her sense of self. Several reasons account for her decision to return to Suther-land's River in the summer of 1900. Whatever were her aspirations in respect to the Rev. D. McG. Gandier, they may have been fading, given he was compelled to resign his Rossland parish because of ill health in September 1900 and shortly thereafter left the ministry. Catherine ensured that all her daughters knew of her tribulations, but she had done so for such a long time that they probably paid less attention than would otherwise be the case. 'My knee has rheumatism in it, & makes it stiff to rise off chair if much on my feet.' Yet Jessie knew, despite not wanting to know, that her mother was finding it increasingly difficult to manage the farm. As Annie hinted to Catherine in a letter home, 'Do

you find butter making pay[s] you for the time and trouble?'[10] In
November 1899, Jane had to be institutionalized again, leaving Catherine on her own.

Worse was to follow a month later. George, the clever but indulged
prodigal son whom Catherine continued to hope would give up the folly
of his ways and return to the farm and to his filial duties, died in a Brooklyn hospital on 1 December 1899. His death certificate gives as the cause
'tubucular pneumonia,' his occupation as mechanic, and his age as just
forty-one. On inquiring of her son's employers about the state of his soul
and his life in his final days, Catherine received a shattering reply.
George had abandoned not just church-going but religion as well. 'No
clergyman visited him during his illness.' The letter continued: 'From
some of his conversation with our Mr. Smith, he spoke in favor of the
Protestant faith, and for those reasons we buried him accordingly.'
George was living alone in a boarding house. 'He left no letters or papers
of any kind,' the account continued, 'and in reference to George having
money, I am sorry to say, he had none.' The letter's reticent wording inti-
mated that there was more about George's life that his employers chose
not to reveal. For Catherine, a woman of seventy-seven, living by herself,
the loss was devastating, sufficient to awaken in Jessie's heart her sense of
duty. Even then, at first Jessie hoped to go home only for a visit and
applied for a six-month leave of absence.[11] Her aspiration of the past several years to get a life certificate, if not a 2nd A, indicates strongly that
she planned to make a teaching career in British Columbia.

For the third time in her life, Jessie travelled east to Nova Scotia. By
the middle of July 1900, she was back on the farm almost as if she had
never left. Returned to Sutherland's River, Jessie found herself stuck
there. Approaching her fortieth birthday, she once again became the
dutiful daughter. Catherine, for her part, had never let go. 'Be sure if
weather gets the least cold to put on warm clothes as tis often cause for
sickness the sudden change from heat to cold, unless warm clothes are
also used,' Catherine had commanded her in Rossland. The next summer as a postscript: 'Don't neglect your health better take a little simple
med – & watch overheat or sudden cold.' A young niece visited Sutherland's River a year after Jessie's return and sensed her plight. On her
departure Kate Wisdom composed a poem in honour of 'Dear little
Aunt Jess,' in which she advised, 'be sure & not work to [sic] hard let
some of your work go and have a rest, try to get as many bathes as you
can.' She wanted Jessie to 'come & see us & leave the old cows behind,'
and, most of all, 'don't be lonesome dear little Aunt Jess.' It was only to

her still beloved younger sister Nan that Jessie was willing to acknowl-edge a deep 'loneliness.' From far away Tobacco Plains, Annie commis-erated how Jessie was 'cutting the sheep's potatoes, feeding and milking the cows etc. all by you alone, in cold weather.' A year later, Annie shared with their mother how 'it makes me feel badly to think of Jessie struggling alone with all those cows, and a scanty supply of fuel.'[12]

According to McQueen descendants, Jessie took another chance on intimacy that again ended in tragedy. Shortly after returning home, in her early forties, she is said to have become engaged to a New Glasgow widower whose wife and child had died of tuberculosis. Before they could wed, he too succumbed of the disease, the story goes. Providence had once again intervened. Whatever the specifics, thereafter Jessie's everyday life did not go much beyond the family farm, caring for the ani-mals, haying, keeping house. In her little spare time, she participated in the work of the local church, hooked rugs out of old rags, and once in a while managed to get away to visit her married sisters spread across the Maritimes. To get needed cash, Jessie considered helping out in the local post office, and for a time she and Catherine boarded the teacher. Every summer, various nephews and nieces would come to visit the farm, for whom Jessie became a favourite aunt. Her niece and nephews in Brit-ish Columbia were not forgotten. Dal kept all his life a miniature illus-trated edition of *Eric; or, Little by Little*, bound in tartan and inscribed, 'To Dal with love from his aunt Jessie, Christmas 1906.'[13]

This time it was Annie who was left behind in British Columbia. At the turn of the century, as Jessie returned home to Pictou County to care for her mother, Annie gave every appearance of having settled down into wifely domesticity as her life's work. She continued to strive, but within the context of a growing family and of what she later termed 'the typical log house of B.C. pioneering days.'[14]

Then Annie's circumstances changed once again. She got no closer to Jessie, but she did manage to manoeuvre her children's future, after five years at Gateway, in the direction she had in mind for them. Marsh had been away for a year at Vancouver High School when in 1907 Jim wran-gled a transfer to the provincial capital of Victoria. It had been twenty years since a boisterous young Annie, just arrived from Pictou County, tripped through its streets. She had changed, and so had the city. The National Policy, which, some considered to have thwarted Nova Scotia's development, had done somewhat the same for British Columbia, as its nascent industries fell into decline. More important to Victoria's destiny was the rise of Vancouver, which as terminus of the transcontinental rail line and of ships heading to Asia, had become the principal city in the province, with a population more than double the capital city's 25,000 or so. Victoria was acquiring its own character, playing on its British colonial origins to become a tourist destination. The city centre was transformed with the construction of an imposing Canadian Pacific hotel near to the recently completed Parliament Buildings, both fronted by an elegant sea promenade. Victoria compared favourably to any place Annie had known in the Maritimes, and now she would be part of it.

In early June 1907, Annie resigned her position as Gateway's postmistress, filled with anticipation that, finally, her children would have the opportunities she considered their due. Jessie was a young woman of eighteen, but the move meant that Marsh, at sixteen, and Dal, who was eleven, could get a proper education. Jim's transfer did not signal a promotion. He remained a 'prevention officer,' but with an annual salary $200 richer at $1,100.[15] The move, however, did benefit the family as a whole.

The Gordons settled at 404 Oswego Street in the long-established James Bay section of Victoria. Their corner house is no longer there, but others on the street and around the corner on Superior Street suggest it was a fairly modest newish one-and-a-half or two-storey shingled or wood-sided structure. Their neighbours were carpenters, grocers, and bakers, longshoremen, painters, and teamsters. The Gordons' house was located only a long block away, along Superior Street, down which ran a tram, from the Parliament Buildings, and beyond that, downtown Victoria. For the first time since their Ontario years, the Gordons could go to church as often as they pleased. 'We attend St. Andrew's regularly and altho the minister is not a great preacher, the services are really quite an inspiration.' Freed of her children's schooling, Annie joined the Ladies' Musical Club. Young Jessie did some teaching and was, according to her father, 'enjoying it very much.'[16]

As well as their offspring's schooling, the move was motivated by Jim and Annie's middling health. Jim enthused to Catherine a year later. 'We all have had better health since coming to the coast. Annie is looking better than she has for years, a fine complexion & clear eyes, also a much more serene mind.' The change did less to ameliorate Jim's stomach ailments, which continued to dog him. Perhaps for that reason he wrote his last will and testament in April 1910, leaving everything to 'my said wife, Annie L. Gordon, for her own use absolutely.' Jim Gordon died eighteen months later, on 10 November 1911, after three weeks' illness followed by an emergency operation.[17] He was just fifty-one years of age.

Annie was devastated. Still in her mid-forties, she turned her grief out-ward into causes intended to smooth British Columbia's rough edges. By virtue of living in the provincial capital, she had opportunities denied her on the frontier. Annie, who had flashed across the sky and then sub-merged herself into marriage and family, came full circle. She learned to take her quarter century on the frontier in stride, reflecting one evening, 'The house is scented with a big bunch of sweet peas. It makes me think of Phillipps.' Within a year of Jim's death, Annie had transformed herself from fitful housewife to an efficient head of household and public fig-ure, so she informed her mother in 1912 in no uncertain terms. 'I have a good many business letters that have to be written and am kept busy with financial affairs, for times are a little slack, and my management of affairs now will make all the difference between comparative comfort and pretty hard scratching for us later.' Annie also moved, taking her three children to 1326 Woodlands Road (later Thurlow), in the Fairfield area, not far from Beacon Hill Park. The Gordons' frame two-storey house was likely newly built, as were most of the other quite presentable houses on the block. It was a respectable middle-class area of Victoria in which to bring up children.[18]

The vitality that characterized Annie as a young woman, first in Nova Scotia and then in the Nicola Valley, returned with renewed vigour. She realized that, for her public self to be effective, the private image also had to be transformed. Annie explained to her sister Jessie in the fall of 1912: 'Jessie and I have not dared to get any clothes this summer, and are looking pretty shabby, but we will get some soon, enough for respectability, and I will have to get my teeth fixed, I have broken one of the front ones.' A year later, she was still tending to her teeth, abused by years of frontier life. 'On Tuesday next I have an appointment with the dentist to have my old stumps removed, and will be thankful when it is done.'[19]

Nothing gave women greater freedom to act in the public realm than did the burgeoning social reform movement. For many women, as well as men, of Annie's and Jessie's generation, the religious piety of their childhood had shifted from a concern with the hereafter to the world on earth. Margaret Prang explains the consequences of this shift. 'A broader network of friendship and interest [than in the churches] was created by women in interdenominational endeavours such as the Woman's Christian Temperance Union and Young Women's Christian Association. Many of the thousands of upper- and middle-class women who were active in these associations also belonged to others of more secular origin such as the Imperial Order Daughters of the Empire (1900) and the Women's Institutes (1897).'[20]

Previously, in her married life, Annie had only fleeting opportunities to effect action. The most significant was in St Thomas, shortly after her marriage, where, just before the Gordons headed back to British Columbia, she took 'a prominent part in the WCTU work' and, her husband later recalled, 'gave an address to a crowded house on missionary work in B.C.' Now Annie had ample opportunity to indulge, and she joined, among other organizations, the Local Council of Women, Imperial Order Daughters of the Empire, Women's Canadian Club, and the Women's Institute. She was involved with the Women's Equality League as it sought to get women the vote. Another public cause was, in 1912, the entry of Sikh women into British Columbia 'both as a matter of justice and as a solution to the unrest of the new Sikh residents.' That was not all. 'I am getting up a paper on Nietszche's philosophy for the Literary Society.'[21]

By acting as she did, Annie made a double contribution to the ongoing work of domestication. Even as she 'played a prominent part in many activities aimed at community betterment,' to quote from her obituary, Annie was gaining acceptability for women as persons in their own right. The Gordons owned some lots in Vancouver, which Annie decided to sell in the summer of 1912. As she put it: 'The agent in Vancouver has been giving me a great deal of trouble, which, however, is pretty well settled now. He did not realise that I was accustomed to doing business, and tried to get the better of me.' Annie was not to be done in. 'I kept my own accounts, and rejected his statement – substituting my own.'[22]

In the summer of 1913, Annie visited the Maritimes. It was too late for a joyous reunion between mother and daughter, especially given that the relationship between them had never been that intense in the first place. Returned to Victoria, Annie pacified her mother: 'I too wish that we could have talked more, but I noticed that every time we got talking about matters you go nervous and worried, so I let it alone.' All the same, Annie considered, she consoled Catherine, that her mother's letter just received 'struck me as being one of the best letters I have had from you for some time.' At least part of the distance between mother and headstrong youngest daughter was closed. The trip also confirmed for Annie how far away she had come from her Nova Scotian roots. She was no longer a sojourner in any sense of the word. She later recalled to her sister Jessie how on her trip home 'I saw very few people.'[23] It was, in part, this dissociation that fuelled Annie's growing determination to remake British Columbia to the advantage of women with views similar to her own.

In 1915 Annie's cousin Jessie Olding Hunter visited Annie in Victoria. She described in graphic detail Annie's endless energy, much as McQueen women had earlier contributed to the Church. Annie regularly volunteered for 'the noon hour on Saturday' to further 'the work "The Daughters of the Empire" are doing for the shop girls.' As retailed by Jessie: 'They have a large cheerful hall, with tables & chairs, a piano and magazines, and good fire in chilly weather, and the shop girls pay 25c for eight tickets, a ticket entitles them to all the tea or coffee with milk & sugar that they wish to drink with their lunch. Annie washed the dishes and I dried and Miss Currie [the other volunteer] waited on the girls. They have white table linen, a nice gas range to make tea & coffee on, and they own the dishes – plates, cups & saucers, spoons, sugar bowls, cream jugs, tea pots etc. It is a great thing for the girls to have a comfortable place to go to eat their lunches, and will aid in keeping them from evil ways.'[24]

The First World War expanded Annie's opportunities to effect change in the public sphere. She was active in relief work, being especially concerned with conditions in military hospitals. She became official visitor to convalescent hospitals on behalf of Victoria's Red Cross Auxiliary, distributing gifts of fruit, cigarettes, and reading material. Writing to Jessie back home in Pictou County at the beginning of 1919, Annie made clear how much of a public person she had become. 'Last week was a perfect nightmare of meetings, and this week is almost as bad. Annual meetings too. I had three meetings today and am "near dead."' In somewhat maudlin fashion, Annie added: 'I think I will try to give up all meetings for a time. I have got to where I just naturally hate them all, and even my sense of duty is wearing thin.'[25]

A month or two later, Annie was again on the offensive, having 'got a recreation room for the Military Isolation Hospital at long last.' All of the connections she had built up during the past several years were called on to achieve her ends. 'The YMCA put up the lumber, the Engineers built it, I hustled the Engineers and have furnished it mostly.' She prided herself on being invited to the opening. 'When the recreation room was opened, there were several YMCA men there, and they had a program. I was, of course, the only woman permitted to enter and as each speaker arose, he solemnly said, "Mr Chairman, Mrs Gordon and gentlemen," until I got so embarrassed and hysterical, that when they called on me to speak, for the first time in my life I was actually tongue tied and could only gasp out a few sentences.' Annie could not resist a little bragging to Jessie in describing the event. 'The boys almost tore the house down with applause, for no matter what I may say, they think it is lovely. I am "Maw" to them all, saints and sinners alike, and for some reason or other the military authorities are fairly eating out of my hand.'[26]

War's end did not stop Annie. 'I had expected to have little or nothing to do after peace was declared, but have had a very busy time.' There was not just the recreation room. 'I have to go to the City hospitals and look after friendless returned soldiers.' Annie juggled numerous voluntary groups. 'The Red Cross sent for me a few days ago, and asked me to add the Red Cross to the organizations which I represent in my hospital work, and to draw on them for what was needed among my boys. Then they pinned a large badge, with a maple leaf on it, on me, and turned me loose.' Annie's 'boys' were soldiers returning from overseas, who had to be clothed as well as housed. 'So I have to come through with some sort of arrangement, and probably with pajamas!'[27]

In the aftermath of the war, Annie's star rose even higher. In August 1919 she was appointed provincial director of the Homes Branch of the Soldiers' Settlement Board. The federal initiative was intended to settle returned soldiers on the land through government-funded loans and agricultural training. Annie explained the Home Branch's rationale. 'Realizing that every man's objective was the home, the Board organized the Homes Branch knowing that the happiness and well-being of the family would tend to the success of the man in his farm work.' According to the official announcement, 'Mrs. Gordon will act in an advisory capacity to the wives of returned soldier settlers, her duties bearing the same relation to the women as do those of the Field Supervisor to the ex-service men under the scheme.' Annie's qualification for the position lay in life experience. 'A teacher before her marriage,' she was 'a pioneer in the then scarcely settled upper country.'[28]

Annie had found a new frontier, and she acted with verve and efficiency. Short days after her appointment, she was at work. 'I have just got back from my first trip in my new job, up to Courtenay, Comox, Oyster River, Little River, Lazo, and Nanoose, working through to Parksville and Errington. All on the [Vancouver] island.' As to the purpose of the trip: 'I taught bread and biscuit making, canning vegetables, preserving fruit, curing meat and fish, care of poultry, preparation for maternity, care of infants, and advised many lines. Altogether did the deuce an' all.'

Very commendably, Annie did it all on her own. 'The only way I could get about was by motor, and I worked from early morn to dewy eve, was up for seven o'clock breakfast every day.' Annie was convinced that she held the key. 'So much depends on the way one meets these women, who are so far away from their old homes and friends, among new conditions and work which so far they are not able to cope with.' As Annie put it, 'it is just like neighbouring in Salmon Arm in the old days.' Annie's trips took her even further back in time, as when she visited friends of thirty years ago in the Okanagan and Nicola Valleys. 'Saw Grace Douglas who asked for you – My Okanagan trip was very [bad], but haven't time to tell except that it was cold & roads dangerous.' Annie was so caught up with her new position she used paper headed 'The Soldier Settlement Board Canada' for her private correspondence.[29]

Newcomer women's domestication into British Columbia and into Canada lay at the heart of Annie's position. The program was open to soldiers' wives from Britain as well as from within Canada. Many of the women were 'recent arrivals from the Old Country, unversed in Canadian ways and customs.' It was her responsibility to 'extend advice and help of a practical nature, thus assisting them to overcome those difficulties which are bound to arise in taking up the threads of a new life.' Annie played an important role in defining the position of, and thereby in imposing her particular biases on, a generation of newcomer women to British Columbia. As she explained after her first trip, 'so far I have found many fine young English women, not any of the dreadful ones I have heard so much about.' English descent did not necessarily make, in her view, a good British Columbian and Canadian. Annie was in no way deferential to these women simply because they came from the former mother country. Differences in social status, or at least Annie's perception of them, may have magnified the differences she felt between herself and some of these women newly arrived from England. Building on her first field trip, Annie developed a series of courses intended to inculcate, even in the 'dreadful ones,' the way of life consistent with her view of Canada as a nation. 'The Homes Branch plans soon to inaugurate a series of short, practical courses for settlers' wives, including canning, simple cookery, and sick room cookery, making and re-modeling of garments, care of infants and young children, dairying, poultry and bee keeping, goat raising, and kindred subjects of value to women on the farms.'[30]

As head of the Homes Branch, Annie became ever more self-assured, taking as her due the sharing of platforms with such dignitaries as suffrage leader Emmeline Pankhurst. Having travelled through 'the outlying, remote districts of the Province,' she claimed an authority that left little room for doubt as to its correctness. Her views both reflected and directed the prejudices of the day as to the boundaries of the nation. 'Canada is still in the making, and what it will be will depend largely on the sort of people allowed to enter and become part of the state.' Annie had a distinct idea of who could be suitably domesticated into the nation. 'We can take a considerable number of the peasant class of Europe every year and develop them into good and prosperous Canadians in course of time, because they know how to do one thing well, and are willing to work, but we must not undertake more than we can assimilate readily.' The economic factor was not to be disregarded and could even trump skin colour. 'We do need a great deal of cheap farm labor to develop the country for the good of all, and it is for this reason that we have admitted numbers from China and Japan.' Like almost all her contemporaries, Annie had become taken up with the need to screen persons for entry into Canada on the basis of perceived mental capacity. 'It is a mistake to allow misfits to enter Canada, whether moneyed or otherwise, ... those men and women who are idle, purposeless, immoral, diseased, or of defective mentality should not be allowed to enter Canada and become a menace and a burden.'[31]

Just as Annie had done when selling her lots in Vancouver a half dozen years earlier, she made clear, in no uncertain terms, that she was not to be done in by virtue of being a woman. Because she 'had been out on the road so much,' Annie's Vancouver office was usurped by someone else even though 'a locked filing cabinet had arrived, also an inkwell packed in a box marked with my name.' Promised an office that 'was to be ready for me the following morning,' she discovered that a male official 'had swiped it.' Annie weighed in. 'I promptly hopped down [the offending] Burrows' throat, and the whole bunch, [and] ordered all my equipment into my present office 534, retrieved my filing cabinet, to which but one key was turned in. I demanded the duplicate. No one knew where it was, so I went to the head of the office equipment and said, "I'll give you until 10 tomorrow to have that key turned in. If it is not, a locksmith will be here to put on a new lock, and that key will be useless." The key was turned in! I also hunted out my inkwell, and took possession. When I came back from my last trip, there was a new desk and swivel chair added.'[32] Annie had become caught up in her own importance.

In public, Annie was all business, though in private she effected modesty, as was still expected behaviour of women in comparison with men. She gloried in the position even as she pretended, in somewhat gendered fashion, to be overwhelmed by its responsibilities. Annie could not resist letting Jessie know how important she had become. 'I am enclosing newspaper comments from the two dailies on the appointment. It was very generous of the [Victoria] Times to say all the nice things they did, for it is a Federal appointment and the Times opposes Federal politics.' Annie had no doubts whatsoever but that she was up to the job. 'My initial trip has shown me that there is a big work to be done, and that I can do it ... I think I'm going to like the work. They are all so glad to see me, wherever I go.' It was equally necessary for Annie to ensure that Jessie knew that she had not been unduly forward in getting the job. 'The position certainly sought me. I did not apply for it, and did not even know that such a position existed, and had to be persuaded that I was the one needed before I would consent to take it.' Reflecting her upbringing, Annie could not appear to enjoy the position too much. 'I cannot get a drop of ink at the wretched little hotels I have to stay at so frequently. And after I have seen women and women and three women, and heard all their troubles, and advised, and given all sorts of instruction, I am the tiredest thing that ever lifted one weary foot after another.'[33]

It was always with Annie half one and half the other. Having decried her obligations, Annie again enthused to Jessie a couple of months later how important she was. 'I address organizations, and write newspaper articles, and go on long journeys sometimes to make confidential reports on certain troublesome situations. Also I interview government people, and wring concessions from them, and do the deuce an' all!' She had 'over twenty letters awaiting me, but with a stenographer that's not so hard.' Annie did a good job, and she knew it. 'The Ottawa authorities are much pleased, but I think they ought to be, for I have not only organized my own field work, my own office, including the filing system, but I have wrung many concessions from the local Govt.' She closed a long letter to Jessie, at home in Sutherland's River, in a fashion that brooked no nonsense. 'Must run, have to be in the office by nine.' It may have been Annie's outspokenness that led to her resignation, about which no correspondence survives, over a disagreement with federal policy.[34]

For Jessie, back home in Sutherland's River, the years of the First World War and its aftermath passed very differently. About the time the war began, Catherine became bedridden. Annie reflected from Victoria in November 1914 how 'these sharp changes of climate have been very hard on old people everywhere.' Catherine McQueen died at home in February 1916, aged ninety-three. Jessie's obligations did not cease, for there was still Jane to be looked after. Doing so was no small responsibility. Neighbour children of these years recall Jane's belief that fairies lived in the back of the garden, and how 'she'd make up her mind and walk,' being in their house when they woke in the morning. They feared her, for she could turn violent, as when she decided the minister was not interpreting the Bible correctly during his sermon, and threw her copy at him so that he could see what it really said.[35] Daughterhood's obligations combined with sisterhood's bonds to keep Jessie minding her older sister as best she could year after year.

Then the cycle was broken. Jessie had kept in contact with her older sister Mary Belle's daughters Kate and Jennie. Jessie had been a year and a half in British Columbia when the family visited Sutherland's River in 1889, and Catherine reassured Jessie about the two girls, then aged eight and five: 'Your memory was fresh in the mind of the little St. John girls. Katie would say, I miss Aunt Jess so much & one day Jane was talking and saying something about you to Jenny, when she says, "I don't want you to be talking to me about her. There is not a week nor a day but I think about her."' A year later, in 1890, Jessie got 'a fine letter' from the older sister and mused: 'Three years is a long time in the life of a little child but Katie seems to have me in her affections just as though she had seen me only three months ago.' The family visited Sutherland's River from time to time, and over the years Jessie became particularly close to Jennie, a quarter century her junior. A graduate of McGill University and of a social work program affiliated with Columbia University in New York City, Jennie Wisdom became in 1916 the first head of the newly established Bureau of Social Services in Halifax. Four years later, Jennie arranged for her Aunt Jessie, who was turning sixty, to go with her and two of her friends to England for several weeks. Jessie was entranced, telling her niece Muriel, who had once cared for Annie's children at Gateway, 'I want to write about everything, & seems I can only write nothings!'[36]

Jessie's interest in the world beyond Pictou County was reawakened. At the beginning of 1922, Jane had to be institutionalized again. For the first time in a long time, Jessie was no longer needed at home. Daughterhood's obligations were no more. Jessie had a chance to do what she wanted, and she knew what it was. She wanted to return to teaching. 'I had some golden dreams of getting my hand in once more, pulling down a few shekels to relieve the general "unpecuniosity."' Now approaching sixty-two years of age, Jessie tried to find a job near home. 'I did a whole lot of thinking in circles, & finally sent for a list of vacant schools, & even wrote a few applications. But to shorten up – "nothing doing" – vacancies were filled before my appeals arrived, so I took it as a sign that I'm no longer able to offer anything in the world's market, & had better go where I can be of some use.'[37]

So, in the spring of 1922, Jessie returned a fourth time to British Columbia. It might be thought that the West would have long since dropped out of her thoughts. Twenty years had passed since she had last seen the province, almost a decade since Annie had visited Pictou County, but Jessie had kept her property in Rossland and she continued to correspond with the friends she had made there. It remained a high-point of her life. One of them, now a successful Rossland businessman, still waxed nostalgic over 'the busy and happy days of the Pioneer mining camp of the Kootenays.'[38] For this group of women and men, Rossland during its heady boom years gave a freedom of action only possible in a frontier setting, and Jessie must have frequently reflected on this special time in her life. Back in British Columbia, Jessie stayed at first with Annie in Victoria.

Sisterhood's bonds were renewed as if there had never been a break. The Soldiers' Settlement position behind her, Annie was turning her energies elsewhere. Her social contacts were extensive, as Jessie soon found out. She was at first impressed and then disenchanted by the bustle. 'Here's another week – worse if anything in the way of "doings." And every time we go down town to any meeting it gets away with hours & hours ... On Monday May 15, we went to the monthly W.M.S. [Women's Missionary Society] meeting ... Tuesday – heard [UBC English professor Garnet] Sedgewick lecture before the Canadian Club, very keen & witty, we N.S. folk quite proud to claim him. Next, refused tea with Annie & Margaret Clay, as I was feeling seedy, so packed off home alone to rest up for an evening at McKillicans. Mrs. McK is an old lady, running a lovely large home & grounds. Her husband used to work with Jim in the customs ... Wed. P.M. Annie had two ladies to tea ... Thursday, Tina McColl had us to her birthday celebration, a picnic to Patricia Bay, about 23 miles out ... Mrs Anderson with her 7-seater, pick[ed] up us two ... I forget what was on Friday & Sat. but Jean McNaughton, her mother & two sisters had tea here Sunday P.M.'[39]

A time free of Annie gave Jessie pause. 'Annie is in Vancouver for a week – Women's National Council.' Jessie realized that her sister's pace was not for her: 'I like *this* busy day – ironing, baking, & my little mending, with a snooze in between, lots better than teas – only I suppose a body shouldn't withdraw from one's kind.' Jessie well understood the fundamental difference which, all their lives, both bound and divided them. With a few exceptions, such as her years in Rossland, Jessie lived through others, and liked it that way, whereas Annie hugged the spotlight or fretted when she could not do so, as during her years on the frontier. Jessie realized that, as ever the case, Nan wanted her for herself. 'Annie says "*don't* go back to the farm, stay here," but they don't need me, & I'm quite able to do "light housework" any how.'[40]

Jessie wanted to fend for herself. 'I ... would like to work & earn my living for a few more years.' The matter of getting a job was not easy, but she was determined to pursue her dream of returning once more to the classroom. 'There *are* schools away up North, in the Cariboo country (& worse) that pay $114.00 per month, if it were a choice between resuming work on the farm, & going up there, I'd go – up – there, if I could.'[41]

Jessie's perseverance paid off. In the fall of 1922, she got the school at the farming community of Beaver Point on southern Salt Spring Island. The large island, lying in the Strait of Georgia between Vancouver Island and the mainland of British Columbia, had a newcomer population going back to the gold rush. The first settlers were miners who decided a better fortune lay in farming and fishing than in scrambling for gold. In a letter to her sister Mary Belle, Jessie described what she found there. 'Salt Spring is one of the largest of the Gulf Is. – there are seven school districts therein, & there are some excellent farms too, & acres of timber.' According to a senior pupil, the teacher the previous year was an Englishman who 'did not think much about the BC curriculum and taught us grammar and some Latin.' The school inspector was unimpressed, and so Jessie was hired to teach the twenty-some pupils for a salary of $840/year. Out of this, she paid $23/month to board about a mile away from the school. There a couple of months, Jessie felt she was doing all right. 'My memory being so faulty is a great drawback, but I'm improving slowly in that respect, though it still takes a lot of time to get up the daily lessons.' She kept to a routine. 'I'm usually at school by 8.30, & kindle the fire & get work down before the children come.' In the information form she sent the provincial government, Jessie described how 'pupils and teacher co-operate' to provide janitorial services.[42]

In a quite remarkable fashion, Jessie came full circle. Returning to Beaver Point by launch from the Thanksgiving weekend spent with Annie in Victoria, Jessie 'met an old chap who said he used to know Nicola thirty years ago or more.' Suddenly her entire teaching career in

British Columbia, both its accomplishments and what it did not achieve, was laid out before her. 'I *didn't* say, "so did I," because it might undermine my reputation as a "modern teacher"; and when he told of [Presbyterian minister] John Chisholm who used "to bring over Nova Scotians & marry them off," I kept stiller than ever!'[43]

It was not just individual incidents that brought Jessie full circle. Beaver Point had a human history very similar to that of Lower Nicola, where she began her British Columbia teaching career over a third of a century earlier. Both areas were based in agriculture and had a founding family that set the pace in the transition from frontier to settlement. The long-established Ruckle family recalled the Woodwards of Lower Nicola with their aura of respectability firmly grounded in hard work. Born in Ireland of German parents, its patriarch, Henry Ruckle, and his sturdily Norwegian wife, Ella, had one of the first and finest farms in the vicinity of the school. Not only that, Henry Ruckle had built the local wharf and was an early postmaster and school trustee. Numerous Beaver Point families were similar in background to the Ruckles, while others were of mixed race, echoing the earlier frontiers where Jessie taught. Attitudes toward hybridity were similar among the various locations across British Columbia. Shortly before the turn of the century, an Anglican minister settled nearby put together a promotional guide to Salt Spring in which he dismissed his neighbours as 'quite a little colony of half-breeds' who 'still gain their livelihood to a considerable extent by hunting.'[44] In the go-ahead future he envisaged, they could not compete and had no role to play.

Two of the principal families with children in Jessie's school were hybrids into the third generation. Over the past half century, they had intermingled and intermarried with their neighbours also of mixed race, huddling together in the face of newcomer settlement. The three Pappenberger brothers she taught were descended from an American of German origin and an Aboriginal woman named Mary who had settled at Beaver Point after the gold rush. The boys' maternal grandmother was likely hybrid Emma Purser, whose father had been a sapper with the Royal Engineers sent out from England during the colonial years. Settled on southern Salt Spring, George Purser begot a large family by a Cowichan woman. Emma's half-brother George Fisher lived on Russell Island just off of Beaver Point with his hybrid wife, Maria Mahoi, of indigenous Hawaiian and Aboriginal descent. Reflecting the close familial ties that bound hybrids together in the face of the racism that pervaded newcomer society in British Columbia, Emma Purser had for the past two decades lived with Maria's oldest son, George Douglas, a bit further away on Lasqueti Island.[45] The grandfather of the three young Kings in Jessie's school was a Greek ship jumper who in the 1860s pre-empted land near Beaver Point, where he and his Saanich wife, Mary, raised five children. As did so many hybrid men, the father of Jessie's pupils, Leon King, scratched out a living through his versatility in farming, fishing, logging, and boat building. His wife was Emma Purser's younger sister Sophie. Jessie once reflected on the meaning of all these lives. 'Looking at the shores of the various small islands as we chugged along past them last week, I wondered how in the world any one ever thought of landing on them, & attempting to farm.'[46]

The recollections of one of Jessie's three pupils in grade eight, Lotus Fraser, whose stepfather had only recently moved his family to Beaver Point, suggest that once again this 'tiny little woman' treated her pupils equitably. Some aspects of Jessie's teaching persona had not changed, as with her 'very sparky blue eyes that could look severe.' She described her teacher. 'In appearance she was getting quite a lot of wrinkles but in her manner she never seemed to be old at all. She had a terrific sense of humor.' The vividness of Lotus Fraser's reflections, seventy-five years later, affirms more than any official record how consummate a teacher was Jessie McQueen. For Lotus, if 'always Miss McQueen,' Jessie was 'such a helpful person, she would stop at your desk, if you were having trouble, she would stop and help.' Jessie was also a very effective teacher. 'She really was the most wonderful teacher. She was most anxious to see us all graduate, she worked very hard. She was suffering from stomach trouble, she worked under stress. I had the highest mark of pupils in the exam at Ganges [for all of Salt Spring Island] so you can see what a good teacher she was.'[47]

Jessie's teaching adventure with her 'little Beaver Pointers,' as she termed them, came to an end after the single year. While on Salt Spring and for many years earlier, Jessie had various stomach complaints, and poor health forced her out of the classroom for the last time. Jessie returned to Nova Scotia and was in December 1923 operated on in Halifax for a gastric ulcer. Her hospital stay lasted a good month, after which she returned to Pictou County. Perhaps because they were her last pupils, Jessie kept in touch with Lotus and her sister Ruth Fraser. Writing to them in the spring of 1928, now in her late sixties, Jessie railed against the effects of aging. 'I have to be careful, & go slow (as though I could do anything else) but when I remember how much slower & more helpless I was two summers ago, I try to be content, & put up with my limitations. One of them is this writing. Never do I feel in the mood for it, this having to feel around for words, & even keep your eye on them as you set them down, plays the dickens with any mood but one of discouragement ... Oh if only I could write as *fluently* as of yore!'[48]

Jessie was seventy years of age when, in 1930, she suffered a stroke that left her disabled. Annie applauded her resilience. 'I was much astonished to see you write so legibly. You must be making good progress which is good to see ... Keep up the good work of getting well. You are doin' fine!' Jessie died three years later, on 30 April 1933, at New Glasgow.[49] She had lived just a dozen of her seventy-three years in British Columbia.

As had Jessie, Annie also came full circle in both her public and her private lives. One of the organizations that long attracted her was the Women's Institute. Begun in Ontario in 1897 and familiar to her from her visit there in 1902, the Women's Institute movement was intended to complement the Farmers' Institute.[50] That organization was committed to improving agriculture, while its female counterpart aimed to help rural women raise better families. The Women's Institute came to British Columbia in 1909. The organization was almost immediately allocated an annual provincial grant from the Ministry of Agriculture comparable to that given to the Farmers' Institute. Activities supported by the Women's Institute ranged from fall fairs to lectures and classes on domestic life to sociability for rural women through regular meetings.

Annie became so caught up that in 1924 she was elected provincial convener of 'Women's Institute Work and Method.' Much as she had done with the Soldiers' Settlement scheme, Annie initiated Women's Institute classes on a variety of topics, including parliamentary procedure, canning, bread making, and childcare. 'I do like teaching groups of grown women, better than anything I have tried for some time.' Writing to her sister Mary Belle in 1925, Annie took particular pleasure that 'requests for my services had been coming in from all over the province.' In 1927 Annie was elected provincial president of the Women's Institute, a position she held for a full decade, to 1936. This activity led to her appointment by the provincial Department of Agriculture as a judge of women's work at district fairs across the province. Through explaining the basis of her adjudication, Annie is said to have improved the standards in the women's section at rural fairs.[51]

In or out of office, Annie repeatedly spoke her mind on behalf of women. Late in 1924, the newly arrived chief of police in Victoria dismissed the city's one policewoman 'for *disobedience.*' By this he meant that she had not given him the names of two venereal disease patients even though it was, in Annie's view, 'against the law of the land' for her to do so. Annie acted as spokesperson 'for a bunch of indignant women.' A newspaper article highlighted her position. 'I quoted from the Attorney Gen.'s ruling on the subject, which supported the Policewoman in her refusal, but the mayor gave the casting vote to dismiss her just the same. *Then*, I lit into him, and without raising my voice, ripped the hide off him.' Perhaps reflecting back to her own experience in the Nicola Valley so many years earlier, on another occasion Annie made an equally fervent 'plea for more co-operation and kindness toward young inexperienced teachers who took their first schools in rural districts.' Two years later, she argued for the abolition of local school boards on the grounds that 'women "on the whole" had not received courteous treatment from school boards,' which were all too often 'composed of "ignorant and illiterate" men.'[52] Annie set herself up as the voice of women, as always according to her own lights.

With time, Annie's strong sense of self caught up with her. She had always been her own person. Now, in the view of critics, she became 'extremely autocratic,' 'a real tartar.' Annie never apologized or admitted to a mistake. The story is told of a frontier housewife bringing an iced fruitcake, too big to fit into a container, a long distance in a horse-drawn open trap to a fall fair. Spotting a tiny speck on the icing, Annie as judge decided a fly had made the spot the previous summer, and thereby disqualified the cake as having been entered the year before. She simply refused to listen to the far simpler explanation of its being a speck of dirt.[53] Annie no longer understood, or cared to understand, the frontier on which she had spent so many years of her life.

In no way did Annie come more full circle than with her children. In a remarkable fashion, she, who had always been the rebellious one, came more and more to resemble her mother. Long before Annie died on 28 May 1941, her and Jim's ambitions for their offspring were realized. Just as Annie's mother had pushed her only son to Dalhousie University and all of her daughters into becoming teachers, so the majority of Catherine's grandchildren achieved the marker of their generation of a university degree. The seventeen grandchildren of Daniel and Catherine McQueen counted among their number five graduates of McGill, three of Dalhousie, one of Acadia, one of Oxford University, and two of teacher training colleges.[54]

For Annie, as it had been for her parents, the 'boys' education' took priority.[55] Marsh studied at Victoria College, affiliated with McGill University, and then headed off to Montreal to complete his bachelor of arts degree in 1912. He had already been at McGill a year when Annie reflected how 'Jessie must have a term at Normal as soon as I can manage it.' In the interim, the hapless Jessie, two years Marsh's senior, was reduced to doing 'a good deal in the house, but needs a regular job or something.' Having finally got her opportunity, Jessie was, Annie wrote a couple of years later, 'getting along very well indeed with her pupils, and conscientiously prepares her work every night.'[56]

Considering she knew best, Annie sought to keep her sons out of the First World War. Writing in November 1914, when Marsh was twenty-three and Dal eighteen, she explained her position to Jessie back home in Pictou County. 'Some think I should let them enlist, but I don't see it that way. They are not in the least of the soldier type, and I frankly don't want to spare them unless I have to.' Giving an interview about her family almost two decades later, Annie was still focused on her 'boys' and their successes with nary a mention of even having a daughter.[57] The gender equity that Annie fought for in the public domain she did not extend to her own children, just as her work among returning soldiers did not echo her sons' experience.

Annie's two oldest children retained their loyalty to the British Columbia of their upbringing. At McGill during the 'unusually mild' winter of 1911–12, Marshall explained to his grandmother how 'the rain always reminds one of B.C.' Bachelor of arts degree in hand, he returned to Victoria to article and was admitted to the bar in 1916. Marsh thereupon began a long career as a lawyer with Crease Brothers, a prestigious firm almost as old as Victoria itself. He became noted for his expertise on administrative law and for never losing a case during his thirty years as municipal lawyer for the Victoria suburb of Oak Bay. Marshall's older sister, Jessie, did finally make it to the Victoria Normal School and, like her namesake aunt, became a career teacher, first in rural schools and then in Victoria. Annie took pride in 1925 how 'Jessie has the normal students to supervise this term in addition to her school work.' By then she had 'taken up golf for recreation.'[58] Both Marsh and Jessie were enthusiastic tennis players at the Victoria Lawn and Tennis Club.

Annie's third child, Eric Valentine, known as Dal, took a very different career path. Perhaps because he was in good part educated at home by his mother, he was bookish from a young age. A friend told a story of how he and Dal went camping. Because Dal was smaller and had asthma, the friend carried their gear only to discover when they made camp why it was so heavy. 'Dal had brought three hefty volumes of the

Philosophy of Kant, being unable to contemplate a weekend with no reading matter.'[59] At Victoria High School, Dal captained the football team and learned Greek on his own. He followed his older brother to Victoria College and in 1915, his second year there, was named Rhodes Scholar for British Columbia. The honour capped Annie's aspirations for her children, permitting Dal to continue his education at Oxford University in England. Her years of hiving off her children into patterns of behaviour consistent with the colonial enterprise had paid off.

Dal left for England in the fall of 1915 and never looked back. He escaped British Columbia much as his mother and Uncle George had Nova Scotia at a similar age. Like both of them, he wrote home infrequently, making his life on his own terms. Dal enlisted in the Canadian Overseas Expeditionary Force, to be invalided out after a short period in France, likely because of his asthma. The rest of the war he spent 'counting bacon-coupons,' so the family story goes, in the Ministry of Food. Annie could only fret from the sidelines. 'Poor little dear, he has had a hard pull of it, and I only hope Oxford may improve his health.' When Jessie visited England in 1920, Dal entertained her at Oxford. His loyalties, Jessie discovered, had shifted from British Columbia and Canada to the former mother country. He simply could not fathom why his older brother, Marsh, had postponed a planned visit. 'I don't think he feels much curiosity about the British Isles, which I can't understand. It seems to me that almost any interests in the end ought to take one to England ... I wouldn't have missed England for anything.'[60]

Dal moved far more quickly than had his mother from being a sojourner to transferring his loyalties. He became impassioned not only by England but by the study of the English language and of language generally. Jessie described how she and her nephew enthusiastically 'prowled around among some bookstores – he had got on the track of a second hand Greek Testament he had been looking for.' By then, Dal had completed his B.A. degree at Oxford and found himself a mentor in Ronald Tolkien, four years his senior, who briefly tutored him before taking up a teaching job at the University of Leeds. Two years later, in 1922, Dal was also offered a position there. Tolkien reported enthusiastically in his diary, 'Eric Valentine Gordon has come and got firmly established and is my devoted friend and pal.' As well as their common interest in philology, or linguistics, they shared personal attributes that may have drawn them together. They were colonials, Tolkien being born in Bloemfontein, South Africa. They lost their fathers when young, Tolkien at the age of four, and were thereafter managed by strong

women. They were men of small stature and had been largely home
schooled, being thereby, more than usually, left to their own devices. All
of these factors may explain their escape into languages existing only in
the imagination, including Old and Middle English and the language
Norwegians took to Iceland in the ninth century, known variously as
Old Norse and Old Icelandic.[61]

Founded in 1904, the University of Leeds spoke to the desire in
England's industrial heartland for independent educational institutions
rather than having to defer to self-satisfied Oxford and Cambridge. The
two young academics encouraged a sense of community by forming a
'Viking Club' for language undergraduates. Its members drank large
amounts of beer, read sagas, and sang comic songs, mostly composed by
Tolkien and Dal. The pair turned nursery rhymes into Anglo-Saxon and
drinking songs into Old Norse. 'When I'm dead don't bury me at all,
just pickle my bones in alcohol,' Dal translated into Old English,
Gothic, and a Scottish dialect. They tracked down local Yorkshire dia-
lects, and Dal made recordings of them. Their more serious moments
were given over to a new edition of the Middle English poem *Sir Gawain
and the Green Knight.* Dal had charge of the notes. Tolkien, who was
responsible for the text and glossary, found it hard to keep up with Dal,
who he characterized as 'an industrious little devil.' The edition,
described as 'a major contribution to the study of medieval literature'
and 'still the standard edition used … throughout the world,' was published in 1925. It secured Tolkien a professorship at the University of
Oxford, and Dal a similar position at Leeds. In 1931, shortly after marrying a talented philology student, Ida Pickles, about to complete her
Ph.D. degree, Dal was named Professor of English Language and Germanic Philology at another of the new 'red brick' comers, the University
of Manchester.[62]

Dal was the more productive of the two scholars, in part because Tolkien had become caught up by creative writing, according to a literary
critic 'reaching back to an imaginative world which he believed had
once really existed, at least in a collective imagination.' In 1927 Dal published *An Introduction to Old Norse,* which remains a standard text. Its
preface paid a special debt 'to Professor J.R.R. Tolkien, who read the
proofs of the Grammar and made valuable suggestions and corrections.'
Dal's interest went further. He visited Iceland, brought students over to
study English at Leeds, and arranged for the university library to acquire
an important Icelandic collection. In 1930 he was knighted by the King
of Denmark 'for his services to the Icelandic nation, their language and

literature' and a year later elected an honorary Fellow of the Icelandic Society of Letters. The relationship between Dal and Tolkien remained close, as attested by their mutual friend C.S. Lewis's verse in the metre of the early English poem *Beowulf* describing how the two conspired during an examination the trio oversaw at Oxford University in 1933:

> Two at table in their talk borrowed
> Gargantua's mouth. Gordon and Tolkien
> Had will to repeat well-nigh the whole
> That they of Verner's law and of vowel sorrows,
> Cares of consonants, and case endings,
> Heard by hearsay.
>   Never at board I heard
> Viler vivas.

Tolkien critiqued the introduction to Dal's edited text of *The Battle of Maldon*, published in 1937. 'I owe my greatest debt of gratitude to ... Professor J.R.R. Tolkien, who read the proofs of my edition and made many corrections and contributions ... [and,] with characteristic generosity, gave me the solution to many of the textual and philological problems discussed in the following pages.'[63]

Collaborative projects were less successful. On the completion of *Sir Gawain*, the pair mapped out joint editions of *Pearl*, possibly written by the same author, and of two Anglo-Saxon elegies *The Wanderer* and *The Seafarer*. According to Tolkien's biographer, the single-minded Dal did a great deal of work on all three projects, so much so they were virtually complete, but nothing had come of them by the time his career was cut short. Even when Jessie visited Dal at Oxford in 1920, he was, in the pattern of his father, 'miserable' from 'indigestion.' Annie lamented a decade later how 'his illness and operation last summer had taken all his savings and more.' Operated on for gallstones in the summer of 1938, Dal's condition suddenly deteriorated, and he died on July 29th of a yet undiagnosed hereditary condition that had also taken his father's life. The University of Manchester arranged an academic position for his widow, Ida, that permitted her not only to bring up their four children on her own but get them a university education. The eldest, Bridget, followed in her parents' footsteps, becoming a lecturer in Old Norse at Glasgow University and a strong supporter of Highlander culture.[64]

'The sudden death of my friend Professor Eric Gordon' shook Tolkien and for good reason. A *Times* of London correspondent praised Dal as

'an untiring worker, quick of eye and penetrating mind' and for 'his var-
ied learning, his wisdom, his lively humor, and his capacity for unselfish
friendship.' Tolkien proved unable to bring their joint projects to frui-
tion, as indicated by his letter of 1945. 'I am in trouble with the widow of
Professor E.V. Gordon of Manchester, whose posthumous work on *Pearl*
I undertook, as a duty to a dead friend and pupil, to put in order; and
have failed to do my duty.' Through the unrelenting efforts of Dal's
widow, *Pearl* finally appeared in 1953 and, like his other works, remains
the standard edition. Ida Gordon explained diplomatically in the introduction how 'many factors combined to delay publication' and added:
'My warmest thanks must go to Professor Tolkien, who had the original
typescript for some time and added valuable notes and corrections; he
has also responded generously to queries.' She was being generous, for
Tolkien had long since given himself over to the fantasy writing that
would make him famous. His children's book, *The Hobbit*, was published
in 1937, one of his author's copies being sent to Dal. Tolkien's *The Lord
of the Rings* trilogy appeared in 1954–5. All of these, according to a critic,
drew on the texts he had worked on with Dal. In 1960 Ida Gordon
brought her husband's legacy full circle by publishing *The Seafarer*, which
he and Tolkien had initiated together. Whether as a result of Tolkien's
other interests, or what his authorized biographer terms his 'passion for
perfection,' not just the collaborative projects to which he committed
himself but 'most of his scholarly work that he pursued on his own never
reached print.' The important exception of *Sir Gawain* grew out of his
symbiotic relationship with Dal, which worked to both their benefits. Ida
Gordon, for one, considered that Tolkien had, compared with her husband, squandered his talents. She confided to a colleague in 1982: 'I
ought to tell you that I have very little interest in the Tolkien of the *Lord
of the Rings*. In my opinion that side of him robbed us of a very fine medieval scholar who might have done so much more work of lasting value
like the *Gawain* & *Pearl* editions.'[65]

Dal's remarkable academic career, truncated into just forty-two years
of life, gave his mother very real pleasure. At the same time, his way of
life, independent of her oversight, was incompatible with Annie's plans
for her children, which harked back a generation. Just as Catherine's
strong personality bound her daughters, particularly Jessie, to her in a
lifetime of obligation, so Annie's dominant character kept two of her
three children at her side. Like Catherine, Annie had known poverty.
Now a widow, she did not intend to experience it again. As a great-niece
has phrased it, 'Annie's children were her security.' About to travel the

province in 1919 in her new Soldier's Settlement position, at a time when Jessie and Marsh were thirty-some years of age, Annie fretted that she might lose control. 'My family intend to try to keep house by themselves for a while. I don't know how long it will last. If I can get a reliable woman I shall put her in at once to keep house, but they are hard to get. Jessie will get breakfast, and take her lunch to school with her, as she has always done. Marsh will take his down town. Then she will come home from school through town and bring the necessary eats with her, and get supper after she gets home. I think it will be too confusing for her, but she wants to try it.' The possibility of generational tension from time to time comes through in Jessie's comment while spending the summer of 1922 with Annie and her family before teaching at Salt Spring. '"It hardly seems enough" is a favorite phrase of Marsh's, when we folk give him a chance to sleep in, but that's a quiet bit of sarcasm from him.' At this point in time, Marsh still took a packed lunch of 'cookies & sandwiches,' made for him at home, to his legal firm each day.[66]

Much like her own mother, Annie simply could not fathom that her children had grown up. The stories that have come down through the family impart a strong sense of deliberation on Annie's part that extended well beyond her offspring's education. 'Annie didn't want any of her children to marry, but expected them to live with her as companions and care-givers as long as she lived. She discouraged any incipient romances of the two older children, who never did marry, but Dal was too far away to be controlled, and he defied her.' Echoing her mother's peremptory response to her own faraway engagement, Annie informed her sister Jessie in 1930 in the most cursory fashion that Dal was 'engaged to be married.' Thereafter, according to Dal's daughter Bridget, 'Annie refused to acknowledge that my father had married in England, she refused to acknowledge his wife, or that they had children.' Bridget added: 'She did not communicate with my mother, nor acknowledge that she had four grandchildren. When I was a child, we were all made to write regularly to Granny Gordon, but she never replied, and never sent messages or presents.'[67]

In the event, both Jessie and Marshall stayed single. Dal's daughter Bridget, who came to know her unmarried aunt and uncle well through letters, considers that 'Annie actively prevented both Marsh and Jessie from marrying – having lost Dal she was taking no more chances.' The two older children didn't have a hope. Annie's grand-niece has recalled how she played up 'the horrors of marriage.' Not only that, she rooted out potential admirers. 'Jessie's followers were severely discouraged –

Annie couldn't carry on her public works without the services of Jessie as housekeeper.' Annie would always find faults in her daughter's boy-friends in such a way as to turn her against them. Much the same occurred with Annie's older son. 'Marsh was very keen on his cousin, Catherine.' Eliza's daughter Kate Cunningham graduated in home economics from a college affiliated with McGill and did further study in Vancouver, perhaps for that reason. His mother was going to have none of this. 'Annie is said to have intercepted his letters (this may not be true), and on more than one occasion saw to it that he was away when Kate was coming to visit. Marsh was her meal ticket, after all, and her insurance for old age.'[68]

Jessie and Marshall lived with Annie at 1326 Woodlands until her death in 1941, and then together until Jessie's death in April 1971. Five years later, the University of Victoria honoured him with a Doctor of Laws degree. Dal's daughter Christine went out to Victoria to visit her uncle and, realizing how ill he was, took care of him until his death in November 1979, being at the age of eighty-nine the oldest practising lawyer in British Columbia. As for his cousin Kate, he still 'had her photo over his bed,' reminding him of the relationship his mother had sufficiently discouraged so that neither of them ever married.[69]

Attempting to assess Annie's life and legacy, her grand-niece, Mc-Queen family historian Relief Mackay, has reflected on how she 'did sacrifice a lot' for her children and her ambitions for them, 'but having suffered herself under a possessive mother, one would expect her to allow her children more freedom.' Annie's granddaughter agrees. 'I'm afraid sprightly, fun-loving Annie became a bitter, quarrelsome old woman.' In Bridget's view, Annie's two older children paid the price for her public image. 'I think she was ruthlessly selfish with both of them, but mothers were, in those days, even mothers less manipulative and domineering than Annie.'[70] If Annie had as a young woman escaped her mother, which Jessie never did, in old age it was Annie and not Jessie who became their mother.

Chapter Twelve

Reflections

The McQueen sisters had far more with them than baggage and some food when they headed west to British Columbia shortly after the completion of the transcontinental railway. They brought a way of life that was so accepted, so expected, it need not be declared, much less questioned. Until then, the sisters had been embedded in a social landscape whose components they took for granted. Normal in Pictou County was to be rural, long settled and committed to family, to be Scots and Presbyterian, and to be literate. Normal in the colonial world to which Nova Scotia and Canada adhered was to be as pale a skin colour as possible and, in the public domain, to be male rather than female. The outlook formed out of these attributes came with the sisters to British Columbia.

Jessie and Annie McQueen had every reason to hold on to the way of life they brought with them from Nova Scotia. They were sojourners with no intention of becoming residents. It was not British Columbia that attracted them, but rather Nova Scotia that drove them out. Like many arrivals from elsewhere, including Asia, they arrived in order to be able to leave again. Because they went to make money and then to return home, the sisters saw little need to adapt to their new settings. Their point of reference long remained Pictou County, as a comment by Jessie made clear: 'Unless I am mistaken & I rather think I'm not this is the sixth anniversary of my leaving home for this wild & woolly west.'[1]

Jessie McQueen would reside a little under a dozen years in British Columbia, and Annie, over half a century. Familiarity did not breed acceptance; nor did it encourage the sisters to change. They genuinely believed that their way of life was far preferable to the frontier character of much of the province. Newcomers like the McQueens tended to cluster together with others of their own kind. The support networks they formed served to confirm the rightness of the practices they brought with them. If memories of Pictou County and of Nova Scotia faded and became, over time, as much mythic as real, that in no way diminished their utility. The sisters accommodated to broader changes taking place around them, as with Jessie taking to 'the wheel' and Annie to social reform, but they did not, for the most part, transfer their allegiance between provinces.

The McQueen sisters were encouraged to maintain their way of life for another reason, as well. For them and many of their contemporaries, including fellow Pictonian George Monro Grant, their outlook equated with Canada as a whole. Scots ethnicity and Presbyterian dogma had long since been refashioned into a way of life. The values associated with Pictou County and Nova Scotia remained for Jessie and Annie a centre of certainty, just as a generally similar outlook originating in Ontario was for many newcomers to British Columbia from that province.[2] Grant, for one, firmly believed that Maritimers were the most influential in nation-making. If referring to a somewhat later time period, historian Ian McKay concurs that 'Atlantic Canadians have often been the most grounded, cogent and sustained Canadian nationalists.'[3] To the extent British Columbia did not conform to the sisters' expectations, it became their responsibility to make it do so. It was for that reason that Jessie and Annie McQueen domesticated in the two linked senses of the word. They moved the locations where they lived from frontier toward settlement, and they helped to make British Columbia more like Canada as they conceived it.

To understand the sisters' contribution to nation-building, it is necessary to recognize that Canada, since Confederation, has extended from coast to coast. Canada as a nation did not radiate out from the centre. Writing shortly after Jessie and Annie McQueen followed the Canadian Pacific Railway west, political commentator Goldwin Smith lamented Canada's condition. Astutely observing that 'to make a nation there must be a common life, common sentiments, common aims, and hopes,' he went on to suggest that perhaps Ontario, as 'a British and Protestant community,' should stride out on its own as 'a nation.'[4] The rest of Canada did not figure in Smith's calculations. He was unable to conceive the nation from other than his own, centrist perspective. The unfortunate aspect of such views is not that they once existed but that they still linger. They continue to influence our thinking about Canada

as a nation. As Ian McKay cogently puts it, 'Canadian intellectual histori-
ography has been seized with the rather pleasing illusion – but it is an
illusion – that words spoken by professors at Queen's University [in
Ontario] resound from coast to coast.'[5] The attention of the last several
decades to gender, race, class, sex, and other human attributes has done
little to shift what fellow historian Phil Buckner terms 'the centralist bias
of Canadian history.'[6]

The role played by persons like the McQueen sisters is also obscured
by its everyday nature. Gerry Friesen argues persuasively in *Citizens and
Nation* that the building of Canada has depended far more on what he
describes as 'common people' than on the pronouncements of the few
occupying formal positions of power. 'Canadians have failed to integrate the achievements of common people into the ideas and symbols
that articulate their sense of nationhood, an omission that dilutes their
understanding of their own strengths.'[7] The McQueen family was typical
of Pictou County's inhabitants in background and outlook, much more
so than were coal miners labouring in the pits outside of New Glasgow
or the few Mi'kmaq struggling to survive on the margins. The sisters'
employment of distinctions based on skin colour or 'race,' willingness to
tolerate gender inequities, and lack of sympathy for the disadvantaged
contradict notions now prevailing about Canada's strengths as a nation,
but their outlook was the common perspective of the time. Jessie and
Annie were, as much as individuals can be, ordinary.

The McQueen sisters' correspondence tells a story whose everyday
character, locations, and gender explain its absence from narratives of
the nation. Goldwin Smith's 'common life, common sentiments, common aims, and hopes' are essential components of Benedict Anderson's
imagined community that is Canada, and it was through 'common people' like Jessie and Annie that they were realized. The ways women
effected change were not nearly so spectacular as were those of men,
who had access to the press, podium, and pulpit. Women acted in the
everyday realm and may have for that reason been even more effective
than men in fostering the invented traditions Eric Hobsbawm associates
with the nation. They shared in the same celebrations as did men, as
with Queen Victoria's birthday on May 24th. More female than male
teachers were molding the next generation. Women's leisure was less
team-based but just as much encouraged a common ethos, as with
Jessie's daily walks and her infatuation with cycling. Women read the
same newspapers as did men, but they also shared in another genre of
writing in the Samantha and Pansy books with their strong base in Prot-

estant values. Sewing and church-going gave other opportunities for developing the shared understandings that feed into the nation. The largely mundane character of most women's lives makes their contribution to the nation more difficult to detect than that of men, except, as with Jessie and Annie, where an exceptional record of everyday events survives. It is through such traces as the McQueen family correspondence that we can begin to understand why Canada survives intact into the twenty-first century.

The McQueen sisters helped to make Canada not just because they came from certainty, from their perspective, but also because they headed into uncertainty. When Jessie and Annie first arrived in British Columbia, Canada was only two decades old and most of the young province still a frontier, a space in time and place open to the imagination. The fur trade and the gold rush had cast one way of life aside, while the next was yet to be. A frontier is by definition a site where peoples, and also the societies of which they are a part, come together and for a time interact before again drawing apart. The frontier must either be occupied or, at the least, divided between competitors, for settlement to occur. However inevitable the eventual outcome might appear in retrospect, so long as there is a frontier the winners and losers have not yet quite been determined.

Much of the McQueen sisters' time in British Columbia was spent on the frontier. They began as teachers in the Nicola Valley, Jessie migrating to Campbell Creek, Salmon Arm, Rossland, and later to Beaver Point on Salt Spring Island. Annie became a quintessential frontier wife, moving among Kamloops, Salmon Arm, Trail, Crow's Nest Landing, Tobacco Plains, and Gateway before tackling reform head on from Victoria. Most actors on the frontier have been evoked as male, and for good reason. In British Columbia, adult male newcomers outnumbered their female counterparts by a ratio of three to one. If women on the frontier, as elsewhere, lived in the shadow of men, this does not mean they were without agency. Women acted in many and diverse ways, within the realms of activity considered appropriate for them, and also in more subtle and unexpected fashion. Both the Woodward and Campbell clans, as Jessie evoked them in her letters, were firmly in the charge of men. Yet, at some critical point in time, a woman took a stand. Agnes Woodward acted to protect her young daughter from sexual abuse; Mary Campbell, to cosset the tiny teacher in their midst.

The notion of the frontier as a contact zone or liminal space is confirmed by the McQueen sisters' experiences. They were each affected by their encounter. Annie, in particular, appreciated that conventions could, for a moment in time, be set aside. She behaved more outrageously than was permissible back home in Pictou County, even though at the same time she did not go much beyond the gender expectations of the day. Her wedding gave newcomers in a settlement still in embryo the opportunity both to demonstrate an exuberance that the frontier condoned and to replicate the home left behind through their choice of gifts. Jessie showed most daring in courting intimacy, in treating her hybrid students with respect, and in permitting herself a home of her own, without male oversight, on the mining frontier of Rossland. To the extent the sisters were altered by their experiences, they served as exemplars to others as to how far it was possible to go without bringing dishonour to their origins.

The McQueen sisters, together with fellow teachers, ministers, and others from Nova Scotia, exercised influence in British Columbia far beyond their numbers. Following the completion of the transcontinental railway, the non-Aboriginal population in British Columbia soared from 24,000 in 1881 to 70,000 a decade later, reaching 150,000 by 1901, the proportion born elsewhere in Canada doubling from 15 to almost 30 per cent.[8] Residents born in Nova Scotia climbed from just 379 in 1881 to 2,656 a decade later and to 4,603 in 1901.[9] They composed 2 per cent of British Columbia's non-Aboriginal population in 1881, and under 4 per cent thereafter. The number of Nova Scotians in British Columbia was never considerable.

Nova Scotians' influence was magnified many times over by their strongly held common values and by their concentration in the two most visible institutions of these years – the school and the church. They were each far closer to most persons' lives than the agents of governance encountered from time to time or the big events experienced once or twice in a lifetime. Religion and education possessed an importance that, in the first instance, we now discount and, in the second, we take for granted. Particularly on the frontier neither was obtained easily, heightening their potential to effect change among ordinary men and women. Referring, half a decade before the sisters headed west, to the central role played by church and school in the westward movement within Canada, George Monro Grant stressed how 'the settler is not expected to come without a live coal from his own venerated altar-fires.'[10]

No group of persons occupied a more pivotal position across British Columbia during these years than did teachers. Just as did clerics, teachers possessed authority external to their settings, in their case a professionalizing body of knowledge and a provincial administrative apparatus. They were in no way neutral beings who simply transmitted knowledge from textbooks to their pupils. Teachers, in Julie Jeffrey's words, 'saw themselves as part of a national effort to save the West for Protestantism and civilization.'[11]

The railway encouraged to come west hundreds of Jessies and Annies, as British Columbia's demand for teachers sharply increased to reach almost 750 by the turn of the century.[12] Teachers born elsewhere in Canada jumped from just over a third of the total at the time of the rail line's completion to about 60 per cent during the 1890s.[13] Only a small part haled from Nova Scotia or even from the Maritimes. Those two proportions rose from about 3 and 10 per cent, respectively, in the 1885/86 school year to 13 and 22 per cent in 1890/91, before falling back, in the face of a teacher surge from Ontario, to 7 and 16 per cent by 1900/01.[14] Much more importantly, fully half of the teachers at work in British Columbia between the McQueen sisters' arrival and the end of the century shared at least one of their three formative values – Scots descent, Presbyterian affiliation, Nova Scotian birth.[15]

Overall, teaching was becoming women's work. The gender balance was roughly equal in British Columbia up to the railway's completion, but by 1890 the proportion of women approached 60 per cent, where it remained through the end of the century.[16] Certainly not all teachers with origins similar to Jessie and Annie's were women. At virtually the same time the sisters left Pictou County for British Columbia, so did Robert James Douglas. His older brother had taken over the family farm upon their father's death, leaving the young man to fend for himself, which he did by sojourning. Douglas was among the many male teachers who taught only as long as it took them to acquire the money to study for a profession, begin a business, or farm full-time. After half a dozen years in British Columbia classrooms, Douglas returned east to attend McGill University to become a Presbyterian minister.[17] Most women also saw teaching as a short-term pursuit, in their case prior to marriage. However long they might spend in the classroom, Maritimers like Robert Douglas and the McQueen sisters shared a common achievement. They gave their pupils a sense of Canada they might not otherwise have acquired. Not only that, teachers, both male and female, retained a self-confidence on which they drew throughout their lifetimes, in Annie's case as a wife, mother, and then a social reformer, domesticating in a very literal sense the brides of the First World War.

Outwardly, Annie was a far more powerful figure in nation-building than was her sister Jessie. Annie understood how to effect change in the political and voluntary realms, and did so with panache before, during, and after the First World War. Her willingness to take leadership roles at a time when women were just emerging out of the home, and to ensure men acknowledged her status, is remarkable. Her long, hard years on the British Columbia frontier, rather than marking her life, became a prelude to another life. She rebounded to her own satisfaction, if at a cost to the personal lives of her children. Annie McQueen Gordon contributed in significant ways to British Columbia and to Canada.

Annie knew what she wanted, whereas Jessie found it extremely difficult and even troubling to be forced to depend on her own resources. Jessie may have been no more than an average teacher during her dozen years in British Columbia, but she was a teacher nonetheless, inculcating into her pupils understandings that reflected her Nova Scotia heritage as much as they did the British Columbia curriculum. Less firmly based in self than Annie, she was more accepting of others, as with the diversity of racial inheritances existing across the frontier. Jessie pushed the boundaries inherent in colonialism when instructing her hybrid charges. She was more able to do so because she did not have to bear the consequences within her own family, as did Annie with her children. The generation of pupils Jessie taught was inevitably influenced by her, even though, apart from a handful – Tina Voght in the Nicola Valley, Ulysses Campbell at Campbell Creek, Lotus Fraser on Salt Spring – we know little about them.

Jessie's lack of self-confidence may have made her the more effective at domestication. She did not harass, as Annie was wont to do, nor was she in the least threatening. Her ways were easily taken for granted, subsumed into others' worlds without their even being aware. Five years in the Nicola Valley, she remained virtually unchanged from the sojourner who half a decade earlier left Pictou County. In the course of time, Jessie verged toward achieving autonomous action and self-expression, while still drawing on, but no longer merely replicating, her Pictonian origins. On the frontier that was Campbell Creek, she was needed as never before and gained courage through responding to others' needs. In boom-town Rossland, Jessie might not have become wholly a 'new woman,' but for the first time she came to appreciate her own self.

However much the McQueen sisters engaged the frontier, they never strayed far from their origins. As their letters indicate, they continued to evoke British Columbia as a place other than their own. Even though Annie eventually settled there, it remained for her principally a site to effect change. Three factors intertwined. The sisters self-monitored.

Their rigid Scots Presbyterian upbringing put in place assumptions about right behaviour that it was extremely difficult to abandon. Pleasure was in and of itself suspect, however much it might momentarily be enjoyed, precisely because it was enjoyed. Secondly, to the extent that Jessie or Annie might have strayed, they were monitored within the family. The letter writing that they took for granted, as a pleasure and also as an obligation, was so integral to their lives that rarely did events get deliberately left out or obscured. When they did so, an element of guilt crept in which, likely more than the telling, removed any pleasure from whatever had been omitted. Thirdly, the McQueen sisters were watched over by every other Nova Scotian and Maritimer, Presbyterian and Methodist, they encountered in British Columbia. Cousins, ministers around every corner, other newcomers – they were so interlinked and so interrelated that Jessie and Annie never quite knew when some event would be retailed back to their families. It was not just their parents but their married sisters across the Maritimes who might serve as the conduits through which some incident made the rounds.

The lives of Annie and Jessie McQueen argue that the freedom the frontier gave was illusory. Congruent with colonialism, the frontier was highly racialized, intended to be experienced by persons of pale skin tones at the expense of Aboriginal people, hybrids, and, in the case of British Columbia, persons from China. The frontier's freedom was also gendered. The sisters domesticated within a set of imperatives designed to control women's lives far more than they were ever encouraged to participate in events equitably with their male counterparts. Even when they strayed, just a little, they indicated by their behaviour how far it was possible for newcomer women to do so without losing their credibility. By their outlooks and actions, the sisters exemplified patterns of behaviour that moved the frontier toward settlement and melded British Columbia into Canada. By the time of Jessie's final departure in 1923, and even more so by Annie's death in 1941, British Columbia had become a largely urban place and Canada had acquired a certain taken-for-granted quality. It would take another generation or two for the racial and gender assumptions the sisters embodied to be challenged and to some extent altered.

The McQueen sisters' lives are equally interesting in and of themselves. They came from a family, and a generation, that assumed daughter-hood's obligations and sisterhood's bonds. The five McQueen daughters, in turn, contributed a decade of labour toward sustaining the family economy. Mary Belle, Eliza, and Dove could each slip away into marriage because there was a younger sister to take her place. Jessie got caught, both because she was their junior and because Annie broke the sequence. Mindful of her intended fate, Annie escaped, first to British Columbia and then into marriage well before she reached the conventional age in Nova Scotia for doing so.

Jessie was not encouraged to marry, and she did not. Her shyness played a role. So did misfortune in terms of the men to whom she became close. Even more important was the nature of the family. Through all the years and all the letters, her mother never urged Jessie toward intimacy with men. Catherine McQueen needed Jessie to remain a single, healthy, working offspring, just as Annie later expected of her children. Catherine's admonitions had much more to do with Jessie's taking care of herself, generating such responses as 'don't be afraid mother of [my] putting myself in dangerous places,' than with encouraging Jessie to join her self to another.[18] A single life came at a cost. Jessie remained a sojourner more so than Annie. Each new teaching job forced Jessie to improvise her living conditions. Only once, at Rossland, did she acquire a home of her own, apart from the one in which she had been born. Returned to the farmhouse at Sutherland's River, she resumed daughterhood's obligations as if she had never been away. She did so, not because she chose to, but as a matter of course. By virtue of staying single, Jessie was expected to provide for her sisters as well as her parents. Hers was a lesser status within the family. The freedom that her brother took for granted was never hers to enjoy.

Gender and piety went hand in hand. The only McQueen son, George, was privileged in terms of education, as were Annie's sons. The men of the two generations responded differently. George squandered that privilege, perhaps aware from his upbringing that the prodigal son was doubly loved, whereas Marsh and Dal Gordon had outstanding careers. The morally righteous ethic that permeated the family's decision-making embodied a strong sense of providence. Things worked out the way they should. One's fate had to be accepted. There was, at the same time, a strong strain of self, which both George and Dal exemplified. Given that what one did was what one was meant to do, it might as well be done according to one's preferences and ascribed to providence. Decisions were justified by virtue of their having been made. Among the McQueen women, Catherine embodied both strains, whereas Jessie verged toward the first and Annie the second.

All their lives, the McQueen sisters were mirror images. Annie, from her earliest years, acted as she dared, and as the youngest child probably had more licence to do so than did any of her sisters. Annie fancied herself and possessed the personality to ensure that those around her did so as well. She travelled across a continent on a whim; she married over parental objections; and she rebounded after her husband's death into a whole new way of life at the expense of her children. Jessie, in contrast, put her obligations as daughter and sister over herself. These demands very conveniently obviated the need for her to be her own person, a circumstance that both reflected and played into her timidity. To the extent Jessie realized the power she possessed to make a difference, she ascribed it to external criteria, principally Christian dogma and her obligations as a teacher. Jessie and Annie each continued their mother's life, but in very different ways. Catherine McQueen was every mother, only more so. Jessie found it easiest to do her bidding, whereas Annie resisted. Over the long term, Jessie remained her mother's child, whereas Annie, in terms of her own children, became her mother.

The McQueen sisters' story also reveals, very importantly, the great extent to which, across Canada, women's lives, no less than those of men, have been driven by material considerations. More than any other factor, it was the difficulty of making a living, for themselves and for their families, that caused the major transitions in Annie's and Jessie's lives. Whether in Nova Scotia, British Columbia, or Ontario, where Annie briefly lived, it was extraordinarily hard, the sisters' experiences testify, for ordinary families to survive financially. Time and again, Jessie and Annie uprooted themselves, and those around them, for no other reason than basic human survival. If the McQueens, who possessed a reasonable education and a strong moral ethic, had such difficulties, then what happened to so many other families across Canada during these years? I don't have any answers except to suggest that examination of more such everyday lives might draw out larger issues that continue to agitate us into the present day.

In the final analysis, Jessie and Annie McQueen are all of us. As Kerwin Lee Klein eloquently sums up in *Frontiers of Historical Imagination,* 'the most modest descriptions of history and culture cannot avoid larger stories of history and culture.'[19] As did the sisters, we each, every woman and man, make a difference. Be it Jessie's effect on her pupils or that of Annie's son Dal on J.R.R. Tolkien, our stories are part of larger stories. Whether or not we leave a trace making it possible for our stories to be told, we count. We effect change merely by virtue of our existence. Everything we do, and do not do, has consequences for others, as for ourselves. We domesticate our settings in ways sometimes unbeknownst to us. In doing so, we help to make and remake the nation of which we are a part.

Chronology

1818	July	Daniel McQueen is born.
1822	Sept. 3	Catherine Collard Olding is born.
1849	March 31	Daniel McQueen marries Catherine Olding in New Glasgow, Nova Scotia.
1850	March 27	Jane McQueen is born.
1851	Sept. 28	Mary Isabel (Belle) McQueen is born.
1852		Daniel and Catherine McQueen settle on farm at Sutherland's River.
1854		Presbyterian church is constructed just across Sutherland's River.
	March 27	Elizabeth (Eliza) McQueen is born.
1856	July 3	Susan Dove (Dove) McQueen is born.
1858	Nov. 6	George McQueen is born.
1860	Aug. 4	James Daniel Gordon, Annie McQueen's future husband, is born in Ontario.
	Dec. 24	Margaret Jane (Jessie) McQueen is born.
1865	July 31	Annie Lowden McQueen is born.
1867		New school is constructed at Sutherland's River.
1868		Mary Belle is first of the McQueen offspring to qualify as a teacher.
1878	Oct.	Jessie gets her first teaching job.
1879	May	George McQueen leaves for New York City.
1880	June	Eliza marries Norman Cunningham of Dartmouth, a medical doctor.
	Sept. 28	Mary Belle marries Freeman Wing Wisdom of Saint John, a businessman.

1881	March	Annie gets her first teaching job, as a substitute.
1884	Jan. 1	Dove marries Edwin Crowell, a Baptist minister, then at Yarmouth.
	Nov.	Jessie enrols at the Truro Normal School.
1885	June	Jessie completes studies at the Truro Normal School.
1886	Nov.	Annie enrols at the Truro Normal School.
1887	June	Annie completes studies at the Truro Normal School and travels from Nova Scotia to British Columbia.
	Aug.	Annie begins teaching at Nicola Lake.
1888	March	Jessie travels from Nova Scotia to British Columbia and begins teaching at Lower Nicola.
	Dec.	Annie leaves teaching at Nicola Lake.
1889	Jan. 1	Annie marries James Gordon at Nicola Lake.
	Jan.	Jessie Olding begins teaching at Nicola Lake.
	Feb.	Annie and Jim Gordon move from Kamloops to Ontario.
	May 13	Jessie's beau, Tom Hall, is killed.
	Oct. 26	Jessie McQueen Gordon is born in Ontario to Jim and Annie Gordon.
1890	July–Aug.	Annie and daughter Jessie visit Nova Scotia from Ontario.
1891	July	Jessie leaves teaching at Lower Nicola.
	summer	Jessie returns home to Pictou County for a visit.
	Sept.	Jessie begins teaching at Nicola Lake.
	Oct.	Jessie Olding marries Hugh Hunter, government official at Granite Creek.
	Oct. 14	Daniel Marshall Gordon is born in Ontario to Jim and Annie Gordon.
1893	March	Gordon family moves from Ontario to Kamloops.
	June	Jessie leaves teaching at Nicola Lake.
	Sept.	Jessie begins teaching at Campbell Creek.
1894	spring	Gordon family moves from Kamloops to Salmon Arm ranch.
	June	Jessie leaves teaching at Campbell Creek.
	Aug.	Jessie McQueen returns home to Pictou County.
	Oct. 3	Daniel McQueen dies.
1896	Feb. 14	Eric Valentine (Dal) is born in Salmon Arm to Jim and Annie Gordon.

	May	Jessie McQueen travels from Nova Scotia to Salmon Arm and begins teaching at Upper Salmon Arm.
	Sept.	Jessie McQueen closes the Upper Salmon Arm school to begin teaching in Rossland.
	Oct.	Jim Gordon is appointed sub-collector of customs, and the Gordon family moves from Salmon Arm to Trail.
1897	summer	Gordon family moves from Trail to Crow's Nest Landing.
1898	Sept.	Gordon family moves from Crow's Nest Landing to Tobacco Plains.
1899	Dec.	George McQueen dies.
1900	spring	Jessie leaves teaching at Rossland and returns to Sutherland's River.
1902	spring	Gordon family moves from Tobacco Plains to Gateway.
	late summer	Gordon family visits Ontario and the Maritimes.
1907	summer	Gordon family moves from Gateway to Victoria.
1911	Nov. 10	Jim Gordon dies in Victoria.
1912		Eliza McQueen Cunningham dies.
1916	Feb. 3	Catherine McQueen dies.
1919	Aug.	Annie is appointed provincial director of the Homes Branch of the Soldiers' Settlement Board.
1920	late summer	Jessie visits Dal Gordon in England with her niece Jennie Wisdom.
1922	spring	Jessie travels from Pictou County to Victoria.
	summer	Eric Valentine (Dal) Gordon begins teaching at Leeds University.
	Sept.	Jessie begins teaching at Beaver Point, Salt Spring Island.
1923	June	Jessie leaves teaching at Beaver Point, Salt Spring Island.
	Dec.	Jessie has operation in Halifax hospital.
1925		J.R.R. Tolkien and E.V. Gordon, eds, *Sir Gawain and the Green Knight*, is published.
1927		Annie is elected provincial president of the British Columbia Women's Institute.
		E.V. Gordon, *An Introduction to Old Norse*, is published.

1928		Mary Belle McQueen Wisdom dies.
1929		E.V. (Dal) Gordon is knighted by the King of Denmark.
1930		Jessie has a stroke, leaving her partially paralyzed.
	July 30	E.V. (Dal) Gordon marries Ida Pickles in Yorkshire.
1933	April 30	Jessie McQueen dies.
1934	Dec. 21	Jane McQueen dies.
1938	July 29	E.V. (Dal) Gordon dies.
1941		Dove McQueen Crowell dies.
	May 28	Annie Gordon dies.
1971	April 7	Jessie McQueen Gordon dies.
1979	Nov. 19	Daniel Marshall Gordon dies.

Notes

The McQueen family correspondence is divided among the Provincial Archives of Nova Scotia, British Columbia Archives, Nicola Valley Archives, and Rossland Archives. Letters are cited by location of the originals. All quotations from the letters reproduce the original, with the exception of the addition of some commas and possessive apostrophes for ease of reading. The following abbreviations are used:

AM	Annie McQueen
AMG	Annie McQueen Gordon
BC	British Columbia
BCA	British Columbia Archives
CC	Campbell [Campbell's] Creek
CCM	Colin C. McKenzie
CM	Catherine McQueen
CNL	Crow's Nest Landing
DE	Department of Education
DnM	Daniel McQueen
DvM	Dove McQueen
DvMC	Dove McQueen Crowell
EM	Eliza McQueen
EMC	Eliza McQueen Cunningham
GM	George McQueen
IC	Incoming Correspondence
JG	James Gordon
JJ	John Jessop

JnM	Jane McQueen
JsM	Jessie McQueen
LN	Lower Nicola
MBM	Mary Belle McQueen
MBMW	Mary Belle McQueen Wisdom
NL	Nicola Lake
NS	Nova Scotia
NV	Nicola Valley
NVA	Nicola Valley Archives
PANS	Provincial Archives of Nova Scotia
SA	Salmon Arm
SB	Spence's Bridge
SDP	Stephen D. Pope
SE	Superintendent of Education
SR	Sutherland's River

1. Sojourning Sisters

1 Jean Barman, *The West beyond the West: A History of British Columbia*, rev. ed. (Toronto: University of Toronto Press, 1995), passim. Unless otherwise cited, general information about British Columbia comes from *The West beyond the West*.

2 Natalie Zemon Davis, *Women on the Margins: Three Seventeenth-Century Lives* (Cambridge: Harvard University Press, 1995), 212; see also Helen M. Buss and Marlene Kadar, eds, *Working in Women's Archives: Researching Women's Private Literature and Archival Documents* (Waterloo, ON: Wilfrid Laurier University Press, 2001).

3 Kerwin Lee Klein, *Frontiers of Historical Imagination: Narrating the European Conquest of Native America, 1890–1990* (Berkeley: University of California Press, 1997), 5.

4 Margaret Prang, 'Networks and Associations and the Nationalizing of Sentiment in English Canada,' in *National Politics and Community in Canada*, ed. R. Kenneth Carty and W. Peter Ward (Vancouver: UBC Press, 1986), 49. Prang restricts herself to English Canada, but this summary applies equally well to Canada as a whole.

5 Gerald Friesen, *Citizens and Nation: An Essay on History, Communication, and Canada* (Toronto: University of Toronto Press, 2000), 228.

6 In the classic text *Imperialism and Nationalism, 1884–1914: A Conflict in Canadian Thought* (Toronto: Copp Clark, 1969), Carl Berger singled out seventeen 'intellectuals' (1), all men, as having written about nationalism in

sufficiently significant fashion to deserve to have their perspectives reprinted.

7 Benedict Anderson, *Imagined Communities: Reflections on the Origin and Spread of Nationalism* (London: Verso, 1983), 6.

8 Eric J. Hobsbawm, 'Introduction: Inventing Traditions,' in *The Invention of Tradition*, ed. Eric J. Hobsbawm and Terrence O. Ranger (Cambridge: Cambridge University Press, 1983), 1; see also Hobsbawm, 'Mass-Producing Traditions: Europe, 1870–1914,' 263–307. On ceremony, see H.V. Nelles, *The Art of Nation-Building: Pageantry and Spectacle at Quebec's Tercentenary* (Toronto; University of Toronto Press, 1999).

9 Daniel Francis, *National Dreams: Myth, Memory, and Canadian History* (Vancouver: Arsenal Pulp Press, 1997); Norman Knowles, *Inventing the Loyalists: The Ontario Loyalist Tradition and the Creation of Usable Pasts* (Toronto: University of Toronto Press, 1997).

10 Robert J.C. Young, *Colonial Desire: Hybridity in Theory, Culture and Race* (New York: Routledge, 1995); Avtar Brah and Annie E. Coombes, eds, *Hybridity and Its Discontents: Politics, Science, Culture* (London: Routledge, 2000).

11 Anne McClintock, *Imperial Leather: Race, Gender and Sexuality in the Colonial Context* (New York: Routledge, 1995), 36; see also Julia Clancy-Smith and Frances Gouda, eds, *Domesticating the Empire: Race, Gender, and Family Life in French and Dutch Colonialism* (Charlottesville: University Press of Virginia, 1998); Frederick Cooper and Ann Laura Stoler, eds, *Tensions of Empire: Colonial Cultures in a Bourgeois World* (Berkeley: University of California Press, 1997); Catherine Hall, *Cultures of Empire: Colonizers in Britain and the Empire in the Nineteenth and Twentieth Centuries* (New York: Routledge, 2000); Ruth Roach Pierson and Nuper Chaudhuri, *Nation, Empire, Colony: Historicizing Gender and Race* (Bloomington: University of Indiana Press,1998).

12 Alexandra Harmon, 'Lines in Sand: Shifting Boundaries between Indians and Non-Indians in the Puget Sound Region,' *Western Historical Quarterly* 26 (Winter 1995): 429–53.

13 James A.H. Murray, *A New English Dictionary on Historical Principles*, vol. 4 (Oxford: Clarendon Press, 1901), 566.

14 Prang, 'Networks and Associations,' 51.

15 JsM to CM, NL, 27 March 1893, NVA; JsM to CM, CC, 2 March 1894, BCA; JsM to CM, Private, 28 February 1889, PANS.

16 For instance, JsM wrote, following a visit home, that 'this is the third [letter], starting with the one I wrote at Spence's Br.,' but it is the first to survive (JsM to CM, NL, 17 September 1891, NVA). On letters being passed through the family, see EMC to CM, Dartmouth, 9 November 1894; EMC to JsM, 20 October 1896, PANS.

17 EMC to JsM, Dartmouth, 20 October 1896, PANS; AMG to CM, Gateway, May 1902, BCA; JsM to CM, LN, 19 August 1889, BCA; JsM to CM, LN, 1 April 1890, PANS; JsM to CM, SB, 2 September 1891, BCA. For other examples, see AMG to JsM, Waterloo, 3 April 1889, St Thomas, 28 October 1889, BCA; AMG to CM, St Thomas, 27 July 1891, BCA.

18 Margaret Conrad, Toni Laidlaw, and Donna Smyth, eds, *No Place like Home: Diaries and Letters of Nova Scotia Women, 1771–1938* (Halifax: Formac, 1988); see also Margaret Conrad, 'Recording Angels: The Private Chronicles of Women from the Maritime Provinces of Canada, 1750–1950,' in *The Neglected Majority: Essays in Canadian Women's History*, ed. Alison Prentice and Susan Mann Trofimenkoff, vol. 2 (Toronto: McClelland and Stewart, 1985), 41–60.

19 Closer to the McQueens in background was Annie Leake, whose memoir is reproduced in Marilyn Fäardig Whiteley, ed., *The Life and Letters of Annie Leake Tuttle: Working for the Best* (Waterloo: Wilfrid Laurier University Press, 1999). Leake went to British Columbia in 1887 as matron of the Methodist Church's Chinese Rescue Home.

20 The best accounts open up the lives of Aboriginal women, including Margaret B. Blackman, *During My Time: Florence Edenshaw Davidson, a Haida Woman* (Vancouver: Douglas & McIntyre, 1982); Lizzie Hall, *The Carrier, My People* (Fort St James: n.p., 1992); Lee Maracle, *Bobbi Lee: Indian Rebel* (Toronto: Women's Press, 1990 [orig. 1975]); Jay Miller, ed., *Mourning Dove: A Salishan Autobiography* (Lincoln: University of Nebraska Press, 1990); Bridget Moran, ed., *Stoney Creek Woman: The Story of Mary John* (Vancouver: Arsenal Pulp Press, 1988); Jean E. Speare., ed., *The Days of Augusta* (Vancouver: J.J. Douglas, 1973).

21 Margaret Ormsby, ed., *A Pioneer Gentlewoman in British Columbia: The Recollections of Susan Allison* (Vancouver: UBC Press, 1976). On this point, see Jean Barman, 'Invisible Women: Aboriginal Mothers and Mixed-Race Daughters in Rural British Columbia,' in *Beyond the City Limits: Rural History in British Columbia*, ed. R.W. Sandwell (Vancouver: UBC Press, 1999), 159–79.

22 Kathryn Bridge, *By Snowshoe, Buckboard and Steamer: Women of the Frontier* (Victoria: Sono Nis, 1998). A welcome exception is Jo Fraser Jones, ed., *Hobnobbing with a Countess and Other Okanagan Adventures: The Diaries of Alice Barrett Parke, 1891–1900* (Vancouver: UBC Press, 2001).

23 Three examples: Sarah Crease of Victoria, who left a treasure trove of letters comparable to the McQueen collection; Eunice Harrison, also of Victoria, who wrote a memoir and visited the Cariboo; and Helena Gutteridge of Vancouver, who left almost nothing at all behind, but lived briefly in the rural Fraser Valley. See Kathryn Bridge, *Henry and Self: The Private Life of Sarah Crease 1826–1922* (Victoria: Sono Nis, 1996); Eunice Harrison, *The Judge's*

Wife: Memoir of a BC Pioneer (Vancouver: Ronsdale Press, 2002); Irene Howard, *The Struggle for Social Justice in British Columbia: Helena Gutteridge, the Unknown Reformer* (Vancouver: UBC Press, 1992).

24 Judith Fingard, 'College, Career, and Community: Dalhousie Coeds, 1881–1921,' in *Youth, University and Canadian Society,* ed. Paul Axelrod and John G. Reid (Kingston and Montreal: McGill-Queen's University Press, 1989), 32.

2. Pictou County Origins

1 On the farmhouse and its construction, see Relief Mackay, *Simple Annals: The Story of the McQueens of Sutherland's River* (Pictou: Advocate Printing, 1986), 9–11, 164. A front porch, three dormer windows above it, and a kitchen at the back were added some years later; the church also has some additions; and the original bridge has been replaced with another a short distance away. General information about the McQueen family comes from *Simple Annals,* meticulously researched by Relief Mackay; Margaret McCurrach, 'The Old House,' 1998, typescript, courtesy of the author; and headstones in Woodburn Cemetery, Little Harbour, Nova Scotia. Information on Pictou County is taken from George Patterson, *A History of the County of Pictou, Nova Scotia* (Montreal: Dawson Brothers, 1877); J.P. MacPhie, *Pictonians at Home and Abroad* (Boston: Pinkham, 1914); James M. Cameron, *Pictou County's History* (New Glasgow: Pictou County Historical Society, 1972); Judith Hoegg Ryan, *The Birthplace of New Scotland: An Illustrated History of Pictou County* (Halifax: Formac, 1995); D. Campbell and R.A. MacLean, *Beyond the Atlantic Roar: A Study of the Nova Scotia Scots* (Toronto: McClelland and Stewart, 1974); and Charles Bruce Ferguson, *Place-names and Places of Nova Scotia* (Halifax: Public Archives of Nova Scotia, 1967).

2 JsM to CM, NL, 30 May 1892, LN, 25 June 1888, NVA.

3 Harry Bruce, *An Illustrated History of Nova Scotia* (Halifax: Nimbus and Province of Nova Scotia, 1997), 127. Marianne McLean perceptively captures the character of Highland Scot emigration in 'Peopling Glengarry County: The Scottish Origins of a Canadian Community,' in *Immigration in Canada: Historical Perspectives,* ed. Gerald Tulchinsky (Toronto: Copp Clark Longman, 1994), 68–85.

4 Demographic data taken from *Census of Canada,* 1871, which includes earlier census data in vol. 4; and *Census of Canada,* 1881. The early population figure for the Mi'kmaq comes from Cameron, *Pictou County's History,* 2–3. Interaction between the Mi'kmaq and early Pictou settlers is described in Patterson, *A History of the County.*

5 DnM to CM, n.p., 1 January 1848, in Mackay, *Simple Annals,* 2. This letter, as

with numerous other early letters reproduced by Mackay, does not appear to have made it into a public archive.

6 Olding could not be located in any list of Oxford University graduates.

7 'Obituary: Mrs. Daniel McQueen,' *Leader* [New Glasgow], 4 February 1916.

8 Patterson, *History of the County*, 125; MacPhie, *Pictonians*, 123.

9 Catherine Gillian Pickles, 'The Life of Girls and Women in Mid-Nineteenth Century Pictou County, Nova Scotia' (M.A. thesis, Department of Geography, University of British Columbia, 1991), 15–16.

10 I have preferred Belle over Bell of the two spellings used interchangeably by family members.

11 *Illustrated Historical Atlas of Pictou County, Nova Scotia* (N.p.: J.H. Meacham, 1879).

12 Frederick Swartwout Cozzens, *Acadia; or, A month with the Blue Noses* (New York: Derby and Jackson, 1859), 198–202.

13 DvM to EMC, Stumpy View School, 12 and 18 September 1877, PANS; GM to CM, Brooklyn, 26 December [1881], PANS; 18 March 1878 entry in JsM, 'Diary, 1878,' PANS, MG1, vol. 3349, file 21; JsM to JnM, NL, 9 June 1892, BCA.

14 Marjorie Scott, 'A Brief History of the Presbyterian Church at Sutherland's River,' 1994, typescript available at the church and at www.arles.ns.ca/ sutherland_river. More generally, see Barbara C. Murison, 'The Kirk versus the Free Church: The Struggle for the Soul of the Maritimes at the Time of the Disrupation,' and John S. Moir, 'From Sectarian Rivalry to National Vision: The Contribution of Maritime Presbyterianism to Canada,' both in *The Contribution of Presbyterianism to the Maritime Provinces of Canada*, ed. Charles H.H. Scobie and G.A. Rawlyk (Montreal and Kingston: McGill-Queen's University Press, 1997); Alexander Maclean, *The Story of the Kirk in Nova Scotia* (Pictou: Pictou Academy, 1911).

15 MacPhie, *Pictonians*, 33.

16 Andrew Learmont Spedon, *Rambles among the Blue-noses* (Montreal: J. Lovell, 1863), 197–8.

17 CM to JsM, n.d. [1899], SR, 14 November 1878, PANS; MBM to CM, 11 May 1879, PANS.

18 CM to JsM, n.d. [1899], PANS; CM to MBM, SR, 26 November 1873, PANS.

19 Michael Gauvreau, *The Evangelical Century: College and Creed in English Canada from the Great Revival to the Great Depression* (Montreal and Kingston: McGill-Queen's University Press, 1991), 20.

20 McCurrach, 'The Old House'; CM to JsM, n.d. [1899], PANS; CM to AM, St John, NB, 4 August 1881, PANS.

21 CM to MBM and EM, 'Sabbath' [April 1878], PANS; CM to DnM, 15 December 1848, in Mackay, *Simple Annals*, 6.

22 JsM to CM, NL, 1 March 1891, NVA; AM to MBM, SR, 19 November 1879, PANS; AM to CM, NL, 10 November 1888, BCA.

23 E.R. Forbes, 'Prohibition and the Social Gospel in Nova Scotia,' *Acadiensis* 1, no. 1 (Autumn 1971): 11–36; but, according to Ryan, *Birthplace of New Scotland*, 37, it was the second in British North America.

24 CM to DnM, 15 December 1848, in Mackay, *Simple Annals*, 6.

25 Mayflower Juvenile Lodge minutes for 1868–70, esp. 18 December 1868 meeting, PANS, MG1, vol. 3349, file 23.

26 Robert Nicholas Bérard, 'Moral Education in Nova Scotia, 1880–1920,' *Acadiensis* 14, no. 1 (Autumn 1984): 49–63.

27 Robert MacKinnon and Graeme Wynn, 'Nova Scotian Agriculture in the "Golden Age,"' in *Geographical Perspectives on the Maritime Provinces*, ed. Douglas Day (Halifax: Saint Mary's University, 1988), 53.

28 GM to CM, New York, 6 August 1884, PANS.

29 Rusty Bitterman, Robert MacKinnon, and Graeme Wynn, 'Of Inequality and Interpendence in the Nova Scotian Countryside, 1850–70,' *Canadian Historical Review* 74, no. 1 (1993): 1–43; Steven Maynard, 'Between Farm and Factory: The Productive Household and the Capitalist Transformation of the Maritime Countryside, Hopewell, Nova Scoita, 1869–1890,' and Danny Samson, 'Dependency and Rural Industry: Inverness, Nova Scotia, 1899–1915,' both in *Contested Countryside: Rural Workers and Modern Society in Atlantic Canada, 1880–1950*, ed. Danny Samson (Fredericton: Acadiensis Press, 1994); L.D. McCann, '"Living a double life": Town and Country in the Industrialization of the Maritimes,' in Day, ed., *Geographical Perspectives*, 93–113.

30 GM to CM, 28 March 1882, New York, 6 August 1884, PANS; JsM to CM, LN, 1 October 1888, NVA.

31 EMC to CM, Dartmouth, 27 January 1888, PANS; Ronald MacDonald to DnM, Mailland, 8 August 1863, PANS, MG1, vol. 3349, file 2.

32 GM to DvMC, New York, 30 December 1892, PANS; Duncan McQueen to DnM, Austin, Indiana, 1 January 1870, PANS, MG1, vol. 3350, file 10.

33 George Herbert, 'The Elixer,' in his *The Temple* (1663).

34 Julie Roy Jeffrey, *Frontier Women: 'Civilizing the West'? 1840–1880*, rev. ed. (New York: Hill and Wang, 1998 [orig. 1979]), 18, 6, 92; Cynthia Comacchio, *The Infinite Bonds of Family: Domesticity in Canada, 1850–1940* (Toronto: University of Toronto Press, 1999), esp. 20–1, 25–6; *Etiquette for Ladies; or, The Principles of True Politeness* (Halifax: Milner and Sowerby, 1852), 9, cited in Elizabeth Langland, *Nobody's Angels: Middle-Class Women and Domestic Ideology in Victorian Culture* (Ithaca: Cornell University Press, 1995), 28.

35 Conversation with Marjorie Scott and Betty MacNeill, SR, 1 August 2001.

36 Jeffrey, *Frontier Women*, 92.

37 JsM to CM, 8 November 1893, BCA; AM to EM, SR, 14 August 1877, PANS; CM to MBM, SR, 28 November 1878, PANS; Alexander McKenzie to DnM, New Glasgow, 31 October 1870, PANS, MG1, vol. 3349, file 2.

38 Pickles, 'Girls and Women,' 39. Also useful on this shift toward women teachers are Alison Prentice, 'The Feminization of Teaching in British North America and Canada, 1845–75,' in *The Neglected Majority: Essays in Canadian Women's History*, vol. 1, ed. Susan Mann Trofimenkoff and Alison Prentice (Toronto: McClelland and Stewart, 1977), 49–69; and Janet Guildford, '"Separate Spheres": The Feminization of Public School Teaching in Nova Scotia, 1838–1880,' in *Separate Spheres: Women's Worlds in the Nineteenth-century Maritimes*, ed. Janet Guildford and Suzanne Morton (Fredericton: Acadiensis Press, 1994), 119–43.

39 Conversation with Marjorie Scott and Betty MacNeill, SR, 1 August 2001; MBMW to CM, St John, 9 June 1882, PANS.

40 School Inspector's Report, *Eastern Chronicle* [New Glasgow], 29 August 1872; CM and JnM to MBM, SR, 3 March [1874], PANS; CM and DvM to MBM, SR, 26 November 1873, PANS.

41 Certificate, PANS, MG1, vol. 3349, file 10; MBM, journal entry cited in *Simple Annals*, 24. The journal does not seem to have made it into PANS.

42 JnM to MBM, SR, 13 March 1874, PANS; MBM to family, 21 March 1874, 10 June [1874], PANS.

43 GM to MBM, Halifax, 10 March 1876, PANS; EM to MBM, 17 September 1877, PANS; JsM, 'Diary, 1878,' PANS, MG1, vol. 3349, file 21.

44 Maggie Thompson to EM, 28 August 1878, PANS; CM to EM, SR, 2 September 1878, PANS; documents in PANS, MG1, vol. 3349, file 2.

45 CM to EM, SR, 2 September 1878, PANS; CM to MBM, SR, 2 June 1879, PANS; CM to DvMC, SR, 25 August 1888, PANS; CM to EM, SR, 4 February 1879, PANS.

46 Louise A. Tilly and Joan W. Scott, *Women, Work, and Family*, rev. ed. (New York: Routledge, 1989), 115.

47 DM to CM, Clyde, 19 June [1882], PANS.

48 Jennie [Blanchard] to EM, Antigonish, 21 August [1878], PANS; GM to CM, New York, 26 April [1880], PANS; Judith Fingard, 'George Munro,' in *Dictionary of Canadian Biography*, vol. 12 (Toronto: University of Toronto Press, 1990), 771–3.

49 GM to JsM and JnM, New York, 17 November 1880, PANS; GM to CM, Brooklyn, 2 December 1881, 18 April [1883], PANS; GM to JsM, New York, 7 March 1882, PANS; GM to CM, New York, 6 August 1884, New York, 19 February 1885, PANS; EMC to CM, Dartmouth, 27 January 1888, PANS.

50 GM to JsM, 4 February 1883, PANS.

51 EM to MBM, SR, 13 March 1874, Glencoe, 17 September 1877, PANS; EM to MBM and DvM, Guysboro, 11 March 1880, PANS.

52 JsM to MBM, SR, 14 March 1874, PANS; MBMW to CM, 10 March 1882, PANS; 17 March 1878 entry in JsM, 'Diary, 1878,' PANS, MG1, vol. 3349, file 21; certificate, PANS, MG1, vol. 2249, file 12; JsM to EM, SR, 1 May 1878, PANS; EM to MBM, SR, 10 October 1877, PANS; JsM to EM, SR, 1 February 1878, PANS; MBM to EM, 18 February 1878, PANS; JsM to EM, SR, 1 May 1878, PANS.

53 CM to EM, SR, 2 September 1878, PANS; JsM to EM, 8 October 1878, PANS; 4 December 1878 entry in JsM, 'Diary, 1878,' PANS, MG1, vol. 3349, file 21; JsM to EM, 18 November 1878, PANS.

54 CM to MBM, SR, 28 November 1878, PANS; CM to JsM, SR, 14 November 1878, PANS; JsM to JnM, 21 November 1878, PANS; JsM to MBM, 14 January 1879, PANS.

55 For instance, CM to MBM, SR, 21 October 1879; AM to MBM, SR, 19 November 1879; AM to CM, Dartmouth, 30 March 1881; EMC to JsM, Dartmouth, 2 October 1882, PANS.

56 12 July 1880 entry in JsM, 'Diary, 1878,' PANS, MG1, vol. 3349, file 21; EMC to CM, Dartmouth, 21 June 1880, PANS; Hent Robertson to JsM, Chelsea, 11 July 1883, PANS; McCurrach, 'The Old House'; EMC to JsM, Dartmouth, 25 October 1882, PANS.

57 JsM to DvMC, Victoria, 10 July 1888, NVA; GM to JsM, Greenville, 7 January 1888, PANS; GM to CM, New York, 30 March 1886, PANS; CM to MBM, SR, 24 May 1878, PANS; GM to JsM, Brooklyn, 8 January 1883, PANS; JsM to CM, LN, 17 May 1888, NVA.

58 AM to CM, NL, 16 March 1888, NVA; JsM to CM, LN, 27 March 1889, NVA; EMC to CM, Dartmouth, 11 January 1888, PANS; AM to EM, SR, 14 August 1877, PANS; AM to CM, Dartmouth, 25 May 1881, PANS; AM to EM, SR, 18 March 1878, PANS; AM to JsM, SR, 14 November 1878, PANS; JsM to EM, 18 November 1878, PANS; AM to CM, Dartmouth, 31 January 1881; trustees of Little Harbour to AM, 14 September 1883, PANS.

59 JsM to CM, Truro, 16 July 1884, PANS; EMC to CM, Dartmouth, 18 July 1884, PANS; AM to JsM, SR, 19 July 1884, PANS.

60 See David E. Stephens, *Truro: A Railway Town* (Hantsport, NS: Lancelot, 1991).

61 JsM to CM, Truro, 17 November 1884, 5 December 1884, PANS; JsM to AM, Truro, 27 February 1885, PANS.

62 Guildford, '"Separate Spheres,"' 121; AM to JsM, Truro, 19 February 1886 [1887], PANS; JsM to AM, Truro, 27 February 1885, PANS; Bérard, 'Moral Education in Nova Scotia,' 49–63.

63 JsM to AMG, Truro, 27 February 1885, PANS; JsM to CM, Truro, 6 March 1885, PANS; JsM to DnM, CM, and AMG, Truro, 22 May 1885, PANS; JsM to AMG, Truro, 3 July 1885, PANS; 'Normal School Register, 1884–85,' Little White Schoolhouse Museum, Truro; JsM to family, Truro, 17 July 1885, PANS.

64 JsM to family, Truro, 17 July 1885, PANS; JsM to CM, Truro, 20 July 1885, PANS; EMC to CM, Dartmouth, 18 September 1885, PANS.

65 AM to JsM, Truro, 19 February 1886 [1887], PANS; 'Normal School Register 1886–87,' Little White Schoolhouse Museum, Truro.

66 EMC to CM, Dartmouth, 15 April 1887, PANS; Christine to JnM, Dartmouth, 3 December 1888, PANS; Mackay, *Simple Annals*, 112–13; F.E. Runnalls, *It's God's Country: A Review of the United Church and Its Founding Partners, the Congregational, Methodist and Presbyterian Churches in British Columbia* (Ocean Park: N.p., 1974), 81, 92.

3. Nova Scotia to British Columbia

1 Margaret Conrad, Alvin Finkel, and Cornelius Jaenen, *History of the Canadian Peoples*, Vol. 1, *Beginnings to 1867* (Toronto: Copp Clark Pitman, 1993), 608.

2 CM to JsM, SR, 14 November 1878, PANS.

3 Both push and pull factors were at work. According to Patricia A. Thornton, in 'The Problem of Out-Migration from Atlantic Canada, 1871–1921: A New Look,' *Acadiensis* 15, no. 1 (Autumn 1985): 3–34, extensive out-migration preceded economic decline, meaning that the loss of workers may have encouraged the decline as well as vice versa.

4 This point is made in Lesley Choyce, *Nova Scotia Shaped by the Sea: A Living History* (Toronto: Viking, 1996), 170, and Campbell and MacLean, *Beyond the Atlantic Roar*, 109. For more nuanced interpretations of changes over time in the Nova Scotia economy, see Julian Gwyn, *Excessive Expectations: Maritime Commerce and the Economic Development of Nova Scotia, 1740–1870* (Montreal and Kingston: McGill-Queen's University Press, 1988); E.R. Forbes and D.A. Muise, eds, *The Atlantic Provinces in Confederation* (Toronto/Fredericton: University of Toronto Press / Acadiensis Press, 1993), esp. chapters 1–4; Margaret R. Conrad and James K. Hiller, *Atlantic Canada: A Region in the Making* (Toronto: Oxford University Press, 2001); P.B. Waite, 'Becoming Canadians: Ottawa's Relations with Maritimers in the First and Twenty-first Years of Confederation,' in Carty and Ward, eds, *National Politics*, 153–68.

5 Michael Katz, *The People of Hamilton, Canada West: Family and Class in a Mid-Nineteenth Century City* (Cambridge: Harvard University Press, 1975), 123. See also Peter Knight, *The Plain People of Boston, 1830–1860: A Study in City Growth*

(New York: Oxford University Press, 1971); and David Ward, *Cities and Immigrants: A Geography of Change in Nineteenth-Century America* (New York: Oxford University Press, 1971).

6 Betsy Beattie, *Obligation and Duty: Single Maritime Women in Boston, 1870–1930* (Montreal and Kingston: McGill-Queen's University Press, 2000). Gary Burrill, *Away: Maritimers in Massachusetts, Ontario, and Alberta: An Oral History of Leaving Home* (Montreal and Kingston: McGill-Queen's University Press, 1992), is perforce limited to the twentieth century.

7 Randy William Widdis, *With Scarcely a Ripple: Anglo-Canadian Migration into the United States and Western Canada, 1880–1920* (Montreal and Kingston: McGill-Queen's University Press, 1998), 75. The specific years of Widdis's observation are 1895–1924.

8 Thornton, 'The Problem of Out-Migration'; Alan A. Brookes, 'Out-Migration from the Maritime Provinces, 1860–1900: Some Preliminary Considerations,' *Acadiensis* 5, no. 2 (Spring 1976): 36; Conrad, Laidlaw, and Smyth, eds, *No Place like Home*, 18–19; Comacchio, *The Infinite Bonds of Family*, 39.

9 Patterson, *History of the County*, 442.

10 Mike Olding to EM, Jamaica Plain, 4 May 1871, PANS.

11 Daniel McQueen to DnM, Medford, MA, 1 May 1849; Daniel McQueen to DnM, Austin, IN, 1 January 1870; Thomas McQueen to parents, Jeffersonville, IN, 15 March 1858, Medford, MA, 1 May 1849, PANS, MG1, vol. 3350, file 10.

12 Brookes, 'Out-Migration,' 35–7.

13 EMC to CM and JsM, Dartmouth, 4 March 1887, PANS; CM to JnM, SR, 14 February 1885, 5 April 1887, PANS; EMC to CM, Dartmouth, 15 April 1887, PANS.

14 NS, DE, *Annual Report*, 1887, x.

15 JsM to AM, LN, 19 April 1888, BCA.

16 *Journal of Education, Nova Scotia*, second series, October 1878–October 1888, supplemented by McQueen correspondence. According to NS, DE, *Annual Report*, 1885, ix–x, 1886, ix, 1887, x, and 1888, x–xi, the average salary per term in Pictou County ranged, depending on qualifications, from $90 to $250 for men, $80 to $135 for women.

17 JsM to MBMW, LN, 29 March 1888, PANS; EMC to CM, Dartmouth, 15 April 1887, PANS.

18 GM to CM, New York, 11 July 1887, PANS.

19 In 1881 British Columbia contained 13,431 non-Aboriginal adult males compared to 4,613 females; in 1891, 41,354 and 14,081 respectively. By 1901 the proportion of males had dropped to 71 per cent, the respective totals being 81,946 and 33,687. For data and basis of calculation, see Table 11 in Barman, *The West beyond the West*, 385.

20 Adele Perry, *On the Edge of Empire: Gender, Race, and the Making of British Columbia, 1849–1871* (Toronto: University of Toronto Press, 2001).
21 See Barman, 'Invisible Women.'
22 See Roderick J. Barman, 'Packing in British Columbia: Transport on a Resource Frontier,' *Journal of Transport History*, 3rd ser., 21, no. 2 (Sept. 2000): 140–67.
23 JsM to CM, LN, 12 November 1888, BCA; JsM to CM, LN, 12 September 1888, 24 June 1889, NVA.
24 See Jean Barman, 'British Columbia's Pioneer Teachers,' in *Children, Teachers and Schools in the History of British Columbia*, ed. Jean Barman, Neil Sutherland, and J. Donald Wilson (Calgary: Detselig, 1995), 189–208.
25 See Runnalls, *It's God's Country*, 67–9.
26 Michael Hagan, 'Notes by the Way,' *Inland Sentinel*, 16 November 1882.
27 D.B. Mack, 'George Monro Grant,' in *Dictionary of Canadian Biography*, vol. 2 (Toronto: University of Toronto Press, 1994), 403–9.
28 Prang, 'Networks and Associations,' 54, 52.
29 Moir, 'From Sectarian Rivalry to National Vision,' 162. Moir is most interested in the generation of Maritimers who acquired leadership positions in post-secondary institutions in Ontario and elsewhere.
30 Prang, 'Networks and Associations,' 52.
31 George M. Grant, *Ocean to Ocean: Sanford Fleming's Expedition through Canada in 1872* (Toronto: James Campbell & Son, 1873), 358, 366.
32 Moir, 'From Sectarian Rivalry to National Vision,' 164.
33 G.M. Grant, 'Churches and Schools in the North-West,' in *Manitoba and the Great North-West*, ed. John Macoun (Guelph: World, 1882), 528.
34 See George L. Cook, 'Educational Justice for the Campmen: Alfred Fitzpatrick and the Foundations of Frontier College, 1899–1922,' in *Knowledge for the People: The Struggle for Adult Learning in English-Speaking Canada, 1828–1973*, ed. Michael R. Welton (Toronto: OISE Press, 1987), 37–51.
35 George Grant, 'Canada First,' in *Canadian Leaves: A Series of New Papers Read before the Canadian Club of New York*, ed. G.M. Fairchild, Jr (New York: Napoléon Thompson, 1887), 251.
36 Prang, 'Networks and Associations,' 55.
37 Moir, 'From Sectarian Rivalry to National Vision,' 162–3.
38 Ian Manson, 'Canada's Presbyterian Legacy,' *Beaver* 80, no. 3 (June–July 2000): 6.
39 G.M. Grant, *Imperial Federation: A Lecture* (Winnipeg: Manitoba Free Press, 1890), 7.
40 EMC to CM, Dartmouth, 15 April 1887, PANS; AMG to CM, St Thomas, 23 June 1890, BCA.

41 EMC to CM, Dartmouth, 13 June 1887, PANS; AM to CM, NL, 10 March 1888, BCA.

42 JsM to AMG, St John, 31 May 1882, PANS; AM to JsM, NL, 1 October 1887, NVA; GM to CM, Greenville, 7 January 1888, PANS; EMC to CM, Dartmouth, 27 January 1888, PANS; DvMC to CM, 14 February 1888, PANS.

43 AM to JsM, NL, n.d. [February 1888], 10 March 1888, BCA; AM to CM, NL, 16 November 1887, NVA.

44 JsM to CM, CC, 12 March 1894, BCA; JsM to AM, LN, 19 April 1888, BCA. Jessie left on Monday, 12 March 1888.

45 JsM to MBMW, LN, 29 March 1888, PANS.

46 JsM to family, Riv-du-Loup, 2 p.m. Wednesday [March 1888], PANS; JsM to CM, Thursday evening [March 1888], PANS.

47 JsM to CM, Sudbury Junction, 16 March 1888, PANS.

48 JsM to MBMW, LN, 29 March 1888, PANS; JsM to AM, Kamloops, 22 March 1888, BCA.

49 JsM to MBMW, LN, 29 March 1888, PANS.

50 JsM to CM, Swift Current, 20 March 1888, Wednesday noon [21 March 1888], PANS; JsM to MBMW, LN, 29 March 1888, PANS.

4. Sisterhood's Bonds

1 EMC to CM, Dartmouth, 25 November 1887, PANS; GM to JsM, Greenville, 7 January 1888, PANS.

2 AM to JsM and CM, Victoria, 13 July 1887, BCA; AM to JsM, NL, 1 October 1887, NVA; AM to CM, NL, 1 October 1887, NVA; JsM to CM, LN, 27 March 1888, PANS.

3 'Questions Set at the Teachers Examination,' BC, DE, *Annual Report*, 1888, lxxxv–xcv.

4 AM to JsM and CM, Victoria, 13 July 1887, BCA.

5 AM to JsM, Dartmouth, 21 January 1881, PANS; AM to JsM and CM, Victoria, 13 July 1887, BCA.

6 AM to JsM and CM, Victoria, 13 July [1887], PANS.

7 Hagan, 'Notes by the Way,' *Inland Sentinel*, 16 November 1882.

8 See Pat Lean, 'The Town at the Foot of the Lake,' *Nicola Valley Historical Quarterly* 4, no. 2 (April 1981): 7; J.A. Bowell to SDP, SE, NL, 22 November 1884, in BC, SE, IC, BCA, GR 1445.

9 AM to CM, NL, 20 October 1888, BCA; Thomas Matthews and A.E. House to SDP, NL, 29 July 1887, in BC, SE, IC, BCA, GR 1445.

10 AM to SDP, NL, 10 August 1887, in BC, SE, IC, BCA, GR 1445.

11 AM to SDP, NL, 10 August, 16 November 1887, in BC, SE, IC, BCA, GR 1445.

12 AM to SDP, NL, 9 December 1887, 20 September, 30 June 1888, in BC, SE, IC, BCA, GR 1445.

13 AM to CM, NL, 7 January 1888, BCA; AM to JsM, NL, n.d. [February 1888], BCA; AM to CM, NL, 16 March 1888, NVA.

14 AM to CM, NL, 1 October 1887, 30 January, 16 March 1888, NVA.

15 AM to JsM, NL, 1 October 1887, NVA; AM to CM, NL, 30 January 1888, NVA; AM to JsM, NL, 18 November 1887, NVA.

16 AM to JsM, NL, 18 November 1887, NVA.

17 AM to JsM, NL, 18 November 1887, NVA.

18 AM to JsM, NL, 1 October 1887, NVA.

19 AM to JsM, NL, 18 November 1887, NVA.

20 AM to CM, NL, 16 November 1887, 10 March 1888, NVA.

21 JsM to CM, Wednesday noon [March 1888], NVA; JsM to AM, Kamloops, 22 March 1888, BCA; JsM to MBMW, LN, 29 March 1888, PANS; *Inland Sentinel*, 24 March 1888; JsM to EMC, LN, 29 March 1888, PANS.

22 'Mainland School Interests,' *Colonist*, 25 June 1874; A. Irwin to JJ, Yale, 2 October 1875, in BC, SE, IC, BCA, GR 1445.

23 A. Irwin to JJ, Yale, 16 November 1878, in BC, SE, IC, BCA, GR 1445; 'Notes of conversations with Albert Elgin Howse, in his home in Princeton, July 11, 13, 15, and 16, 1930,' typescript in BCA, ms. 1346.

24 Interview with Bertha Corkle, cited in Pat Lean, 'Nicola Valley Profile: Bertha Van Norman (Woodward) Corkle,' *Nicola Valley Historical Quarterly* 4, no. 1 (Jan. 1981): 1; JsM to CM, LN, 19 September, 24 December 1889, BCA; A. Irwin to JJ, Yale, 2 October 1875, 17 January 1876, in BC, SE, IC, BCA, GR 1445.

25 James Turner, NV, 15 November 1875, in *Missionary Notices*, March 1876, p. 94; James Turner, NV, 30 December 1876, in *Missionary Notices*, April 1877, p. 201; A. Irwin to JJ, Yale, 17 January 1876, in BC, SE, IC, BCA, GR 1445.

26 Pat Lean, 'Alexander Coutlie (1826–1901),' *Nicola Valley Historical Quarterly* 6, no. 2–3 (1983): 3; Pat Lean, 'The Garcia Story,' *Nicola Valley Historical Quarterly* 6, no. 4 (1984): 2–5; F.W. Laing, *Colonial Farm Settlers on the Mainland of British Columbia 1858–1871* (Victoria, 1939), 230, 423–4, 426; 'William Charters,' *Merritt Herald*, 1967 Centennial edition; AM to JsM, NL, 1 September 1887, NVA; F.M. Buckland, *Ogopogo's Vigil: A History of Kelowna and the Okanagan* (Kelowna: Okanagan Historical Society, 1966), 37.

27 A. Irwin to JJ, Yale, 17 January 1876, quarterly return of December 1877, 16 November 1878, in BC, SE, IC, BCA, GR 1445.

28 28 May 1877 entry, Jessop Diary, BCA, GR 1468; A. Irwin to JJ, NV, 8 March 1878; A. Irwin to CCM, NV, 16 November 1878; Charles J. Hamilton to CCM, NV, 15 May 1883, in BC, SE, IC, BCA, GR 1445; Michael Hagan, 'Notes by the Way,' *Inland Sentinel*, 30 November 1882.

29 Harvey H. Woodward to NV trustees, 25 February 1881; Charles J. Hamilton
    to CCM, NV, 22 April 1882; Henry Woodward to CCM, NL, 12 March 1882;
    Agnes Woodward to Charles J. Hamilton, n.d., copy in Charles J. Hamilton
    to CCM, NV, 22 April 1882; H.D. Green Armytage to Henry Woodward, NL,
    7 February 1882; H.D. Green Armytage, to CCM, NV, 31 March 1882, in BC,
    SE, IC, BCA, GR 1445; CCM to Henry Woodward, n.d., in BC, SE, Outward
    Correspondence, BCA, GR 450; JsM to CM, LM, 2 February 1891, NVA.
30 Hagan, 'Notes by the Way,' *Inland Sentinel*, 30 November 1882.
31 A. Irwin to JJ, Yale, 2 October 1875, in BC, SE, IC, BCA, GR 1445; JsM to CM,
    LN, 27 March 1888, PANS; JsM to CM, LN, 17 January 1889, BCA.
32 JsM to JnM, 21 November 1878, PANS; JsM to MBMW, LN, 29 March 1888,
    PANS; JsM to CM, LN, 12 September 1888, NVA.
33 AM to SDP, NL, 20 September 1888, in BC, SE, IC, BCA, GR 1445; AM to
    CM, NL, 31 March 1888, BCA.
34 Harvey H. Woodward to SDP, LN, 25 September 1888; JsM to SDP, LN,
    2 October, 31 October 1888, in BC, SE, IC, BCA, GR 1445.
35 JsM to CM, LN, 27 March 1888, PANS.
36 JsM to CM, LN, 19 April 1888, 'Private,' n.d. [August 1888], 'Private,' n.d.,
    BCA; also MBM to EM, 18 February 1878, PANS.
37 JsM to CM, NL, 19 April 1888, BCA; AM to CM, NL, 31 March 1888, BCA; JsM
    to CM, LN, 27 March 1888, PANS.
38 AM to CM, NL, 13 June 1888, NVA; JsM to CM, LN, 11 June 1888, 1 October
    1888, NVA.
39 JsM to CM, LN, 20 April 1893, 17 May, 4 June 1888, NVA; JsM to DnM, LN,
    4 June 1888, NVA; JsM to JnM, LN, 16 August 1888, NVA.
40 JsM to CM, LN, 27 March, 19 April, 11, 18 June, 8 August 1888, NVA; JsM to
    CM and DvMC, LN, 16 August 1888, NVA.
41 JsM to CM, LN, 14 April 1888, BCA; AM to CM, NL, 22 August, 20 October
    1888, BCA.
42 JsM to CM, LN, 26 December 1888, 17 January 1889, BCA.

5. Taking a Chance on Love

1 AM to JsM, n.d. [Victoria, 15 July 1887], BCA; EMC to CM, n.d., PANS.
2 AM to JsM and CM, Victoria, 13 July [1887], PANS.
3 AM to CM, NL, 7 January 1888, BCA; JsM to MBMW, LN, 29 March 1888,
   PANS; John Chisholm to AMG, Kamloops, 8 February 1888, BCA; AM to CM,
   NL, 10 March 1888, SR, NVA.
4 *Industries of Canada: Historical and Commercial Sketches* (Toronto: Railway
   Steamship Publishing Co., 1890), 162; *Inland Sentinel*, 19 January 1894, 2 Feb-

ruary 1889; Mary Balf, *Kamloops: A History of the District up to 1914*, 3rd ed.
(Kamloops: Kamloops Museum Association, 1989), 39; AM to CM, NL,
16 March 1888, NVA. I am grateful to Bridget Gordon Mackenzie for information on the Gordon family.

5 JsM to CM, LN, 27 March 1888, PANS; JsM to CM, NL,19 April 1888, fragment, n.d., BCA; AM to CM, NL, 31 March, 23 April 1888, BCA.

6 AM to CM, Kamloops, 4 August 1888, BCA.

7 JsM to CM, Private, n.d. [early August 1888], PANS.

8 JsM to CM, Private, n.d. [early August 1888], PANS.

9 JsM to CM, Private, n.d. [early August 1888], n.d. [mid-late August 1888],
PANS. CM's letters, perhaps understandably, do not survive.

10 JsM to CM, LN, n.d. [August 1888], BCA; JsM to CM, n.d. [mid-late August
1888], PANS.

11 AM to CM, 20 September 1888, BCA; AM to JnM, 20 September 1888, BCA.

12 AM to SDP, NL, 1 November 1888, in BC, SE, IC, BCA, GR 1445.

13 Peter Ward, *Courtship, Love, and Marriage in Nineteenth-Century English Canada*
(Montreal and Kingston: McGill-Queen's University Press, 1990), 129.

14 JG to DnM, Kamloops, 10 November 1888, PANS.

15 AM to CM, NL, 10 November 1888, BCA; JsM to CM, SB, 2 January 1889,
NVA.

16 JsM, likely to a sister, n.d. [likely autumn 1888], NVA; JsM to CM, LN,
26 December 1888, NVA.

17 JsM to CM, LN, 22 October, 12 December 1888, NVA.

18 AM to CM, LN, 26 December 1888, NVA; JsM to CM, SB, 2 January 1889,
NVA. Weddings' importance on the frontier is exemplified in Nancy Millar,
*Once upon a Wedding: Stories of Weddings in Western Canada, 1860–1945, for Bet-
ter or Worse* (Calgary: Bayeux Arts, 2000).

19 AMG to CM, Kamloops, 7, 19 January, 4 February 1889, BCA.

20 JsM to CM, SB, 2 January 1889, NVA; AM and JsM to CM, LN, 26 December
1888, BCA; JsM to CM, SB, 2 January 1889, NVA.

21 Ward, *Courtship, Love, and Marriage*, 110.

22 'Gordon-McQueen,' *Inland Sentinel*, 6 January 1889; JsM to CM, SB, 2 January
1889, NVA.

23 JsM to CM, SB, 2 January 1889, NVA.

24 A.E. Howse to SDP, NL, 7 January 1889, in BC,SE, IC, BCA, GR 1445.

25 JsM to CM, no date [mid-late August 1888], PANS; JsM to CM, LN, 17 January 1889, BCA; AM to CM, NL, 20 October 1888, BCA.

26 AMG to CM, Kamloops, 19 January 1889, BCA.

27 JsM to CM, LN, 13 February 1889, NVA; *Inland Sentinel*, 2 February 1889;
AMG to CM, Kamloops, 4 February 1889, BCA.

28 JsM to CM, 28 February 1889, BCA; EMC to CM, Dartmouth, 18 May 1888, PANS; Thomas Duke to SDP, Metchosin, 9 August 1888, in BC, SE, IC, BCA, GR 1445.

29 AM to CM, NL, 10 November 1888, BCA; George Murray to SDP, NL, 26 November 1888; A.E. Howse to SDP, NL, 12 November 1888, 7 January 1889, in BC, SE, IC, BCA, GR 1445.

30 Hattie Macleod to SDP, Stump Lake, Kamloops, 10 December 1888, in BC, SE, IC, BCA, GR 1445.

31 JsM to CM, LN, 12, 26 December 1888, NVA.

32 JsM to CM, LN, 24 June 1889, NVA.

33 GM to JsM, Greenville, 7 January 1888, PANS; EMC to JsM, Dartmouth, 20 May 1889, PANS.

34 JsM to CM, Wednesday noon [March 1888], PANS; JsM to EMC, LN, 29 March 1888, PANS; JsM to DnM, LN, 4 June 1888, NVA.

35 JsM to EMC, LN, 29 March 1888, PANS; JsM to CM, LN, 28 May 1888, NVA.

36 JsM to CM, LN, 12 September 1888, NVA; JsM to JnM, LN, 12 September 1888, NVA.

37 JsM to CM, LN, 28 May, 27 September 1888, NVA; Census of Canada, 1881, 89 Yale (Nicola-Okanagan), household 36; Census of Canada, 1891, EA 5, Yale and Nicola, household 196; 26 February and 25 September 1877 entries in R.M. Clemitson, Notebook, typescript in Kamloops Archives; A. Irwin to JJ, Nicola Valley, 8 March 1878; undated enrolment list from A. Irwin, in BC, SE, IC, BCA, GR 1445; JsM to CM, LN, 16 October 1888, NVA.

38 JsM to CM, LN, 24 January 1889, NVA.

39 'Terrible Accident,' *Inland Sentinel*, 18 May 1889; JsM to CM, Private, 22 May 1889, PANS; JsM to CM, LN, 5 November, 1888, BCA.

40 McCurrach, 'The Old House'; JsM to CM, LN, 5 November 1888, BCA; JsM to CM, SB, 2 January 1889, NVA.

41 JsM to CM, LN, 11 March 1889, NVA; JsM to CM, CC, 29 January 1894, PANS.

42 JsM to CM, Private, 22 May 1889, PANS; JsM to CM, LN, 26 December 1888, NVA; JsM to CM, LN, 28 February 1889, BCA; JsM to DnM and CM, LN, 23 March 1889, BCA.

43 JsM to CM, LN, 27 March, Private, 22 May, Private, 29 May 1889, PANS.

44 AMG to JsM, Waterloo, 2 April 1889, BCA.

45 JsM to CM, Private, 22 May, Private, 29 May 1889, PANS; 'Terrible Accident.'

46 'Terrible Accident'; McCurrach, 'The Old House.'

47 JsM to CM, Private, 22 May 1889, PANS.

48 AMG to JsM, St Thomas, 4 June 1889, BCA.

49 McCurrach, 'The Old House'; JsM to CM, Private, 22 May 1889, PANS.

50 JsM to CM, Private, 29 May 1889, PANS; CM to JsM, SR, 4, 11 June 1889, PANS; JsM to CM, LN, 24 June 1889, NVA.

51 JsM to DnM and CM, LN, 24 December 1889, BCA.

6. Domesticating Everyday Life

1 JsM to CM, LN, 17 May 1888, NVA.

2 JsM to DvMC, Victoria, 10 July 1888, BCA; JsM to CM, LN, 6 August 1888, BCA; AM to CM, NL, 10 November 1888, BCA.

3 JsM to CM, LN, 16 March 1891, BCA.

4 AMG to JsM, St Thomas, 22 April 1889, BCA; JsM to CM, LN, 27 March 1888, PANS.

5 JsM to CM, LN, 18 April, 17 May, 1 October 1888, 18 March 1889, NVA; JsM to CM, LN, 19 August 1889, BCA.

6 JsM to CM, NL, 19 April 1888, BCA; JsM to CM, LN, 5 November 1888, NVA; JsM to DnM and CM, New Westminster, 22 July 1889, BCA; JsM to CM, LN, 23 September 1889, NVA.

7 JsM to CM, LN, 14 April 1888, NVA; JsM to CM, LN, 18 May 1891, BCA; JSM to CM, LN, 17 May 1888, NVA.

8 JsM to CM, LN, 8 August 1888, NVA; R.M. Woodward in A.R. Carrington, 'Nicola Pioneers' Column,' no. 9, *Merritt Herald*, 9 November 1934; JsM to JnM, LN, 16 August 1888, NVA; JsM to CM and DvMC, LN, 16 August 1888, NVA; JsM to JnM, LN, 20 September 1888, PANS; JsM to CM, LN, 27 September, 29 August, 1 October 1888, NVA.

9 JsM to CM, LN, 14 October, 3 October [November] 1889, NVA; JsM to DnM, LN, 13 November 1889, NVA.

10 JsM to CM, LN, 8 January, 26 February 1890, NVA; JsM to CM, LN, 1 April 1890, PANS.

11 JsM to CM, LN, 14 April 1888, BCA; JsM to CM, LN, 25 June 1888, NVA; AM to JsM, NL, 1 October 1887, NVA; JsM to CM, LN, 12 December 1888, NVA.

12 JsM to CM, LN, 25 June, 22 October, 14 April, 5 November 1888, NVA; JsM to CM and DvMC, LN, 16 August 1888, NVA; JsM to CM, LN, 16 October 1888, NVA.

13 JsM to CM, LN, 14 April 1888, 8 December 1890, NVA.

14 JsM to CM, LN, 27 September 1888, NVA.

15 JsM to CM, LN, 12, 27 September 1888, 4 March 1889, NVA; JsM to CM, LN, 14 October 1889, BCA; JsM to McQueen family, LN, 11 August 1890, BCA.

16 JsM to CM, LN, 2 February 1891, NVA.

17 JsM to CM, LN, 30 June 1890, 4 June 1888, BCA.

18 JsM to CM, LN, 23 September 1889, BCA; JsM to CM, LN, 28 May 1888, NVA; JsM to AMG, LN, 28 July 1890, BCA.

19 JsM to CM, LN, 28 May, 6, 22 August 1888, NVA.

20 JsM to CM, LN, 27 March 1888, PANS; JsM to CM, Victoria, 12 July 1888, NVA.

21 JsM to CM, LN, 18 June 1888, NVA; JsM to JnM, LN, 20 September 1888, PANS.

22 JsM to CM, LN, 27 March 1888, PANS; JsM to CM, LN, 14 April 1888, BCA; JsM to CM, LN, 29 August 1888, NVA; JsM to CM, LN, 1 June 1891, 1 January 1893, BCA.

23 JsM to CM, LN, 28 May 1888, NVA; JsM to CM, LN, 11 March, 30 October 1889, BCA.

24 JsM to CM, LN, 12 September 1888, NVA; JsM to CM, LN, 9 September 1889, BCA.

25 JsM to CM, LN, 23 October 1890, NVA.

26 JsM to CM, LN, 1 June 1891, BCA. Diana C. Archibald makes this point, using literary sources, in 'Angel in the Bush: Exporting Domesticity through Female Emigration,' in *Imperial Objects: Essays on Victorian Women's Emigration and the Unauthorized Imperial Experience*, ed. Rita S. Kranidis (New York: Twayne, 1998), 228–47.

27 CM to JsM, SR, 14 October 1889; JsM to CM, LN, 25 November 1889, BCA; JsM to CM, LN, 1 October 1888, 12 June 1890, NVA.

28 JsM to CM, LN, 5 November 1888, NVA; JsM to family, LN, 11 August 1890, NVA; JsM to JnM, LN, 20 September 1888, PANS; JsM to CM, LN, 26 December 1888, NVA.

29 JsM to JnM, LN, 16 August 1888, NVA; DvMC to JsM, Canning, 7 June 1893, PANS; JsM to CM, CC, 8 November 1893, BCA.

30 JsM to CM, LN, 25 June, 16 October 1888, 30 June 1890, 14 April 1888, NVA.

31 JsM to CM, LN, n.d. [August 1888], 4 April 1889, BCA; EMC to JsM, Dartmouth, 20 May 1889, PANS; JsM to CM and DvMC, LN, 16 August 1888, NVA; JsM to CM, CC, 28 March 1894, BCA.

32 JsM to CM, LN, 17 May 1888, NVA; JsM to family, LN, 3 December 1888, NVA.

33 Moir, 'From Sectarian Rivalry to National Vision,' 169. For the orientation of these newspapers, see Jerry N. Pittman, 'Darwinism and Evolution: Three Nova Scotia Religious Newspapers Respond, 1860–1900,' *Acadiensis* 22, no. 2 (Spring 1993): 40–60.

34 JsM to CM, LN, 14 November, 9 September 1889, NVA.

35 Isabella Alden, *Mrs. Solomon Smith Looking On* (Boston: Lothrop, 1882); J.B. Dobkin, 'Isabella Alden (Pansy),' in *American Writers for Children before 1900,*

ed. Glenn E. Estes, vol. 42 of *Dictionary of Literary Biography* (Detroit: Gale, 1985), 37–41.

36 Langland, *Nobody's Angels*, 3.

37 JsM to CM, LN, 6 August, 27 September, 22 October 1888, NVA.

38 JsM to CM, LN, 25 June 1888, NVA; CM to JsM, SR, 4 June 1889, NVA; AMG to CM, NL, 30 October 1888, BCA; EMC to CM, Dartmouth, 11 November 1887, PANS.

39 JsM to CM, Victoria, 12 July 1888, New Westminster, 19 July 1893, Kamloops, 27 June 1893, BCA; JsM to EMC, LN, 29 March 1888, PANS; JsM to AM, Kamloops, 22 March 1888, BCA; JsM to CM, LN, 6 August 1888, NVA; MBMW to CM, St John, 3 September 1888, PANS; JsM to CM, LN, 29 September 1890, PANS; JsM to CM, LN, 5, 12 November 1888, NVA.

40 JsM to family, New Westminster, 22 July 1889, BCA; AM to SDP, NL, 16 November 1887, in BC, SE, IC, BCA, GR 1445; AM to CM, NL, 10 November 1888, BCA; JsM to DvMC, Victoria, 10 July 1888, NVA.

41 JsM to CM, Private, 22 May 1889, PANS; JsM to CM, LN, 14 April 1889, BCA; CM to JsM, SR, 4 June 1889, PANS; JsM to CM, LN, 24 June 1888, NVA.

42 EMC to CM, Dartmouth, 15 April 1887, PANS.

43 AMG to CM, NL, 31 March 1888, BCA; JsM to CM, LN, 22 August, 12 September 1888, NVA; JsM to CM, LN, 11 March 1889, BCA; JsM to CM, LN, 30 June 1890, NVA.

44 JsM to CM and DvMC, LN, 22 August 1888, NVA.

45 JsM to DnM, LN, 4 June 1888, NVA; JsM to CM, LN, 28 May, 5 November 1888, NVA; JsM to CM, LN, 15 September 1889, BCA.

46 James Turner, NV, 15 November 1875, in *Missionary Notices*, March 1876, p. 94; 'Editorial Notes,' *Missionary Outlook* 11, no. 8 (Aug. 1891): 114.

47 AM to CM, NL, 10 March 1888, NVA; JsM to CM, Victoria, 28 May, 4 June, 12 July 1888, NVA; JsM to CM, LN, 15 September 1889, BCA.

48 J.W. Winslow, NL, 29 January 1890, *Missionary Outlook* 10, no. 3 (March 1890): 47.

49 JsM to DnM, LN, 4 June 1888, NVA; JsM to DvMC, Victoria, 10 July 1888, NVA; JsM to DnM and CM, New Westminster, 22 July 1889, BCA; JsM to CM, LN, 18 May 1891, BCA.

50 JsM to DnM and CM, New Westminster, 22 July 1889, BCA; JsM to CM, LN, 14 April 1888, BCA; JsM to CM, LN, 24 January 1889, NVA; JsM to CM, LN, 1 April 1890, PANS.

51 JsM to CM, LN, 1 April 1890, Private, 29 May 1889, PANS; JsM to CM, LN, 1 June 1891, BCA.

52 JsM to CM, LN, 5 November 1888, NVA.

53 J.M.D. Meiklejohn, *The First Primer* (Toronto: Gage, 1881), 24–6.

54 *The Practical Speller* (Toronto: Gage, 1881), iv, 10, 15; *The Canadian Readers, Book III* (Toronto: W.J. Gage & Co., 1883).

55 JsM to CM, LN, 30 June 1890, NVA; JsM to CM, LN, 14 April 1888, BCA; JsM to CM, LN, 8 August 1888, NVA.

56 JsM to SDP, LN, 1 May 1890, in BC, SE, IC, BCA, GR 1445; JsM to CM, LN, 23 September 1889, BCA; JsM to family, LN, 11 August 1890, BCA.

57 JsM to CM, LN, 14 April 1888, BCA.

58 JsM to CM, LN, 17 January 1889, BCA; JsM to CM, LN, 4 March 1889, NVA. The observation about Jessie's strengths as a teacher comes from my reading of the inward and outward correspondence of BC, SE, 1872–96, BCA, GR 1445 and 450.

59 JsM to DnM and CM, LN, 23 March 1889, BCA; JsM to CM, NL, 15 February 1892, NVA; JsM to CM, LN, 29 August 1889, BCA; Jessie Olding to JsM, NL, 28 April 1890, PANS; JG to CM, St Thomas, 27 May 1890, BCA; JsM to CM, LN, 16 March 1891, NVA; JsM to CM, NL, 19 April 1888, BCA.

60 JsM to CM, LN, 12 June 1890, NVA; JsM to CM, LN, 18 May, 24 June 1891, BCA.

61 M. Hunter Mitchell, 'Jessie (Olding) Hunter,' *Nicola Valley Historical Quarterly* 3, no. 4 (1980): 1.

7. Daughterhood's Obligations

1 JsM to SDP, LN, 23 March 1891, in BC, SE, IC, BCA, GR 1445; fragment of JsM to CM [spring 1891], BCA; JsM to CM, NL, 24 September 1891, NVA.

2 Ed Olding to JsM, Kohala, Hawaii, 22 April [1893], PANS.

3 JsM to CM, SB, 2 September 1891, BCA; JsM to CM, Montreal, 16 August 1891, Owen Sound, 27 August 1891, PANS; JsM to CM, SB, 2 September 1891, BCA.

4 CM to MBMW, SR, 31 August 1891, PANS; EMC to JsM, Dartmouth, 20 May 1889, PANS; CM to JsM, n.d. [October 1891], PANS.

5 JsM to CM, NL, 10 April 1893, NVA; CM to JsM, n.d. [October 1891], PANS; JsM to CM, LN, 1 January 1893, BCA.

6 CM to JsM, n.d. [October 1891], PANS.

7 CM to JsM, 28 March 1892, n.d. [August 1892], PANS; JsM to CM, NL, 3 October 1892, NVA; JsM to CM, NL, 6 March 1893, BCA.

8 CM to JsM, n.d. [October 1891], SR, 21 February 1893, PANS.

9 CM to JsM, SR, 2 December 1889, PANS; CM to MBMW, SR, 31 August 1891, PANS.

10 CM to JsM, SR, 26 December 1891, PANS; JsM to CM, NL, 22 February 1892, NVA; GM to CM, New York, 18 March 1892, PANS; CM to JsM, n.d. [August 1892], PANS.

11 GM to DvMC, New York, 30 December 1892, PANS; marriage certificate, New York Municipal Archives; DvMC to CM, Private, Canning, 5 January 1893, PANS; DvMC to JsM, Canning, 7 June 1893, PANS; CM to JsM, SR, 3 October 1893, PANS; Williams, *Simple Annals*, 135.

12 JsM to SDP, LN, 30 June 1890; Harvey H. Woodward to SDP, LN, 9 July 1890, in BC, SE, IC, BCA, GR 1445.

13 Thomas Carrington to SDP, NL, 27 June 1891, in BC, SE, IC, BCA, GR 1445; JsM to CM, LN, 24 June 1891, BCA; A. Irwin to SDP, LN, 15 July 1891, in BC, SE, IC, BCA, GR 1445.

14 'Post Offices – Nicola Valley,' *Nicola Valley Historical Quarterly* 2, no. 4 (Oct. 1979): 2; JsM to CM, NL, 17 September, 8 October 1891, NVA.

15 JsM to CM, NL, 14 January 1892, PANS; JsM to CM, NL, 22 February, 21 April 1892, NVA; JsM to CM, NL, 20 June 1892, BCA.

16 JsM to CM, NL, 12 November 1891, PANS; JsM to CM, NL, 28 April 1892, NVA.

17 JsM to JnM, NL, 9 June 1892, BCA; JsM to CM, NL, 8 October 1891, NVA.

18 JsM to CM, LN, 5 November 1888, NVA; JsM to CM, LN, 28 July 1890, BCA.

19 JsM to CM, NL, 24 September, 29 October 1891, NVA.

20 JsM to CM, NL, 19 May 1892, 24 September, 26 November 1891, NVA; CM to MBMW, SR, 26 December 1891, PANS; JsM to CM, NL, 9 May 1892, NVA.

21 JsM to CM, NL, 1 October 1891, BCA; JsM to CM, NL, 22 October, 26 November, 1 March 1891, NVA; JsM to CM, NL, 11 April, 3 October 1892, 27 March 1893, BCA.

22 AM to CM, LN, 26 December 1888, NVA; JsM to CM, Kamloops, 18 July 1892, BCA; JsM to CM, NL, 7 January 1892, PANS; JsM to CM, NL, 26 January 1893, NVA. On the Rileys, see 'Notes of Conversations with Albert Elgin Howse'; 'Bill Riley,' *Merritt Herald*, 1967 Centennial edition; AM to CM, NL, 30 January, 13 June 1888, BCA; JsM to CM, NL, 7 January, 1 March, 14 March, 2 April 1892, NVA.

23 JsM to CM, NL, 12 November 1891, PANS; JsM to CM, NL, 26 November 1891, 26 January 1893, NVA.

24 JsM to CM, NL, 20 June, 19 May 1892, BCA.

25 JsM to CM, NL, 24 September 1891, 1 March, 15 February 1892, NVA.

26 JsM to CM, NL, 8 October, 12 November 1891, 14 January 1892, PANS; JsM to CM, NL, 9 May 1892, 6 March 1893, NVA; JsM to CM, NL, 27 October 1892, BCA; JsM to CM, NL, 20 April 1893, NVA.

27 JsM to CM, NL, 1 October 1891, BCA; JsM to CM, NL, 2 April 1892, NVA.

28 JsM to CM, NL, 12 November 1891, PANS; JsM to CM, NL, 26 November 1891, 9 May 1892, NVA.

29 JsM to CM, NL, 21 September 1892, PANS; JsM to CM, NL, 3 October 1892, NVA.

30 Runnalls, *It's God's Country*, 76; JsM to CM, NL, 11 April 1892, NVA; JsM to CM, NL, 17 December 1891, PANS; JsM to CM, NL, 2 April 1892, NVA.

31 JsM to CM, NL, 25 August 1892, BCA; Isabella Alden, *Chrissy's Endeavor* (Boston: Lothrop, 1889); JsM to CM, NL, 21 April 1892, NVA.

32 JsM to CM, NL, 7 January 1892, PANS; JsM to CM, LN, 2 January 1893, BCA; Marietta Holley, *My Opinions and Betsy Bobbet's* (Harford: American Publishing, 1873; London: Ward & Lock, 1891); Kate H. Winter, *Marietta Holley: Life with 'Josiah Allen's Wife'* (Syracuse: Syracuse University Press, 1984), 47; and Marietta Holley, *Samantha Rastles the Woman Question*, ed. Jane Curry (Urbana: University of Illinois Press, 1983), xiii, 4–16, 43, 134.

33 From *The Widder Doodle's Love Affair*, quoted in Holley, *Samantha Rastles*, 6.

34 JsM to CM, NL, 6 March 1893, NVA. On Holley, see Jane A. Curry, 'Marietta Holley,' in *American Humorists, 1800–1950*, Part 1: A–L, ed. Stanley Trachtenberg, vol. 11 of *Dictionary of Literary Biography* (Detroit: Gale, 1982), 206–10.

35 JsM to CM, NL, 28 April, 14 March, 11, 21 April 1892, NVA; JsM to CM, NL, 12 September 1892, PANS; JsM to CM, NL, 14 November 1892, NVA.

36 JsM to CM, NL, 22 February, 11 April 1892, NVA.

37 JsM to CM, NL, 11 April 1892, NVA.

38 JsM to CM, NL, 12 September 1892, PANS; AMG to CM, St Thomas, 7 October 1891, BCA.

39 JsM to CM, NL, 21 November 1892, 6 March 1893, NVA.

40 JsM to CM, NL, 14 November 1892, NVA; JG to CM, St Thomas, 20 October 1892, BCA.

41 JsM to CM, NL, 21 January 1892, NVA.

42 JsM to CM, NL, 21 September, 21 April 1892, NVA.

43 JsM to CM, NL, 12 November 1891, PANS.

44 JsM to CM, NL, 12 November 1891, PANS; JsM to CM, NL, 21 January 1892, NVA.

45 Hobsbawm, 'Mass-Producing Traditions,' 300–6.

46 CM to MBM, SR, 1 March 1875, PANS; JsM to CM, NL, 3 December 1891, 26 January 1893, 26 November 1891, NVA; JsM to CM, NL, 14 January 1892, PANS.

47 JsM to CM, NL, 20 February, 6, 27 March 1893, NVA; JsM to CM, NL, 6 March 1892, BCA.

48 JsM to CM, NL, 20 February, 6 March 1893, NVA.

49 JsM to CM, NL, 26 November 1891, NVA; JsM to CM, NL, 7 January 1892, BCA; JsM to CM, NL, 14 January 1892, PANS; JsM to CM, NL, 21 January, 15 February, 28 April, 30 May 1892, NVA; JsM to CM, CC, 18 January 1894, BCA.

50 JsM to CM, NL, 28 April, 20 June 1892, NVA.

51 JsM to CM, NL, 27 March 1893, NVA.

52 JsM to CM, NL, 28 December 1891, PANS; JsM to CM, NL, 3 December 1891, 22 February 1892, NVA.

53 JsM to CM, LN, 11 June 1888, SB, 2 January 1889, NVA; JsM to CM, LN, 12 June, 29 August, 29 October 1889, BCA; JsM to CM, LN, 8 January, 26 February 1890, NVA.

54 JsM to CM, NL, 3 December, 26 November 1891, NVA; JsM to CM, NL, 28 December 1891, PANS; JsM to CM, NL, 2 April 1892, NVA.

55 JsM to CM, NL, 20 June 1892, Kamloops, 18 July 1892, BCA.

56 JsM to CM, NL, 14 March 1892, BCA; JsM to CM, NL, 18 April 1892, 3 December 1891, 29 May 1893, NVA.

57 JsM to CM, NL, 30 May 1892, NVA; Mitchell, 'Jessie (Olding) Hunter,' 1; JsM to CM, Kamloops, 11 July 1892, BCA; JsM to CM, NL, 12 September 1892, PANS.

8. Enduring Bonds of Sisterhood

1 AMG to CM, Kamloops, 4 February 1889, BCA.

2 AMG to JsM, Waterloo, 2 April 1889, BCA; *The Industries of Canada: Historical and Commercial Sketches* (Toronto: M.G. Bixby, 1887), 129, 121; EMC to CM, Dartmouth, 16 September 1889, PANS.

3 CM to JsM, SR, 14 October 1889, PANS; AMG to MBMW, St Thomas, 17 October 1889, BCA; JsM to CM, LN, 3 October 1889, BCA; CM to JsM, SR, 2 December 1889, PANS; AMG to CM, St Thomas, November 1889, BCA.

4 *Ontario Gazatteer and Directory, 1892–93* (Toronto: Might's Directory Co., 1892), 1045, passim; AMG to CM, St Thomas, 15 September 1892, BCA; JG to CM, St Thomas, 27 May, 28 November 1890, 28 May 1892, BCA.

5 AMG to JsM, Waterloo, 2 April 1889, BCA; AMG to CM, St Thomas, 27 July 1891, 15 September 1892, BCA.

6 JsM to CM, NL, 10 April 1893, NVA; DvMC to JsM, Canning, 7 June 1893, PANS; JsM to CM, Kamloops, March 1893, BCA; JsM to CM, NL, 10 April 1893, NVA; CM to JsM, SR, 21 February 1893, PANS.

7 JsM to CM, NL, 6, 27 March 1893, NVA; AMG to CM, Kamloops, 4, 29 April, 29 October 1893, BCA; JsM to CM, Kamloops, March 1893, BCA; JsM to CM, NL, 10 April 1893, PANS.

8 JsM to CM, NL, 10 April 1893, PANS.

9 AMG to CM, Kamloops, 5 May, 27 June 1893, BCA; JsM to CM, NL, 10 April 1893, PANS.

10 JsM to CM, Kamloops, 27 June 1893, BCA.

11 JsM to CM, Kamloops, 22 August 1893, NL, 7 August 1893, NVA; JsM to CM, Kamloops, 9 August 1893, BCA.

12 JsM to CM, Kamloops, 22 August 1893, NVA; JsM to SDP, New Westminster, 24 July 1893, in BC, SE, IC, BCA, GR 1445; JsM to CM, LN, 4 September 1893, NVA.

13 JsM to CM, CC, 23 November 1893, NVA; Albert W. Duck to SDP, Duck, 20 September 1893, in BC, SE, IC, BCA, GR 1445; *Inland Sentinel*, 23 September 1893; ad, *Kamloops Sentinel*, 30 July 1892.

14 Mary Balf, *Kamloops: A History of the District up to 1914*, 3rd ed. (Kamloops: Kamloops Museum Association, 1989), 125; Oblate register of baptisms, 1867–82, and marriages, 1873–4, in Kamloops Archives; Census of Canada, 1881, 189 Yale (Lytton, Cache Creek), household 9; Census of Canada, 1891, 5 Yale (Kamloops), household 138; Census of Canada, 1901, Yale & Cariboo, K11, Yale North, household 98; Laing, *Colonial Farm Settlers*, 396; JsM to CM, CC, 18 March, 10 May, 8 June 1894, BCA.

15 JsM to CM, CC, 23 November 1893, 29 January 1894, PANS.

16 JsM to CM, CC, 23 November 1893, 29 January 1894, PANS; JsM to CM, CC, 2 March 1894, BCA.

17 I.W. Mackay to A.W. Vowell, Kamloops, 24 September 1892, in Canada, Department of Indian Affairs, Black Series, RG 10, vol. 3867, file 87,125; Morley Roberts, *The Western Avernus* (Westminster: Archibald Constable, 1896 [orig. 1887]), 126.

18 *Kamloops Sentinel*, 8 July 1886, 3 September 1887; 'Campbell Creek School,' *Kamloops Sentinel*, 7 May 1897, 9 April 1898.

19 JsM to CM, CC, 26 May 1894, 27 September, 10 October 1893, BCA.

20 JsM to SDP, CC, 27, 30 September, 3 November 1893, in BC, SE, IC, BCA, GR 1445; JsM to CM, CC, 29 January 1894, PANS. The superintendent of education's letters were not located in his outgoing correspondence.

21 JsM to CM, CC, 27 September 1893, BCA; JsM to SDP, CC, 30 September 1893, in BC, SE, IC, BCA, GR 1445.

22 CM to JsM, SR, 3 October 1893, PANS; JsM to CM, Kamloops, 29 October 1893, NVA; JsM to CM, CC, 23, 27 November 1893, 2 March 1894, BCA.

23 JsM to CM, CC, 10 October, 27 September 1893, BCA.

24 JsM to CM, Kamloops, 8 January 1894, CC, 8, 14 November 1893, BCA; JsM to CM, CC, 29 January, 15 February 1894, 23 November 1893, PANS.

25 JsM to CM, CC, 27 September 1893, BCA; CM to JsM, SR, 3 October 1893, PANS.

26 JsM to CM, CC, 27 September 1893, Kamloops, 30 September 1893, BCA; JsM to CM, CC, 23 November 1893, PANS.

27 JsM to CM, CC, 12 March 1894, BCA; CM to JsM, SR, 3 October 1893,

15 February 1894, PANS; JsM to CM, CC, 14 December 1893, 12 March 1894, BCA.

28 JsM to CM, CC, 14 December 1893, BCA; CM to JsM, SR, 3 October 1893, PANS; JsM to CM, Kamloops, 8 January 1894, BCA.

29 JsM to CM, Kamloops, 29 October 1893, NVA; AMG to CM, Kamloops, 29 October 1893, BCA; JsM to CM, CC, 8 November 1893, BCA; JsM to CM, CC, 23 November 1893, 15 February 1894, PANS; JsM to CM, CC, 10 October 1893, BCA.

30 JsM to CM, CC, 28 March, 21 June 1894, BCA; JsM to CM, CC, 23 November 1893, PANS.

31 JsM to CM, CC, 27 September 1893, Kamloops, 14 October 1893, 8 June 1894, BCA.

32 British Columbia, Division of Vital Statistics, Death registration, 1926–4224, BCA, GR 2951; I.W. Mackay to A.W. Vowell, Kamloops, 24 September 1892, in Canada, Department of Indian Affairs, Black Series, RG 10, vol. 3867, file 87,125. I am grateful to Bruce Watson for information on the fur trade from his biographical dictionary in process.

33 JsM to CM, CC, 10 October 1893, 2 March 1894, BCA.

34 Untitled biography, *Kamloops Sentinel*, 19 October 1894; 'Pioneer Today Recalls His Adventurous Past,' *Colonist*, 25 December 1931; BC pioneer form, c.1933, BCA, vertical files.

35 JsM to CM, CC, 14 December 1893, Kamloops, 8 January 1894, BCA.

36 JsM to CM, CC, 29 January 1894, 23 November 1893, PANS; JsM to CM, CC, 10 October 1893, Kamloops, 8 January 1894, CC, 28 March 1894, BCA.

37 JsM to CM, CC, 27 September 1893, BCA; JsM to CM, CC, 15 February 1894, PANS; JsM to CM, CC, 2 March 1894, 10 May 1894, BCA.

38 JsM to CM, CC, 2 March 1894, BCA.

39 JsM to CM, CC, 29 January 1894, PANS; JsM to CM, CC, 8 November 1893, BCA; JsM to CM, CC, 23 November 1893, PANS.

40 JsM to CM, CC, 18 January 1894, BCA; JsM to CM, CC, 29 January 1894, PANS.

41 J Marietta Holley, *Samantha at the World's Fair* (New York, London, and Toronto: Funk & Wagnalls, 1893); JsM to CM, CC, 14 December 1893, 28 March, 11 April 1894, BCA.

42 JsM to CM, CC, 21 June 1894, Kamloops, 6 July 1894, BCA; JsM to CM, Dartmouth, 9 January 1895, PANS.

43 JsM to CM, CC, 15 February 1894, PANS; JsM to CM, CC, 28 March 1894, BCA; *Inland Sentinel*, 10 August 1894; JsM to CM, CC, 14 December 1893, 18 January, 26 May 1894, BCA.

44 'Campbell Creek School,' *Kamloops Sentinel*, 9 April 1898; Winifred Swan to

SDP, CC, 24 March 1897, and William Burns to SDP, Shuswap, 24 March 1897, in BC, SE, IC, BCA, GR 1445; 'Campbell Creek School,' *Kamloops Sentinel,* 9 April 1898.

45 Lewis Campbell to SDP, Kamloops, 18 June 1897, and J. Wilson to SDP, Kamloops, 12 April 1897, in BC, SE, IC, BCA, GR 1445.

46 AMG to CM, St Thomas, 19 November 1892, BCA.

47 AMG to CM, Kamloops, 29 October 1893, BCA; AMG to CM, Kamloops, 6 February 1894, PANS; JsM to CM, CC, 17 March 1894, BCA.

48 JsM to CM, CC, 28 March, 10 May 1894, BCA.

49 AMG to CM, CC, 17 March, 10 April 1894, BCA.

50 AMG to CM, Kamloops, 6 February 1894, PANS.

51 AMG to CM, CC, 10 April 1894, BCA.

52 George H. Melvin, *The Post Offices of British Columbia 1858–1970* (Vernon, 1972) 106; 'Salmon Arm Notes,' *Inland Sentinel,* 23 February 1894; 'Salmon Arm – Land of Orchards,' *Province* [magazine], 12 April 1925.

53 Daniel Marshall Gordon, 'An Autobiography,' c. 1908, manuscript courtesy of Bridget Mackenzie; 'Salmon Arm Notes,' *Inland Sentinel,* 23 February 1894; AMG to CM, CC, 10 April 1894, BCA.

54 AMG to JsM, SA, 18 August 1894, BCA; Cecil Scott, 'No Royal Road to Learning for This B.C. Lad,' *Province,* 20 April 1930; 'Salmon Arm Notes,' *Inland Sentinel,* 23 February 1894; AMG to CM, CC, 10 April 1894, BCA.

55 AMG to CM, SA, 11 June 1894, PANS; Gordon, 'An Autobiography.'

56 AMG to CM, SA, 11 June, 7 October 1894, PANS.

57 JsM to CM, SA, 21, 18 July 1894, BCA; JsM to CM, SA, 1 August 1894, PANS.

58 JsM to CM, SA, 1 August 1894, PANS; JsM to CM, SA, 18 July 1894, BCA; AMG to JsM, SA, 18 August 1894, BCA; JsM to CM, SA, 18 August 1894, BCA.

59 JsM to CM, SA, 18 August 1894, Brandon, 31 August 1894, BCA; JsM to CM, St John, 12 September 1894, PANS.

60 JsM to CM, CC, 23 November 1893, BCA; EMC to CM, Dartmouth, 12 October 1894, PANS; Mackay, *Simple Annals,* 185.

61 AMG to JsM, n.d., quoted in Mackay, *Simple Annals,* 165; AMG to JsM, SA, 6 February 1895, BCA; JM to JsM, SA, 18 October 1894, BCA.

62 CM to MBMW, SR, 19 March 1896, PANS; AMG to JsM, SA, 27 November 1894, NVA; AMG to JsM, SA, 6 February 1895, BCA.

9. Annie on the Frontier

1 AMG to JsM, SA, 27 November 1894, NVA.

2 *Inland Sentinel,* 20 June, 9 September 1893; AMG to JsM, SA, 7 September [1895], BCA.

3 AMG to CM, SA, 7 October 1894, 6 February, 19 April 1895, BCA.
4 AMG to CM, SA, 7 October, 12, 25 December 1894, BCA. On women's roles in agriculture, see Marjorie Griffith Cohen, *Women's Work, Markets, and Economic Development in Nineteenth-Century Ontario* (Toronto: University of Toronto Press, 1988).
5 AMG to CM, SA, 7 October 1894, 6 February 1896, BCA; AMG to JsM, SA, 7 September [1895], 17 April 1895, BCA.
6 AMG to CM, SA, 27 November 1894, NVA; AMG to CM, SA, 9 January 1895, 22 November 1895, 1 September 1896, BCA; AMG to JsM, SA, 17 April 1895, BCA.
7 AMG to JsM, SA, 6 February 1895, BCA.
8 AMG to JsM, SA, 6 February 1895, 17 April 1895, 7 September [1895], BCA; AMG to CM, SA, 6 February, 19 April 1895, BCA.
9 AMG to CM, SA, 25 December 1894, BCA.
10 AMG to CM, SA, 19 April 1895, BCA; AMG to JsM, SA, 7 September [1895], BCA.
11 AMG to CM, SA, 22 November 1895, BCA.
12 AMG to CM, SA, 22 November 1895, BCA; Scott, 'No Royal Road to Learning.'
13 JsM to CM, Dartmouth, 27 April 1896, PANS; EMC to CM, 27 April 1896, PANS.
14 JsM to CM, Dartmouth, 27 April 1896, PANS; EMC to CM, 27 April 1896, PANS.
15 CM to JsM, SR, n.d. [May 1896], 20 June 1896, 12 November 1897, PANS. Daniel McQueen was buried in Woodburn Cemetery near Little Harbour, where he lies not far from his grandparents, parents, wife, eldest daughter, Jane, namesake son, who died at a year of age, and more distant family members. His headstone contains his name, date of death, and age.
16 MBMW to JsM, St John, 25 May 1896, PANS; JsM to CM, St John, 13 May 1896, BCA.
17 JsM to CM, SA, 20, 29 May, 10 June 1896, BCA; MBMW to JsM, St John, 25 May 1896, PANS.
18 JsM to SDP, Upper SA, 29 May, 1 June 1896, in BC, SE, IC, BCA, GR 1445; CM to EMC, SR, 1 June 1896, PANS; JsM to CM, SA, 29 May 1896, BCA.
19 JsM to CM, SA, 29 May, 10 June 1896, BCA.
20 JsM to CM, SA, 26 June 1896, BCA.
21 JsM to CM, SA, 20, 29 May, 10, 26 June, 9 August 1896, BCA.
22 JsM to CM, SA, 9 August 1896, BCA; AMG to CM, SA, 1 September 1896, BCA.
23 JsM to CM, SA, 26 June 1896, Rossland, 10 April 1898, BCA.

24 AMG to CM, SA, 1 September 1896; JsM to SDP, Rossland, 7 September, 2 October 1896, in BC, SE, IC, BCA, GR 1445.

25 AMG to CM, SA, 1, 10 September 1896, BCA; JsM to SDP, Rossland, 7 September 1896, in BC, SE, IC, BCA, GR 1445; BC, DE, *Annual Report*, 1895/96, 273, BCA; Gordon, 'An Autobiography.'

26 *Inland Sentinel*, 16 October 1896; Herbert Legg, *Customs Services in Western Canada 1867–1925: A History* (Creston: n.p., 1962), 224, 250, 253. Notepaper Jim used was headed Customs Canada, as with JG to JsM, CNL, 20 September 1897, BCA.

27 Gordon, 'An Autobiography'; JsM to JnM, Rossland, 10 February 1897, NVA.

28 Legg, *Customs Services*, 248, 253; Gordon, 'An Autobiography'; P.O. Inspector to Postmaster General, Victoria, 19 March 1897, Canada Post Office correspondence in National Archives of Canada, RG3, Series D-3, vol. 17, 1897–871, reel C-7232; AMG to JsM, CNL, 19 October 1897, BCA. The development of this area is described in Wayne Norton and Naomi Miller, eds, *The Forgotten Side of the Border: British Columbia's Elk Valley and Crowsnest Pass* (Kamloops: Plateau Press, 1998). I am grateful to Edward Affleck for tracking down the location of Crow's Nest Landing.

29 JG to JsM, CNL, 20 September 1897, BCA; AMG to CM, CNL, 2 December 1897, BCA.

30 AMG to JsM, CNL, 19 October 1897, BCA; JG to JsM, CNL, 20 September 1897, BCA; AMG to CM, CNL, 4 January 1898, 2 December 1897, BCA.

31 AMG to JsM, CNL, 19 October 1897, BCA; AMG to CM, CNL, 4 January 1898, BCA.

32 JG to JsM, CNL, 20 September 1897, BCA; AMG to JsM, CNL, 19 October 1897, BCA.

33 AMG to CM, CNL, 4 January 1898, BCA.

34 AMG to CM, CNL, 4 January 1898, BCA; Gordon, 'An Autobiography.'

35 AMG to CM, CNL, 21 April 1898, Tobacco Plains, 1 November 1898, BCA.

36 *The Civil Service List of Canada, 1899* (Ottawa, 1900), in *Sessional Paper*, no. 16a (1900); 83; Dave McIntosh, *The Collectors: A History of Canadian Customs and Excise* (Ottawa: NC Press and Revenue Canada, Customs and Excise, 1984), 292, 328; for an example, AMG to CM, Gateway, May 1902, BCA.

37 AMG to CM, Phillipps, 4 December 1898, Tobacco Plains, 1 November 1898, BCA; AMG to JnM, Port Phillipps, 20 February 1899, BCA; AMG to CM, Phillipps, 14 August 1899, BCA.

38 AMG to CM, Phillipps, 23 September 1900, 17 May 1901, BCA.

39 AMG to CM, Phillipps, 4 December 1898, BCA; AMG to JnM, Port Phillipps, 20 February 1899, BCA; AMG to CM, Phillipps, 14 August 1899, BCA; AMG to family, Phillipps, 8 July 1900, BCA.

40 AMG to EMC, Phillipps, 8 November 1899, BCA; AMG to JnM, Port Phillipps, 20 February 1899, BCA; AMG to CM, Phillipps, 14 August 1899, BCA.

41 AMG to CM, Tobacco Plains, 1 November 1898, BCA; AMG to MBMW, Phillipps, 8 November 1898, BCA; AMG to CM, Phillipps, 4 December 1898, 14 August 1899, BCA.

42 AMG to CM, Phillipps, 17 May 1901, Gateway, May 1902, Phillipps, 4 December 1898, 14 August 1899, BCA; CM to JsM, SR, 27 December 1898, PANS.

43 AMG to JnM, Port Phillipps, 20 February 1899, BCA; AMG to CM, Phillipps, 17 May 1901, Tobacco Plains, 1 November 1898, BCA; AMG to MBMW, Phillipps, 8 November 1898, BCA.

44 AMG to CM, Phillipps, 11 February 1899, BCA; AMG to JnM, Port Phillipps, 20 February 1899, BCA; AMG to CM, Gateway, May 1902, Phillipps, 23 August, 17 May 1901, BCA.

45 AMG to MBMW, Phillipps, 8 November 1898, BCA; AMG to CM, Phillipps, 14 August 1899, 23 September 1900, 17 May 1901, BCA; AMG to MBMW, Phillipps, 8 November 1898, BCA.

46 AMG to CM, Phillipps, 14 August 1899, 23 September 1900, 17 May 1901, BCA.

47 *Missionary Outlook* (Toronto: Missionary Society of the Methodist Church, 1880–); *Youth's Companion* (Boston: Willis, 1836–).

48 AMG to CM, Phillipps, 4 December 1898, Tobacco Plains, 1 November 1898, BCA.

49 AMG to JnM, Port Phillipps, 20 February 1899, BCA; AMG to CM, Phillipps, 14 August 1899, BCA.

50 AMG to CM, CNL, 21 April 1898, BCA; AMG to JnM, Port Phillipps, 20 February 1899, BCA.

51 'Relative Claims Historical Name Spelled Incorrectly,' *Cranbrook Courier*, n.d., in BCA, vertical files; Dave Kay, '$45,000 Shipped by Pack Train,' *Cranbrook Courier*, 22 June 1977; Laing, *Colonial Farm Settlers*, 499; Naomi Miller, 'Michael Phillipps: Prominent Kootenay Citizen,' in Norton and Miller, eds, *The Forgotten Side of the Border*, 32; undated clipping, reproduced in Candace L. House, *The Galbraiths and the Kootenays* (New York: Vantage Press, 1969), 114; Olga Weydemeyer Johnson, *Flathead and Kootenay: The Rivers, the Tribes and the Region's Traders* (Glendale, CA: Arthur H. Clark, 1969), 335–6; Census of Canada, 1901, Yale & Cariboo, E6-SE Kootenay, household 44.

52 Frederick Norbury to father, Tobacco Plains, 13 November 1887, BCA, Ms. 877; Miller, 'Michael Phillipps,' 31, 35.

53 Frederick Norbury to father, Tobacco Plains, 13 November 1887; Frederick Norbury to mother, n.d., BCA, Ms. 877.

54 Edna Wallace to Jean Barman, Victoria, 9 March 1988; Miller, 'Michael Phillipps,' 35.

55 Frederick Norbury to father, Tobacco Plains, 13 November 1887, BCA, Ms. 877; AMG to CM, Phillipps, 4 December 1898, BCA.
56 Charles N. Edwards, in Olga Weydemeyer Johnson, *The Story of the Tobacco Plains Country: The Autobiography of a Community* (Caldwell, ID: Caxton Publishers for The Pioneers of the Tobacco Plains Country, 1950), 56; AMG to CM, Phillipps, 14 August 1899, BCA.
57 AMG to CM, Phillipps, 14 August 1899, 17 May 1901, BCA; Johnson, *Flathead and Kootenay*, 297; AMG to CM, JnM, and JsM, Phillipps, 8 July 1900, NVA; AMG to family, Phillipps, 8 July 1900, BCA; AMG to CM, Phillipps, 23 September 1900, BCA. I am grateful to Elizabeth Gravelle of Grassmere, BC, for identifying Paul David.
58 Miller, 'Michael Phillipps,' 36; Jurors to Attorney General D.M. Eberts, Sand Point, 8 June [1898], in BCA, GR 429, 1067/98; Frederick Norbury to father, Fort Steele, 12 June 1898, BCA, Ms. 877; AMG to CM, Tobacco Plains, 1 November 1898, Phillipps, 4 December 1898, BCA.
59 AMG to CM, Tobacco Plains, 1 November 1898, BCA; AMG to MBMW, Phillipps, 8 November 1898, BCA; AMG to CM, SA, 25 December 1894, Phillipps, 4 December 1898, BCA; AMG to JnM, Port Phillipps, 20 February 1899, BCA.
60 BC, DE, *Annual Reports*; 'Visitation by Schools of Inspector William Burns during Month of October, 1898,' BC, DE, Correspondence, BCA, GR 1468; Edna Wallace to Jean Barman, Victoria, 9 March 1988.
61 Edna Wallace to Jean Barman, Victoria, 9 March 1988; 'Visitation by Schools of Inspector William Burns during Month of October, 1898,' BC, DE, Correspondence, BCA, GR 1468; AMG to JnM, Port Phillipps, 20 February 1899, BCA.
62 AMG to MBMW, Phillipps, 8 November 1899, BCA.
63 AMG to family, Phillipps, 8 July 1900, BCA; AMG to CM, Phillipps, 23 September 1900, BCA; BC, DE, *Annual Report*, 1901, 269; AMG to CM, Phillipps, 17 May 1901, BCA; AMG to JsM, Phillipps, 27 December 1901, BCA.
64 AMG to CM, Phillipps, 23 August 1901, BCA.
65 AMG to JnM, Phillipps, 20 February 1899, BCA; AMG to family, Phillipps, 8 July 1900, BCA; AMG to CM, Phillipps, 23 September 1900, BCA; Post Office Inspector's Report, Victoria, 15 March 1897, National Archives of Canada, RG3, Post Office, file 1897–873, reel C-7232; Acting Post Office Inspector to Postmaster General, [August] 1899, National Archives of Canada, RG3, Post Office, file 1899–175, reel C-7237; Report, Victoria, 19 November 1898, National Archives of Canada, RG3, Post Office, file 1898–494, reel C-7233; Acting Post Office Inspector to Postmaster General, Vancouver, 26 May 1899, file 1895–175, reel C-7237; Melvin, *Post Offices*, 93; AMG to CM, Phillipps, 17 May 1901, 7 June 1901, BCA; AMG to CM and JsM, Phillipps, 26 July 1901, BCA.

66 AMG to CM, Phillipps, 7 June, 23 August 1901, BCA; AMG to family, Phillipps, 8 July 1900, BCA.
67 David Davies, 'The Crows Nest Southern Railway,' in Norton and Miller, eds, *The Forgotten Side of the Border*, 58–65; AMG to CM, Gateway, May 1901, BCA; Legg, *Customs Services*, 248, 253; Gordon, 'An Autobiography'; *The Civil Service List of Canada, 1903* (Ottawa, 1904), in *Sessional Paper*, no. 30 (1904): 90
68 AMG to JsM, Phillipps, 27 December 1901, BCA; AMG to CM, Gateway, May 1901, BCA; Legg, *Customs Services*, 248, 253; Gordon, 'An Autobiography.'
69 AMG to CM, Gateway, May 1902, BCA; Legg, *Customs Services*, 248.
70 Gordon, 'An Autobiography.'
71 AMG to CM, Gateway, May 1902, Phillipps, 23 August 1901, BCA; Legg, *Customs Services*, 248, 253;
72 AMG to CM, Gateway, May 1902, 11 January 1903, BCA.
73 Melvin, *The Post Offices*, 44; AMG to CM, Victoria, 16 December 1913, BCA.
74 AMG to JsM, Gateway, 21 August 1905, BCA; Scott, 'No Royal Road to Larning'; AMG to CM, Gateway, 11 January 1903; AMG to CM, Gateway, May 1902, BCA.
75 AMG to JsM, Gateway, 21 August 1905, BCA; Legg, *Customs Services*, 248, 253; Gordon, 'An Autobiography'; Scott, 'No Royal Road to Learning.'
76 EMC to CM, Dartmouth, 19 March 1902, PANS.

10. Jessie in Charge

1 Chapter 10 JsM to CM, NL, 20 February 1893, NVA.
2 CM to JsM, SR, 21 July 1893, PANS; EMC to JsM, Dartmouth, 27 November 1894, PANS.
3 AMG to CM, SA, 1 September 1896, BCA.
4 *Rossland Miner*, 2 March, 13 July 1895. Information on Rossland has been taken from Jeremy Mouat, *Roaring Days: Rossland's Mines and the History of British Columbia* (Vancouver: UBC Press, 1995); Michael Ripmeester, 'Everyday Life in the Golden City: A Historical Geography of Rossland, British Columbia' (M.A. thesis, Department of Geography, University of British Columbia, 1990); Lance H. Whittaker, ed., *Rossland: The Golden City* (Rossland: Rossland Miner, 1949); J.D. McDonald and Joyce Austin, comps., *Rossland Centennial Photo Album, 1897–1997* (Rossland: Rossland Historical Museum, 1996); Rosa Jordan and Derek Choukalos, *Rossland: The First 100 Years* (Rossland: Harry Lefevre, 1995).
5 *Rossland Miner*, 2 March, 28 September, 12, 19 October, 30 November, 7, 14, 21, 28 December 1895, 18 January 1896, historical edition; BC, DE, *Annual Report*, 1896/97, 235; S. Forteath to SDP, Rossland, 12 January 1897; JsM to

SDP, Rossland, 7 September 1896; D. Wilson to SDP, Trail, 5 October 1896, in BC, SE, IC, BCA, GR 1445.

6 D. Wilson to SDP, Trail, 5 October 1896, in BC, SE, IC, BCA, GR 1445; Runnalls, *It's God's Country*, 101, 103; BC, DE, *Annual Report*, 1895/96, 271; JsM to CM, Rossland, 11 December 1898, BCA; JsM to CM, Rossland, 25 February 1897, PANS.

7 JsM to SDP, Rossland, 7 September 1896, in BC, SE, IC, BCA, GR 1445; JsM to CM, Rossland, 22 September 1896, BCA; 'Rossland,' *Saturday Globe* [Toronto], 6 February 1897.

8 D. Wilson to SDP, Trail, 5 October 1896, in BC, SE, IC, BCA, GR 1445; JsM to JnM, Rossland, 10 February 1897, PANS.

9 S. Forteath to SDP, Rossland, 12 January 1897, Rossland class lists to SDP, Rossland, 1897, in BC, SE, IC, BCA, GR 1445; JsM to CM, Rossland, 15 January 1897, BCA.

10 S. Forteath to SDP, Rossland, 12 January 1897, in BC, SE, IC, BCA, GR 1445; JsM to CM, Rossland, 14 November 1897, BCA; JsM to CM, Rossland, 25 February 1897, PANS.

11 JsM to CM, Rossland, 14 November, 31 October 1897, BCA.

12 JsM to CM, Rossland, 14 January 1897 [1898], 14 November 1897, BCA; *Rossland Miner*, 16 December 1897; BC, DE, *Annual Report*, 1897/98. A handful of children were taught privately.

13 JsM to CM, Rossland, 14 January 1897 [1898], BCA; 'Visitation by Schools of Inspector William Burns during Month of April, 1898,' BC, DE, Correspondence, BCA, GR 1468.

14 JsM to CM, Rossland, 20 March 1898, BCA.

15 JsM to CM, Rossland, 8 May 1898, PANS; JsM to CM, Rossland, 11 December 1898, BCA; AMG to CM, Phillipps, 4 December 1898, BCA; BC, DE, *Annual Report*, 1897/98, 1273; JsM to CM, Rossland, 16 May 1899, PANS.

16 JsM to CM, Rossland, 10 April 1898, 8 October 1899, BCA; *British Columbia Mining Record* 4, no. 111 (Nov. 1898): 14–15, cited in Ripmeester, 'Everyday Life in the Golden City,' 81.

17 'Visitation by Schools of Inspector William Burns during Month of September, 1898,' BC, DE, Correspondence, BCA, GR 1468 (also November and December 1898); *Rossland Miner*, 29 August 1899.

18 CM to JsM, letter fragment, n.d. [likely late May or early June 1896], SR, 6 July 1898, PANS.

19 JsM to CM, Rossland, 10 November 1898, BCA; BC, Department of Vital Statistics, Death registration, 65–09–00806, BCA, GR 2951.

20 Mouat, *Roaring Days*, 24.

21 'The Mining Camp,' 14 July 1897, unidentified press clipping headed 'The

Civil & Military,' in BCA, Ms 1877, Box 1, 1897 file; 'Rossland,' *Mining Record* 2, no. 8 (Aug. 1896): 20, cited in Mouat, *Roaring Days*, 39–40; Father Held, in *Spokane-Spokesman Review*, reprinted as 'A Priest's Impressions,' *Vancouver Daily World*, 13 August 1896; J.A. Forin, cited in Whittaker, ed., *Rossland: The Golden City*, 44.

22 Mouat, *Roaring Days*, 127, 111.

23 JsM to SDP, Rossland, 7 September 1896, in BC, SE, IC, BCA, GR 1445.

24 JsM to SDP, Rossland, 7 September 1896, in BC, SE, IC, BCA, GR 1445; EMC to JsM, Dartmouth, 20 October 1896, PANS; JsM to CM, Rossland, 14 November 1897, BCA; 'JNO' to JsM, Boston, 22 December 1897, Rossland Archives; JsM to CM, Rossland, 15 January 1897, BCA.

25 'The Mining Camp,' 14 July 1897, BCA, Ms 1877, Box 1, 1897 file; bill from Campbell Brothers, Rossland, 17 October 1896, Rossland Archives; JsM to CM, Rossland, 15 January 1897, BCA.

26 JsM to JnM, Rossland, 10 February 1897, PANS; JsM to CM, Rossland, 15 January 1897, BCA.

27 JsM to CM, Rossland, 25 February 1897, PANS; JsM to CM, Rossland, 15 January 1897, BCA; JsM to JnM, Rossland, 10 February 1897, BCA; JsM to CM, Rossland, 31 October 1897, 14 January 1897 [1898], BCA.

28 JsM to CM, Rossland, 15 January 1897, BCA; JsM to CM, Rossland, 25 February 1897, PANS.

29 JsM to CM, Rossland, 15 January 1897, BCA; JsM to JnM, Rossland, 10 February 1897, NVA.

30 JsM to JnM, Rossland, 10 February 1897, NVA; JsM to CM, Rossland, 15 January 1897, BCA.

31 Ian Maclaren [John Watson], *Kate Carnegie and Those Ministers* (Toronto: F.H. Revell, 1896); Ian Maclaren [John Watson], *Beside the Bonnie Brier Bush* (Toronto: F.H. Revell, 1894); Jep C. Johnson, 'John Watson (Ian Maclaren),' in *British Short-Fiction Writers, 1880–1914: The Romantic Tradition* (Detroit: Gale, 1996), vol. 156 of *Dictionary of Literary Biography*, 365–74; W. Robertson Nicoll, *'Ian Maclaren': Life of the Rev. John Watson* (Toronto: Westminster, 1908), esp. 166–86.

32 JsM to JnM, Rossland, 10 February 1897, PANS; EMC to JsM, Dartmouth, 20 October 1896, PANS; JsM to CM, Rossland, 10 April 1898, BCA.

33 JsM to JnM, Rossland, 10 February 1897, BCA; 'The Mining Camp,' 14 July 1897, BCA, Ms 1877, Box 1, 1897 file; JsM to CM, Rossland, 15 January 1897, BCA.

34 JsM to CM, Rossland, 25 February 1897, PANS.

35 JsM to CM, Rossland, 15 January 1897, BCA.

36 JsM to CM, Rossland, 15 January 1897, BCA.

37 JsM to CM, Rossland, 15 January 1897, BCA; JsM to CM, Rossland, 25 February 1897, PANS; JsM to CM, Rossland, 22 May 1898, 14 January 1897 [1898], BCA.

38 'The Mining Camp,' 14 July 1897, BCA, Ms 1877, Box 1, 1897 file; 'JNO' to JsM, Tacoma, 17 August 1897, Boston, 22 December 1897, Rossland Archives.

39 J.D. Helm to JsM, Seattle, 5 December 1897, PANS; JsM to CM, Rossland, 20 March 1898, BCA.

40 JsM to CM, Rossland, 15 January 1897, BCA.

41 JsM to CM, Rossland, 14 November 1897, 14 January 1897 [1898], 20 March 1898, BCA.

42 JsM to CM, LN, 6 August 1888, Rossland, 20 March, 10 April 1898, BCA.

43 JsM to CM, Rossland, 14 November 1897, 14 January 1897 [1898], 20 March 1898, BCA.

44 BC, DE, *Annual Report*, 1897/98, 1241, 1243; Jessie Olding Hunter to JsM, Granite Creek, 28 August 1898, BCA; Public Schools Act, 1891, section 54; 'Visitation by Schools of Inspector William Burns during Month of January, 1898,' BC, DE, Correspondence, BCA, GR 1468.

45 JsM to CM, Private, 22 May 1889, PANS.

46 JsM to CM, Rossland, 10 April 1898, BCA; JsM to CM, Rossland, 8 May 1898, PANS; JsM to CM, Private, Rossland, 10 November 1898, BCA; *Rossland Miner*, 29 August 1899.

47 'The Mining Camp,' 14 July 1897, BCA, Ms 1877, Box 1, 1897 file; JsM to CM, Rossland, 10 November, 11 December 1898, BCA.

48 JsM to CM, Private, Rossland, 10 November 1898, BCA; JsM to CM, Rossland, 16 May 1899, PANS; John Keen to JsM, Kaslo, 14, 20 April, 2 May 1899, Rossland Archives.

49 JsM to CM, Rossland, 10 November 1898, 14 February 1899, BCA.

50 JsM to CM, Rossland, 14 February, 7, 21 March 1899, BCA.

51 JsM to CM, Rossland, 7 March, 16 May 1899, PANS.

52 JsM to CM, Rossland, 11 December 1898, 14 February 1899, 10 April 1898, BCA.

53 Glen Norcliffe, *The Ride to Modernity: The Bicycle in Canada, 1869–1900* (Toronto: University of Toronto Press, 2001), esp. 190–3; also Ellen Gruber Garvey, *The Adman in the Parlor: Magazines and the Gendering of Consumer Culture, 1880s to 1910s* (New York: Oxford University Press, 1996), 106–34.

54 JsM to CM, NL, 26 November 1891, BCA; JsM to CM, Rossland, 25 February 1897, PANS; JsM to CM, Rossland, 18 June, 31 August 1899, BCA. Frances Willard, head of the Women's Christian Temperance Union, put forth her views in *A Wheel within a Wheel: How I Learned to Ride the Bicycle* (New York: Fleming H. Revell, 1895).

55 JsM to CM, Rossland, 14 February 1899, 11 December 1898, BCA.

56 Alden, *Mrs. Solomon Smith Looking On*; Dobkin, 'Isabella Alden (Pansy),' 37–41.

57 JsM to CM, Rossland, 11 December, 10 November 1898, 14 February 1899, BCA.

58 JsM to CM, Rossland, 11 December 1898, BCA; 'Visitation by Schools of Inspector William Burns during Month of January, 1898,' BC, DE, Correspondence, BCA, GR 1468.

59 BC, DE, *Annual Report*, 1898/99, 237; JsM to CM, Rossland, 18 June, 2 July 1899, BCA; Mrs. Frank Harris, conversation with J.S. Matthews, Vancouver, 16 June 1937, in J.S. Matthews, comp., *Conversations with Khahtsahlano, 1932–1954* (Vancouver: City Archives, 1955), 276.

60 JsM to CM, Rossland, 18 June, 31 August, 9 November 1899, BCA.

61 JsM to CM, Rossland, 15 January 1897, 20 March 1898, BCA.

62 JsM to CM, Rossland, 31 October 1897, BCA.

63 JsM to CM, Rossland, 11 December 1898, BCA.

64 JsM to CM, Rossland, 14 November 1897, 8 May 1898, PANS.

65 JsM to CM, Rossland, 10 November 1898, 14 February 1899, BCA.

66 JsM to JnM, Rossland, 10 February 1897, BCA; JsM to CM, Rossland, 9 November 1899, BCA.

67 JsM to CM, Rossland, 11 December 1898, 14 February 1899, BCA.

68 CM to JsM, SR, 7 July 1897, PANS; JsM to CM, Rossland, 15 January 1897, BCA.

69 'The Mining Camp,' 14 July 1897, BCA, Ms 1877, Box 1, 1897 file; JsM to CM, Rossland, 15 January, 31 October 1897, 20 March 1898, BCA.

70 Lynne Marks, *Revivals and Roller Rinks: Religion, Leisure, and Identity in Late-Nineteenth-Century Small-Town Ontario* (Toronto: University of Toronto Press, 1996).

71 JsM to CM, LN, 27 September 1888, 13 February 1889, BCA; Elsie G. Turnbull, *Church in the Kootenays: The Story of the United Church of Canada in Kootenay Presbytery* (Trail: Trail Times for Kootenay Presbyterian United Church Women, 1965), 17; CM to JsM, SR, 12 November 1897, 6 July 1898, PANS; Runnalls, *It's God's Country*, 103.

72 JsM to CM, Rossland, 25 February, 31 October 1897, BCA; JsM to CM, Rossland, 8 May 1898, PANS.

73 JsM to CM, Rossland, 31 October 1897, BCA; CM to JsM, SR, 12 November 1897, PANS. I am grateful to the Rossland Museum and Archives for checking the minutes of St Andrew's Presbyterian Church for information; and to the Presbyterian Church of Canada Archives and Bob Stewart of the United Church Archives in the Vancouver School of Theology for attempting to trace down information about Rev. D. McG. Gandier.

74 JsM to CM, Rossland, 14 November 1897, 10 April 1898, BCA.
75 JsM to CM, Rossland, 14 January 1897 [1898], BCA.
76 JsM to CM, Rossland, 20 March 1898, BCA.
77 JsM to CM, Rossland, 10 April, 8, 22 May, 11 December 1898, BCA.
78 JsM to CM, Rossland, 31 August, 9 November 1899, BCA.

11. Sisters Full Circle

1 Chapter 11 EMC to JsM, Dartmouth, 20 October 1896, PANS.
2 JsM to CM, Rossland, 15 January 1897, 14 January 1897 [1898], BCA.
3 JsM to CM, Rossland, 20 March 1898, BCA; AMG to CM, CNL, 21 April 1898, BCA; CM to JsM, SR, 6 July 1898, PANS.
4 CM to JsM, SR, 7 July 1897, PANS; AMG to CM, Phillipps, 4 December 1898, BCA; JsM to CM, Rossland, 14 February 1899, BCA.
5 AMG to CM, Tobacco Plains, 1 November 1898, BCA.
6 JsM to CM, Rossland, 11 December 1898, BCA; AMG to CM, Phillipps, 11 February, 14 August 1899, BCA.
7 JsM to CM, Rossland, 16 May 1899, 8 May 1898, PANS.
8 JsM to CM, Rossland, 31 October 1897, BCA; CM to JsM, SR, 12 November, 4 September 1897, PANS; JsM to CM, Private, Rossland, 10 November 1898, BCA.
9 JsM to CM, Rossland, 14 February 1899, BCA; CM to JsM, SR, 2 May 1899, PANS; JsM to CM, Rossland, 16 May 1899, PANS; AMG to MBMW, Port of Phillips, 8 November 1899, BCA.
10 CM to JsM, SR, 12 November 1897, PANS; AMG to CM, Phillipps, 14 August 1899, BCA.
11 Death certificate, New York Municipal Archives; Golliek and Smith to CM, New York, 26 December 1899, PANS; *Rossland Miner*, 22 December 1899.
12 CM to JsM, SR, 4 September 1897, 6 July 1898, PANS; Katherine Wisdom to JsM, n.d. [1901], PANS; AMG to JsM, Phillipps, 27 December 1901, BCA; AMG to CM, Gateway, 11 January 1903, BCA.
13 Mackay, *Simple Annals*, 163; McCurrach, 'The Old House'; Bridget Mackenzie to Jean Barman, Dornoch, Sutherland, Scotland, 8 November 1999.
14 Annie McQueen, quoted in Scott, 'No Royal Road to Learning.'
15 Melvin, *The Post Offices of British Columbia*, 44; McIntosh, *The Collectors*, 328; *The Civil Service List of Canada, 1909* (Ottawa, 1910), in *Sessional Paper*, no. 30 (1910): 130.
16 'Mr. J.D. Gordon Passes Away,' *Colonist*, 11 November 1911; personal inspection, 22 January 2001; *Henderson's Great Victoria Directory, 1910–11* (1910), 143; JG to CM, Victoria, 16 September 1908, BCA.

17 JG to CM, Victoria, 16 September 1908, BCA; JG, will, BCA, GR 1052, box 18, file 2671; BC, Department of Vital Statistics, death registration 1911-09-024074, BCA, GR 2951; Mackay, *Simple Annals*, 167; 'Mr. J.D. Gordon Passes Away,' *Colonist*, 11 November 1911.

18 AMG to family, Victoria, 2 August 1913, BCA; AMG to CM, Victoria, 6 September 1912, BCA; *Henderson's Great Victoria City Directory, 1913* (1913), 545; personal inspection, 29 January 2001. I am grateful to Lyn Tait and Patricia Roy for their perceptive comments on the neighbourhood.

19 AMG to CM, Victoria, 6 September 1912, BCA; AMG to family, Victoria, 2 August 1913, BCA.

20 Prang, 'Networks and Associations,' 55.

21 JG to CM, St Thomas, 20 October 1892, BCA; 'Pioneered in Women's Work,' *Colonist*, 30 May 1941; AMG to JsM, Victoria, 15 November 1914, BCA.

22 'Pioneered in Women's Work'; AMG to CM, Victoria, 6 September 1912, BCA.

23 AMG to CM, Victoria, 16 December 1913, BCA; AMG to JsM, Victoria, 6 February 1930, BCA.

24 Jessie Olding Hunter to CM, Princeton, 3 December 1915, PANS.

25 AMG to JsM, Victoria, 8 February 1919, PANS.

26 AMG to JsM, Victoria, 18 April 1919, BCA.

27 AMG to JsM, Victoria, 18 April 1919, BCA.

28 'Mrs. J.D. Gordon Has Important Post,' *Victoria Times*, 26 August 1919; 'Plea for Sympathy for Settlers and Their War-Brides,' *Victoria Times*, 5 May 1920; 'Pioneered in Women's Work.' On the Soldiers' Settlement Board, see Kent Fedorowich, *Unfit for Heroes: Reconstruction and Soldier Settlement in the Empire between the Wars* (Manchester: Manchester University Press, 1995), esp. 77–9.

29 AMG to JsM, Victoria, 31 August, 10 November 1919, BCA.

30 'Pioneered in Women's Work'; AMG to JsM, Victoria, 31 August 1919, BCA; 'Plea for Sympathy.'

31 Annie Gordon, quoted in 'Plea for Sympathy for Settlers and Their War-Brides,' *Victoria Times*, 5 May 1920.

32 AMG to JsM, Victoria, 10 November 1919, BCA.

33 AMG to JsM, Victoria, 31 August, 10 November 1919, BCA.

34 AMG to JsM, Victoria, 10 November 1919, BCA; *Modern Pioneers, 1909–1959: British Columbia Women's Institute* (Vancouver: Evergreen Press, c. 1959), 28

35 AMG to JsM, Victoria, 15 November 1914, BCA; Allan, Ethel, and Kate Cunningham to JsM, Halifax, December 1917, PANS; AMG to JsM, Victoria, 8 February 1919, BCA; conversation with Marjorie Scott and Betty MacNeill, Sutherland's River, 1 August 2001.

36 CM to JsM, SR, 9 September 1889, PANS; JsM to CM, LN, 23 October 1890, NVA; JsM to Muriel Cunningham, Oxford, 31 August 1920, BCA.
37 JsM to Katherine Wisdom, Victoria, 4 September 1922, PANS. With one short break, Jane would remain institutionalized until her death in December 1934.
38 W.F. McNeill to JsM, Rossland, 14 March 1923, Rossland Archives.
39 JsM to Mary, Victoria, 26 May 1922, BCA.
40 JsM to Mary, Victoria, 26 May 1922, BCA; JsM to Katherine Wisdom, Victoria, 4 September 1922, PANS.
41 JsM to Mary, Victoria, 26 May 1922, BCA; JsM to Katherine Wisdom, Victoria, 4 September 1922, PANS.
42 W.F. McNeill to JsM, Rossland, 14 March 1923, Rossland Archives; JsM to 'Mary,' Beaver Point, 10 November 1922, BCA; conversation with Lotus Fraser Ruckle, Beaver Point, 29 July 1997; JsM, 'School District Information Form,' 12 March 1923, BCA, GR 461, box 1, file 1, Beaver Point. On Salt Spring, see Charles Kahn, *Salt Spring: The Story of an Island* (Madeira Park: Harbour, 1998).
43 JsM to 'Mary,' Beaver Point, 10 November 1922, BCA.
44 Rev. E.F. Wilson, *Salt Spring Island British Columbia* (Saltspring Island: E.F. Wilson, 1895), 72, 77, 80.
45 Beaver Point school register, 1922–3, in Salt Spring Archives; church records, St Andrew's Catholic Church, Victoria, 1849–1934, in BCA, Ms. 1; 'St. Ann's Baptisms-Marriages, 1886–1896,' held at St Edward's Church, Duncan; Shirley Morrison to Jean Barman, Chemainus, 1 July 1994.
46 Interview with Gladys Margaret King, 14 June 1977, BCA, tape 4061; JsM to 'Mary,' Beaver Point, 10 November 1922, BCA.
47 Conversation with Lotus Fraser Ruckle, Beaver Point, 29 July 1997.
48 JsM to MBMW and family, Halifax, 21 December 1923, PANS; conversation with Lotus Fraser Ruckle, Beaver Point, 29 July 1997; JsM to MBMW, Halifax, 19 January 1924, PANS; E.P. Hopgood to JsM, Dartmouth, 30 January 1923, PANS; JsM to Ruth and Lotus Fraser, New Glasgow, 24 April 1928, courtesy of Lotus Fraser Ruckle, Beaver Point, Salt Spring Island.
49 AMG to JsM, Victoria, 6 February 1930, BCA; certificate of death, Nova Scotia, Division of Vital Statistics.
50 See Linda M. Ambrose, *For Home and Country: The Centennial History of the Women's Institutes in Ontario* (Erin, ON: Boston Mills Press, 1996), 20–1.
51 AMG to MBMW, Victoria, 21 February 1925, BCA; *Modern Pioneers*, 16, 28; 'Pioneered in Women's Work.'
52 AMG to MBMW, Victoria, 21 February 1925, BCA; '"Superiority Complex" Retards Canada, W.I. Head Charges,' *Sun*, 27 August 1936; 'Would Abolish School Boards of Province,' *Victoria Times*, 8 July 1838.

53 Story told to Bridget Mackenzie, as related in her letter to Jean Barman, Dornoch, Sutherland, Scotland, 8 November 1999.
54 Mackay, *Simple Annals*, 168, 189–95; BC, Department of Vital Statistics, death registration 1941–09–588957, BCA, GR 2951.
55 AMG to CM, Victoria, 6 September 1912, BCA.
56 'Oldest City Lawyer Dies after Stroke,' *Colonist*, 20 November 1979; AMG to CM, Victoria, 6 September 1912, BCA; AMG to JsM, Victoria, 15 November 1914, BCA.
57 AMG to JsM, Victoria, 15 November 1914, BCA; Scott, 'No Royal Road to Learning.'
58 Marshall Gordon to CM, Montreal, 26 December 1911, PANS; 'Oldest City Lawyer Dies after Stroke'; 'B.C. Oldest Lawyer Dead,' *Times*, 20 November 1979; AMG to MBMW, Victoria, 21 February 1925, BCA; JsM to 'Mary,' Beaver Point, 10 November 1922, BCA.
59 Story told to Bridget Mackenzie, as related in her letter to Jean Barman, Dornoch, Sutherland, Scotland, 8 November 1999.
60 Jennie Wisdom to JsM, Brooklyn, 5 October 1915, PANS; Bridget Mackenzie to Jean Barman, Dornoch, Sutherland, Scotland, 8 October 2000; AMG to JsM, Victoria, 31 August 1919, BCA; Dal Gordon to JsM, Oxford, 22 October 1920, BCA. Dal's letters to his family in British Columbia have not survived.
61 JsM to Muriel Cunningham, Oxford, 31 August 1920, BCA; Humphrey Carpenter, *J.R.R. Tolkien: A Biography* (London: George Allen & Unwin, 1977). Information on Tolkien's relationship with Dal is taken from Carpenter, *J.R.R. Tolkien*; Daniel Grotta-Kurska, *J.R.R. Tolkien: Architect of Middle Earth* (Philadelphia: Running Press, 1976); John and Priscilla Tolkien, *The Tolkien Family Album* (London: HarperCollins, 1992); and Douglas A. Anderson, '"An Industrious Little Devil": E.V. Gordon As Friend and Collaborator with Tolkien,' in *Tolkien the Medievalist*, ed. Jane Chance (London: Routledge, 2002).
62 Carpenter, *J.R.R. Tolkien*, 105; Katharyn W. Crabbe, *J.R.R. Tolkien*, rev. ed. (New York: Continuum, 1988), 17; J.R.R. Tolkien and E.V. Gordon, eds, *Sir Gawain and the Green Knight* (Oxford: Clarendon Press, 1925). Songs composed during the Viking Club days, distributed on stenciled sheets, were privately published by one of their students as J.R.R. Tolkien and E.V. Gordon, *Songs for the Philologists* (London: Department of English, University College, 1936).
63 T.A. Shippey, *J.R.R. Tolkien: Author of the Century* (London: HarperCollins, 2000), xv; E.V. Gordon, *An Introduction to Old Norse* (Oxford: Clarendon Press, 1927), viii; 'Professor E.V. Gordon,' *Times*, 1 August 1938; Humphrey Carpenter, *The Inklings: C.S. Lewis, J.R.R. Tolkien, Charles Williams, and Their friends* (London: George Allen & Unwin, 1978), 55; E.V. Gordon, ed., *The*

Battle of Maldon (London: Methuen, 1937), vi. Dal played a major role in the translation of Stella M. Mills and E.V. Gordon, *The Saga of Hrolf Kraki* (Oxford: Blackwell, 1933), and Haakon Shetelig, Hjalmar Falk, and E.V. Gordon, *Scandinavian Archaeology* (Oxford: Clarendon Press, 1937).

64 AMG to JsM, Victoria, 6 February 1930, BCA; JsM to Muriel Cunningham, Oxford, 31 August 1920, BCA; conversation with Bridget Mackenzie, Dornoch, Scotland, 7 August 2001.

65 J.R.R. Tolkien to C.A. Furth, Allen & Unwin, Oxford, 12 February 1939, in *Letters of J.R.R. Tolkien*, ed. Humphrey Carpenter and Christopher Tolkien (London: George Allen & Unwin, 1981), 42; 'Professor E.V. Gordon,' *Times*, 4 August 1938; J.R.R. Tolkien to Stanley Unwin, Oxford, c. 18 March 1945, in Carpenter and Tolkien, eds, *Letters*, 114; E.V. Gordon, ed., *Pearl* (Oxford: Clarendon Press, 1953), iii; Shippey, *J.R.R. Tolkien*, passim; Ida Gordon, ed., *The Seafarer* (London: Methuen, 1960); Carpenter, *J.R.R. Tolkien*, 137–8; Ida Gordon to John D. Ratcliff, 1982, cited in Anderson, '"An Industrious Little Devil."'

66 Conversation with Margaret McCurrach, Victoria, 30 November 1999; AMG to JsM, Victoria, 31 August 1919, BCA; JsM to 'Mary,' Victoria, 26 May 1922, BCA.

67 Relief Mackay to Jean Barman, Merigomish, Nova Scotia, 13 June 1993; AMG to JsM, Victoria, 6 February 1930; telephone conversation with Bridget Mackenzie, Dornoch, Scotland, 31 October 1999; Bridget Mackenzie to Jean Barman, Dornoch, Sutherland, Scotland, 8 November 1999.

68 Bridget Mackenzie to Jean Barman, Dornoch, Sutherland, Scotland, 8 November 1999, 8 October 2000; telephone conversation with Margaret McCurrach, Victoria, 31 July 2000.

69 BC, Department of Vital Statistics, death registration 1971–09–005229, BCA, GR 2951; death notice, *Colonist*, 9 April 1971; 'Oldest City Lawyer Dies after Stroke'; story told to Bridget Mackenzie, as related in her letter to Jean Barman, Dornoch, Sutherland, Scotland, 8 November 1999.

70 Relief Mackay to Jean Barman, Merigomish, Nova Scotia, 13 June 1993; Bridget Mackenzie to Jean Barman, Dornoch, Sutherland, Scotland, 8 November 1999.

12. Reflections

1 JsM to CM, CC, 12 March 1894, BCA.
2 Some of the best descriptions of Ontario's role are still found in F.H. Armstrong, H.A. Stevenson, and J.D. Wilson, eds, *Aspects of Nineteenth Century Ontario: Essays Presented to James J. Talman* (Toronto: University of Toronto

Press, 1974), including Allan Smith, 'Old Ontario and the Emergence of a National Frame of Mind,' 194–217. On migration out of Ontario, see Widdis, *With Scarcely a Ripple*, 50–64.

3 Ian McKay, 'A Note on "Region" in Writing the History of Atlantic Canada,' *Acadiensis* 29, no. 2 (Spring 2000): 99.

4 *The Bystander*, n.s., no. 3 (Dec. 1889): 78–9.

5 McKay, 'A Note on "Region,"' 93.

6 P.A. Buckner, '"Limited Identities" Revisited: Regionalism and Nationalism in Canadian History,' *Acadiensis* 30, no. 1 (2000): 7.

7 Friesen, *Citizens and Nation*, 228.

8 Unless otherwise noted, demographic data comes from Barman, *The West beyond the West*. The exact proportion of the non-Aboriginal population born elsewhere in Canada was 14.9 per cent in 1881, 29.2 per cent in 1891, and 27.4 per cent in 1901. Not until the mid-twentieth century would the proportion born elsewhere in Canada again approach 30 per cent.

9 *Census of Canada*, 1881, vol. 1, 396; 1891, vol. 1, 362; 1901, vol. 1, 416.

10 Grant, 'Churches and Schools,' 523.

11 Jeffrey, *Frontier Women*, 46.

12 See British Columbia, Department of Education, *Annual Reports*.

13 Birthplace calculations are derived from combining teachers' names from Department of Education, *Annual Reports*, with birthplaces located in the manuscript census for British Columbia in *Census of Canada*, 1881, 1891, 1901. Percentages are calculated based on the two-thirds of qualified teachers whose birthplaces were located for 1885/86 and 1900/91, and three-quarters for 1890/91. The exact proportions born in Canada were 35.2 per cent in 1885/86, 57.6 per cent in 1890/91, and 60.5 per cent in 1900/01.

14 The proportion of qualified teachers born in Nova Scotia went from 3.3 per cent in 1885/86 to 13.0 per cent in 1890/91 to 7.3 per cent in 1900/01; in the Maritimes, from 9.9 per cent to 21.7 per cent to 15.7 per cent; in Ontario, from 22.0 per cent to 34.2 per cent to 42.3 per cent. The proportions born in Quebec and the Prairies were miniscule.

15 Data compiled from British Columbia, Department of Education, *Annual Reports*, and *Census of Canada*, 1881, 1891, 1901.

16 The exact proportions of women were 44.7 per cent in 1880, 50.4 per cent in 1885, 57.6 per cent in 1890, and 58.2 per cent in 1901 (data compiled from British Columbia, Department of Education, *Annual Reports*).

17 Ross Douglas to Jean Barman, White Rock, 30 October 1999; Barman, 'British Columbia's Pioneer Teachers.'

18 JsM to CM, NL, 22 February 1892, NVA.

19 Klein, *Frontiers of Historical Imagination*, 295.

Illustration Credits

Index

McQueen, Isabella Chase (sister-in-law), 112–13

McQueen, Jane (sister), 14, 23, 46, 96, 151, 157, 164, 210–12, 222

McQueen, Jessie
- appearance, 30
- attitudes: to Aboriginal people, 64, 93–5, 123, 141–2, 171–3; British Columbia, 87, 123, 127–9, 180, 236–7, 242–3; Canada, 87, 193; Chinook, 64–5, 94, 123; cycling, 197, 199, 206–7, 237–8; daughterhood's obligations, 31–3, 47, 62, 70–1, 85, 96–7, 109–12, 128–9, 151–3, 158, 200, 207, 210–13, 222, 235, 244; domestication, 86–7, 109, 117–18, 135, 141, 200–3, 237, 242–3; fellow Nova Scotians, 65, 79, 95, 99–101, 115–16, 122–3, 145, 194–5, 198, 204–5, 210, 237; frontier, 7, 63–5, 68, 70, 79, 82–5, 87, 92, 115, 126, 135, 182, 187–8, 200, 236–42; gender, 30, 32, 79–81, 110, 126–8, 205; hybridity, 80–1, 83, 92–3, 106–7, 123–4, 129, 135–46, 170, 179, 186–7, 203, 225–6, 240, 242; letter writing, 63, 96, 126, 210–11, 243; nation building, 92, 237–42; Nova Scotian things, 86, 89, 95, 97–8, 125, 180; Nova Scotian ways, 87, 90–1, 95–7, 126–7, 129, 159, 180; persons from China, 93–4, 97; race, 92, 238, 242; sisterhood's bonds, 25, 46–7, 63–4, 69–70, 108, 112, 131–4, 140–1, 150–1, 158–9, 162, 180, 208–10, 212–13, 222–4; social activism, 201–2; United States, 193, 205; walking, 124–5, 143, 238
- character, 10, 28, 30–1, 86, 208, 224, 242–5
- contributions to family economy,

29, 32, 47, 62–3, 79, 86, 96, 107–11, 139, 151, 211
- health, 30, 38, 124–6, 158, 226, 242–5
- life course: birth, 11, 14; upbringing, 22, 28, 243; courtships, 30, 81–5, 127–8, 205–7, 213, 240; singledness, 95, 110, 115–16, 120–1, 123, 126, 159, 164, 244; as a teacher in Nova Scotia, 28–31, 33, 39, 61, 222–3; at Truro Normal School, 32–3; departures west from Nova Scotia, 34, 46–7, 109–10, 157–9, 180–1, 223; trips across Canada, 47–9, 56, 79, 108, 110; teaching at Lower Nicola, 56, 60–2, 104–7, 113–14, 134, 137; living at Lower Nicola, 60–1, 87–92, 117–18, 122, 139; teaching at Nicola Lake, 109, 113–15, 118, 122, 128–9, 133–4; living at Nicola Lake, 116–18, 134; teaching at Campbell Creek, 135–8, 142–6, 149; living at Campbell Creek, 138–44, 147, 242; teaching at Upper Salmon Arm, 157, 159–62; teaching at Rossland, 161, 180–7, 200, 205, 207; living at Rossland, 182, 187–211, 223, 240, 242, 244; visiting England, 222, 230, 232; teaching at Beaver Point, 224–6; back home at Sutherland's River, 109, 150–2, 212–13, 221–13, 226–7, 244; death, 227
- piety, 48, 101–4, 118–23, 140, 144–5, 201, 203–7
- reliance on providence, 85, 110, 134, 160, 213, 244
- salaries as a teacher, 30, 39, 63, 109, 128, 133, 135, 137–8, 158, 224
- sojourning, 46, 86–7, 100–1, 108–10, 128–30, 145, 150, 180, 210–12, 236–7, 242, 244